2nd Edition

Where to Stay and Eat
for All Budgets

Must-See Sights
and Local Secrets

Ratings You Can Trust

Fodor's Travel Publications   New York, Toronto, London, Sydney, Auckland
www.fodors.com

FODOR'S DOMINICAN REPUBLIC

Editor: Douglas Stallings

Editorial Contributors: Eileen Robinson-Smith, Elise Rosen, Michael de Zayas

Production Editor: Evangelos Vasilakis

Maps & Illustrations: David Lindroth, Ed Jacobus, *cartographers;* Bob Blake, Rebecca Baer, *map editors;* William Wu, *information graphics*

Design: Fabrizio La Rocca, *creative director;* Guido Caroti, Siobhan O'Hare, *art directors;* Tina Malaney, Chie Ushio, Ann McBride, Jessica Walsh, *designers;* Melanie Marin, *senior picture editor*

Cover Photo: David Deas/DK Stock/Getty Images

Production Manager: Amanda Bullock

SPECIAL SALES

This book is available at special discounts for bulk purchases for sales promotions or premiums. Special editions, including personalized covers, excerpts of existing books, and corporate imprints, can be created in large quantities for special needs. For more information, write to Special Markets/Premium Sales, 1745 Broadway, MD 6-2, New York, New York 10019, or e-mail specialmarkets@randomhouse.com.

AN IMPORTANT TIP & AN INVITATION

Although all prices, opening times, and other details in this book are based on information supplied to us at press time, changes occur all the time in the travel world, and Fodor's cannot accept responsibility for facts that become outdated or for inadvertent errors or omissions. So **always confirm information when it matters,** especially if you're making a detour to visit a specific place. Your experiences—positive and negative— matter to us. If we have missed or misstated something, **please write to us.** We follow up on all suggestions. Contact the Dominican Republic editor at editors@fodors.com or c/o Fodor's at 1745 Broadway, New York, NY 10019.

PRINTED IN THE UNITED STATES OF AMERICA

10 9 8 7 6 5 4 3 2 1

Be a Fodor's Correspondent

Your opinion matters. It matters to us. It matters to your fellow Fodor's travelers, too. And we'd like to hear it. In fact, we need to hear it.

When you share your experiences and opinions, you become an active member of the Fodor's community. That means we'll not only use your feedback to make our books better, but we'll publish your names and comments whenever possible. Throughout our guides, look for "Word of Mouth," excerpts of your unvarnished feedback.

Here's how you can help improve Fodor's for all of us.

Tell us when we're right. We rely on local writers to give you an insider's perspective. But our writers and staff editors—who are the best in the business—depend on you. Your positive feedback is a vote to renew our recommendations for the next edition.

Tell us when we're wrong. We're proud that we update most of our guides every year. But we're not perfect. Things change. Hotels cut services. Museums change hours. Charming cafés lose charm. If our writer didn't quite capture the essence of a place, tell us how you'd do it differently. If any of our descriptions are inaccurate or inadequate, we'll incorporate your changes in the next edition and will correct factual errors at fodors.com immediately.

Tell us what to include. You probably have had fantastic travel experiences that aren't yet in Fodor's. Why not share them with a community of like-minded travelers? Maybe you chanced upon a beach or bistro or B&B that you don't want to keep to yourself. Tell us why we should include it. And share your discoveries and experiences with everyone directly at fodors.com. Your input may lead us to add a new listing or highlight a place we cover with a "Highly Recommended" star or with our highest rating, "Fodor's Choice."

Give us your opinion instantly at our feedback center at www.fodors.com/feedback. You may also e-mail editors@fodors.com with the subject line "Dominican Republic Editor." Or send your nominations, comments, and complaints by mail to Dominican Republic Editor, Fodor's, 1745 Broadway, New York, NY 10019.

You and travelers like you are the heart of the Fodor's community. Make our community richer by sharing your experiences. Be a Fodor's correspondent.

Happy traveling!

Tim Jarrell, Publisher

CONTENTS

MAPS

ABOUT THIS BOOK

Our Ratings

Sometimes you find terrific travel experiences and sometimes they just find you. But usually the burden is on you to select the right combination of experiences. That's where our ratings come in.

As travelers we've all discovered a place so wonderful that its worthiness is obvious. And sometimes that place is so unique that superlatives don't do it justice: you just have to be there to know. These sights, properties, and experiences get our highest rating, **Fodor's Choice**, indicated by orange stars throughout this book.

Black stars highlight sights and properties we deem **Highly Recommended**, places that our writers, editors, and readers praise again and again for consistency and excellence.

By default, there's another category: any place we include in this book is by definition worth your time, unless we say otherwise. And we will.

Disagree with any of our choices? Care to nominate a place or suggest that we rate one more highly? Visit our feedback center at www.fodors.com/feedback.

Budget Well

Hotel and restaurant price categories from to $$$$ are defined in the opening pages of each chapter. For attractions, we always give standard adult admission fees; reductions are usually available for children, students, and senior citizens. Want to pay with plastic? **AE, D, DC, MC, V** following restaurant and hotel listings indicate whether American Express, Discover, Diner's Club, MasterCard, and Visa are accepted.

Restaurants

Unless we state otherwise, restaurants are open for lunch and dinner daily. We mention dress only when there's a specific requirement and reservations only when they're essential or not accepted—it's always best to book ahead.

Hotels

Hotels have private bath, phone, TV, and air-conditioning and operate on the European Plan (aka EP, meaning without meals), unless we specify that they use the Continental Plan (CP, with a continental breakfast), Breakfast Plan (BP, with a full breakfast), or Modified American Plan (MAP, with breakfast and dinner), or are all-inclusive (AI, including

all meals and most activities). We always list facilities but not whether you'll be charged an extra fee to use them, so when pricing accommodations, find out what's included.

Many Listings
★ Fodor's Choice
★ Highly recommended
⊠ Physical address
✛ Directions or Map coordinates
⌂ Mailing address
☎ Telephone
🖷 Fax
⊕ On the Web
✆ E-mail
🖅 Admission fee
🕓 Open/closed times
Ⓜ Metro stations
🚍 Credit cards

Hotels & Restaurants
🕮 Hotel
🖙 Number of rooms
⚴ Facilities
🍽 Meal plans
✕ Restaurant
⚲ Reservations
🏛 Dress code
⚲ Smoking
🍸 BYOB

Outdoors
🏌 Golf
⛺ Camping

Other
♨ Family-friendly
⇨ See also
⊠ Branch address
☞ Take note

1

Experience the Dominican Republic

WORD OF MOUTH

"Santo Domingo['s Zona Colonial] is a UNESCO World Heritage Site. There is a tropical wonderland at Saona Island. . . . Great golf in the Dominican Republic if that interests you."

—jmelzie

WHAT'S NEW

Santo Domingo a Cultural Capital
Santo Domingo won the distinction of being the American Capital of Culture in 2010, awarded annually by Buro Internacional de Capitales Culturales (BICC) in Barcelona, Spain.

B&Bs in Santo Domingo's Zona Colonial
For decades there were few hotels in this most appealing quarter of the city, but now there are more than a half-dozen petite hotels to please travelers. In most instances these urban sanctuaries are owned by artsy, intellectual expats, and the properties often reflect the personality of their charismatic owners.

Regenerated Beaches and Alluring New Condos
Two modern engineering feats, the regeneration of the beaches at Cabarete (broadened by some 114 feet) and Juan Dolio (lengthened by nearly 11,500 feet) have proven to be key elements in renewing tourism in the two towns. New oceanfront condos in Cabarete have added top-notch housing stock for expats and vacationers in the former backpacker's haven. Juan Dolio has seen an even more miraculous rebirth, with a new wave of luxurious, beachfront condos. Six miles east of Juan Dolio, Costablanca will have an 18-hole Greg Norman Signature Golf Course, a luxury marina, and a Chris Evert Tennis Center.

Ecotourism Is a Draw in the Southwest
The natural beauty of this unspoiled province, where the mountains and rivers meet a pristine coastline, is an enticement for all tourists who think green. The region is a crossroads for bird-watchers, nature photographers, bush pilots, volunteers and workers stationed in Haiti, and other globetrotters who take the roads less traveled. Three national parks preserve the landscape, while small, eco-oriented lodges and villas are sprouting up.

Cap Cana Keeps Growing Up
In 2008, Sanctuary Cap Cana Golf & Spa, the flagship hotel for the Cap Cana development south of Punta Cana, opened its doors with 177 posh ocean-view suites. In early 2010 the Sanctuary was relaunched and renamed Secrets Sanctuary Cap Cana Golf & Spa. The Golden Bear Lodge and Spa, a luxury condo-style hotel, is also now open.

Early 2011 is expected to bring the first phase of the Fishing Lodge Cap Cana, another midsize luxury hotel on the marina. AMResorts has announced a $400-million project, a four-resort complex called the Gems at Cap Cana. Slated for completion in late 2012, it will have a total of 1,100 suites. Also part of the complex will be a major convention center, a spa, a 20,000-square-foot casino, gourmet restaurants and lounges, boutiques, an Explorers Club for kids, and an artists' square.

The Dominican Republic Is Now a Top Cruise Destination
Pirates once sailed these waters, but these days it's cruise passengers you'll find, some 600,000 of them in 2010. This increase means that the island's cruise traffic now rivals Puerto Rico's. Now every major line pulls into various ports on the island, and some offer cruises from Santo Domingo. The revitalization of the Don Diego Cruise Terminal near the Zona Colonial was a key element in the growth of the capital's cruise business. Nearby, the Sans Souci Port, with its terminal, tourist shops, convention center, and more, became the capital's major port after a renovation.

DID YOU KNOW?

A Growing Multiracial Mix

Multiculturalism characterizes the Dominican Republic, where the official language is Spanish and where 73% of the Dominicans are classified as mixed-race. Add to that the 11% who are of African origin and 16% who are of European descent, and the cultural variety continues to grow. The next census will have to catch up with the number of *Norte Americanos* and other expats who have chosen to live here, often after retirement.

Just What Is Island Time?

You've heard tell of the phenomenon called island time, and in the Dominican Republic this generally refers to the mindset that there is no point in hurrying. But the Dominican Republic is really on a different island time than the United States. The local time zone is Eastern Caribbean Time. In winter the Dominican Republic is one hour ahead of Eastern Standard Time (the rest of the year it's on the same time). Since the Dominican Republic does not observe daylight savings time, you might say it's in an endless summer. But what this means in reality is that at sunset in winter, darkness really does fall . . . and suddenly.

The Peso Is a Good Deal for Americans

Since the Dominican Republic has such strong economic ties to the United States, U.S. greenbacks are not only widely accepted but also desired. Although the island's currency—the peso—has increased in value, the Dominican Republic is one place where the dollar is still quite strong. Independent *cambios* (currency-exchange offices) often give a better rate than banks and have longer hours.

The Dominican Republic Has a Prosperous Japanese Community

Thanks to Generalissimo Rafael L. Trujillo, who implemented an immigration program in the 1950s, descendants of the 200 Japanese families that he "imported" to the fertile mountain region of Constanza have prospered. Trujillo's original intention was to establish a strong agricultural community and bolster the area's economy. These industrious immigrants did just that, and today, amid strawberry fields and flower farms, the prominent but still small community of Japanese-Dominican families has prospered and built substantial homes in the Dominican "Alps."

Juan Luis Guerra Is Merengue's Superstar

In 2007 the classically trained Juan Luis Guerra won four Grammys at the Latin Grammy Awards. He blends jazz-influenced merengue and sentimental *bachatas* (traditional country ballads) with his own hip lyrics. Merengue, invented in the Dominican Republic, combines the sounds of the aboriginal *guiro* (a metal "grater" that is scratched), the *tambora* (an African lap drum), and the accordion. Indeed, Guerra's renditions are refinements. As Guerra has grown more religious, there have been significant changes in his lyrics; they are more like prayers, but they are still poetry. In 2009 he shared the stage at Santo Domingo's Olympic Stadium in a concert to raise money for Haitian children after their devastating earthquake. Guerra pleased the crowd by singing some of his original classics, and millions of dollars were raised.

WHAT'S WHERE

Numbers refer to chapters.

2 Santo Domingo. Santo Domingo is a sprawling metropolis of close to 3 million, but its soul is within the historic blocks of its famous Zona Colonial. Southwest is the undeveloped ecoparadise around Barahona and its three national parks.

3 The Southeast Coast. East of Santo Domingo, Boca Chica gives way to the luxury condos of "new" Juan Dolio. Beyond La Romana and the famous Casa de Campo are beautiful Bayahibe Bay and Dominicus Beach.

4 Punta Cana. First-timers usually head to the all-inclusives in this East Coast enclave, which stretches from densely developed Baváro all the way north to Uvero Alto.

5 Samaná. The haunt of independent travelers has now been discovered and is no longer so remote. A new toll road just east of Santo Domingo now makes a fast route to the Samaná Peninsula. The region is traditionally known for its idyllic beaches, small inns, beachside restaurants, waterfalls, and excellent whale-watching.

6 The North Coast. This coast still has something for everyone. There are the all-inclusive enclave of Playa Dorada, the authentic city of Puerto Plata, German-influenced Sosúa, and Cabarete, known for its windsurfing, kiteboarding, and nightlife.

7 Santiago and the Cibao Valley. Santiago's charm is its historic, Victorian-style downtown square. Nearby, the mountainous Cordillera Central offers white-water rafting, kayaking, and other adventure sports, while the fireplaces at several small ecolodges help thwart the nightly chill.

ATLANTIC OCEAN

Playa Cofresí
Playa Dorada **6**
Puerto Plata
◆✈ Sosúa
Gregorie Luperón ○
Pico Isabel de Torres ▲ **Int'l Airport**
Cabarete
Santiago ○
Moca ○
Cabo Francés Viejo
○ Cabrera
7 CIBAO VALLEY
Nagua ○
Bahía Escocesa
Playa Bonita
Santa Bárbara de Samaná
Jarabacoa ○
La Vega ○
San Francisco de Macorís
Samaná Peninsula ✈
5
Bahía de Samaná

HISPANIOLA
Bonao ○
Sabana de la Mar ○
Miches ○
Los Haitises National Park

Monte Plata ○
Hato Mayor ○
El Seibo ○
El Macao ○
Punta Cana International Airport
✈

2 Santo Domingo
Boca Chica
San Pedro de Macorís
Higüey ○
4
Punta Cana
Punta Cana
Azua ○
San Cristóbal
La Romana ○
Mona Passage

Bahía de Ocoa
Bani ○
Pto. Palenque
Las Américas International Airport
✈
Juan Dolio
3
La Romana International Airport
✈
Bahía de Yuma

Playa Bahoruco
Isla Saona

Caribbean Sea

ata

0   40 miles
0   40 kilometers

THE DOMINICAN REPUBLIC TODAY

Leonel Is President Once Again

Locals just call him Leonel (lee-o-*nel*), but the full name of the Dominican Republic's president is Dr. Leonel Fernández Reyna. In 2008 the head of the Dominican Liberation Party (PLD) was reelected for his third term, which will be over in 2012. (He won his first four-year term in 1996, at the age of 42, but was not reelected until 2004). An intellectual politico *and* a former New Yorker, he put the country on a sound economic path in the 1990s, curbing waste, fostering privatization, lowering unemployment and illiteracy, and awakening tourism. Leonel was defeated in 2000 by Hipólito Mejí, a so-called man of the street, whose reign proved disastrous. It is said that when Leonel took over again in 2004, the treasury was nearly empty. The sales tax was raised to an unpopular 16%, and to reduce crime in the capital a midnight curfew on weeknights (2 AM on weekends) was established. Although the curfew has put some nightclubs out of business, the city is a safer place, and the extra money in government coffers is devoted to tourism infrastructure developments. These days, Leonel doesn't rate as high in the popularity pools as he originally did, and rumor has it that he has fallen into some of the typical political pitfalls.

Tourism Is Expanding the Middle Class

The past 20 years have improved the income and standard of living for many Dominicans. Since 1992 tourism has grown to encompass 24% of the country's GDP, and car dealerships are opening up all over the island, this in a place where a car—never mind a luxury import—was inconceivable for most families. The government plans to invest some $1 billion in tourism infrastructure developments by 2012. For many, education and social mobility have come through tourism. Although they may have grown up in a palm-thatched hut with a dirt floor, many tourism workers now own a home in a middle-class, suburban neighborhood. Poverty, however, is still omnipresent, from city slums to the most remote areas, especially near the Haitian border.

Dominican New Yorkers Return Home

Many Dominicans who have been living in New York—sometimes for decades—are now starting to come home to retire and/or invest their hard-earned money. For decades, those sons and daughters who chose to try and get ahead in the States have sent their dollars home to their families. Remittances from Dominicans who live outside the country, particularly those one million brothers and sisters in New York, were calculated to amount to $1 billion annually. Although they are still a top source of revenue for the country, the Dominican New Yorkers have been negatively impacted by the world economic downturn, like so many others.

Dominican Players Are Synonymous with Good Baseball

Osvaldo "Ozzie" Virgil was the first Dominican to enter the U.S. Major Leagues when he made the NY Giants in 1953. He paved the way for the 82 players who now populate our majors, including the ever-popular Manny Ramirez. The famous Alou "baseballing" family started its sporting history when Felipe Alou debuted for the San Francisco Giants in 1958. Mateo (Matty) made the Giants two years later; Jesus followed Matty into the Giants in '63 and now Moises is "the man."

Superstar athletes can be credited with bringing both their fame and hard-earned cash to their homeland. Their substantial salaries contribute to the country's economy, too, from the luxury penthouses they buy to the philanthropic donations that can turn around a whole hometown. Sammy Sosa, who started life as a shoeshine boy in San Pedro Macorís, has donated a sizeable fortune to that mighty town that spawns baseball greats. He owns an apartment in the capital's classy Malecón Center and a villa at Casa de Campo, as does Juan Marichal. Known for his flamboyant style, Marichal was one of the early Dominican record-breaking pitchers and the first Dominican Hall of Famer (1983). His Juan Marichal Golf Tournament at Los Marlins Golf Course, held annually in Juan Dolio, has raised millions for the island's needy families.

Larimar and Amber Gain International Recognition

These indigenous semiprecious stones are starting to bring in big bucks to the island. For years amber was the more popular product, but as the novelty of wearing fossilized resin has held steady, interest in larimar has grown. Larimar, a pectoline that is the color of the Caribbean Sea, is being set in sterling silver with more upscale designs and is especially gaining popularity in Europe. Jewelers are having difficulty meeting demand. There's only one larimar mine in the world, and that's in Bahoruco, in the Southwest.

High Energy Prices Foster Innovation

Electricity all over the Caribbean is more expensive than in the United States, but rates are among the world's highest in the Dominican Republic. And despite these exorbitant prices, regular power outages occur; in some neighborhoods they even occur daily. (The power company justifies this by saying that if everyone actually paid for their electricity, there wouldn't be any outages.) This has forced innovation. Wealthy homeowners have always had generators, but the growing cost of diesel fuel has created a surge in sales of efficient, compact fluorescent bulbs and solar hot-water heaters to both homeowners and small inns and bed-and-breakfasts. Apartment dwellers, particularly in Santo Domingo, have small, battery-operated generators. People are also resorting to wind power. As prices rise at the pump, more taxi drivers are turning their vehicles over to propane, which is a third of the cost; at approximately RD$10,000 (US$275, which is still real money in the Dominican Republic), a propane conversion is an investment to save over the long haul. Larger resort complexes that use a lot of power enter the sustainable realm by growing some of their own food and planting heat-absorbing trees to shade buildings.

DOMINICAN REPUBLIC TOP EXPERIENCES

Strolling Through Santo Domingo's Zona Colonial

(A) If you believe in magic, you'll be enchanted with the Zona Colonial. Walk down Calle Las Damas, which may make you feel as if it were still 1590. The Zone is not just a medieval museum piece with cobblestone streets, but a hip, contemporary neighborhood. Tourists head to the bars and restaurants on Plaza de España, all with outdoor cafes. In-the-know travelers have their own favorites, including some landmark Dominican restaurants and the bar and fine-dining restaurant in the Hostal Nicolas de Ovando.

Whale-Watching Is Big in Samaná

(B) To cruise alongside a school of whales and photograph their playful antics is an experience you won't soon forget. The season lasts from January to March, when the humpbacks delight in the warm waters of the Bahía de Samaná, their breeding ground for centuries. By the end of January, as many as 4,000 whales are courting and cavorting in the Bay of Samaná.

Beaching It in Punta Cana

(C) Punta Cana is justifiably famous for its beautiful beaches, which ring the eastern-most cape over the course of 35 unbroken miles of sand, from Playa Uvero Alto in the north all the way to Playa Juanillo in the south, now a resort area with the luxurious Cap Cana development. The beaches are sandy, white, and beautiful, and some of them are still unspoiled.

White-Water Rafting Is an Adrenaline Rush

(D) For travelers with a bigger taste for adventure, the Dominican Republic's adventure-sport center is Jarabacoa, in the so-called Dominican Alps. From here several companies offer white-water rafting trips on the Rio Yaque del Norte's Class II rapids, a trip that will take you through

wild canyons, past soaring waterfalls, and on to Class III rapids.

Playing Golf on an Illustrious Course

(E) Golfers have long been drawn to the acclaimed courses at Casa de Campo in La Romana, but there are many other notable courses, including Playa Dorada's on the North Coast; Punta Cana's many great greens, such as the Rōco Ki, La Cana, and Punta Espada at Cap Cana; and the Guavaberry and Los Marlins courses in Juan Dolio. More new courses are in development all over the Dominican Republic, including Las Iguanas, a Cap Cana course designed by Jack Nicklaus.

Snorkeling off Isla Saona

(F) This beautiful national park off the island's Southeast Coast has beautiful beaches and is surrounded by crystal-clear, aquamarine waters that teem with sea life, particularly starfish. A day here is an extremely popular excursion for

travelers in La Romana and Bayahibe, and even for visitors from as far away as Punta Cana.

Renting a Beachfront Villa

(G) A superb option for family reunions, destination weddings, golf forays, corporate retreats, and other reunions, the Dominican Republic's beautiful villas will get you out of the all-inclusive throngs. Some of these are fully staffed with chef, butler, maids, and more. And you can have a luxurious vacation on the Dominican Republic's north shore for less than the cost of a comparable villa on most other Caribbean islands.

Kite- and Windsurfing Are Great Highs

(H) Strong, steady winds and a clean shoreline have made Cabarete—especially Kite Beach—the North Coast's center for windsurfing, putting it on the map for sporty travelers with an adventurous spirit (and excellent upper-body strength).

QUINTESSENTIAL DOMINICAN REPUBLIC

If you want to get a sense of Dominican culture and indulge in some of its pleasures, start by familiarizing yourself with the rituals of daily life.

Sample Some Sancocho

If there is a single Dominican specialty that could be called the national dish, it is this protein-rich stew that traditionally includes chicken, pork, pumpkin, yucca, plantain, corn on the cob, and cilantro. The best version is served alongside hearty portions of rice and sliced avocado. After clubbing, *capitaleños* (Santo Domingoans) pile into late-night restaurants for their sancocho fix—it's thought to absorb alcohol and lessen hangovers. Stop at any popular local restaurant at midday on Sunday, and it's almost a sure bet that you'll find sancocho on the menu. Of course, the best way to experience this soupy stew is to get yourself invited to someone's home and have it family-style, with homemade pepper sauce.

Ride the Guaguas

If you want to feel what it's like to be a real Dominican, then you have to brave the local transportation. Guaguas are local buses, which are often minivans, especially in the smaller towns. In Cabarete, for example, you just stand on the side of the road and wait for what looks like a speeding ambulance—a white van with a red light on top and a man hanging off the running board. Wave violently. The hanging man (often called a tigre) will bang his hand on the side, making the driver stop short. Watch what the other passengers give the hanger-on, and do likewise. It's usually *diez* pesos (RD$10), on up to about 30. In Santo Domingo, guaguas are buses, often beat-up school buses, though never yellow. As taxi rates increase, there's even more reason to take a guagua. And it's a trip to see what locals bring aboard—produce from the market,

kettle drums, a stack of Haitian artwork, full-size baby carriages.

Get Saturday Night Fever at a Colmodon

If you want to have a real peek through a window of Dominican culture, then you have to go dancing. A *colmodon* is larger than your average corner *colmado* (a small grocery store) and serves a larger purpose. It's part supermarket, part bar, and part social center. The colmodon will have tables and chairs, a TV always tuned to a baseball game or *telenovela,* and loud merengue and bachata music playing in the background. On weekends the colmadons come alive, when many add a makeshift kitchen serving authentic Dominican fare, including *tostones* (fried green plantains), fried chicken, *platanos* (fried sweet plantains), or *arroz con pollo* (rice with beans and fried chicken parts). Patrons dance in the street, and shots of local rum—chased by Presidente beer—help you feel the rhythms that you may never knew you had.

Take Yourself Out to a Ball Game

Dominicans are mad about baseball. Taking in a game is definitely doable, and will help you get on down with the locals. For the full whammy, go to one of the top parks—in Santo Domingo, La Romana, or San Pedro de Macorís, the so-called City of Shortstops. The betting is fast and furious, the bookies (who hang out in the area) are remarkably astute. Vendors have their individual style, whether they're peddling souvenirs, local snacks, Presidente beer, or minibottles of rum. The spectacle is like nothing you have ever seen. Mascots go through bizarre, often ribald antics. Merengue is played at ear-splitting levels, and fans dance hedonistically. This is one social event where you can make new friends as long as you pledge allegiance to their team.

IF YOU LIKE

All-Inclusive Resorts

The all-inclusive concept, where your accommodations, meals, drinks, entertainment, tips, and activities are included in one price tag, may be one of the most popular tourism promotions in recent history, even more successful than the swim-up bar. Although this crowd pleaser began in Jamaica, the AI has reached its zenith in the Dominican Republic (particularly in Punta Cana).

Casa de Campo. The Dominican Republic's original luxury resort offers its best value to those guests who choose the all-inclusive plan; the side benefit is access to Casa's wonderful facilities and amenities, though golf is an additional cost.

Dreams La Romana Resort & Spa. A multi-million-dollar renovation upgraded the resort to luxury status, with the Club level available for additional amenities and perks. The Core Zone (for teens) and activity-filled Explorers Club for kids and the great gourmet restaurants make this the hot property at Bayahibe.

Excellence Punta Cana. A sumptuous lovers' lair, this adults-only resort exudes romance and sensuality. The open-air, tropical lobby looks out on the heavenly beach. Swim-out suites open directly onto the lazy river pool that snakes around the grounds.

Paradisus Palma Real. At this impressive resort there are three elements that make it truly stand out. The Reserve is a private self-contained sanctuary of 190 luxurious suites that's a glamorous option for families. The YHI Spa combines atmospheric lagoons and boardwalks with an Asian atmosphere and hushed serenity. The third element is the Gabi Beach restaurant, noted for its classic cuisine and impressive presentation.

Beautiful Beaches

The Dominican Republic's beaches are among the world's best. Beaches lined with coconut palms, with pearl-white to amber sands; beaches with looming, dramatic cliffs; pebbled beaches where mountain streams meet the sea; the country's coastline has them all.

Bahía de las Áquilas. This is the remote beach in the Southwest that everyone hears about and longs to go to. It takes some doing to get here, but it's oh so worth the effort.

The Coconut Coast. The beaches of Punta Cana—Juanillo, Punta Cana/Bávaro, El Cortecito, Arena Gorda, Macao, and Uvero Alto—are joined together in a 35-mi-long unbroken stretch of pearly sand with turquoise water.

Orchid Bay Beach. Near Cabrera on the North Coast, and named for the wild orchids that grow on its cliffs, it offers a large public beach seldom used by anyone but the residents in the luxury villas lining it. Swimmable in a couple of choice locations, this is an underutilized gem.

Playa Bahoruco. In front of the Southwest fishing village of the same name, this gorgeous stretch of virgin beach goes on for miles with unobstructed views. Taupe sand is under and around those white stones.

Playa Bayahibe. This glorious half-moon cove is where you'll find the area's best all-inclusive resorts. At night, when no one is on it and the silver moon illuminates the phosphorescence, it is what Caribbean dreams are made of.

Partying All Night

If you love nightlife, you're going to love the Dominican Republic. Dominicans are a fun-loving people, who like to drink,

party, and dance. Dancing is a national passion—even more than baseball! Here happy hour starts as early as 4 PM. Some then take a second siesta, so they can rest up before the usual late dinner and dancing after.

Casino Diamante Dominicus Bayahibe. This sparkling Las Vegas–style casino in Bayahibe reopened in early 2010 under enthusiastic, new management. It all has a Caribbean flamboyance.

Hemingway's Café. Since the 1980s, this bar and restaurant has been the spot in Playa Dorada to party if you're young or fun, offering a safe haven for both AI guests and expats. Merengue bands, a DJ, karaoke, and American food keep the crowds coming.

Lax. It's one big beach party in Cabarete, with barhopping the name of the game. Open-air Lax spills onto the sand, attracting both the young and the ageless. The fun begins at happy hour, but the scene really comes alive after 10, when a DJ spins or a live band rocks.

LED. The Hispaniola Hotel & Casino can stay open past normal curfews. That in itself has made this a favorite of young party-hardys, who like their music loud 'til the wee small hours of the morning.

The Freshest Seafood

Seafood—eaten with views of the water it came from—is one of the best aspects of dining in the Dominican Republic. Price is another plus. Although Dominican cuisine can be heavy, lighter, fresher cuisine can be found at upscale restaurants all over the island, particularly those owned by expats.

Jellyfish. Shaped like a double-decker yacht, this sophisticated open-air restaurant on the sands of Bávaro focuses on fresh seafood caught by local fishermen. Soothing music and soft lighting set the mood for romantic dining, from fish right off the grill to the oven-baked lobster.

Lucía. At this Playa Dorada stunner, within Casa Colonial, the large and creative menu includes sea bass, a tuna and lobster seviche, tamarind lamb, and something called a molten chocolate volcano.

Mesón D' Bari. For decades, Señor Marisol has been feeding the locals in the capital's Zona Colonial using the recipes of his grandmother. Everyone is welcome at this late-night hangout.

Peperoni. Casa de Campo's Marina has a classy and contemporary Italian-accented restaurant that ranges from osso bucco and risotto to wood-oven pizzas and even some Asian specialties.

La Terrasse. This casually charming Samaná restaurant offers one of the best beachfront dining experiences in the Dominican Republic. It's a standout primarily because of the caring European owner and the "sun-inspired" Mediterranean cuisine.

HISTORY YOU CAN SEE

Colonial Times Are Mirrored in the Present

Christopher Columbus claimed the island for Spain on his first New World voyage in 1492, when he came looking for riches for his Spanish patrons; Columbus's brother Bartolomeo founded Santo Domingo in 1496, and it became the cradle of Western civilization in the Americas. Columbus's son Don Diego, resided here grandly before returning to Spain in 1532. Nicolas Ovando, the first governor, was an able ruler, but his mistreatment of the indigenous people was his black mark.

What to See: You can see some 300 surviving structures from the period in Santo Domingo's Zona Colonial (a UNESCO World Heritage Site). Although key buildings, such as the hospital and monastery, are now artistic ruins, some buildings have been beautifully restored. The **Plaza de España,** formerly the colony's warehouse row, now houses trendy restaurants with popular outdoor cafés. The urban mansion of the Governor of the Americas is now a luxury hotel, the **Hostal Nicolas de Ovando.** The focal point of Parque Colón, **Basílica Catedral Metropolitana Santa María de la Encarnación,** was the first cathedral in the Americas. **El Museo de las Casas Reales** is one of the Zone's most handsome colonial edifices; built in the Renaissance style, it was the seat of Spanish government and now functions as an art gallery and museum. The **Casa del Cordón** is the oldest surviving stone house from the early colonial period in the Western Hemisphere.

The Victorian Era Was a Golden Age

The 19th-century was a golden age for the island's tobacco-growing regions, when world prices reached their heights in the 1870s. While tobacco was grown in the fertile Cibao Valley around Santiago, it was shipped from such ports as Puerto Plata, bringing great wealth to that city, too. The trade made tobacco traders and merchants rich, and several Germans built impressive dwellings in the region. Although many such mansions are in disrepair, some have been restored; others are in the works.

What to See: The tobacco trade spawned opulent homes and handsome wooden buildings decorated with gingerbread fretwork and painted in eye-stopping Caribbean colors, which is notably present in all their faded glory in **Puerto Plata.** You can get a feeling for this bygone era in the magnificent Victorian-style gazebo in the central **Parque Independencia,** the **Museo del Ambar Dominicano** (originally the home of a German tobacco entrepreneur), and **Casa de La Cultura** (now a Dominican art gallery and performance space). The old Victorian neighborhoods continue northeast about eight blocks and also east toward the ocean. Many of the millionaire families in the charming, provincial city of Santiago still owe their fortunes to tobacco. Santiago's Old Town is also centered around its central park, **Parque Duarte.** Santiago's colorful past is seen in the facades of its 19th-century gingerbread houses that are scattered through the streets surrounding the park all the way to the **Fortaleza de San Luis.**

Reminders of the Trujillo Era

Generalissimo Rafael L. Trujillo ruled the Dominican Republic with an iron fist from 1930 until he was assassinated in 1961. His reign was one of the bloodiest in the 20th century. After gaining power, he entered into several pushes to "whiten" the mixed-race nation. He was particularly against the immigration of Haitians to the Dominican Republic, and his

policies caused the deaths of thousands. At the same time, he had an open-door policy for Europeans, welcoming Jewish refugees during World War II and Japanese colonists afterward. He had a flamboyant style, drove yellow, big-finned Cadillacs, and was intent on leaving an architectural legacy behind. Indeed, he left a vast infrastructure in the country, including highways and other public works and monuments.

What to See: The most notable of Trujillo-commissioned structure is Santiago's massive **Monumento a los Héroes de la Restauración de la Republica,** a 230-foot monument topped by an allegorical figure of Victory. The excellent, modern **Autopista del Este** (Highway 3) that connects Santo Domingo with Juan Dolio and La Romana was built in the late 1950s, in part so that Trujillo's son Rafael would have a place to drive his race cars. The impressive **Palacio Nacional,** the white, neoclassical seat of government in Santo Domingo, which was completed in 1947, is emblematic of Trujillo's love of grandeur. It's not open to the public.

The New Millennium Awakens Architects' Creativity

It was as if the year 2000 signaled an awakening in the artistic sensibilities of Dominican architects, as their talent burst forth in compelling ways. The island nation was emerging as a tourist destination, and the revenue from tourism began to seep into the economy at every level. Neither architects nor developers were satisfied with the bland, concrete buildings and cookie-cutter mentality that predominated across the island. And upscale second-home buyers demanded something more interesting. The millennial revival has positively affected both

the resort and residential categories, and can be seen in important public works projects as well. In some cases, Dominican design has taken inspiration from its historic past, beginning with the 16th-century Spanish architecture.

What to See: The **Centro León** is the most impressive, new, architectural landmark in Santiago, a world-class museum and art gallery that was also designed to promote sensorial emotions. **Secrets Sanctuary Cap Cana Golf & Spa,** with its palatial main lobby and gorgeous stone facade, was inspired by 16th-century colonial styles. **Casa Colonial Beach & Spa Resort** in Playa Dorada may look like a restored colonial mansion, but as you can see on the inside, it's also a contemporary marvel. After many a renovation, **Casa de Campo** now has a minimalist design in its public areas. Three of the top design professionals in the country participated in the transformation that included the reception, the pool area, fitness center, main restaurant and lounge, and 80 of its rooms, which are designated "Elite." The complete renovation of another 75 rooms and 10 suites is underway.

WHEN TO GO

The high season in the Dominican Republic—and the rest of the Caribbean—is traditionally from mid-December to the week after Easter, when northern weather is at its worst. During the winter high season you'll find a fairly even mix of Americans, Canadians, and Europeans at many resorts, though each group has its pet locales. There's a spike in travel by Europeans in the summer months, so even June through August can be busy in the Dominican Republic, unlike much of the rest of the Caribbean. This means that the island's resorts have no real low season, but you'll generally find the cheapest prices from September through November, during the height of hurricane season.

Carnival is an important event in this predominately Catholic country; the most famous carnival celebration is in La Vega, followed by the one in Santiago. The Dominican Republic Jazz Festival is an annual event in Cabarete each November.

Climate

Weather in the Dominican Republic is warm year-round, but temperatures are generally cooler from November through April and warmer from May through October. The average daily temperature ranges from 78°F to 88°F. The coolest region is the Cordillera Central, around Jarabacoa and Constanza, where high temperatures can be in the 60s. The North Coast is rainier during the winter months from November through April, the southern coast from May through October. Barahona, in the Southwest, is the driest part of the country and often chilly at night. Punta Cana is about average, with peaks of precipitation in May, June, October, and November. La Romana and the nearby Bayahibe area have some of the island's best weather, sunny and warm.

Toward the end of summer, hurricane season begins in earnest, with the first tropical wave passing by in June; the season does not end until late November. The tropical storms passing by leave behind the sunniest and clearest days you'll ever see.

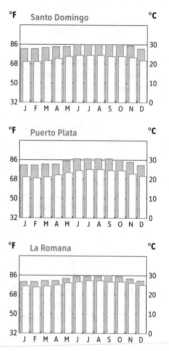

Santo Domingo

WITH AN EXCURSION TO BARAHONA

WORD OF MOUTH

"I can absolutely recommend the [Hostal Nicolas Ovando]. This property is on the oldest street in the city, so [you] would be right in the heart of the Zona Colonial, with all its history and sightseeing potential. . . .The rooms/bathrooms are gorgeous, excellent breakfast buffet, charming pool."
—lifes2short

"I do not recommend driving too much in Santo Domingo . . . [take a taxi instead]: it's much more enjoyable than driving through yourself. Santo Domingo is as safe as any other big city in the world. If you stay in the touristy area, you will be fine."

—demi56

By Eileen Robinson Smith

Santo Domingo is the vibrant seaside capital of this emerging country. As the Dominican Republic grows up, this city, which for decades has had a cosmopolitan atmosphere and infrastructure that distinguished it from the rest of this island nation, only becomes more sophisticated. It's known throughout the Caribbean for its upscale hotels and restaurants—and certainly for its nightlife. Simply put, it's urbane, historic, and hip.

There are many reasons why you might choose to fly into Santo Domingo instead of directly to Punta Cana or La Romana. It's often less expensive, and there are more convenient flights into Las Américas International Airport than into some of the beach destinations. If this is the case, you can easily take a few days for an urban vacation and then couple it with a beach stay elsewhere on the island.

You might also be sent down by your company or have your own business dealings in this growing metropolis. Or you may be scheduled to attend an international conference at one of the deluxe high-rise hotels on the Malecón, the seaside boulevard that's one of the city's main thoroughfares. Plan on having your spouse or a special friend join you for a romantic getaway, and add a couple of days to your itinerary.

Perhaps you've heard about the city's Zona Colonial and, being a history buff, want the ambience and romanticism of such an Old World setting. That one square mile was the location of the original Spanish settlement to the island, and was ruled in the 16th century by the family of its founder, Christopher Columbus. Architectural landmarks include a number of firsts for the New World: the first cathedral, monastery, seminary, military fort, and university. These are among the reasons why the Buró Internacional de Capitales Culturales (BICC), based in Barcelona, chose Santo Domingo as the American Capital of Culture for 2010. The Dominican Republic's capital is the first city in the Caribbean or Central America to receive the distinction; it's planning a schedule of cultural events to mark the occasion. Head to the Web site of the Dominican Republic Tourist Office (⊕ *www.godominicanrepublic.com*) to find out what's being planned.

If you're bound for faraway ports on a cruise ship, and Santo Domingo is your port of embarkation, you may have to overnight here. Don't hesitate to extend your stay for a pre- or post-trip sojourn. Though it can be overwhelming, Santo Domingo is a genuine place, not simply a tourist area. It's the largest city in the Caribbean (with 3 million residents, both poor and rich); it's where the Dominican Republic's movers and shakers can be found. And as the country's economy has grown ever stronger, the old smoky cars are giving way to decent automobiles, the litter has decreased, and the hotels just keep getting better.

TOP REASONS TO GO

The Zona Colonial. In one of the most appealing historic districts in the Caribbean, you can check out the Casa Reales, the Alcazar de Colón at Plaza de España, and the New World's oldest cathedral—still in service at Parque Colón.

Wining and dining. Partake of the city's sophisticated restaurant scene, from the Zona Colonial to restaurants in the top hotels along the Malecón, and best yet, in upscale residential districts like Piantini.

Quality shopping. Whether souvenir shopping on Calle El Conde, buying Dominican cigars and rum, or designer clothing in Piantini, you can find bargains here on quality goods.

Love the nightlife. Start at a small, artsy bar in the Zona, then go dancing at one of the clubs. When they close, carry on to one of the hotel bars, like Meliá's club Coppa, which is a late-night haunt.

If you like getting dressed up and doing the town, the nightlife here is comparable to the glory days of the late 1950s and early '60s in the United States. People go out—couples, singles, and in groups—to have dinner and then go dancing at one of the clubs. Going a couple of rounds at one of the glitzy casinos is another option, as are theaters and live music venues. Instead of hitting the diners for breakfast, Dominicans pile into late-night restaurants for *sancocho,* the protein-rich stew that is the national dish.

ORIENTATION AND PLANNING

GETTING ORIENTED

Parque Independencia separates the Old City from modern Santo Domingo, a sprawling, noisy city with a population of over 2 million. Avenida Independencia is inland from the Caribbean and cuts through the neighborhood of Gazcue. This wide boulevard comes to an end at Parque Independencia, which is just west of the Zona Colonial. This park has rotating art (often replicas or poster art) and photography exhibits, too. These large "works of art" are lit up at night and hung on the wall that encircles the park. Miraculously, people respect what the city is doing here and it never seems to disappear in the night.

Within two blocks of this park, the Zona Colonial begins, with the end of Calle El Conde, a major pedestrian street that's lined with shops, restaurants, fast-food outlets, and Internet centers.

Zona Colonial. The 12 cobblestoned blocks of Santo Domingo's Colonial Zone contain most of the major sights in town. It's one of the most appealing historic districts in the Caribbean. The Zone ends at the seafront, called the Malecón.

El Malecón. Running parallel to Avenida Independencia, Avenida George Washington is more commonly referred to as the Malecón, the word for a seaside boulevard. Running along the Caribbean for nearly five miles, it has tall palms, cafés, high-rise hotels, and sea breezes. It begins at, and is considered part of, Gazcue.

Gazcue. Within walking distance of the Malecón and the Colonial Zone, this blend of residential and commercial areas has many houses from the 1940s and 1950s, when it was a wealthy residential neighborhood. Pleasantly shaded by trees, Gazcue is where the majority of the modern museums are concentrated.

Piantini. Northwest of Gazcue is Piantini, one of the most expensive neighborhoods in Santo Domingo. It's highly urbanized, with apartment towers and offices, as well as a number of fine restaurants and shops.

PLANNING

WHEN TO GO

Any time is the right time to go to Santo Domingo. It is a destination for all seasons, and its warm but temperate climate is only a few degrees cooler in the winter months. Although it gets its share of rainfall during the rainy season, from September through November, that does not matter as much here as it does in a beach destination. One can just go by taxi from hotel to shop to restaurant—no problem. In addition, hotel rates are traditionally the same year-round.

GETTING HERE AND AROUND
AIR TRAVEL

The busy Las Américas International Airport (SDQ), about 15 mi (34 km) east of the city, has many daily flights from the United States. Allow a full two hours to check in for an international flight. La Isabela International Airport (JBQ), also called Higüero for the northern Santo Domingo suburb in which it's located, services mostly charter and domestic flights, with a few international flights.

AIRPORT TRANSFERS If you book a package through a travel agent, your airport transfers will almost certainly be included in the price you pay. Look for your company's sign as you exit baggage claim. If you book independently, then you may have to take a taxi (approximately $40 for two people from either airport) or rent a car. Caribe Tours now has a bus that goes from the airport to downtown Santo Domingo for $10, if you're not burdened by much luggage. (Caribe will take you to its bus station, which is not near any of the hotels, and from there you will have to take a taxi to your accommodations. It makes more sense, especially for solo travelers, to ask someone else in the taxi line if they want to share a cab.) Prieto Tours also offers an airport shuttle service ($18 per person to Las Américas, $20 to La Isabela), with a minimum of two people); you must reserve this service in advance by phone or e-mail, and pay in advance with a credit card. A private driver is also an option.

Airports La Isabela International Dr. Joaquin Balaguer (DHG⊠ *Higüero* ☎ *809/826–4003).* **Las Américas International Airport (***SDQ* ⊠ *Santo Domingo* ☎ *809/412–5888).*

Airport Transfers Caribe Tours (✉ *Av. 27 Febrero, esq. Leopoldo Navarro, Naco* ☎ *809/221-4422* ⊕ *www.caribetours.com.do*). **Prieto Tours** (✉ *Av. Francia 125, Gazcue* ☎ *809/685-0102*).

BUS TRAVEL

Public transit is not one of Santo Domingo's strong points. A system of local buses called *guaguas* runs through the city. They're a lot less fun than walking. Should you want to brave them—and, yes, they will get you out to Juan Dolio and Boca Chica beaches for a fraction of what a taxi costs—your hotel staffers will be able to point out the nearest stops.

Similarly, there are *publicos*, old run-down cars that drive the main drags, picking up as many people as they can squeeze in—seven, eight, or more. Even though the ride may not seem too bad if you're one of the first ones in, as it goes along it will get progressively more crowded until you will want to jump out no matter where you are.

CAR TRAVEL

You do not want a car in Santo Domingo itself, where both parking and traffic are a definite problem, but you can rent a car in Santo Domingo to explore the country at your own pace. Most major car-rental companies have outlets at Las Américas Airport outside Santo Domingo, since this is the airport of choice for most independent travelers who are likely to rent cars.

You can expect to pay as little as $55 for a manual compact car, $85 for an automatic with insurance, or $125 for an SUV from a major agency like Budget. But don't rent the cheapest model, even from a major entity. Chances are that even a two-year old cheapie will be badly beaten up and perhaps even dangerous. You may save money by renting from a local agency, but some travelers prefer the comfort of renting from a known quantity. It's usually cheaper to book your car in advance or book in conjunction with your hotel stay. If you want to rent a car for a day, you can often do so at a car-rental desk at your hotel and have it delivered.

Local Agencies MC Auto Rental Car (✉ *Las Américas Airport* ☎ *809/549-8911* ⊕ *www.mccarrental.com*). **Nelly Rent-a-Car** (✉ *Las Américas Airport* ☎ *809/530-0036; 800/526-6684 in U.S.*).

Major Agencies Avis (✉ *Las Américas Airport* ☎ *809/549-0468*).**Budget** (✉ *Las Américas Airport* ☎ *809/549-0351*). **Europcar** (✉ *Las Américas Airport* ☎ *809/549-0942*). **Hertz** (✉ *Las Américas Airport* ☎ *809/549-0454* ✉ *Calle José Maria Heredia 1, Santo Domingo* ☎ *809/221-5333*).

TAXI TRAVEL

Taxis, which are government regulated, line up outside hotels and restaurants. They're unmetered, and the minimum fare is about $4.50, but you can bargain for less if you order a taxi away from the major hotels. Though they're more expensive, hotel taxis are the nicest and the safest option. Freelance taxis, which are technically illegal but tolerated, aren't allowed to pick up from hotels, so they hang out on the street in front of them and can be half the cost per ride (in a hotel taxi) depending on the distance. Carry some small bills, because drivers rarely seem to have change.

Recommendable radio-taxi companies in Santo Domingo are Tecni-Taxi (which also operates in Puerto Plata) and Apolo. Tecni is the cheapest, quoting RD$80 as a minimum per trip, Apolo RD$90. Hiring a taxi by the hour—with unlimited stops and a minimum of two hours—is often a better option if you're doing a substantial sightseeing trip. Tecni charges RD$240 per hour, but will offer hourly rates only before 6 PM; Apolo charges RD$280 per hour, day or night. When booking an hourly rate, be sure to establish clearly the time that you start. There are also set rates to most out-of-town locations. Call Tecni-Taxi for a rate quote.

Contacts Apolo Taxi (☎ *809/537–0000; 809/537–1245 for a limo, which must be booked far in advance*). **Tecni-Taxi** (☎ *809/567–2010; 809/566–7272 in Santo Domingo*).

INTERNET

Paid Internet access of some kind is available in almost every hotel, though you may sometimes have access to only one slow and old terminal in the lobby, maybe with a Spanish keyboard. Wi-Fi is becoming more prevalent in the better hotels and smaller boutique properties; it's usually free, but generally available only in the lobby and some public areas, rather than in your room—but that is slowly coming. There are dozens of Internet cafés in Santo Domingo, particularly on Calle El Conde. Look up; they're generally on the second stories.

TOURS

When considering a tour, make certain that you're aware of how much time is involved. For example, local tour companies sell city visitors excursions to La Catalina. They typically leave at 6:30 AM and return some 12 hours later! It can take you three hours just to get to where the boat disembarks, because you will usually have a long stop in at least one area all-inclusive resort. You arrive back in the city, exhausted, at nearly 7 PM, and you will pay about $130.

The Audio Guide is a self-guided walking tour of the Zona Colonial. For US$30 you get information about 25 historic sights, admission to three museums, and a nonalcoholic beverage at the Hard Rock Cafe. The company targets cruise-ship passengers with its booth at the cruise pier, but anyone with a major credit card can rent the audio tour.

DomRep Tours, a European-owned travel agency, specializes in individual tours and eco-adventures—even to Jarabacoa and Barahona. With an office in the Zona Colonial, the company offers city-breaks of two or three nights that include airport transfers, hotels, tours, and lunch. Guided private tours of the historic sights in the Zone are available, as are tours to nearby beaches and sights, including some multiday trips.

EcodoTours, as the name implies, specializes in eco-adventures, but also brings groups into the capital for city tours and will pick up individual travelers at their hotels. One excellent option is a "Santo Domingo Night Tour." Included is a drink, two disco admissions, and time at a casino for $49, a good deal, since taxis to all these places can easily cost $40.

The well-established Prieto Tours, an agent for American Express, gives tours of the city and surrounding area in English. For the latter, these

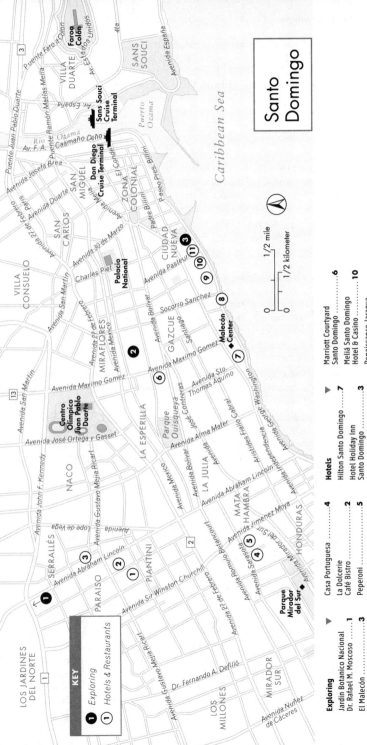

Santo Domingo

Caribbean Sea

0   1/2 mile

0   1/2 kilometer

Exploring

Jardin Botanico Nacional
Dr. Rafael M. Moscoso **1**
El Malecón **3**
Plaza de la Cultura **2**

Restaurants

Adrian Tropical **8**
Casa Portuguesa **4**
La Dolcerie
Café Bistro **2**
Peperoni **5**
Sophia's **1**

Hotels

Hilton Santo Domingo **7**
Hotel Holiday Inn
Santo Domingo **3**
InterContinental
V Centerario **11**
Marriott Courtyard
Santo Domingo **6**
Meliá Santo Domingo
Hotel & Casino **10**
Renaissance Jaragua
Hotel & Casino **9**

KEY

● Exploring
① Hotels & Restaurants

large bus tours usually include guests from the all-inclusive resorts outside the city. The company offers a good three-hour tour of the Zona Colonial for about US$25. If you have the stamina for it, a six-hour tour takes in the Zone, El Faro, the Aquarium, and "modern" Santo Domingo, including lunch, museum entrances, and an hour of shopping time for $50.

Tours, Trips, Treks & Travel specializes in educational, adventure, and company programs for groups. Although based in Cabarete, it operates all over the Dominican Republic, including Santo Domingo. The company is especially good at helping to organize cultural excursions. One recent project had TTT&T setting up remote camps for volunteer workers who came to build a community center. They will also help plan creative, non-cookie-cutter weddings.

Private tour guides are another option, and you'll have to pay approximately $125 a day for a guide (more if the guide uses a private driver). Your hotel concierge will know the good English-speaking guides, though you may pay more than if you organized the tour yourself. Dré Broeders is a multilingual, licensed tour guide with 16 years of experience in the Dominican Republic who can give a customized tour for two people or a group. His late-model car is clean and well maintained, and he is very reliable. He will also pick up passengers from any of the area airports and bring them to any destination on the southeast coast. Although he lives in Juan Dolio, he's an expert on the Colonial Zone and runs a great tour.

Kate Wallace, a recognized birding authority who leads tours in various parts of the country, will lead private bird-watching tours in the Jardin Botanico Nacional Dr. Rafael M. Moscoso.

Contacts Audio Guide (✉ *Don Diego Cruise Terminal, Av. del Porto, Zona Colonial* ☎ *809/221–2221 for CTN television network*). **DomRep Tours** (✉ *Plaza Paseo del Conde, Calle El Conde 360, Zona Colonial* ☎ *809/686–0278; 829/367–7421 cell* ⊕ *www.domreptours.com*). **Dré Broeders** (☎ *809/526–3533; 809/399–5766 cell* ✍ *drebroeders@hotmail.com or peralta162@gmail. com*). **EcodoTours** (☎ *809/815–1074* ⊕ *www.ecodotours.com*).**Kate Wallace** (☎ *809/686–0882* ⊕ *www.todytours.com* ✍ *katetody@gmail.com*). **Prieto Tours** (✉ *Av. Francia 125, Gazcue* ☎ *809/685–0102* ⊕ *www.prietotours. com*). **Tours, Trips, Treks & Travel** (✉ *Cabarete* ☎ *809/867–8884 in Cabarete* ⊕ *www.4Tdomrep.com*).

VISITOR INFORMATION

Contacts Dominican Tourism Office (✉ *Palacio Bortello, Isabel la Catolica 103, across from Parque Colón, Zona Colonial* ☎ *809/686–3858* ⊙ *Mon.–Sat. 9–3*).

EXPLORING SANTO DOMINGO

The easiest away to start your trip to this fascinating city is to fly into Las Américas International Airport and proceed by taxi or prearranged transfer to downtown. Chances are you'll be staying in a hotel either in the Zona Colonial or on the Malecón. Much of your exploration can be done on foot—that's certainly true in the Zone—and it's easy to walk from one Malecón property to another. In other areas, including Piantini, you'll need to drive or be driven. At night it's not really safe to walk the Malecón alone, but if you're with a group it's usually fine. To be safe, take a hotel taxi. The most important thing is to have fun!

THE ZONA COLONIAL

Fodor'sChoice
★ Spanish civilization in the New World began in Santo Domingo's 12-block **Zona Colonial.** As you stroll its narrow streets, it's easy to imagine this old city as it was when the likes of Columbus, Cortés, and Ponce de León walked the cobblestones, pirates sailed in and out, and colonists started settling. Tourist brochures claim that "history comes alive here"—a surprisingly truthful statement. Almost every Thursday to Sunday night at 8:30 a typical "folkloric show" is staged at Parque Colón and Plaza de España. During the Christmas holidays there are an artisans' fair and live music concerts. A fun horse-and-carriage ride throughout the Zone costs $25 for an hour, with any commentary in Spanish. The steeds are no thoroughbreds, but they clip right along. You can also negotiate to use them as a taxi, say to go down to the Malecón. The drivers usually hang out in front of the Hostal Nicolas de Ovando. History buffs will want to spend a day exploring the many "firsts" that happened here. You can get a free walking-tour map and brochures in English at the Secretaria de Estado de Turismo office at Parque Colón (Columbus Park), where you may be approached by freelance, English-speaking guides who will want to make it all come alive for you. They'll work enthusiastically for $20 an hour for four people. Wear comfortable shoes. Make certain that your guide-to-be is wearing a government-issued, pictured I.D. around his neck. Their "uniform" is khakis and blue shirts.

Numbers in the margin correspond to points of interest on the Zona Colonial Exploring map. Note: Hours and admission charges to sites are erratic.

WHAT TO SEE

❹ Alcazar de Colón. The castle of Don Diego Colón, built in 1517, has 40-inch-thick coral-limestone walls. The Renaissance-style structure, with its balustrade and double row of arches, has strong Moorish, Gothic, and Isabelline influences. The 22 rooms are furnished in a style to which the viceroy of the island would have been accustomed—right down to the dishes and the viceregal shaving mug. Multilingual audio guides, which can be rented for RD$50, are worth it. Costumed "docents" appear on Saturday morning, and on Saturday night the Colón family walks through the castle again, as actors in period costume play the role of Diego and his family from 8 PM to midnight. ⌂ *Plaza de España off Calle Emiliano Tejera at foot of Calle Las Damas, Zona Colonial* ☎ *809/682–4750* ⌷ *RD$60* ☉ *Mon.–Sat. 9–5, Sun. 9–4. Closed if no cruise ship in port.*

❾ Calle Las Damas. "Ladies Street" was named after the elegant ladies of
★ the court: in the Spanish tradition, they promenaded in the evening. Here you can see a sundial dating from 1753 and the Casa de los Jesuitas, which houses a fine research library for colonial history as well

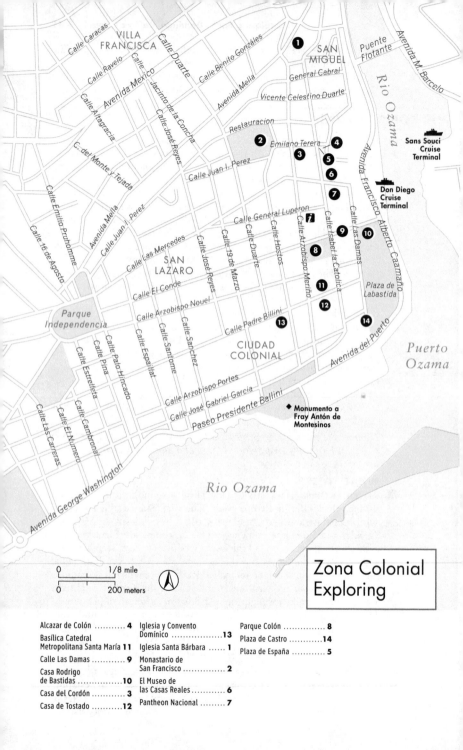

Zona Colonial
Exploring

0   1/8 mile
0   200 meters

as the **Institute for Hispanic Culture**; admission is free, and it's open weekdays from 8 to 4:30. If you follow the street going toward the Malecón, you will pass a picturesque alley, fronted by a wrought-iron gate, where there are perfectly maintained colonial structures owned by the Catholic Church.

 Casa Rodrigo de Bastidas. There's a lovely inner courtyard here with tropical plants and galleries for temporary exhibitions.

Within the Casa Rodrigo de Bastidas, the brilliant **Museo Infantils Trampolin** is a great destination for your kids even if they do not speak Spanish. This is the most kid-friendly venue in the city, and the interactive experience (for parents, too) delves into paleontology, geology, ecology, biodiversity, water, and technology. It's a fun place and certainly stimulating, with earthquake and volcano simulations and a jungle gym made with giant, pretend body parts. Call in advance, and you may be able to get a bilingual guide. ⊠ *Calle Las Damas off Calle El Conde, Zona Colonial* ☎ *809/685–5551 for Casa Rodrigo de Bastidas, 809/685–5551 for Museo Infantils Trampolin* ⊕ *www.trampolin.org. do* ☜ *Casa free, Museo Infantils Trampolin RD$125; children RD$60* ☾ *Tues.–Sun. 9–5.*

 Casa del Cordón. This structure, built in 1503, is the western hemisphere's oldest surviving stone house. Columbus's son, Diego Colón, viceroy of the colony, and his wife lived here until the Alcazar was finished. It was in this house, too, that Sir Francis Drake was paid a ransom to prevent him from totally destroying the city. ⊠ *Calle Emiliano Tejera at Calle Isabel la Católica, within Banco Popular, Zona Colonial* ☎ *809/544–8915* ☜ *Free* ☾ *Weekdays 9–4.*

⑫ **Casa de Tostado.** The house, built in the early 16th century, was the residence of writer Don Francisco Tostado. Note its unique twin Gothic windows. It houses the Museo de la Familia Dominicana (Museum of the Dominican Family), which has exhibits on well-heeled 19th-century Dominican society. The house, garden, and antiquities have all been restored. ⊠ *Calle Padre Bellini 22, near Calle Arzobispo Meriño, Zona Colonial* ☎ *809/689–5000* ☜ *RD$40* ☾ *Mon.–Sat. 9–4.*

⑪ **Basílica Catedral Metropolitana Santa María de la Encarnación.** The coral-limestone facade of the first cathedral in the New World towers over the south side of the Parque Colón. Spanish workmen began building the cathedral in 1514, but left to search for gold in Mexico. The church was finally finished in 1540. Its facade is composed of architectural elements from the late Gothic to the lavish Plateresque style. Inside, the high altar is made of hammered silver. At this writing, a museum is being built for the cathedral's treasures. ⊠ *Calle Arzobispo Meriño, Zona Colonial* ☎ *809/689–1920* ☜ *Free* ☾ *Mon.–Sat. 9–4; Sun. masses begin at 6* AM.

⑬ **Iglesia y Convento Domínico.** Founded in 1510, this graceful building is still a Dominican church and convent. Note the prominent and beautiful rose window. In 1538 Pope Paul III visited here and was so impressed with the lectures on theology that he granted the church and convent the title of university, making it the oldest institution of higher learning in the New World. ⊠ *Calle Padre Bellini and Av. Duarte, Zona Colonial* ☎ *809/682–3780* ☜ *Free* ☾ *Tues.–Sun. 9–6.*

❶ **Iglesia Santa Bárbara.** This combination church and fortress, the only one of its kind in Santo Domingo, was completed in 1562. ⊠ *Av. Mella, between Calle Isabel la Católica and Calle Arzobispo Meriño, Zona Colonial* ☎ *809/682–3307* 🖳 *Free* ⊙ *Mon.–Sat. 6:00–6:45; Sun. masses begin at 8, 9, and 10* AM.

❷ **Monasterio de San Francisco.** Constructed between 1512 and 1544, the St. Francis Monastery contained the church, convent, and hospital of the Franciscan order. Sir Francis Drake's demolition squad significantly damaged the building in 1586, and in 1673 an earthquake nearly finished the job, but when it's floodlit at night, the eerie ruins are dramatic indeed. The Spanish government has donated money to turn this into a beautiful cultural center, but we are still waiting. In the meantime, on certain Sunday nights, at 7 PM, the music, often live, plays, and it becomes an old-fashioned block party. Zone residents mingle with expats and tourists, who snap pictures of the octogenarians dancing the merengue and the bachata. Others who come are content to just sit in white plastic chairs, swaying and clapping. It's nice. ⊠ *Calle Hostos at Calle Emiliano, Zona Colonial* ☎ *809/687–4722.*

❻ **El Museo de las Casas Reales.** This is a remarkable museum that will
★ help you comprehend the discovery of the New World by Christopher Columbus and the entire 16th-century epic. Housing Taino finds, colonial artifacts, coins salvaged from wrecks of Spanish galleons, authentic colonial furnishings, as well as a collection of weapons, the museum also has one of the handsomest colonial edifices in the Zone. Built in the Renaissance style, it was the seat of Spanish government, housing the governor's office and the Royal Court. It has beautiful windows, for example, done in the Plateresque style. A frequent wedding venue, it also functions as an art gallery, with rotating shows. When candlelit at night, it's truly magical. ⊠ *Calle Las Damas, end of street, right before Plaza de España, Zona Colonial* ☎ *809/682–4202* 🖳 *RD$50* ⊙ *Tues.–Sun. 9–5.*

❼ **Pantheon Nacional.** The National Pantheon (circa 1714) was once a Jesuit monastery and later a theater. The real curiosity here is the military guard, who stays as still as the statues, despite the schoolchildren who try to make him flinch. ⊠ *Calle Las Damas, near Calle de Las Mercedes, Zona Colonial* ☎ *809/689–6010* 🖳 *Free* ⊙ *Mon.–Sat. 8* AM *to 9* PM.

❽ **Parque Colón.** The huge statue of Christopher Columbus in the park named after him dates from 1897, and is the work of sculptor Ernesto Gilbert. Like all the parks in the Zona Colonial, this one is quite a social gathering place. ⊠ *El Conde at Arzobispo Meriño, Zona Colonial.*

⓮ **Plaza de Castro.** Calle Las Damas dead-ends as it goes in the direction of the Malecón. Few people ever make it past the junction of Calle Padre Bellini, thinking there's nothing to see. If you keep walking past the convent (you may hear the nuns singing in the chapel), just keep going until the street actually stops; make a right turn, and you'll find yourself in this delightful little park. Known almost solely to residents of the Zone, the Plaza de Castro was not named after the Cuban dictator but rather a Dominican poet, Arturo Bautista Pellerano Castro. It's an enchanting green space, peaceful, and free of litter. The new Coco Boutique

Hotel fronts the park, and the co-owner, Eduardo, is probably the best bartender in the Zone. Have one of his fresh strawberry *mojitos* or a perfect martini. Sit at the table on the deck facing the plaza or have it on the rooftop. Up there you can get comfy in a Balinese sun bed and count the ships that go sailing by. ⊠ *At end of Calle Las Damas.*

5 **Plaza de España.** This wide esplanade, which goes past the Casas de Reales in front of Don Diego Columbus's former palace, El Alcazar de Colón, is the area in the Zona Colonial where national holidays

DID YOU KNOW?

Santo Domingo was once a walled city. In centuries past the enormous walls surrounding Santo Domingo safeguarded the city from attacks by pirates and buccaneers. Behind these massive stone walls lay the Plaza de España and the Alcazar of Don Diego Columbus. The beautiful San Diego gates can still be seen, as can remains of the fort that bears the same name.

are celebrated. The annual Coca-Cola–sponsored Christmas tree is here. It's bordered by what once were the ramparts of the original walled city. People enjoy the views of the Ozama River from here, and watch the cruise-ship activity below at the terminal. Lovers stroll here by night, sharing a kiss under the gas lamps. When many people talk about the Plaza de España, they are often referring to the half-dozen restaurants in a row, which are on the upper level of these 16th- and 17th-century warehouses. The popular tables are on their outdoor decks. ⊠ *Bordered by Calle Las Damas and Calle La Atarazana, Zona Colonial.*

NEED A BREAK? Your explorations will surely take you to the Plaza de España, and you'll want to take a breather in one of its restaurants. **Angelo's (⊠ *Plaza de España, Zona Colonial* ☎ 809/686–3586)** has a gregarious, hands-on owner, and consequently service is better than good. From the old school, he's a suave and gracious host. Although the restaurant is overly elegant and pricey, with some entrées around $20, you can make a nice lunch from a cold beer and an appetizer. The third-floor terrace, with its lion's-head fountain, is where the "in" crowd sits.

ELSEWHERE IN SANTO DOMINGO

If you only have two or three days, you should probably just take in the sights in the Colonial Zone. But if you're looking to explore some of the city's major museums, most of them can be found in the Gazcue neighborhood, north of the Malecón.

Numbers in the margin correspond to points of interest on the Santo Domingo map. Note: Hours and admission charges to sites are erratic.

1 **Jardín Botánico Nacional Dr. Rafael M. Moscoso.** A tranquil, green oasis in a frenetic city, this is also one of the best botanical gardens in the Caribbean. A petite train will take you around for RD$45 (every half hour until 4:30), or you can just stroll. If you have limited time, then just hit the high points that interest you. There's an arboretum, a small forest reserve, a Japanese garden, an orchid garden, and more. This is

also the best place for bird-watchers in Santo Domingo; you can see the common endemic birds and the palm chat, the only member of its taxonomic family and the national bird of the Dominican Republic. The Hispaniolan Ornithological Society offers a free walk the first Sunday of every month at 7 AM. ⊠ *Av. República de Colombia, corner Los Proceres, Jardines de Norte* ☎ *809/385–2611* ▨ *RD$45* ⊘ *Daily 9–6.*

❷ **Plaza de la Cultura.** Landscaped lawns, modern sculptures, and sleek buildings make up the Plaza de la Cultura. There are several museums and a theater here. The works of 20th-century Domini-

> **A BOOK OF REAL-LIFE INTERIORS**
>
> While at the Museo de Arte Moderno look for the photography book *Interiors*, by Polibio Díaz, whose photography won him a place at the Fifth Biennial of the Caribbean. The prize money enabled him to create this memorable photo essay, which is far more than a coffee-table book. He has a series of three photos each of interiors of humble, Dominican *casitas*. It's colorful, revealing, and often ribald, not to mention a real slice of Dominican life.

can and foreign artists are displayed in the **Museo de Arte Moderno** (☎ *809/682–2153*). One of the native sons is Elvis Aviles, an abstract painter whose works have a lot of texture. His art combines Spanish influences with Taino Indian and other Dominican symbols. Tony Capellan is one of the best-known artists, representing the Dominican Republic in major international exhibitions. The **Museo del Hombre Dominicano** (☎ *809/687–3622*) traces the migrations of Indians from South America through the Caribbean islands. The **Teatro Nacional** (☎ *809/687–3191*) stages fascinating performances in Spanish only, but don't let that stop you. When in Rome, you would go to an Italian opera, right? ⊠ *Plaza de la Cultura, Gazcue* ▨ *Museo de Arte Moderno RD$50, Museo del Hombre Dominicano RD$75* ⊘ *Tues.–Sun. 10–5.*

WHERE TO EAT

Santo Domingo's dining scene is the best in the country and probably as fine a selection of restaurants as you can find anywhere in the Caribbean. If you avoid the touristy places in the Zona Colonial that have mediocre fare and just-ok service, you can instead focus on one of the capital's great fine-dining options, such as La Residence. By ordering carefully, you can have a nice dinner here for less than $30 per person. Most notably, you'll have caring service and be sequestered in luxe surroundings away from the tourist hustle.

Some of the best restaurant choices are not in the tourist zones but in the business districts of the modern city and in the upscale residential neighborhoods where the wealthy *capitaleños* reside. They typically dress for dinner and dine late. The locals usually start eating after 9:30 PM, when the Americans are just finishing their desserts.

Restaurants tend to be more formal in Santo Domingo than in the rest of the country, so worn-out khakis and flip-flops are simply not acceptable, especially at dinner. For lunch in a casual café in the Zone,

Cruising Into Santo Domingo

Santo Domingo has two stellar cruise-ship terminals, and has become a growing port for cruise passengers. Despite the sluggish economy, in 2009 cruise-ship visits were up 24%. The final tally of cruise-ship passengers for 2010 throughout the country is expected to be close to 600,000.

The **Port of Don Diego** is on the Ozuma River, facing the Avenida del Puerto, and across the street are steps that lead up to the main pedestrian shopping street of the Zona Colonial, Calle El Conde. A lovely yellow-and-white building, with stained-glass windows and faux gaslights, it has a small cafeteria, and potted palms soften the cordoned-off lines where passengers wait to have their tickets checked and go through immigration. The reception area has telephones, Internet access, and a currency exchange. Just down the dock is an ATM machine; in front of that is a counter where you can get cold drinks and snacks. Across from it is a booth offering self-guided audio tours.

The **Sans Souci Terminal** complex, diagonally across the Ozama River from Don Diego Terminal, on Avenida España, has been operational since early 2010, but this long-term rede-velopment project is still a work in progress. Its mezzanine level accom-modates immigration and customs, duty-free shops, and both Internet and information centers. Like the Port of Don Diego, it has stunning lighting systems that cover the exterior and perimeter areas for greater security and visibility for visitors. When com-pleted, the complex will have finished its marina, have a full complement of stores, a 122-acre real-estate development, a new sports arena, and more. This major project is aimed at integrating the port area and the Colonial Zone to create an appealing destination for cruisers, yachtsmen, and high-end tourists.

for example, shorts (though never short shorts) are acceptable, but not at the better, fine-dining establishments, either for lunch or dinner. Similarly, at night in the better establishments trousers and collared shirts are required for men, and skirts, dresses, or resort-casual slacks appropriate for women. Ties aren't required anywhere, and few places still require jackets, even the finer establishments.

ABOUT THE FOOD

The city's culinary repertoire includes Spanish, Italian, Middle East-ern, Indian, Japanese, and *nueva cocina Dominicana* (contemporary Dominican cuisine). If seafood is on the menu, it's bound to be fresh. Among the best Dominican specialties are *queso frito* (fried cheese), *sancocho* (a thick meat stew served with rice and avocado slices), *arroz con pollo* (rice with beans and fried chicken parts), *mofango* (mashed green plantains and shredded pork or chicken and chittlins), *pescado al coco* (fish in coconut sauce), *plátanos* (fried sweet plantains), and *tos-tones* (fried green plantains). On this sugar-producing island the local candies are 98% sugar, the populace consumes far more Coca-Cola than Americans do, but when it comes to dessert, they come up short. It's the quiet corner of the menu, where you may have three, possibly four choices, one of them being flan.

Shacks and stands that serve cheap eats are an integral part of the culture and landscape, but eat street food at your own risk. Presidente is the most popular local beer, but try a Bohemia, which has more flavor. Brugal rum is popular with the Dominicans. Barceló *anejo* (aged) is as smooth as cognac, and Barceló Imperial is so special it's sold only at Christmas.

WHAT IT COSTS IN U.S. DOLLARS					
	¢	$	$$	$$$	$$$$
RESTAURANTS	under $8	$8–$12	$12–$20	$20–$30	Over $30

Restaurant prices are per person for a main course at dinner and do not include the 16% tax (*ITBIS*) and 10% service charge (*ley*).

ZONA COLONIAL

$$–$$$
ITALIAN
✕ **La Briciola.** This high-profile restaurant has continually attracted a clientele of well-heeled residents and international visitors, including President Leonel, Andy Garcia, and Sammy Sosa. In the early 1990s a group of friends from Milan made the momentous decision to restore a trio of 16th-century buildings in the Zone. This historical ambience, with seating in the brick-arched, Spanish courtyard, continues to be the magnet—much more than the food. The menu has not kept up with contemporary trends, nor are the plates garnished artistically. Still, if you go with the house-made pastas and gnocchi; the oversized Briciola salad of arugula, shrimp, and shaved Parmesan cheese; and a grappa to cap your meal, you can have a lovely and romantic night out. The man playing the baby grand and the white twinkle lights add to all this. ⊠ *Arzobispo Meriño, corner of Padre Bellini (across from Plazoleta Park), Zona Colonial* ☎ *809/688–5055* ⚓ *Reservations essential* ▤ *AE, MC, V* ☯ *Closed Sun. and from 3–7 PM Mon.–Sat.*

$–$$
CARIBBEAN
✕ **Mesón D' Bari.** Dominicans call this one a "long hitter"—as in baseball, which will inevitably be on the TV at the bar. For more than 25 years, owner Sr. Marisol has been feeding the local Zoners the recipes of his grandmother. This simple, two-story Dominican restaurant has become a number-one hangout for artists, baseball players, politicians, businessmen, tourists, and even unaccompanied *gringas*, who feel comfortable here. The menu has really flavorful dishes, including creole-style eggplant, empanadas of crab and conch, grilled crabs, and stewed, sweet orange peels. Sadly, the presentations are dated, so expect garnishes of shredded carrots and iceberg lettuce, but now on white geometric plates. Prices are up even though the culinary ambition is not. Live music usually happens on the weekends; otherwise, you'll hear some soothing music from decades past (think "Moonglow"). Some of the owner's artworks are among the wall-to-wall local paintings. ⊠ *Calle Hostos 302, corner of Salomé Ureña, Zona Colonial* ☎ *809/687–4091* ▤ *AE, MC, V.*

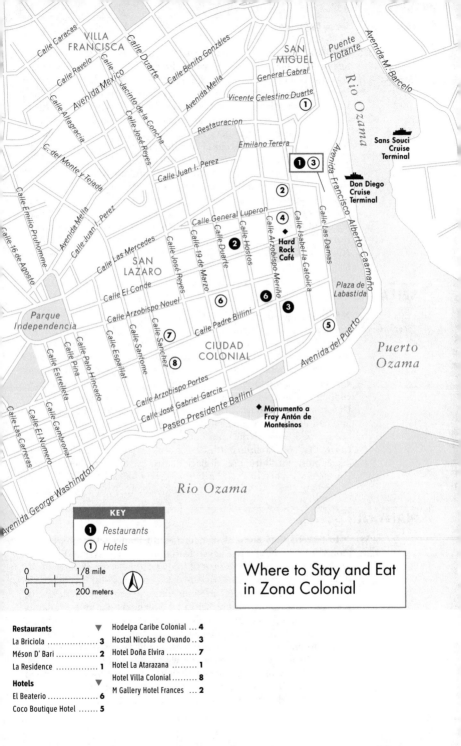

Where to Stay and Eat
in Zona Colonial

KEY

1 *Restaurants*

1 *Hotels*

0   1/8 mile

0   200 meters

Restaurants ▼

La Briciola **3**

Méson D' Bari **2**

La Residence **1**

Hotels ▼

El Beaterio **6**

Coco Boutique Hotel **5**

Hodelpa Caribe Colonial ... **4**

Hostal Nicolas de Ovando .. **3**

Hotel Doña Elvira **7**

Hotel La Atarazana **1**

Hotel Villa Colonial **8**

M Gallery Hotel Frances ... **2**

$$$ ✕**La Residence.** This fine-dining enclave has always had the setting—
FRENCH   Spanish-colonial architecture, with pillars and archways overlooking a
Fodor's Choice   courtyard—but an esoteric lunch-dinner menu with high prices that did
★   not always deliver offset it. Now it has a French Certified Master Chef,
Denis Schetrit (there are only 300 such designated chefs), who serves
classically grounded yet innovative cuisine. He also cleverly utilizes
local produce and offers many moderately priced choices. An amuse-
bouche arrives before your meal, and there is an excellent bread service.
The three-course daily *menu de chef* is less than $28, including tax. It
could be brochettes of spit-roasted duck, chicken au poivre, or vegetable
risotto. You could start with a salad of pan-fried young squid and leave
room for a luscious French pastry. Veer from the daily specials menu,
and prices can go higher, but they remain fair; even the grilled Angus
fillet and braised oxtail with foie-gras sauce and wild mushrooms is
reasonable. Often, musicians romantically serenade diners. ⊠ *Hostal
Nicolas de Ovando, Calle Las Damas, Zona Colonial* ☎ *809/685–9955*
▤ *AE, MC, V.*

BELLA VISTA

$$$ ✕**Casa Portuguesa.** Near the Hotel Embajador, this is a darling of the
PORTUGUESE   privileged set. The decor is staged to resemble a house, with shawls
from Portugal, white lace, and shutters. Portuguese tiles are even found
in the restrooms. Authentic dishes include *bacalhua* (salt cod), *feijoada*
(a hearty bean and pork stew from Brazil), and shellfish, notably clams
and shrimp. Everything's flavorful, and the portions are usually large
enough to share, which is good, since this is not an inexpensive place.
Unfortunately, products are not always imported from Portugal, service can be mediocre, and much of what's on the wine list may have
already said *"adios"* (the list is not kept up to date). Ask in advance to
ensure that your favorite bottle or dish is available that evening to avoid
disappointment. But if you sit back and enjoy the Portuguese ballads,
you can have a fine time. ⊠ *Av. Jardins del Embajador 10B, Bella Vista*
☎ *809/508–2063* ⌦ *Reservations essential* ▤ *AE, MC, V* ⊗ *No lunch.*

PIANTINI

$–$$ ✕**La Dolcerie Café Bistro.** This cutesy, kid-friendly restaurant/bakery
ECLECTIC   looks like a modern-day English tearoom. A new player in Piantini's
growing restaurant inventory, it's buzzing and busy for all three meals
(it's the "in" brunch place for well-heeled residents of this fashionable
neighborhood). Happily, it's also moderately priced, even for delicious,
generous dishes like Montechristo's Medianoche Croque Madame,
which includes pulled pork, the eggs Benedict dishes and the Cubano.
At breakfast, they squeeze your juice and tempt you with house-made
croissants and beignets. For lunch there's grilled *churasco* (a spicy sau-
sage) and such sides as homemade waffle-cut fries in silver baskets.
From the litany of pureed potato options, try those with caramelized
onions and Manchego cheese. Finish with a rich profiterole. Now if
only they would remember that silverware comes with the linen napkins

and consider turning down the music. ✉ *Rafael Augusto Sanchez 20, Piantini* ☎ *809/338–0814* ▤ *AE, MC, V.*

$$$ ✕**Peperoni.** One of Santo Domingo's long-standing destination restau-
ECLECTIC rants, Peperoni continues to evolve, which keeps it on the list of "in" places for the well heeled of all ages. The menu is contemporary and multinational, and only the highest-quality ingredients are used. You may not make it past the appetizers, like a warm goat-cheese salad, and, from the menu's "Asian Market," a sushi roll of sweet plantain, tuna, and avocado. But try to get to the main courses, giving the gnoc-chi, pastas, and risottos your first consideration. Many of the Ital-ian offerings date back to 1999, the restaurant's beginning. The meat dishes, including the fig-glazed veal chop in a mushroom demi-glace with spaghetti squash and haricots verts, are often exceptions. Service is laudable. Take the savvy wine steward's recommendations; an Italian or Chilean reserva works well with much of the menu. Sit out on the deck under a market umbrella or in the indoor dining room, decorated with food-related artwork and painted with contrasting, contemporary colors. ✉ *Sarasota 23, at Plaza Universitaria, Piantini* ☎ *809/508–1330* ▤ *AE, MC, V.*

$$$ ✕**Sophia's.** Don't ask for Sophia; she doesn't exist. "Her" high-profile
ECLECTIC restaurant is actually owned by a prime Dominican family that appreci-ates fine food and wine, both of which are on exhibit there. Although there's a certain formality expressed in suited doormen and profes-sional waiters, the setting is chi-chi and contemporary, with orchids galore and crisp white linens. When you see the first page of the menu you may be amazed that prices are so reasonable (gourmet burgers, *nueva ensaladas,* and creative sandwiches go for around $10). Both lunch and dinner share the same menu. Keep reading, and the prices increase. Starters begin at $10, and the mains range from $12 to $34, the top spot being held by a rack of lamb; sides are additional. To keep expenses down, order an innovative appetizer such as Japanese-style miso eggplant or a ceviche tasting, accompanied by a memorable bottle from the extensive wine list. Wrap it up with warm guava cheesecake and an aged port. (A new chef has been hired, so expect some menu changes). If so inclined, you can join the young lovelies and the *guapos* (handsomes) at the granite bar 'til late (3 AM on Friday and Saturday and 1 AM the rest of the week). ✉ *Paseo de los Locutores 19, Piantini* ☎ *809/620–1001* ▤ *AE, MC, V.*

GAZCUE

$$ ✕**Adrian Tropical.** Hotel concierges still recommend this Malecón institu-
CARIBBEAN tion as having the best Dominican food (it's now a local chain of four). It's touristy, yes, but Dominicans still make up the majority of custom-ers. You may want to try it for the three-tiered setting overlooking the ocean, as well as the opportunity to see if the excellent *sancocho* (a rich, meaty stew), *mofongo* (stuffed mashed plantains), and other local favorites are as good as you hear. The *sopa de pescado* (fish soup) is the best this side of Mexico. You can also get wild and try the goat or pig's feet, or play it safe with grilled items and tropical sides like yucca. The restaurant serves breakfast (from 7:30) and lunch (a buffet), as well as

Sancocho Dominicano

The Dominican national dish was traditionally made with seven different meats. The following recipe, which serves eight, is courtesy of Villa Pajon, a rustic lodge in the mountains of the Valle Nuevo.

Ingredients:

- 1 chicken (with bones), cut into pieces

- 8 pork chops

- 2 limes, juiced

- 4 cloves of garlic, mashed

- 1 large onion, chopped

- 1 habanero pepper, chopped

- 1 bunch cilantro, chopped

- 1 tablespoon salt

- 1 tablespoon bitter orange juice (fresh or bottled)

- 1 tablespoon apple cider vinegar

- 1 teaspoon oregano

- 2 tablespoons cooking oil

- 1 green plantain, peeled and cut into 1" pieces

- 1 lb. yucca, peeled and cut into 2" pieces

- 1 lb. calabaza (auyama), peeled and cut into 2" pieces (butternut squash works, too)

- 1 corn on the cob, cut in half

- 8 to 12 cups water

Season the chicken pieces and pork chops with lime juice, garlic, onion, salt, cilantro, pepper, and oregano. Then sauté the meat and chicken in a large pot with the cooking oil for approximately 20 minutes. Add the water and cook until meat is almost done. Adjust the cooking time, if necessary, so you do not overcook the meat. Remove the meat from the cooking liquid, and strain the liquid, returning it to the pot. On high heat, bring the liquid to a boil, and add the plantain pieces, immediately reducing the heat to medium-high. Cook for five minutes, then add the yucca and pumpkin and cook for 10 minutes more. Finally, add the corn. When the vegetables are almost done, add the chicken and pork chops, vinegar, and bitter orange juice. Adjust the season-ing, if necessary, and cook for 20 more minutes on high.

Serve with white rice, *concon**, avo-cado slices, and hot-pepper sauce if you like.

*Concon: The concon is the golden, crispy rice at the bottom of the pot that is leftover after the bulk of the cooked rice has been removed from the pot. If you crisp the rice yourself, be sure it does not burn.

dinner: it's open 24 hours, and the clubbers come calling for late-night sancocho. Note: Be careful crossing the street here: use the crosswalk. At night on the Malecón, be alert for muggers, too. ⊠ *Av. George Wash-ington 2, Gazcue* ☎ *809/221–1764* ⊟ *AE, MC, V.*

WHERE TO STAY

Most of the better hotels are on or near the Malecón, a short taxi ride from the Zona Colonial. But increasingly visitors want to stay in the Zone itself. The petite boutique hotels in the Zona Colonial are all reconstructions, some of architecturally significant colonial-era buildings. The five-star Hostal Nicolas Ovando, one of only two full-service hotels in the neighborhood, was built to resemble the residence of the city's first governor, Nicolas Ovando. Always make your reservations at the smaller properties as far in advance as possible, because the posh surroundings, good service, and favorable pricing keep them full.

The Malecón's high-rise hotels continue to offer a deluxe experience, at prices that are reasonable for a capital city. Seldom do you have to pay as much as $200, and that would be for the concierge level or a suite. Moderately priced American chains have made inroads into the country. They offer stateside amenities, even luxury bedding programs and in-city pools, for less than the Malecón majors. Although these chain hotels may not have the same glamour or the primo locations, they're good choices, especially for budget-conscious, cruise-ship passengers who must spend a night before embarking. The pre- and post-cruise business has increased the weekend occupancy of some participating hotels by 20%. In 2009 more than 500,000 cruisers came to the Dominican Republic, a large percentage of them to Santo Domingo.

WHAT IT COSTS IN U.S. DOLLARS					
	¢	$	$$	$$$	$$$$
HOTELS*	under $80	$80–$150	$150–$250	$250–$350	over $350
HOTELS**	under $125	$125–$250	$250–$350	$350–$450	over $450

*EP, BP, CP **AI, FAP, MAP

Hotel prices are per night for a double room in high season, excluding 16% tax and 10% service charge.

ZONA COLONIAL

$
HOTEL

El Beaterio. As you sit in the coral stone lobby, with high ceilings, brick archways, and Spanish wrought-iron chandeliers, you're enmeshed in 500 years of history. Once a convent, this boutique hotel has beautifully quiet (albeit petite and dark) second-floor rooms with stone floors and small windows. In each room hangs a unique painting done on linen-like fabric. The once-heavy lobby furniture has been elegantly reupholstered, and better still, the ugly bedspreads in the rooms replaced with cream-colored satin ones and paired with earth-toned drapes. Using the same linen-like fabric, an artist has made a unique painting for each room. A French owner (absent) and French-speaking staff make El Beaterio attractive to Francophiles. In addition to the tranquil courtyard, there is also a rooftop terrace with a bar. You'll pay an extra $17 per night for air-conditioning, but room prices include tax and service. **Pros:** breakfast is quite good (comes with classical music); convenient location with Duarte Park across the street; free Wi-Fi. **Cons:** the lobby and breakfast room are too dark; hotel doesn't accept credit cards or traveler's checks. ⊠ *Calle Duarte 8, Zona Colonial* ☎ *809/687–8657* ⊕ *www.elbeaterio.com* ⏎ *11 rooms* ⚹ *In-room: a/c, no phone, safe. In-hotel: Wi-Fi hotspot* ═ *No credit cards* ⏘ *BP.*

$ ⌨ **Coco Boutique Hotel.** Behind the soft, Caribbean turquoise façade
HOTEL   you'll find a very untypical bed-and-breakfast, not to mention earth tones with white—almost everywhere: the reception and lounge, the stark wooden staircase, the grillwork on the French doors; it's breathtaking, actually, with the zebra-skin rug and dark green plants offering contrast. Coco, which is a handsome renovation of a circa-1920s house, has developed a soul, and the silver-and-gold furnishings give it a hint of Miami glitz as well. The charismatic owners, Elizabeth and Eduardo, who runs the hotel and food service, give it personality. She did the decorating and after so many raves, went back into the design business. The snack menu includesshrimp and avocado salad and crêpes at the breakfast table. **Pros:** amazingly quiet for the Zona Colonial; opposite the picturesque Plaza Pellerano Castro; rooftop terrace with Balinese sun beds from which you can wave to the cruise ships. **Cons:** not full of creature comforts; bathrooms are small, as is one of the front rooms; heels on the wooden staircase sound noisy in the morning. ⊠ *Arzobispo Porte 7, corner of Las Damas, Zona Colonial, Santo Domingo* ☎ *809/685–8467* ⊕ *www.cocoboutiquehotel.com* ⏎ *5 rooms* ⚹ *In-room: a/c, no phone, no TV. In-hotel: bar, laundry service, Wi-Fi hotspot* ═ *AE, MC,* ⏘ *BP.*

$ ⌨ **Hodelpa Caribe Colonial.** When you leave this hideaway, the caring
HOTEL   staff will say "Why so soon?" The art deco–style lobby and the Internet center both make clever use of blue objets d'art. Rooms have white-gauze canopies on king-size beds; an all-white honeymoon suite has a Jacuzzi. Splurge for a suite or a Superior room (though even those have tight bathrooms), rather than a subterranean standard. Sit out on your balcony and wave to the neighbors. Or better yet: head up to the new rooftop terrace/solarium, plop yourself into a chaise, and relax. Check out the packages online, which throw in extras like breakfast. **Pros:** friendly staff; well managed and efficient. **Cons:** small bathrooms; standard rooms not on par with the rest; subsequent renovated buildings in the area have been done better. ⊠ *Isabel La Católica 59, Zona Colonial* ☎ *809/688–7799 or 888/403–2603* ⊕ *www.hodelpa.com* ⏎ *52 rooms, 2 suites* ⚹ *In-room: a/c, safe. In-hotel: restaurant, room service, bar, laundry service, Internet terminal, parking (free)* ═ *AE, MC, V* ⏘ *BP.*

$$$–$$$$ ⌨ **Hostal Nicolas de Ovando.** This branch of the M Gallery, a chain of
Fodor'sChoice   historic boutique hotels, was sculpted from the residence of the first gov-
★   ernor of the Americas, and it just might be the best thing to happen in
HOTEL   the Zone since Diego Columbus's palace was finished in 1517. Not only did the governor sleep here, but (much more recently) so have Brad Pitt, Robert De Niro, Colin Farrell, and Jamie Foxx. Colonial rooms have canopied queen-size beds, tall ceilings, original stone window benches, and shutters. Some guests prefer the sunny (smaller) rooms in the contemporary annex; with river views, these are smart examples of French minimalist style. Overlooking the river, trees and tropical plantings

shade the pool, and swimmers leave the sun for a fitness break in the gym. The bar is a social scene, particularly when the music man plays at cocktail hour, which includes complimentary hors d'oeuvres. When he's not there, he can be found in the laudable restaurant La Residence (⇨ *Where to Eat*). Special rates are available for cruise-ship passengers who want a pre- or post-stay. ■TIP➜ **Jazzy Thursday at the Nicolas O. is the buzz among the hip Zone residents. It has a two-for-one cocktail hour from 6–8 pm, with live jazz. On every other night but Thursday, the Hora Dominica has two-for-one cocktails at the same time but not necessarily music.** Pros: lavish breakfast buffet; beautifully restored historic section. Cons: pricey; rooms could be larger. ⊠ *Calle Las Damas, Zona Colonial* ☎ *809/685–9955 or 800/763–4835* ⊕ *www.mgallery.com* ⇩ *100 rooms, 4 suites* ⚭ *In-room: a/c, safe, refrigerator. In-hotel: restaurant, room service, bars, pool, gym, laundry service, Internet terminal, Wi-Fi, parking (free), some pets allowed* ⊟ *AE, MC, V* ⏐◎⏐ *BP*.

$–$$ ⌦ **Hotel Doña Elvira.** Housed in a colonial beauty some 500 years young,
HOTEL   this family-owned hotel is noteworthy for its exposed stone and brick walls with 20-foot high, mahogany-beamed ceilings. That look carries through to the best room in the house, No. 11, where an open-air Moroccan tiled bath and shower leads to a normal bathroom. A swimming pool shaded by a mammoth mango tree is flanked by two stories of guest rooms, the better ones being Nos. 2, 3, 6, and 7; the loft rooms you don't want. The rooftop solarium and Jacuzzi are especially attractive when the orchids are in bloom. In 2004 this was the dream project of the owners Marc Bautil, now Honorary Consul of Belgium, and his wife Elvira, a Philippine-American businesswoman. Everything looks neat and tidy, and the bedding, towels, and in-room artwork have been recently upgraded. The prices include tax and service. Ask about the two-bedroom apartment nearby, which is available for short-term rental. Pros: as atmospheric as a Mexican hacienda; excellent location in the Zone; new flat-screen cable TVs. Cons: employees are not polished professionals, and have limited to no English skills; open closets. ⊠ *Padre Bellini 209, Zona Colonial* ☎ *809/221–7415* ⊕ *www.dona-elvira. com* ⇩ *13 rooms* ⚭ *In-room: a/c, no phone, safe. In-hotel: restaurant, bar, pool, laundry facilities, Wi-Fi hotspot* ⊟ *MC, V* ⏐◎⏐ *BP*.

$ ⌦ **Hotel La Atarazana.** A white wrought-iron gate opens to a small foyer
★   with a large mirror and long stems of tropical flowers at this artistically
HOTEL   renovated town house. To the left is the kitchen and bar, to the rear is a courtyard furnished with outdoor tables and market umbrellas; there's a coral-stone wall with bamboo and exotic greenery—it's an urban oasis, and one with a waterfall that flows into a dipping pool. Your hosts are Susanne and Bernie. She's a German economist; he's a German architect who designed the hotel and the contemporary lighting fixtures. Rooms, all upstairs, are minimalist and clean, with new plush towels. The courtyard is the setting for the healthy, European-style breakfast and the rum-soaked cocktail hour. Massage services are now available by a trained therapist. Pros: superior service; excellent location near Plaza de España but not on a touristy block; rooftop terrace has views and both sunny and shaded sitting areas. Cons: front rooms (particularly the one closest to the police station) are noisy in the early morning,

although double-paned balcony doors should soon help this; no luxurious creature comforts beyond cable TV and Wi-Fi; no restaurant (but the license for a new lobby/lounge has been received and it should be open soon). ⊠ *Vicente Celestino Duarte 19, next door to police station, Zona Colonial* ☎ 809/688–3693 ⊕ *www.hotel-atarazana.com* ⇗ 7 *rooms* ⌂ *In-room: a/c, no phone, Wi-Fi. In-hotel: bar, laundry service, Internet terminal, Wi-Fi hotspot* ▤ *AE, MC, V* ⏐◎⏐ *BP.*

$ 🏨 **Hotel Villa Colonial.** Owner Lionel Biseau has kept as much of the origi-
HOTEL   nal structure here as feasible. This includes the second-floor veranda, the columns, and the patterned tile floors that are so distinctive of the Zone circa 1920. Room 8 has the most beautiful mustard-color replica tiles, based on the damaged originals, which were fabricated by Dominican artist Candido Bido. The reception area features contemporary art, and a Balinese sun bed provides a comfort zone. All the furnishings in this restoration are Indonesian, including the beds, with nouveau wooden canopies. Each room is unique, with colorful bedspreads matching the tile floors and modern bathrooms. Room rates include breakfast, tax, and service. **Pros:** stylish breakfast room and bar overlooking the petite pool; all rooms have Wi-Fi; low rates make this an exceptional value. **Cons:** owner and staff have limited English; no sign out front, hotel takes no credit cards. ⊠ *Calle Sanchez 157, near Padre Bellini, Zona Colonial* ☎ 809/221–1049 ⊕ *www.villacolonial.net* ⇗ 13 *rooms* ⌂ *In-room: a/c, no phone, Wi-Fi. In-hotel: Wi-Fi* ▤ No credit cards ⏐◎⏐ BP.

$$ 🏨 **M Gallery Hotel Frances.** Discerning business travelers, American vaca-
HOTEL   tioners, celebs, and other luminaries (including Oscar de la Renta) opt for the intimate, refined luxury of this small, well-run hotel. French and Dominican flags fly over the arched, coral-stone entrance of what's a local landmark, a former French mansion. Dark, hacienda-like rooms with tall, beamed ceilings overlook the courtyard, an urban refuge with cast-iron balustrades and hanging ferns. (Ask for second-floor corner room No. 205—it's large, with an anteroom, and completely sound-proof.) Now all the windows have been made soundproof, which was just one of the many long-awaited improvements. Also new are a lobby with stylish furnishings and many other in-room amenities, including new linens and now duvets, king-size beds, and bedside lamps. Service throughout is exceptional, with English spoken. A romantic hideaway, it's probably not the best place for children. **Pros:** many fun, celebratory events; long-term, hospitable employees; historic Zone ambience. **Cons:** some furnishings remain dated; menu needs some sprucing up. ⊠ *Calles Las Mercedes and Arzobispo Meriño, Zona Colonial* ☎ 809/685–9331 or 800/763–4835 ⊕ *www.mgallery.com* ⇗ 19 *rooms* ⌂ *In-room: a/c, safe, refrigerator. In-hotel: restaurant, room service, bar, Wi-Fi hotspot, parking (free)* ▤ *AE, MC, V* ⏐◎⏐ *BP.*

GAZCUE

$–$$ 🏨 **Hilton Santo Domingo.** This has become *the* address on the Malecón
★   for businesspeople, convention attendees, and leisure travelers. Rooms
HOTEL   on the six luxurious executive floors have three phones, Internet ports, actual corner offices with imposing desks and ergonomic leather chairs, and DSL lines. Suites are geared for longer stays, and have kitchenettes.

Creature comforts are satisfied with the plush duvets, rain showers, and surround sound in the bathrooms, large flat-screen TVs, and gorgeous sea views. Service might just be the best in the country, and rates are surprisingly moderate, particularly with online packages that include a lavish buffet breakfast with healthy options. **Pros:** Sunday brunch is one of the city's top tickets; luxe bedding; totally soundproof rooms; the executive-level lounge. **Cons:** little about the property is authentically Dominican; live music at cocktail hour has left the lobby for the unatmospheric upstairs bar. ⊠ *Av. George Washington 500, Gazcue* ☎ *809/685–0000* ⊕ *hiltoncaribbean.com/santodomingo* ⤴ *228 rooms, 32 suites* ⚉ *In-room: a/c, safe, refrigerator, Internet. In-hotel: 2 restaurants, bars, pool, gym, spa, Internet terminal, Wi-Fi hotspot* ▤ *AE, D, MC, V* ☉|*EP.*

$$
HOTEL

▦ **InterContinental V Centenario.** This major Malecón property does a lot right. All rooms—not just the deluxe ones on the Club Level that have sea-view balconies—are in subtle earth tones, more masculine than tropical cheery. Rooms on the 10th–15th floors have 32-inch plasma TVs. Bedding and pillows have been upgraded throughout, and there is lovely turndown service. The international cuisine at the hotel restaurants is memorable, from the ample breakfast buffet to gastronomic dinners. Service is professional, and conferences run smoothly. Leisure time can be spent on the swanky pool deck, where discerning attendants dispense frosty drinks (including smoothies) and plush, pastel towels, or at the classy casino. There's also a 24-hour fitness center and a spa and beauty salon at this amenities-heavy hotel. **Pros:** good security; beautiful pool area; professional English-speaking staff. **Cons:** rooms could be in a large chain hotel anywhere; service can be impersonal. ⊠ *Av. George Washington 218, Gazcue* ☎ *809/221–0000* ⊕ *www.ichotelsgroup.com* ⤴ *165 rooms, 31 suites* ⚉ *In-room: a/c, safe, refrigerator, Internet. In-hotel: 2 restaurants, bars, tennis court, pool, gym, spa, Internet terminal, parking (free)* ▤ *AE, MC, V* ☉|*EP.*

$
HOTEL

▦ **Marriott Courtyard Santo Domingo.** This American outpost near the U.S. Consulate is warm, friendly, and welcoming, making it suitable for a short layover. The architecture and its hot coral facade, which includes details such as wrought-iron lighting, are characteristic of a Mexican hacienda style, especially in the courtyard, where a fountain continually ejects water into the swimming pool. Dominicans take advantage of the special weekend and holiday packages, and if you do, opt for one that includes the *delicioso* breakfast buffet. Rooms are cookie-cutter, but have laptop-size safes and coffeemakers; the bedding is high-end, and you'll enjoy the fluffy pillows. The staff is warm, caring, and efficient—and most are bilingual. Many cruise passengers overnight here or add a weekend stay after their cruise because of the reasonable prices; however, you're still 3 mi from the Zona Colonial and the cruise-ship terminals. **Pros:** ATM machine in the lobby; handy for baseball games at Quisqueya Stadium. **Cons:** neighborhood is not exciting for tourists; not a luxury property. ⊠ *Maximo Gomez Av. 50-A, La Esperilla* ☎ *809/685–1010* ⊕ *www.marriott.com* ⤴ *243 rooms, 159 suites* ⚉ *In-room: a/c, safe, refrigerator, Internet. In-hotel: restaurant, room service,* *bar, pool, laundry facilities, laundry service, Internet terminal, Wi-Fi hotspot, parking (free)* $\equiv$ *AE, MC, V* ¶◎¶ *EP.*

$–$$ ⊞ **Meliá Santo Domingo Hotel & Casino.** With a good location on the
HOTEL   Malecón, this deluxe high-rise is among those closest to the Zona Colonial. The concierge-level rooms have always offered a pleasurable way to do business or have a pampered urban vacation. For about 15% more per person (above the cost of a regular room), you can get your clothes ironed, shoes shined, hookup to a DSL line, have a free breakfast in the ocean-view lounge, and enjoy premium cocktails and hors d'oeuvres during happy hour. A major (and necessary) renovation, starting with the lobby and its domes and moving on to the meeting rooms and club level and then the remainder of the guest rooms, is still a work in progress, floor by floor, and it should be finished by early 2011. When reserving, be sure to ask for a newly renovated room. Meliá's Coppa Bar is popular. Sashay in around midnight or beyond and dress up. As a hotel bar, it's not subject to the normal curfew. **Pros:** nightly lobby cocktail hour; free Wi-Fi in the lobby and concierge lounge; professional service staff and management. **Cons:** unrenovated rooms are tired; hotel's large size means less personal service; could use another restaurant. ✉ *Av. George Washington 365, Gazcue* ☏ *809/221–6666* ⊕ *www.solmelia.com* ↝ *241 rooms, 14 suites* ⟳ *In-room: a/c, safe, refrigerator, Internet. In-hotel: restaurant, room service, bars, pool, gym, laundry service, Internet terminal, Wi-Fi hotspot, parking (free)* $\equiv$ *AE, MC, V* ¶◎¶ *EP.*

$–$$ ⊞ **Renaissance Jaragua Hotel & Casino.** This sprawling pink oasis is peren-
HOTEL   nially popular, particularly with Americans, for its beautiful grounds and huge free-form pool. Fountains splash and hot tubs gurgle. Saunas bake in what is the capital's largest fitness club/spa. Everything is bigger than life, from the rooms, where executive-size desks face the satellite TV, to the gigantic suites in the renovated main building, to the generous lobby and huge, lively casino, where bands heat up the action. It also has the town's only cabaret theater. European linens and duvets provide supreme comfort for sleeping. Management and staff are professional and caring. Check the Web for weekend deals, including golf packages. **Pros:** hotel is busy and lively; hotel will match any discount Internet rate; optional all-inclusive plan (rare in Santo Domingo) available. **Cons:** can be a bit too busy at times; nothing understated about the decor; some rooms outdated. ✉ *Av. George Washington 367, Gazcue* ☏ *809/221–2222* ⊕ *www.marriott.com* ↝ *292 rooms, 8 suites* ⟳ *In-room: a/c, safe, kitchen, refrigerator (some), Internet (some). In-hotel: 3 restaurants, bars, tennis courts, pool, gym, spa, Internet terminal* $\equiv$ *AE, D, MC, V* ¶◎¶ *EP.*

PIANTINI

$–$$ ⊞ **Hotel Holiday Inn Santo Domingo.** This contemporary marvel, which
HOTEL   opened in late 2009 in fashionable Piantini, is the Caribbean prototype for Holiday Inn's new line of upscale inns meant for central urban zones. The edgy, industrial metal style wows with splashes of purple in the lobby, juxtaposed with paper art and chrome sculptures. In the health-conscious Mediterranean restaurant the buffet is locally

popular at lunch. The business center, with laptops and a printer, is conveniently located in the Level 2 Bar, which has a creative tapas menu. Guest rooms are chic, with digitally controlled lights. A good spirit prevails: on your way down to a hearty breakfast, the carpet in the elevator says GOOD MORNING; at night the carpet's been changed to one wishing you GOOD EVENING. **Pros:** everything is new and clean; rooftop infinity pool has panoramic views; 24-hour gym with adjacent sauna and massage room. **Cons:** hard mattresses; glass-walled suites face a main avenue and are noisy with late-night traffic on busy weekends. ⊠ *Abraham Lincoln 856, Piantini* ☎ *809/621-0000* ⊕ *www.holidayinn.com* ⇗ *121 rooms, 20 suites* ⋔ *In-room: a/c, safe, refrigerator, Internet, Wi-Fi. In-hotel: restaurant, room service, bars, pool, gym, laundry service, Internet terminal, Wi-Fi hotspot, parking (free).* ⊟ *AE, DC, MC, V* ⵁ *EP.*

> **COMPUTER HELP**
>
> If you have a laptop problem or need parts or repair, go see Carlos Florian at **Host Computers** (⊠ *Calle El Conde, at Plaza Conde, basement level, across from Mercure Hotel, Zona Colonial* ☎ *809/685–2132; 809/867–8202 mobile*), who is the top hombre in Santo Domingo when it comes to computers. It's a Hewlett-Packard repair center, too. Carlos doesn't speak English (an assistant does), but he certainly knows computers.

SPORTS AND THE OUTDOORS

Don't come to Santo Domingo for an active vacation; you simply won't find the wide range of outdoor activities that are everywhere in the resort areas. All the large, modern hotels have fitness centers and swimming pools. ■ **TIP** ➜ **It's not safe to swim off the Malecón.** For tourists, the closest beaches to Santo Domingo are in Juan Dolio or, in a more limited way, Boca Chica. *For information on Boca Chica and Juan Dolio, see* ⇨ *Chapter 3, The Southeast Coast.*

BASEBALL

Baseball is a national passion, and even after retiring in 2009, Sammy Sosa remains a legend in his own time. But he is just one of many celebrated Dominican baseball heroes, including pitcher Odalis Revela. Triple-A Dominican and Puerto Rican players and some American major leaguers hone their skills in the Dominican Republic's professional Winter League, which plays from October through January. Some games are held in the Tetelo Vargas Stadium in the town of San Pedro de Macorís, east of Boca Chica; others are held in Estadio Francisco A. Michelli in La Romana (about two hours east of Santo Domingo).

Ticket prices fluctuate, and often change with the advent of the new season. If you go to the stadium, tickets range from US$1 to US$20. Always buy the most expensive seats, and try to go with a group, preferably with some new Dominican friends. When the Santo Domingo Liceys and Santiago Aquilas play, scalpers are in full force; it's akin to the Yankees playing the Mets in New York City.

CLOSE UP

Take Me Down to the Ball Game

Béisbol is the Domincans' passion, and their pride in it has brought recognition, fame, and fortune to their shores. Try not to miss the opportunity to take in a game—even if you might usually prefer shopping over a sporting event. This is a cross-cultural experience that can be unforgettable. Expect passionate and sometimes rowdy crowds, as well as great playing and a strong, competitive spirit.

David Keller, a coach for the Chicago Cubs, lives in Tampa, and has been coming down to the Dominican Republic during the winter season since the late 1990s. As he explains, "The first three weeks in December, the big kahunas come down, like Tony Batista, Juan Acevedo, Migel Tejada, and Alberto Castillo. The Texas Rangers were down in December and rented a couple of penthouses on the new Juan Dolio Beach. I come down four to five times a year myself to coach and am now a hitting instructor. There is quite a competitive relationship between the Dominican and American players."

During one game that David attended, former Dominican President Hipolito threw the first ceremonial pitch for an Aquilas-Licey matchup. Dave saw the president making his way to the dugout and started to silently rehearse his Spanish, to be certain that his greeting would be *correcto*. Instead, when Hipolito saw him, he said: *"Hola, gringo! Deme cinco!"* ("Give me five!"). So much for protocol.

"One thing that differentiates a Dominican ball game is the fans," David emphasized. "To say they are enthusiastic doesn't cover it. They do love their teams! They don't get out of control so much now that the ruling

was made that if a bottle or can is thrown from the home bleachers, the home team has to forfeit the game. Before, they had been known to throw things at the umpires when they made a bad call."

No peanuts and popcorn here, but *empanadas* with pepperoni and cheese and *pastellas* (seasoned ground beef with mashed plantains wrapped in a plantain leaf, to which you can add ketchup or mayo) are on the menu. The mascot for the home team, the Toros del Oeste (nicknamed Azucareros, as this is sugarcane country) rides around on a scooter. Between innings, fans dance wildly. The beer and rum flow. As passionate as Dominicans can be for the game, though, they are still on island time; even *aficionados* often come late, straggling in as late as the fourth inning.

Going to your first game might be a little overwhelming, with the noise, the craziness in the stands, and the high-decibel merengue playing. **Tropical Tours** (☎ *809/523–2028 at Casa de Campo; 809/556–5801 in La Romana*), a tour operator based at Casa de Campo, takes groups to the midsize Francisco A. Michelli Stadium in La Romana from October through January, often pairing a game with a civilized dinner in town.

Estadio Francisco A. Michelli (✉ *Av. Padre Abreu, near monument, La Romana* ☎ *809/556–6188; 809/556–6188 to buy tickets by credit card*) is two hours east of Santo Domingo and not really suitable for a day trip, but if you decide to spend some time in Boca Chica or Juan Dolio, it might be a possibility; and it's certainly doable if you're staying in one of the resorts in the La Romana/Bayahibe area.

Estadio Quisqueya (✉ *Av. Tieradentes at San Cristóbal, Naco, Santo Domingo* ☎ *809/540–5772; 809/616–1224 to purchase tickets by credit card* ⊕ *www.lidom.com*) is Santo Domingo's main baseball stadium. Because of the traffic and general chaos, it's usually easier to hire a driver for the night if you're planning to attend a game independently. Taxis can be difficult to hail after games, when the demand is very high. The lines at the box office and time to get into the stadium vary depending on who is playing. You'll find few good dining options near the stadium, so plan on hot dogs and beer and empanadas.

Estadio Tetelo Vargas (✉ *Av. Francisco Caamano Denó, San Pedro de Macorís* ☎ *809/529–3618; 829/529–3618 to purchase tickets by credit card*) is the main stadium in San Pedro de Macorís. From Santo Domingo, you might pay as much as $80 each way for the 90-minute trip, but the fares are more reasonable if you're staying 20 minutes away in Juan Dolio, from which the round-trip fare is about $30. From San Pedro de Macorís, it's $8 to the stadium by taxi.

Liga de Béisbol Stadiums (✉ *San Domingo* ☎ *809/567–6371*) can be a helpful information source if you're planning an independent trip to a baseball game.

GOLF

The Dominican Republic has some of the best courses in the Caribbean, designed by some of the world's top course designers. Courses in Juan Dolio are the most easily accessible to clients of Santo Domingo hotels, which can arrange a golf outing for you. If you don't mind the distance (1½ hours one way), the courses at Casa de Campo are stellar, but you must make advance reservations.

SHOPPING

Shopping in the capital is perhaps the best in the country. You can buy everything from inexpensive souvenirs to Italian designer shoes. *Mamajuana*—an herbal extract that is usually mixed with rum—is said to be the Dominican answer to Viagra. Brugal and Barceló rums make good gifts or reminders of your island experience. Cigars, of course, are great guy gifts. Amber and larimar jewelry are lady pleasers, and make reasonably priced jewelry gifts for young girls. Wood carvings of mahogany (although most are Haitian), as well as local and Haitian artwork and ceramics—notably the faceless dolls—are popular. High-end boutiques have fashions from Spain, France, Italy, and the United States, as well as from such noted Dominican designers as Oscar de la Renta and Jenny Polanco. If you go to a flea market or public market, yes, you can haggle, saying: *"Gracias no, es demasiado caro para mi!"*

(No thanks, it's too expensive for me). But most prices in shops are set, except perhaps in some of the gift shops on Calle El Conde; if you must haggle, do it graciously.

AREAS AND MALLS

One of the main shopping streets in the Zone is **Calle El Conde**, a pedestrian thoroughfare. With the advent of so many restorations, the dull and dusty stores with dated merchandise are giving way to some hip, new shops. The offerings, including those in local designer shops, are still affordable by many Dominicans. Some of the best shops are on **Calle Duarte,** north of the Colonial Zone, between Calle Mella and Avenida de Las Américas. **Piantini** is a swanky residential neighborhood that has an increasing number of fashionable shops and clothing boutiques. It extends from Avenida Winston Churchill to Avenida Lope de Vega and from Calle Jose Amado Soler to Avenida 27 de Febrero.

Acropolis Mall, between Winston Churchill and Calle Rafael Augusto Sanchez, has become a favorite shopping arena for the young and/ or hip capitaleños (residents of Santo Domingo). Stores like Zara and Mango, from Spain, have today's look without astronomical prices. The **Malecón Center,** the latest complex, adjacent to the classy Hilton Santo Domingo, will house 170 shops, boutiques, and services, plus several movie theaters, when it's completely occupied. In the tower above are luxury apartments, as well as Sammy Sosa, in one of the penthouses. **El Mercado Modelo,** a covered market, borders Calle Mella in the Zona Colonial; vendors here sell a dizzying selection of Dominican crafts. **Plaza Central,** between avenidas Winston Churchill and 27 de Febrero, is where you can find many top international boutiques. **Unicentro,** on Avenida Abraham Lincoln, is a major Santo Domingo mall.

EVARISTO MORALES

ART

Galería de Arte Mariano Eckert (⊠ *Av. Winston Churchill and Calle Luis F. Tomen, 3rd fl., Evaristo Morales* ☎ *809/541–7109*) focuses on the work of Eckert, an older Dominican artist who's known for his still lifes.

GAZCUE

CIGARS

Santo Domingo Cigar Club (⊠ *Renaissance Jaragua Hotel & Casino, Av. George Washington 367, Gazcue* ☎ *809/221–1483*) is a great place to find yourself a good smoke.

NACO

ART

Casa Jardin (⊠ *Balacer Gustavo Medjía Ricart 15, Naco* ☎ *809/565– 7978*) is the garden studio of abstract painter Ada Balacer. Works by other women artists are also shown; look for pieces by Yolarda

Naranjo, known for her modern work that integrates everything from fiberglass, hair, rocks, and wood to baby dresses.

CIGARS

★ **Cigar Club** (✉ *Av. 27 Febrero 211, Naco* ☎ *809/683–2770*) is one of the only places in the country where you can buy authentic Arturo Fuentes cigars. The club has a walk-in humidor as well as a lounge with a full bar, where you can enjoy fine wines, an aged rum, and Dominican coffee. The striking renovations make this bi-level club truly impressive. On some nights the hip owner takes to the piano. It's open weekdays from 9 AM to midnight, and from 9 AM to 3 AM on Saturday.

PIANTINI

ART

Galería de Arte Nader (✉ *Rafael Augusto Sanchez 22, between Ensanche Piantini and Plaza Andalucia II, Piantini* ☎ *809/687–6674 or 809/544–0878*) showcases top Dominican artists in various mediums. The gallery staff are well known in Miami and New York, and work with Sotheby's.

Lyle O. Reitzel Art Contemporaneo (✉ *Plaza Andalucia II, Piantini* ☎ *809/227–8361*) has, since 1995, specialized in contemporary art. The gallery showcases mainly Latin artists from Mexico, South America, and Spain, and some of the most controversial Dominican visionaries.

CLOTHING

Casa Virginia (✉ *C/Av. Roberto Pastoriza 255, Piantini* ☎ *809/566–1535 or 809/566–4000*), one of the Dominican Republic's leading department stores, was founded in 1945 by the mother of the present Virginia, who took it to the next level, adding a great day spa. The store is stocked mostly with high-end designer clothing (including a Jenny Polanco department) and fashion finds, but also has Italian jewelry and some moderately priced gift items.

Plaza Central (✉ *Avs. Winston Churchill and 27 de Febrero, Piantini* ☎ *809/541–5929*) is a major shopping center with high-end shops, including offerings from upscale Dominican designer Jenny Polanco, who has incredible white linen outfits, artistic jewelry, and purses.

ZONA COLONIAL

ART

Building on a Taino, African, and European heritage, artisans creating modern Dominican art forms often employ seeds, fiber, bones, coconut skin, cow horns, and African motifs. A good selection is found at **Jorge Caridad** (✉ *Arzobispo Meriño, corner of General Cabral, Zona Colonial*).**Plaza Toledo Bettye's Galeria** (✉ *Isabel la Católica 163, Zona Colonial* ☎ *809/688–7649*) sells a fascinating array of artwork, including Haitian voodoo banners and metal sculpture, and souvenirs, chandeliers, and estate jewelry. The American expat owner, Bettye Marshall, has a great eye, and can also rent you a room in one of her bed-and-breakfasts.

CIGARS

Cigar King (✉ *Calle El Conde 208, Baguero Bldg., Zona Colonial* ☎ *809/686–4987*) keeps its Dominican and Cuban cigars in a temperature-controlled cedar room.

HANDICRAFTS

Felipe & Co. (✉ *Calle El Conde 105, Zona Colonial* ☎ *809/689–5810*) has a fascinating assortment of Dominican crafts and artwork, coffee, inexpensive "free spirit" jewelry, and some tropical clothing.

HOME FURNISHINGS

The exquisite **Nuovo Rinascimento** (✉ *Plazoleta Padre Billini, Zona Colonial* ☎ *809/686–3387*), replete with contemporary furniture and antiques, has a trove of Venetian linens and towels. Shipping can be arranged. The wooden hacienda doors open to a wonderful world of white sculptures and an inner courtyard with a lily pad–dotted pool.

JEWELRY

Ambar Tres (✉ *La Atarazana 3, Zona Colonial* ☎ *809/688–0474*) carries high-end jewelry made with amber and larimar, the country's other indigenous, semiprecious stone. If you tour the in-house museum, you'll have a deeper appreciation of the gem.

L'Ile Au Tresor (✉ *Calle El Conde, at Conde Plaza, lower floor, across from Mercure Hotel, Zona Colonial* ☎ *809/685–3983*) has a *Pirates of the Caribbean* theme, but that aside, it's fun. Its owner, a talented Frenchman named Patrick, has some of the most attractive and creative designer pieces in native larimar and amber. If you have never bought any of these lovely stones because of cheesy settings or too high a price tag, then this is your chance. His innovative custom work, with sterling or gold, can be done in 48 hours.

NIGHTLIFE

Santo Domingo's nightlife is vast and ever changing. To get up to speed, check with concierges and hip *capitaleños*. Get a copy of the free newspapers *Touring* or *dr1guide* (⊕ *www.dr1guide.com*)—available free at the tourist office and at hotels—to find out what's happening. At this writing, there is still a curfew for clubs and bars; they must close at midnight during the week and at 2 AM on Friday and Saturday nights. There are some exceptions to the latter, primarily for clubs and casinos in hotels. The curfew has put some clubs out of business, but it has also cut down on the crime and late-night noise, particularly in the Zone. You will also see a lot of action on weekends at the neighborhood colmados (grocery stores that can serve beer and rum) and at large liquor stores, where you can also buy chasers, plastic cups, and ice. The party goes on in the parking lot, with car stereos providing the music.

In the city's casinos the action can heat up, but gambling here is more a sideline than a raison d'être. Most casinos are in the larger hotels of Santo Domingo, and they all offer slot machines, blackjack, craps, and roulette. With a few exceptions, they are generally open daily until midnight (2 AM on Friday and Saturday). You must be 18 to enter, and jackets are required at the chic casinos in the capital. In Santo Domingo,

Amber and Larimar—The D.R.'s Indigenous Gems

As attractive as precious gems—and increasingly popular for jewelry both here and in France, the mineral larimar looks particularly attractive when paired with silver. This semiprecious stone is mined in the mountains of the Southwest, in Bahoruco—the only place that this Caribbean blue pectolite has been found.

The national gem, amber, is actually a fossil—petrified tree resin that has been fossilized over a million or so years. Most amber is a golden color with brown tones, but it can be yellow and even black. It may have oddities like spiders and flies trapped inside.

Fakes are everywhere, with plastic being pawned off as amber (it will float in water) and blue beads as larimar. Stick to the better jewelry shops, especially the Euro-owned ones, which have classy pieces with artistic designs. So much of what is sold in the local shops has cheapie settings, which can ruin the stone's beauty.

---

several upscale hotels have casinos: Barceló Gran Hotel Lina; Meliá Santo Domingo; Hispaniola Hotel & Casino (attracting a younger crowd); Renaissance Jaragua; and the Hilton Santo Domingo.

Dancing is as much a part of the culture here as eating and drinking. As in other Latin countries, after dinner it's not a question of *whether* people will go dancing but *where* they'll go. Move with the rhythm of the merengue and the pulsing beat of salsa (adopted from neighboring Puerto Rico). Among the young, the word is that there's no better place to party in the Caribbean than Santo Domingo's Zona Colonial. Cover charges on Friday and Saturday can range from free up to $20, which usually includes a drink or two.

BELLA VISTA

DANCE CLUBS

Guácara Taina (⊠ *Av. Mirador del Sur 655, Bella Vista* ☎ *809/533–0671*) is a landmark—it's the only *discoteca* to be inside a cave, once inhabited by Taino Indians and . . . bats. (Santo Domingo has a network of natural caves within city limits.) As you descend, you see hundreds of heads bobbing and bodies gyrating among the stalactites: it's a unique sight. Banquettes and seating are carved into the limestone walls ornamented with Taino pictographs. However, these days it's open only for special events (a recent one was sponsored by a new vodka brand and an energy drink, for instance. These are often open to the public, or whoever wants to pay the cover, which can be $20. Lights and videos flash, and apparently it's not subject to curfew. To find out what's going on, talk to your concierge.

GAZCUE

BARS AND CAFÉS

Marrakesh Café & Bar (⊠ *Hotel Santo Domingo, Av. Abraham Lincoln at Av. Independencia, Gazcue* ☎ *809/221–1511*) is where a sophisticated after-work crowd gathers for American and international music and style straight out of *Casablanca*. Complimentary tapas come to the table, and you can get top-shelf liquors.

CASINOS

Atlantis World Casino (⊠ *Av. George Washington 218, Gazcue* ☎ *809/688–8080*), adjacent to the Intercontinental Hotel, is one of the newest. It also has slots that accept dollar bills. Although there's no charge to enter the gaming room, the table minimums are higher than most, so the casino attracts a more upscale crowd. Closing doesn't come until 6 AM.

Majestic Casino (⊠ *Hilton Santo Domingo, 1st Level, Av. George Washington, Gazcue* ☎ *809/685–0000*) is the newest of the Malecón casinos, and it is almost on a par with its Las Vegas counterparts. You'll find 20 gaming tables (including baccarat), a VIP salon, 200 video slots, live music (national and international talent), a bar, and more. Note: If you're staying at the Hilton here, you still can't charge what you consume at the bar or restaurant to your room.

DANCE CLUBS

Cha (⊠ *George Washington 165, Gazcue* ☎ *809/912-1918* At the moment Cha is the happening gay club in town. With a South Beach concept, it draws large crowds every day that it's open (Fri.–Sun.). Live performances get the applause.

The **LED** (⊠ *Hispaniola Hotel & Casino, Av. Abraham Lincoln at Av. Independencia, Gazcue* ☎ *809/476–7733*) Because this disco is in a hotel, it is able to stay open later than the other clubs, and that in itself is what has made this a favorite of the young and well-to-do partiers who take their music loud. Many a graduation is celebrated here until the wee small hours of the *mañana*.

> ### THE POLITUR IS YOUR FRIEND
>
> You may see white SUVs with the word POLITUR cruising the streets; this is the tourist police, and their role is to protect and guide international tourists. Most have a working knowledge of English; some are trilingual. They play a leading role in making the tourist sector safer by eradicating unlicensed street vendors and controlling prostitution by both sexes.

NACO

BARS AND CAFÉS

Trio Cafe (⊠ *Av. Abraham Lincoln Norte 12A, at Plaza Castilla Ensanche, Naco* ☎ *809/412–0964*) is one of those places where the cool, older crowd comes to graze, drink, and dance, even though there's no real dance floor. They just stand around and groove, and chances are they will make new friends—as might you.

PIANTINI

BARS AND CAFÉS

Punto Y Corcho (✉ *Av. Abraham Lincoln at Gustavo Mejía Ricart, Piantini* ☎ *809/683–0533*), on Plaza Andalucia, is where wine (by the glass and bottle) and local and international liquors are the order of the night. This is a great date and late-night spot, and it tends to appeal to mature and sophisticated types.

★ **Wine Tasting Room at El Catador** (✉ *Calle Jose Brea Péna 43, Avaristo Morales, Piantini* ☎ *809/540–1644*) is an avant-garde wine bar and wine store created by the major wine distributor El Catador. Cushy leather armchairs and hardwood floors help create a clubby atmosphere. There's a well-chosen selection of hors d'oeuvres, canapés, and tapas, both hot and chilled. Check out their calendar, as the events here include well-priced, prix-fixe dinners paired with wine on designated nights. You will want to buy one of the 500 bottles of wine from around the wine-making world. It's open until 11 PM on weekdays, but only until 6 on Saturday. If you opt to buy a bottle, you have to do it by 10:15 (or 5:15) so as to finish up by closing time.

> ### BAILE! BAILE!
>
> Dance! Dance! The merengue is regarded as the Dominican national dance. Traditionally, it combines the sounds of the aboriginal *guiro* (a metal tube that is scratched to produce a continuous grating sound) and the *tambora* (a double-skinned African drum played on the lap) for rhythm, as well as the accordion. Over time, saxophones, trumpets, and trombones were added to produce the first merengue orchestras. The 1970s saw the introduction of electric pianos, and since then, synthesizers have given merengue a new sound, which increased its popularity even more abroad.

DANCE CLUBS

Amika (✉ *Ave. Abraham Lincoln, corner of Gustavo Mejía Ricart Plaza, Local 40 B, Piantini* ☎ *809/563–2003*) does a lot to attract the young and moneyed with special theme nights and events, including sexy fashion shows, Viva Sundays, and I Love Reggaeton. It's high-tech everything—the decor, the DJ stand, the sound system, and the couches. There are also shades of the '70s, with the chrome and mirrored balls and chicas in low-cut cocktail dresses. And everyone dances—well.

SERALLES

BARS AND CAFÉS

Don't think of the sandwich when you visit **Monté Cristo** (✉ *Av. José Armado Soler at Av. Abraham Lincoln, Serralles* ☎ *809/542–5000*), although the crowds can sandwich you in. The pub's clientele spans the decades, music crosses the Americas, and there's a small dance floor. Both hot and cold tapas and sandwiches are served. It's open after work until late, and there's no cover. It's the only club where there's anything happening on a Tuesday night, when there's a wine tasting.

ZONA COLONIAL

BARS AND CAFÉS

Doubles (⊠ *Calle Arzobispo Meriño 54, Zona Colonial* ☎ *809/688-3833*) looks like a friend's place—that is, if you have a French friend who has a hip sense of interior design and who's prone to mixing rattan furniture, antiques, subdued lighting, and candles in a space that's centuries old. Spanish tiles add interest to this atmospheric bar, where a DJ spins mainly for patrons in their twenties.

Hard Rock Café Santo Domingo (⊠ *Calle El Conde 103, Zona Colonial* ☎ *809/686-7771*), more and more of a night spot, has live, mainly local bands that play on Tuesday and Sunday, starting at 10. It's a good place for times when you may just want to feel at home, have some bar food, and a really strong American napkin. Nachos are supreme, and they pair well with a perfect Rockarita, a huge margarita served in a big goblet with a salted rim. The music videos are loud, but you can understand the words and sing right along. You can take a break from the bands and music videos by adjourning to the front terrace, which faces Parque Colón. The sound system still easily reaches there, but the sounds drop a decibel and you can people-watch. Servers even sweep up the litter.

DANCE CLUBS

Atarazana #9 (⊠ *Atarazana 9, Zona Colonial* ☎ *809/688-0969*), just down the hill from Plaza de España toward the river, has an ideal location if you're staying in the Zone. The first level of this dance club has a bar and a stage, as well as large windows overlooking the historic streetscape. This place opens early, at 8 PM, and a light menu is served, but there's no real action here until at least 10:30. Reggaeton, bachata, and merengue are on the dance menu. Admission can be cheaper on Thursday nights due to promotions.

El Sartan (⊠ *Calle Hostos 153, Zona Colonial* ☎ *809/686-9621*) may seem like a hole in the wall, but the crowd covers all classes of Dominicans, from the poorer Zone residents and the old men playing dominoes on the plastic tables on up to a wealthy and well-dressed group stopping by after an art opening. It's as funky and real a slice of life as it was before the neighborhood became so gentrified. When the traditional dancing begins, you will see all ages moving to the Cuban beat, with some of the oldsters seriously proficient in their merengue moves.

DRESSING DOMINICANA

Dominican women tend to be flashy dressers. Expect to see a lot of glitter, with too-short skirts and too-tight slacks, not to mention a great deal of cleavage, wherever you go. And these are the good girls! Though outwardly flamboyant, they'll act in a ladylike manner. Treat them like ladies, or you may have to answer to their brothers.

TOP REASONS TO GO

Ecotourism. Nature in all its most beautiful forms is one of the major draws.

Pristine, unspoiled environments. Far from the tourist trail and with no all-inclusive resorts, the area is a reminder of how the whole island used to be.

Bird-Watching. The three national parks in the Barahona region are all super birding destinations.

Horseback Riding and Trekking. Saddling up or going on a hike is the best way to get to some of the smaller villages up in the mountains, far from any tourist haunts.

Amazing Beaches. They can be hard to get to, with amenities approaching zero, but the untouched sand of beaches such as Bahía El Cabo Rojo and Bahía de las Águilas makes it all worth the hassle.

2

BARAHONA AND THE SOUTHWEST

Think of a trip to the Dominican Republic's southwestern provinces as an exotic safari. The variety of flamingos, crocodiles, iguanas, and many other kinds of animals is truly amazing. If you come to this wild part of the island, you can experience nature the way you were meant to, whether on solitary walks into the mountains or on daylong ecotours.

Left behind are the long lines and overpriced piña coladas. You will find friendly people who have not been jaded by tourism, and you'll also experience food straight from the earth or the sea. Fishermen, farmers, and tradesmen still work and live here with their families, away from the established tourism zones. As we overheard one guest exclaim, "This has to be as beautiful as heaven, but I don't think heaven could be this beautiful!"

This is the part of the Dominican Republic where rivers, still clear and cold from their mountain springs, meet the sea at pebbly beaches washed by gentle waves. And you can see for miles and miles down the undeveloped coastline. Try the various beaches and investigate villages like La Bahoruco, San Rafael, Paraíso, and Los Patos. Ecotourism is on the rise here, and the Southwest continues to draw visitors looking to commune with nature, including ardent bird-watchers. Right now, this is a Dominican destination without the crowds (although it is getting more popular), and it's so physically beautiful and unspoiled that each day will amaze you.

ORIENTATION AND PLANNING

GETTING ORIENTED

You'll need three to five days to really appreciate what the region has to offer. If you put yourself in the hands of a guide or ecotour company that knows its way around, you'll be able to make the most of your time. But you can also do it on your own, preferably in a 4x4 vehicle, which can be reserved in advance from Hotel El Quemaito.

Barahona. This gateway to the Southwest is about 209 km (129 mi) southwest of Santo Domingo. The drive here from the capital (primarily on Highway 44 through the towns of Bani and Azua) takes between 3 and 3½ hours.

Pedernales. A three-hour drive south from Barahona, this peninsula is known for the vivid beauty of its three national parks.

Lago Enriquillo. To the northwest of Barahona, this large, shallow lake has islands filled with flamingos, iguanas, and other creatures.

PLANNING

WHEN TO GO

Anytime is the right time to go to this region. One exception might be rainy season—primarily September to November—because it is more difficult to hike or go bird-watching or ecotouring if there are heavy rains. That said, the sometimes-heavy rainfall usually stops as abruptly as it started. It is best to go midweek, as some inns not only book up but raise their rates on weekends.

GETTING HERE AND AROUND

AIR TRAVEL

Aeropuerto Internacional Maria Montez in Barahona is open only for charter flights. Unless you're paying the big bucks, you'll be flying into Santo Domingo first, and then making the three-hour-plus drive from there.

BUS TRAVEL

Caribe Tours leaves from its terminal in Santo Domingo four times daily, with service to the town of Barahona; at this writing, there were buses at 6:15, 9:45, 1:45, and 5:15 (returns are at the same times from Barahona). All buses make a pit stop in Azua, but there's no reason for independent travelers to head here. The populace here is unaccustomed to tourists, although they're accommodating and friendly.

The trip, a modest RD$250 each way, is considered first-class transportation in these parts; it even has a bathroom (but bring your own paper, wipes, and hand sanitizer, because the water in the sink never runs). The air-conditioning on these buses is strong, so be prepared for the cold. The 3½-hour drive is reasonably efficient, not that much longer than driving yourself.

Information Caribe Tours (✉ *Av. 27 de Febrero and Leopoldo Navarro, Santo Domingo* ☎ *809/521–5088 or 809/221–4422* ✉ *Av. Uruguay and Calle Maria Montez, Barahona* ☎ *809/524–4952* ⊕ *www.caribetours.com.do*).

CAR TRAVEL

About half of the region's tourists rent a car and tour the area for three to five days, picking up their cars in Santo Domingo or at the airport. At this writing, there are almost no rental-car agencies in the Barahona area, so you pick up a car before coming. (Hotel El Quemieto has a few cars and trucks for rent, but they must be reserved in advance.) *For more information, see ⇨ Car Rentals in Santo Domingo Essentials, below.* ⚠ **Don't attempt to drive the nearly four hours from Santo Domingo to the Southwest after dark. If you arrive in Santo Domingo in the afternoon or evening, stay in a reasonably priced hotel and head out in the morning, whether by rental car or by bus. The truly scenic journey to Barahona by day is a treacherous run on unlighted, unfamiliar roads after dark. Livestock wanders the roads as if it were out to pasture.**

GUAGUA TRAVEL

These local buses are actually white or beige minivans that can pack 'em in like chickens in a coop. They run hourly to Santo Domingo and have air-conditioning but no bathrooms. Expect to pay about half the price of a Caribe Tours bus, but take one only in an emergency.

They are a different story for shorter trips. The cost of one trip is about RD$5 to RD$10, and they offer a viable way to get between the little towns. In Barahona they leave from the east end of the central park, on Avenida 27 de Febrero. In the small towns, just stand on the side of the highway and wave them down. The going rate from, say, Bahoruco to Los Patos is about RD$60. You can actually take a guagua all the way from Barahona to Pedernales. You would then get off and take a moto-concho (motorcycle taxi) to Bahía de las Aguilas. Good luck, however!

TAXI TRAVEL

If you don't want to do the driving but still want a private transfer to the Southwest, you can hire a taxi. Expect to pay at least US$180 plus tip. If you take a tour with ECO-Tours or another company, transportation may be included. Don't expect to be able to arrange transportation if you arrive late in the day, or especially after dark.

Once you get to Barahona, taxis are not particularly organized. There are no metered cabs, and all of them seem to be on their last axle. If you arrive on the Caribe Tours bus with luggage, expect to pay RD$350 to RD$400 to get to the towns of Juan Esteban, Bahoruco, or La Cienega, RD$950 to Los Patos. In town, you should have to pay only RD$100.

Once up in the countryside, the hotels have trusted drivers they will call on their cell phones for you. In La Cienega, there's a taxi stand where they all hang out right as you get into the town on the highway.

Motoconchos are motorcycle taxis—half the price and twice the risk. They are usually in bad condition, just like the car taxis. In Barahona they can be found at the central park, in front of Los Robles restaurant, and along Avenida Luis E. Delmonte. In the country, you just flag them down. If they stop and are going where you want to go, then they are for hire. Ask at your lodging what the fare should be.

INTERNET

Cybernet has the best Internet service in Barahona, with a bank of computers; it's open from 8 AM to 9 PM and charges about US$1.25 per hour. Guanaba.net in La Cienega has nine computers with Skype to make Internet calls; it's open from 8:30 AM to 7:30 PM from Monday through Saturday, from 8:30 to 3 on Sunday. Expect to pay about $1 per hour.

Information **Cybernet** (⊠ *Av. Uruguay, between Calles Cabral and Messon, Barahona*). **Guanaba.net** (⊠ *Calle Duarte 35, across from Catholic Church, La Cienega*).

MONEY MATTERS

The only ATMs are in the city of Barahona, so stock up on pesos before heading to el campo (the countryside). Use the ATM at Banreservas (the one at Banca Agricultura doesn't accept American cards). Banreservas, like many other banks, has limited the amount of each withdrawal to RD$4,000, which you can obtain twice a day. All considered, it's a good idea to bring some pesos from Santo Domingo to be sure you have enough.

TOURS

The Aguinape organization is made up of experienced youths who offer guide services for Bahía de las Águilas. They include college students, athletes, and young men active in their churches. They have taken classes with birding expert Kate Wallace. The guides only speak Spanish, but a Peace Corps volunteer is usually available to go as a translator. Some are taking English classes.

A Peace Corps volunteer has worked to help set up the Association of Eco-Tourism Guides of Lago Enriquillo, many of whom were previously with the Parks Department. There are three boats on Lago Enriquillo, which carry 10, 15, and 25 passengers. The guide association, which works in conjunction with ECO-Tour Barahona, does a creditable job of offering useful guided tours of the lake and Isla de Cabritos. Some tours visit a small Haitian village on the Dominican border called Mal Passe; it can be upsetting to see the poverty and trash on the other side of the border, but it's an experience nonetheless. The cost of these boat tours is RD$3,500 regardless of the size of the party, which is why it often pays to make advance arrangements through ECO-Tour Barahona to take a prearranged group tour; otherwise, show up in the morning and make your own arrangements, seeing whether you can get a group together. The guide association can help you make local reservations if you're coming on your own from Barahona.

At this writing, there is only one full-service tour agency in the area, but it's a good one. For any of its full-day tours, ECO-Tour Barahona charges about US$65 to US$75 per person per day (if six or more persons, which they organize), including pick-up at your hotel, lunch (with nonalcoholic drinks), national park entrance fees, and boat tours (when applicable). Tours tend to be long (averaging 8 to 12 hours). The company employs English-, French-, and Spanish-speaking guides and organizes trips to all the national parks, Bahía de las Águilas, and Lago Enriquillo (also Isla de Cabritos). They will also drive clients to the annual coffee festival in Polo.

Information AGUINAPE (☎ *809/214–1575 or 829/394-7556*). **Association of Eco-Tourism Guides of Lago Enriquillo** (☎ *809/816–7441* ⊕ *www. lagoenriquilloguides.com*). **ECO-Tour of Barahona** (✉ *Carretera Enriquillo, the Malecón, Edificio 8, Apt. 306, Paraiso* ☎ *809/243–1190 or 809/395–1542* ⊕ *www.ecotour-repdom.com*).

> ### CHICKENS DEAD OR ALIVE
>
> Stuck in traffic in Azua, you may be able to glimpse through the crowds a *pollera* (chicken shop) advertising *pollos vivo* (live chickens) for RD$20; *pollos matando* (dead chickens), on the other hand, are RD$26. If they ring its neck, apparently, it's six pesos extra—money well spent.

RESTAURANTS

The hotel Casa Bonita has the only fine-dining restaurant in the Southwest. The table d'hôte dining room at Casablanca (also near Barahona) and the Hotelito Oasi Italiano (in Los Patos) both serve some fine meals. There are also many good local and seafood restaurants with welcoming owners and staff.

Expect simple local food for the most part: a lot of sancocho, mofongo, and *chicharrones* (crispy pig skin fried with garlic), which come packaged here like potato chips. Restaurants are not too big on desserts; they keep it simple, with flan, white cheese and guava, *majarete* (corn pudding), and boiled orange peels, which can be quite tasty. Food tastes like it just came from the earth or the sea; when you see a 4-foot silver *dorado* (mahimahi) paraded through a restaurant to the kitchen, you know what you should be having for dinner. Bring cash, because credit cards are not accepted at many establishments.

HOTELS

Most hotels in the Southwest are simple; almost all the recommendable hotels in the region are small inns, and many offer meals (though breakfast is not always included in the base price). Hotels in the Southwest normally quote rates in both pesos and dollars, though you'll be able to pay with either local or U.S. currency. Some hotels do not take credit cards.

WHAT IT COSTS IN U.S. DOLLARS					
	¢	$	$$	$$$	$$$$
RESTAURANTS	under $8	$8–$12	$12–$20	$20–$30	over $30
HOTELS*	under $80	$80–$150	$150–$250	$250–$350	over $350
HOTELS**	under $125	$125–$250	$250–$350	$350–$450	over $450

*EP, BP, CP **AI, FAP, MAP

Restaurant prices are per person for a main course at dinner and do not include 16% tax and 10% service charge. Hotel prices are per night for a double room in high season, excluding 16% tax and 10% service charge.

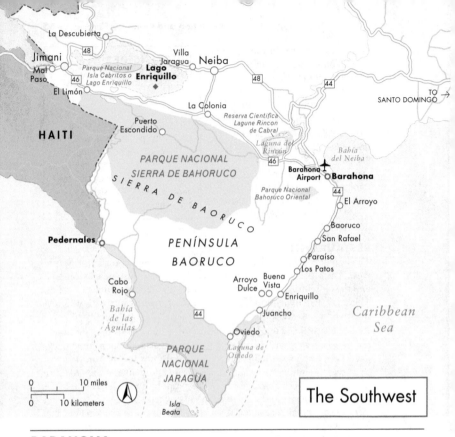

BARAHONA

209 km (120 mi) southwest of Santo Domingo; approximately 3½ hours by car.

Barahona is a noisy, smoky midsize city; it's the least cosmopolitan city of its kind in the Dominican Republic. The primary mode of transportation is the motor scooter or motorcycle, and there's an eternal buzz from them, which escalates on Friday nights when everyone in the entire region seems to come into town to party. It's also a college town with two centers of higher learning, UCATEBA (Universidad Catolica y Tecnologica de Barahona) and the Barahona campus of the UASD (Universidad Autonoma de Santo Domingo). There's a Malecón (seafront promenade) that comes alive on weekends. You'll find some of the more popular Dominican seafood restaurants there. The colorful and lively market, open daily, is a good photo opportunity and great place to meet the locals. Victorian houses give Barahona a little charm, and there's a lovely central park, but some of the streets are still unpaved. A relatively young city in a country whose roots reach back to Christopher Columbus's family, Barahona was founded in 1802 by General François-Dominique Toussaint Louverture, an important leader of the Haitian revolution.

The Pride of My Country (⊕ *www.orgullodemitierra.com.do*), a tourism awareness program sponsored by Centro Cuesta Nacional (CCN), which owns major supermarkets, has chosen to highlight the provinces of Barahona and Pedernales for their environmental characteristics, cultural diversity, ecotourism potential, artistic richness, and folklore. CCN successfully escalated tourism in Samaná, and it is hoped will do the same here through events such as gastronomic festivals, craft exhibitions, the development of a clothing line, area excursions, and video and photography exhibits.

GETTING HERE AND AROUND

Barahona is a very walkable city, although it's best to stroll during daylight. Many of Barahona's motorcycle drivers act as motoconchos, meaning they are for hire for short distances. There are also taxis (some vans). Most of these are "freelance" or street taxis, and all of them are quite beat up.

NEED A BREAK? *Frituras,* the makeshift cooking stands along Highway 44, start frying at noon, when they open for lunch almost every day of the week. On the menu are fish, chicken, and tostones.

At Barahona's colorful **Mercado** (⊠ *Between J.-J. Pena Gomez and Jaime-Mota*) you can find good prices on locally made handicrafts, Haitian art, wooden *pilones* (mortars and pestles), and *giras* (a musical instrument that looks like a kitchen grater; a knife is stroked across it to make a metallic sound), which can be hung as wall decorations.

The city's characteristic **Parque Central**, in the center of town, holds some ancient shade trees, park benches, and a kiosk. Around it are some little wooden creole houses painted Caribbean colors (some of these creole houses are little stores). Around the square are also the banks and a guagua stop.

Larimar is a semiprecious stone the color of the sea that is found only in the Southwest region of the Dominican Republic. The **Larimar Mine** (⊠ *Carretera de la Costa, Km 18, Bahoruco* ✍ *cristianvargas78@ yahoo.com* 🖅 *RD$2,000/3,000 for full-day tour* ☉ *Daily 8–6*) can be visited. With the aid of a grant from U.S.A.I.D. and the assistance of Peace Corps volunteers, a Bahoruco community collaboration gives visitors real-life tours of the mine, as well as a hands-on orientation of the history of larimar mining and processing, and visits to local workshops that make larimar jewelry. You'll be transported in the back of a 4x4 truck, and unless a Peace Corps volunteer is with you, English will be limited. Eco-Tours *(see ⇨ Tours in Planning, above)* offers organized group tours from Barahona and surrounding hotels. The cost of the full-day tour includes lunch, drinks, a multilingual guide, and the mine visit with a token larimar stone. You can find help getting your stone polished at a local shop that processes the blue treasure. The best prices on larimar are in this region; you may pay as much as three times more for the same item in Santo Domingo.

EN ROUTE Go southwest out of Barahona on Carretera de la Costa (also called Carretera Barahona-Paraiso, Carretera Enriquillo, Highway 44, and Carretera Barahona–Pedernales) and watch the beauty unfold. Keeping

Down Under in the Larimar Mines

A larimar mine is not like any mine you have ever seen, whether in West Virginia or Wales. While the larimar that comes from the mine is beautiful, the mine is not. It is, as they say, earthy, even odiferous.

Try to ignore the heaps of litter, especially around the cooking shacks, and the disarmingly loud noise from the diesel generators that keep the lights on and help bring in fresh air. Despite these drawbacks, the mine can be fascinating. There are some 25 holes in a given mine, many owned by small investors. Everyone knows whose hole is whose, despite the seeming disorganization. The individual miners are welcoming to visitors and will sometimes let them go down their shafts. The miners, who work 12 hours a day, range in age from 45 down to

teenagers; all are Dominican or Haitian. The work itself can be hazardous, as two teenage miners discovered in 2007, when their oxygen supply failed and they died.

Each hole is perhaps the size of a typical table in a restaurant and about 20 to 30 feet deep, at which point the shaft narrows until it becomes horizontal, forcing you to crawl. Miners chip away at the larimar deposits, which are brought up in a bucket by a rope and pulley system. The miners ascend and descend foot by foot on wooden pegs. Armed security guards at the top ensure that no one takes a rock that doesn't belong to him.

The next time you see a display of larimar in a jewelry case, you may wonder why the prices aren't higher.

the sea to your left and the mountains to your right, you'll pass through a series of seaside villages: Juan Esteban, Bahoruco, La Cienega (towns where five of the small hotels listed are found) and then onto San Rafael, then Paraiso and Los Patos, and Enriquillo, until you eventually go around the tip of the Pedernales Peninsula and on to the national parks.

WHERE TO EAT

The region's best restaurants are all found in or around Barahona, but not all good food is cooked in "real" restaurants. In Bahía de las Águilas, a pristine beach about two hours from Bahouruco by car (road to Pedernales), you can find rustic restaurants serving the freshest seafood you can find.

$ ✕ **Las Brisas del Caribe.** This dining room, which was built by Catholic
CARIBBEAN medics in 1947, has an old-fashioned charm. It's upscale and pricey by Barahona standards, with professional service that can be slow. Appetizers, such as the flavorful pumpkin soup, are well priced, however. Fresh fish is the obvious choice here, with shellfish a known specialty. A French expat always orders either the paella (for two) or the wonderful garlicky *parrillada mixta* for two, which has grilled lobsters, squid, shrimp, and *lambi* (conch), for about US$22. That is living *la vida buena*! The restaurant is on a knoll with a loop of a driveway at the end of the seafront; the views of the water are best from the open-air terrace. ⊠ *Av. Enriquillo 1, next to Politur, Barahona* ☎ *809/524–2794* 🖃 *MC, V.*

¢ ✕**Melo Café.** You could easily pass by this nondescript three-story
CAFE building, a former office that now houses a charming café owned by
Rafael of the Melo Coffee family and his wife, Teresa. It's a clean-living
(alcohol-free) place, with good plates of eggs, omelets, and pancakes
(a rarity here) for breakfast. On the menu, priced low enough for a
Peace Corps volunteer's budget, the best beverages are the fresh fruit
batidas (smoothies); try papaya, pineapple, or milk and bananas, all
for less than 40 pesos. The *plato del día* always offers rice and beans
with perhaps a chicken fricassee or stewed pork, and a little salad, for
just RD$170. You can get a club sandwich here, too (another rarity).
Monday through Wednesday the hours are 8–2, and then it reopens for
dinner from 6–9. Look for the blue awnings. ⊠ *Anacaona 12, Barahona*
☎ *809/524–5437* ▭ *No credit cards* ⊗ *Closed Sun. No dinner Thurs.,
Fri., and Sat.*

$–$$ ✕**Restaurant at Casa Bonita.** Whether it's lunch poolside shaded by a
CARIBBEAN market umbrella or in the open-air dining room, all white with sleek
Fodor'sChoice furnishings, it's a joy just to be in this glorious environment. The pan-
★ oramic view of the sea here looks extra dramatic after one of the house
drinks—the rum-laced Casa Bonita. By night, tables are draped in white
linen, and attentive waiters dressed in white guayabera shirts serve
food with as many influences as the international music playing in the
background. The Caribbean fusion menu utilizes fresh fish and local
produce. The Barahona-style ceviche and the shellfish spaghetti usually
include conch and octopus. Waiters often suggest such creative house
favorites as a fish fillet wrapped with ripe plantains and then battered
and deep-fried, with coconut sauce on the side. Saturday is barbecue
night, with everything from hamburgers to lobster (US$15–US$35), as
well as a tempting lineup of vegetables and starches. It's divine, especially when accompanied by a good match from the wine cooler. Finish
with a perfect flan. ⊠ *Casa Bonita Tropical Lodge, Km 17, Carretera
de la Costa, Bahoruco* ☎ *809/476–5059* ▭ *AE, MC, V.*

$ ✕**Restaurant at Playa Azul.** Blue-and-white gingham tablecloths are just
CARIBBEAN about the only decoration in the dining room, where you can see the
Caribbean by day and hear its serenade by night. Glistening floor tiles
are the color of larimar, and there's an open kitchen. Keep your order
simple—perhaps lobster, fish, or fillet of beef on the grill, or a Dominican specialty like cream of pumpkin or fish soup, fillet of dorado in
coconut sauce, or lambi vinaigrette—and you'll be fine. There's no
wine by the glass—only bottles—but the bar does serve fresh juices
and nicely garnished, tropical cocktails, including perfect piña coladas.
Local music is played, and when it's not too loud, it's pleasant. ⊠ *Playa
Azul, Km 7, Carretera de la Costa, Juan Esteban* ☎ *809/204–8010*
▭ *No credit cards.*

$ ✕**Restaurant Hotelito Oasi.** Giordano Mettifogo is as good a chef as he
ITALIAN is a photographer, which is how he made his living in his native Italy.
After he "retired" to the Dominican Republic with his young Dominican bride, Eva, this caballero became a restaurateur and hotelier. Pastas
are his specialty; while other restaurants may do a so-so carbonara, this
is the real thing. Similarly, he makes his own gnocchi and authentic
pizzas. A delicious sauce of fresh-peeled tomatoes with Italian olive

oil arrives on fresh fish, and his octopus is marinated with the same fine oil and imported vinegar. Lambi in a tomato sauce with polenta is memorable; ask whether there are some lobsters to throw on the grill to go with the parsley butter sauce. Chicken Milanese is a delightful change, and there are great ice creams and lemon sorbet for dessert. Giordano's three children make this a real family affair. The delicious bread? Giordano's teenage daughter makes that. Dinner, served nightly, is open to the general public; breakfast and lunch service is only for hotel guests. ☒ *Hotelito Oasi Italiano, Calle Jose Carrasco, Los Patos* 🕾 *809/918–6969* ▭ *No credit cards.*

¢–$ ✕ **Restaurant Los Robles.** On a Friday night this Malecón eatery is abuzz,
CARIBBEAN and not just from the drone of the motor scooters. Patrons watch sports on the TV out on the patio; a pizza oven in the corner spits out orders to go, while a grill turns out simple dishes like shrimp or chicken breast on a wooden board with fries or tostones. "Loaded" grilled sandwiches are man-size (and available 24 hours). This rough and rustic joint tries to please everyone, and it often does. It's best known for *mofongo* (of many varieties like chicken, lobster, and lambi). *Asopao,* a thick soup with rice, comes with shellfish. The good news is that tax is included in prices, and a Presidente is only RD$60. The bad news is the cleanliness, which leaves something to be desired. ☒ *Av. Enriquillo, corner Av. Nuestra Santa del Rosario, Barahona* 🕾 *809/524–1629* ▭ *MC, V.*

WHERE TO STAY

The best hotels in the Southwest are around Barahona. Most of these are small and owner-managed, and some are quite good. Although we have recommended the best that the region has to offer, we've also stretched our standards to make some of these recommendations; please read both the pros and cons of each hotel here before making a reservation. Three small hotels have recently opened, which attests to the region's increased popularity, especially on weekends. The good news is that lodging in this part of the island is still relatively cheap, although prices have all gone up, and some prices often increase on weekends.

Destin (🕾 *809/967–5209*) offers a unique option for lodging in Barahona, offering home stays with local families that have been trained how to host international guests. A grant from the U.S. Chamber of Commerce in nearby Banai funded this project. Priced for budget travelers, the home stays cost 1,000 pesos for two people, including three meals.

¢   🖭 **Casa Blanca.** Named after the similarly titled movie, this little hotel is
HOTEL just as much a crossroads for intriguing international visitor as Rick's Bar Americain. Your fellow guests might be a French philosophy prof, diplomat types, or a globetrotter from Finland. Susanna Knapp, a charming Swiss woman, transformed this former doctor's home into a fine little inn. In the main building are the reception and dining area, while two guesthouses contain two double rooms and four rooms that each have three beds. (Some guests complain that there's not enough ventilation in the latter, but the hotel is working on the problem.) The six rooms are spartan, but colorful and pristine, and are set amid palm and almond orchards. Pathways lead to the cliffs and down steep steps to the virgin, private beach. You could literally walk for miles along

the (stony) beach and the rock formations. Susanna sets a lovely table strewn with bougainvillea, and for guests there's an appealing three-course prix fixe for dinner that fosters camaraderie. Dinner possibilities may be fresh-caught fish and shellfish with pasta, a fish soup with coconut, or sancocho. Occasionally, the restaurant is open to nonguests for a three-course dinner for RD$60 to RD$1,000 (beg for a reservation). And now there is a public laptop and Wi-Fi in the public spaces as well as TV/DVD. **Pros:** an outpost of civility; good value for the price; food, including a healthy and energizing breakfast, is among the area's finest. **Cons:** lots of "nots" (a lack of phones, in-room TVs, air-conditioning, pool, hot water); the only access is by an unpaved road; car is almost a must to stay here. ⊠ *Km 10, Carretera Barahona-Paraiso, Juan Esteban* ☎ *809/471–1230* ⊕ *www.hotelcasablanca.com.do* ⋧ *6 rooms* ⚂ *In-room: no a/c, no phone, no TV. In-hotel: restaurant, room service, bar, Wi-Fi hotspot, beachfront, laundry service, parking (free)* ⊟ *No credit cards* ⏉ *BP.*

$–$$
Fodor's Choice
★
HOTEL

⛬ **Casa Bonita Tropical Lodge.** This small gem was once the country house of the Schiffino family. Still in the family, it's been reborn as a small luxury hotel that's now run by Virginia (the daughter of the family) and her husband. There are now some Indonesian design elements, and the thatched-roof cabanas have gone deluxe, with contemporary lighting and natural materials like *tabla de palma* (wood slats of palm). Private balconies allow you to hear the river below and see the cloud forest above. You can have the lovely breakfast served on your balcony or in the *palapa*-topped (grass hut) restaurant that merges into the salon. Both overlook an infinity pool (with its own palm on a tiny island) and the sea beyond. Unquestionably, this is the most stellar option in the entire Southwest. **Pros:** celestial, panoramic vistas allow you to chill and enjoy the area; service is attentive and caring; iPod-ready clock radios in rooms and Jacuzzi poolside. **Cons:** hotel is up a short but rough dirt road; not all staffers are fluent in English. ⊠ *Km 17, Carretera de la Costa, Bahoruco* ☎ *809/476–5059; 809/540–5908 reservations* ⊕ *www.casabonitadr.com* ⋧ *12 rooms* ⚂ *In-room: a/c, no TV, Wi-Fi. In-hotel: restaurant, bar, pool, bicycles, parking (free)* ⊟ *AE, MC, V* ⏉ *BP.*

$$
PRIVATE VILLA

⛬ **Casa de Tarzan.** The innovative, trilevel Tarzan's House is deep in the tropical forest, with decks overhanging a river. The ultimate escape for adventurous types, it's accessible only by a 4x4, horseback, or mountain bike, and all food and other necessities must be brought in. This eco-friendly house has its own spring water aqueduct, a generator, and barbecue. Cell phones can now get a signal, a plus that came with its total renovation in 2009. New bamboo furniture has been added, as well as *hamacas* (hammocks); one bedroom has three bunk beds. Reservations can be made directly through the English-speaking owner or through Eco-Tour Barahona. To reach the house, you go up the drive to Casa Bonita but make a hard left before the hotel, onto a dirt road for some 30 minutes. Five rivers must be forded, but you will eventually get there. **Pros:** you're at one with nature (the sound of the rushing river is omnipresent); can be romantic, especially with a full moon; a nearby local family acts as caretaker and can provide maid service or cook for you.

Cons: a hard-core adventure only for the self-sufficient; the long trek here isn't feasible after dark. ✉ *Km 17, Carretera de la Costa, Bahoruco* ☎ *809/977–4280, 809/476–5059, or 809/540–5908* ✍ *polidiaz@codetel.net.do* *4 bedrooms, 2½ bathrooms* *In-room: no a/c, no phone, kitchen, no TV* *No credit cards* ☞ *Two-day minimum.*

$ INN **Coral Sol Resort.** This is the only real eco-inn in the Southwest. In fact, it may remind you of the rustic cabins found in U.S. national parks, except with palm trees instead of evergreens. The Dominican owners have creatively utilized the round white stones from their beach for the pathways and steps, sometimes painting them black to make a pattern. "Resort" is too grand a description for this place, but there's a pool with mismatched furniture and what would be an inviting clubhouse for mingling if the sofas were reupholstered. Cabins are large and bisected with a slatted wood partition, each section with its own double bed and bathroom. In the rustic open-air restaurant, the ladies do turn out some especially flavorful Dominican meals, such as fried fish with tomato sauce and both white beans and black beans. (You may want to just get breakfast for some of the days you stay here. This will reduce the rate by US$20 for those days.) A major renovation is in the works. If you're thinking of making a reservation (the only way guests are accepted), make sure that the fixes and updates have happened. **Pros:** caring resident owner is a true Barahona caballero; soothing and stress-free atmosphere; attractive to families, students, and ecotourists. **Cons:** This is roughing it with no creature comforts; style and decor need help. ✉ *Km 19, Carretera Paraiso, La Cienega* ☎ *809/233–4882* *www.coralsolresort.com* *9 rooms* *In-room: no a/c, no phone, no TV. In-hotel: restaurant, room service, bar, pool, beachfront, parking (free)* *No credit cards* *MAP.*

¢ HOTEL **Hotel/Comedor Kalibe.** If you're used to four and five stars, this new hotelito may look too basic, but it's now the town's finest. It is an offshoot of the owners' successful restaurant next door, the equally rudimentary Teresa's (aka Comedor Kalibe). Teresa, a Dominicana, is married to a Frenchman, J.P. Raguideau, and in late 2009 they took a giant step and built this two-story stucco edifice and its swimming pool. Rooms, particularly the ones with double beds, are oversized, with kitchenettes, a tiny desk, and an impressive shower. For now, all is new and squeaky clean. The comforters and curtains are less appealing, along the lines of the decoration in the restaurant—plastic tablecloths, plastic flowers. The open-air lobby is a better story, with attractive tropical furnishings, handsome tile floors, and a little bar. At this writing, neither the bar, the Wi-Fi, satellite TV, the Web site, nor the credit-card machine were operational, but (hopefully) will be by the time you read this; in the meantime, use e-mail for making reservations. **Pros:** full electricity; reliable generator and air-conditioning. **Cons:** no water view, although it's close; limited English. ✉ *Calle Arzobispo Meriño 16, Paraiso* ☎ *809/243–1192* ✍ *contact@ecotour-repdom.com* *7 rooms* *In-room: a/c, kitchen, refrigerator. In-hotel: restaurant, pool, laundry service.* *No credit cards* *EP.*

¢ HOTEL **Hotel Costa Larimar.** Although it's one of the best options in downtown Barahona, this is not a destination hotel. The sign says that this is WHERE

YOUR DREAMS COME TRUE, but it's doubtful that this will be your idea of a sweet dream. However, a recent change in ownership has brought significant improvements. What's broken was fixed, the new lobby furniture is attractive, everything is clean, and the elevators now go up and down. The facade and layout, including a pool within steps of a beach fronting a small tree-covered isle, is quite inviting, but swimming in Barahona's own bay is not advisable. Guest rooms are spacious and have American cable TV and new, nice bedding. You will be treated nicely, and the breakfast buffet may be uninspired, but it is served by the pool. (Don't add a full meal plan to your stay; the regular buffet grub isn't worth it.) Business travelers are often here midweek, and Dominican families prevail on weekends. **Pros:** bed with breakfast is a good value; nice children's playground; some rooms have private balconies and sea views (request one). **Cons:** little English spoken; noisy families take over on weekends. ⊠ *Av. Enriquillo 6, Barahona* ☎ *809/524–1111* ⊕ *www.hotelcostalarimar.com* ⇩ *109 rooms* ⌂ *In-room: a/c (some), safe, Wi-Fi (some). In-hotel: 2 restaurants, bars, pool, beachfront, laundry service, Wi-Fi hotspot, parking (free)* ▭ *MC, V* ⏇ *BP.*

¢ ⛾ **Hotel El Quemaito.** Now under new ownership, this unassuming hotel
HOTEL is best for groups who don't mind doubling up and for families. There are five suite-like family rooms: in the lovely Suite 7, seven people are allowed, and some rooms have sea views. Other big pluses here are the panoramic views of the nearby Quemaito Beach, the pool complex with a kids' pool, and the sun terrace. Open to outside guests, the unadorned dining room looks like an officers' mess hall, with the Dominican flag the only decoration. However, the international meals with a criolla influence—fish, lobster and classics like chicken cordon bleu—are enjoyable. A standout dessert is the chocolate crêpes with Campari sauce and vanilla ice cream. The hotel's wrought-iron gates are locked and opened by security guards. Hotel prices include 16% tax, 26% at the restaurant. **Pros:** clean and well maintained; owners and chef are multilingual; car rentals available; TV room. **Cons:** down a rough dirt road; a car is almost a necessity; more could be done to improve the atmosphere and decor. ⊠ *Km 10, Carretera Barahona–Paraiso, Juan Esteban* ☎ *809/649–7631* ⊕ *www.hotelelquemaito.com* ⇩ *14 rooms* ⌂ *In-room: a/c (some), no phone, safe. In-hotel: restaurant, bar, pool, laundry service, Wi-Fi hotspot, parking (free); some pets allowed* ▭ *V* ⏇ *BP.*

¢ ⛾ **Hotelito Oasi Italiana.** A true oasis in a neighborhood of simple, one-
HOTEL room wooden casitas, this walled and gated complex is impressive from the street. Inside the compound are two buildings, with a pool between. The first two-story building houses a restaurant and the owner's dwelling; the other building, the family's former home, has the seven hotel rooms. The ones on the first floor are centered around a salon with Italian leather furniture and an attractive mural of exotic birds and banana trees. These bedrooms, with the exception of the family room (which sleeps four), have the same decor as the three newer (and smaller) rooms upstairs. These have sea views and handsome desks and furnishings from the owner's native Italy. What is certain is the sincere hospitality of Giordano and his family. **Pros:** location that's closer to the national

parks than hotels near Bahoruco; authentic Italian food at restaurant; proximity to a fun beach; hospitable owners. **Cons:** no phones; rooms and appliances have some maintenance issues; no English spoken (Spanish and Italian). ⊠ *Calle José Carrasco, Los Patos* ☎ *809/918–6969* ⊕ *www.lospatos.it* ↷ *7 rooms* ↺ *In-room: a/c, no phone. In-hotel: restaurant, room service, pool* ▤ *No credit cards* ⦿| *BP.*

¢ ▦ **Loro Tuerto Hotel & Cafe.** Barahona city is fortunate to have this
HOTEL hotelito, which opened in 2009. The savvy Europeans and Americans who discover it are mad about the red, Havana-style café, which has shuttered doors that are usually opened. The fascinating photographs and artifacts that line the brightly painted walls belong to the globetrotting owner, a Spaniard. After ordering from the long list of international drinks, you may become mesmerized by the Haitian lion mask, with its long mane. The menu is limited to tapas and pastas, and rooms in the two-story block are limited in size and creature comforts. They are simple, new, and clean, with hand-hewn furnishings and small TVs that do get American channels. You can adjourn to the inner courtyard to take a siesta in a hammock, tune into the Wi-Fi, or just escape the street noise that invades the café. However, the sound system for the fab international and American music is in the café, so the courtyard can be a little noisy, too. **Pros:** hip, hospitable owner (he's often in Spain); sweet, caring staff; five minutes to Caribe Tour's buses—ideal for early morning runs. **Cons:** wood furniture is unstained, beds and bedding could be bigger; only safe is at reception. ⊠ *Luis E. Delmonte 33, Barahona* ☎ *809/524–6600; 809/909–2262* ⊕ *www.lorotuerto.com* ↷ *9 rooms* ↺ *In-room: a/c, no phone. In-hotel: restaurant, bar, laundry service, Wi-Fi hotspot* ⦿| *EP.*

¢ ▦ **Playa Azul.** Opened in 2006 and overlooking a secluded beach snug in
HOTEL its tranquil cove, this is one of the Southwest's newer and better lodging options. The rooms are quite comfortable, and there's cable TV, though no English-language channels. The hotel itself, two stucco blocks of units, is unattractive. Reserve the first tier of rooms: the second tier, right behind them, has no sea views. The two new casitas, Nos. 19 and 20, are the best. They're spacious and have great design, but why didn't they build them so that they both faced the water? Still, these two are indicative of an upward movement here. Kudos for the new bedding and outdoor massage cabanas. Although two of the three owners are French (the couple's partner is Dominican), for the most part, the decor is strictly local, and the only thing French here is the crêpes. **Pros:** good value; nice rocking chairs on front porch and under thatch-capped gazebos; substantial improvements. **Cons:** lacks class or much spirit; cash only. ⊠ *Km 7, Carretera Barahona–Enriquillo, Enriquillo* ☎ *809/424–5375* ✉ *playaazulbarahona@hotmail.com* ↷ *20 rooms* ↺ *In-room: a/c, no phone. In-hotel: restaurant, bar, pool, beachfront, laundry service, Wi-Fi hotspot, parking (free)* ▤ *No credit cards* ⦿| *CP.*

¢ ▦ **Ponte Vedra.** This stucco hotel with stone details looks good from
HOTEL the outside, as does the bar-restaurant under a palapa next to the pool, which looks out to the sea. It even has a beach with sand rather than pebbles. As an "apartotel," Ponte Vedra has apartment-like rooms with kitchenettes. Some of them, such as the two-room No. 201, which

sleeps six, are OK. Others, however, desperately need a fresh paint job and have rusty stovetops, dated furniture, and a musty smell. No rooms have true water views, and the awnings over the guest rooms' exterior doors are ragged. Although the hotel is family owned, the employees are not outstanding, and there's nothing eco about it. However, on a weekend, sometimes it's the only place with vacancies. **Pros:** convenient location; nice pool and beach. **Cons:** not very welcoming; plastic flowers everywhere are indicative of decor; the little restaurant is not so good (skip the meal plan). ⊠ *Km 12, Carretera Paraiso, El Arroyo* ☎ *809/341–8462 or 809/341–4698* ⊕ *www.pontevedracaribe. com* ⇥ *16 rooms* ⚹ *In-room: a/c, kitchen. In-hotel: restaurant, bar, pool, beachfront, parking (free)* ⊟ *MC, V* ⦿ *EP.*

BEACHES

The reason the Dominican government has been slow to develop the Southwest, despite election promises, is that its *playas* are predominantly white stones and pebbles, with some patches of white sand. Water shoes are necessary for safe walking and swimming on most beaches. That aside, the water, the sun, the unspoiled coastline, and the lack of hotels and development is inviting to the very types who are now discovering ecotourism here. ⚠ **While this is still one of the safest areas in the country, petty theft, especially at beautiful, deserted beaches, has become more common.**

Playa El Quemaito. Although just down from Casa Blanca and Hotel El Quemaito, this beach is seldom populated during the week, so never swim alone. It's usually dead calm because of a small reef; consequently, it's safe even for small children to swim here. White stones are interspersed with white patches of sand where you can put down your towel—but be sure to keep your belongings safe. There are no facilities, but you could take lunch or have drinks at Hotel El Quemaito. ⊠ *Km 16, Carretera de la Costa, Juan Esteban, 9 mi (16 km) southwest of Barahona.*

Playa Bahoruco. In front of the fishing village of the same name, this gorgeous stretch of virgin beach goes on for miles with unobstructed views. Taupe sand surrounds the white stones that are underfoot. Turn left at the sign for the former Barceló Bahoruco Hotel. Surfers come for the small waves, and there is some undertow. You may see some small blue larimar pebbles on the beach (otherwise you can buy them from local children). You may want to take lunch (or dinner) at Restaurant Luz, and leave your belongings there when you swim. Locals and some expats love this homey seafood eatery, and don't seem to mind that they are eating on tables covered with bed throws. ⊠ *Km 17, Carretera de la Costa, Bahoruco, 8 mi (17 km) southwest of Barahona.*

Playa St. Rafael. The joy at this spot, a few kilometers past Playa Bahoruco, is that a river comes right into the sea, and a rock dam makes a small waterfall, which, in turn, forms a pool. Little children scamper in and out of its frigid waters, and you certainly can join them. It's cold, yes, but safer than swimming in the sea, which has quite a strong undertow beneath the mild waves. Beach shacks here turn out tasty fried fish and tostones. You may even be able to get red snapper fillets in coconut sauce. Parking is RD$50, which pays for the security guard. Litter here, from Styrofoam containers to Presidente bottles, can be a definite negativo, particularly on Sundays, when it is packed with locals. You may enjoy this slice of Dominican life on weekends; midweek, it's blissfully quiet and you can have the place to yourself. ⊠ *Km 17, Carretera de la Costa, St. Rafael* ⊕ *25 km (12 mi) southwest of Barahona.*

NEED A BREAK?

Villa Mariam, formerly a private house up the steep hill from St. Rafael Beach, has a wonderful icy waterfall. You can bathe in its pools as you drink aged rum (it's BYOB, and you may need it to brave the chilly waters). Lanai vines and tropical flowers, even orchids, grow wild and make it look like Eden. There's no restaurant or bar, but there are picnic tables, and you can bring your fried-fish plates up from the beach. Admission is RD$100, free to guests of Casa Bonita.

SPORTS AND THE OUTDOORS

The Southwest is one very sporty place, with bird-watching and spectator sports like cockfighting, as well as horseback riding, trekking, mountain biking, snorkeling, surfing, and a host of other possibilities. *For information on the major tour companies that offer organized excursions in the region, see* ⇨ *Tours in Planning, above.*

BIRD-WATCHING

Hispaniola has 30 endemic bird species, not to mention many others that can be found throughout the Caribbean region. Kate Wallace, an American living in Santo Domingo, is an expert in this birding frontier and organizes birding tours through her company **Tody Tours** (⊠ *Calle Jose Gabriel Garcia 105, Zona Colonial, Santo Domingo* ☎ *809/686–0882* ⊕ *www.todytours.com*). When her groups first arrive in Santo Domingo, she houses them at hotels in the Colonial Zone. A four-wheel-drive vehicle is hired, and they travel to the Southwest, staying at Hotel El Quemaito (cheaper camping options are also available at her own Villa Barrancoli). She now has two new wood/screen cabins with real beds. Bird-watching can be an expensive hobby, but tours are all individually designed and priced, depending on duration and choice of lodging.

COCKFIGHTING

Cockfighting is a tradition that persists in the Spanish islands of the Caribbean—in Puerto Rico, Cuba, and the Dominican Republic. The fact that these birds are put in a ring with spurs on their ankles and are expected to fight until death—and it is hoped that only one has to die—may seem like a horrid blood sport to the outsider, but it is a long-held tradition here, and like Spanish bullfights, it's definitely authentic (albeit something that is not for everyone). The high season for fights is June through November (roosters cannot fight during molting season, from December to January). February through May are usually reserved for training. Given the tendency for blood splatters, you might want to avoid the front row. Bets are taken, but first-timers should sit out their first time in the *gallera* until they get the system down.

Birds in the Barahona Region

The national parks in the southwestern part of the country provide the last remaining habitats for some 300 bird species in the Dominican Republic, including 30 that are endemic to Hispaniola. You have never seen anything like these Caribbean birds outside of an exotic pet store. Take the little tody, which has both a narrow- and broad-billed variety. These diminutive beauties are predominately green with red, pink, and yellow markings on white or gray breasts. They're very sweet.

Both the Hispaniolan parrot (*cotorra*) and its smaller cousin, the Hispaniolan parakeet (*perico*) can be sighted here. The Hispaniolan trogon (*papagayo*), which has a verdant green back and head and gray chest that segues into ruby-red plumage, has a bright blue tail and is accented with black and white stripes on its wings. Should you see a low-flying vain hummingbird (*zumbador Cito*) suspended in motion over a fuchsia flower, you may need to catch your breath. Even more rare is his relative, the Antillean mango (*zumbador grande*); the male has a black mask, green face and throat, and purple tail. And then there are other birds normally associated with

northern climes—owls, hawks, swallows, pigeons, quail-doves—though far more beautiful than their northern cousins, with vibrant colorings.

Birders come here in all sizes and shapes, from teenage students to fortysomethings and seniors. The ardent bird-watchers, including "twitchers," as some British aficionados are called, are in their own little feathered world here. They will arrive with tripods for their expensive cameras, not to mention equally expensive binoculars. Their floppy hats act as sunscreens. Of course, all true bird-watchers have their logbooks in which they record their sightings. They travel to exotic countries and spend thousands of dollars to be able to log views of nearly extinct species. The Dominican Republic—and much of the Caribbean (with the exception of Trinidad), actually—is a sleeper for bird-watching, often passed over for better-known places like Costa Rica.

Expert guide Kate Wallace is the queen of the birders. At an age when most ladies are content to garden, she drives a four-wheel-drive vehicle like a professional truck driver at all hours of the morning, up steep mountain trails.

The main cockfighting ring closest to Barahona is **La Gallera** (⊠ *Km 21, Carretera de la Costa, La Cienaga*). Fights (in season) are held on Saturday and Sunday nights, from 4 PM until the wee hours. If you want to take in a cockfight, you'll pay RD$500 for a front-row seat, RD$300 for a second-row seat; elsewhere, you'll pay RD$200 for a chair or RD$75 for standing room.

HIKING AND HORSEBACK RIDING

Horseback riding and hiking tours are popular with those who are fit and who want to have a real eco-experience. Since feet and hooves are the usual mode of locomotion in the mountains, certainly for those who live "in the bush," you'll have a chance to visit many small villages along the way and meet locals, who genuinely enjoy these visits. They may offer you coffee or fruit, a trademark of true Dominican hospitality since they have precious little for themselves. Guides can identify the different species of wild orchids and often do bird calls that attract beauties such as parrots, hummingbirds, papagayos, and even jilgueros (finches), which can make nine different sounds. You will also learn how the residents live off the land and survive; some are coffee-bean pickers, while others cultivate mangoes, avocados, and cacao. These villages are high up in the cloud forest (*Cachote*), which can be chilly and humid. Dress in layers. Lunch breaks for some all-day hikes and horseback riding treks are taken either at the new visitors' center in Cachote, built by volunteers from the University of Ohio, who also constructed campground sites and installed solar panels. Another lunch option is Rancho Platone, which is an impressive wooden compound with a waterslide that goes into a pool—perfect when you're hot and sweaty.

A new tour for athletic types, orchestrated by Eco-Tour Barahona, begins in Santo Domingo's Colonial Zone and includes three days of biking (two in Higuero, and one in the Zone). Participants are then transferred by van to the Southwest for three days of nature hiking. Hotels and meals are included in the price.

ECO-Tour Barahona (⊠ *Carretera Enriquillo, The Malecón, Edificio 8, Apt. 306, Paraiso* ☎ *809/243–1190; 809/395–1542 cell* ⊕ *www. ecotour-repdom.com*) organizes such tours for all levels of trekkers, from greenhorn to advanced. Trips can either be a full day (5 to 8 hours), or several days, including camping at night and a vehicle to help you during the trip. Hiking treks cost $60 for a full-day tour with lunch. Horseback riding costs $70 for a full day with lunch if there are more than three people, $100 a person if just one or two. The horseback riding isn't for small children, pregnant women, or anyone who isn't at least a little horse savvy.

SHOPPING

The best products to buy in the Southwest are indigenous and locally created. Different volunteer groups have spearheaded artisans' cooperatives and training programs to help the locals to help themselves.

La Asociaciòn de Artesania de Paraìso, Arte Natural is one such group. Recently they extended their market to Barahona, to the city's gift shops and restaurants.

Another group of local artisans makes products under the label Arte Natural–Artisans of Paraiso, using only materials that are from the immediate area, including coconut, banana leaves, gourds, bamboo, coffee, rock, wood, feathers, palm leaves, and the like. Look for their label as you browse for gifts and souvenirs.

Melo Coffee (⊠ *Anacaona 14, Barahona* ☎ *809/524–2440*) is a family-owned company, and both the factory and offices of the company are here. Watch the workers sort the beans. Organic coffee is their business, and that is all they sell, beautifully packaged in dark-green one-pound bags for a mere RD$85. This beats taking home an ashtray with the name of the city.

At **Taller Artesanal de Larimar Banesa** (⊠ *Carretera Enriquillo 156, Bahoruco* ☎ *829/401–8668 or 829/401–8591*) Mari and Cesar Feliz, who also own and run theonly pharmacy in their little fishing village, sell their handmade larimar jewelry right in the little *farmacia*. Simple but attractive are the *bolitas* (necklaces of little larimar beads strung like pearls), which make perfect gifts for young girls. The larimar "eggs" make great paperweights. Many other designs are done with silver, and they also sell small wire sculptures.

NIGHTLIFE

In Barahona, nightlife consists mostly of local merengue clubs and discos in town and on the Malecón. Tourists should probably stick to the main restaurant and hotel bars unless accompanied by Dominican friends.

In *el campo* (the countryside), mostly on weekends, evenings are spent at the *colmados* (little grocery stores, most with outdoor seating, on the coastal road). Locals can be seen drinking Presidente beer or *traigos* (shots of Dominican rum), eating plates of *pollo frito* (fried chicken) or *pescado frito* (fried fish) with tostones. Some of these turn into regional dance spots on weekends as well; during the week, you might see the same people watching a baseball game on TV. If you're looking for a good place to dance, ask any local or taxi driver, who can tell you about the best places and how to find them. A new place in Los Patos is the Hollywood Café, somewhat surprisingly owned by an Italian. It's about five minutes up from the river, overlooking the beach. This wooden casita painted turquoise is one hot bar on weekends, with events that include karaoke and bachata contests, with muchos pesos in prize money. The local young, expats, tourists, and oldsters all vie to be couple numero uno. The kids watch enthralled as they take their fruit smoothies through a straw.

PEDERNALES

135 km (84 mi) southwest of Barahona; approximately 3 hours from Barahona by car.

Pedernales is the name of the peninsula on the DR's southernmost shore, the location of three national parks. They are the biggest reason why ecotourists are starting to gravitate here. The physical beauty and diversity of landscape is not inconsiderable. Pedernales is also the name of the town on the DR's border with Haiti, where the best of the natural sites are located, particularly in Parque Nacional Jaragua and the famous Bahía de las Águilas.

Much of the Pedernales region—namely Parque Nacional Jaragua and Parque Nacional Bahoruco—has been declared a Global Biosphere Reserve by UNESCO because of its vast and diverse habitats (a biosphere is an area of the planet where unique forms of earth, water, air, plants, and animals coexist). **Parque Nacional Jaragua** is one of three national parks in this region (the third is Lago Enriquillo). The park is named after a famous Taino chief Jaragua, who defied the Spanish for more than a decade. (If you go on a guided trip, you can see some Taino cave drawings.) Many scientists and hobbyists come here regularly for bird-watching, butterfly-watching, and even palm- (tree) watching. It's a place where you might spot flamingos, iguanas, and crocodiles, among other endemic, protected species in the surrounding lakes, mountains, rivers, and pristine beaches.

From Barahona to the park, you'll drive nearly 3 hours; from the small hotels in the Bahoruco/La Cienega area 2½ hours; from Los Patos 2 hours. (One older Italian couple went from Los Patos with two motoconchos and found the ride exhilarating, the coastal scenery breathtaking,)

There is now one decent hotel in Pedernales, where you can stay if traveling independently. It can beat getting up at dawn to make the drive. The park is a straight shot down Highway 44, the coastal road, from either Barahona or Pedernales. There's good signage for the entrance to the park as well as **Laguna de Oviedo**, about 1½ mi (3 km) from the little town of Oviedo. If you have to choose just one ecotour, this might be the best.

The park occupies the southern part of the Pedernales Peninsula, with its stark and striking contrasts of seascapes and arid desert-like terrain, including a thorn forest, and there are marine turtles and the greatest variety of bird species on the island of Hispaniola. The flocks of pink flamingos that roam the shores of the Laguna de Oviedo on their spindly legs are the most photographed.

The park is a vast area of 1,500 square km (579 square mi), and to reach the interior you must have a strong, four-wheel-drive vehicle and a means of communication should you get stuck or break down. ■ TIP→ Don't attempt this trip on your own without the help of a seasoned guide or tour company.

When you arrive at the park's entrance, you'll be greeted by guides, who will direct you to parking and will line you up to get the boat tour to Laguna de Oveido, which takes about 3 hours. The cost of the boat trip is the same whether you have 2 people or 8, so it's cost-effective to buddy up with strangers. If you have time, climb the tower for a view of the shallow, brackish lagoon. It's best to arrive in the morning, between 8 and 9 AM, before the wind gets up. The lagoon is so shallow that once you reach the mangroves, the boatman has to turn off the motor and push the boat. It makes a wonderful way to quietly approach the flamingos and the roseate spoonbills, the pelicans, egrets, and frigate birds. Tours will take you to visit the flamingo colony, a couple of islets, and a cave with Taino petroglyphs. The birds are more active at dawn, which means it's easier for you if you spend the night in Pedernales (see ⇨ Where to Stay, below). The trip can include the south end of the lagoon, where the endemic iguana Ricordi, only found on Hispaniola, can be seen. (Feed them only leaves, not anything else.) It's hot here, so bring plenty of water, sunscreen, and a hat.

The Alcoa Road, indicated by a park sign on the right, is one of the entrance points for the 800 square-km, mostly mountainous **National Park Sierra de Bahoruco.** The intersection is actually about 10 km (6 mi) before the town of Pedernales. The road leads up to a pine forest and the site of former bauxite mines. The view from the Hoyo de Pelempito of a wide rift valley is justly famous. The other entrance to the Sierra Park is on the north side, passing through Duverge on the south side of Lago

Enriquillo, to Puerto Encondidio. This dusty road is also the entrance to Kate Wallace's camp. You must have a strong four-wheel drive to get to see the wild orchids (some 166 species) and 49 species of birds (including the Hispaniolan parrots) in the pine forests of this interior park. It's definitely not advisable to do it on your own. Wallace's Tody Tours is one of the few recommendable alternatives.

At this writing, ECO-Tour of Barahona and Tody Tours offer excursions here, but two local guides' associations assisted by Peace Corps volunteers are also a possibility if you really want to go it alone *(see* ⇨ *Tours, above)*. ⊠ *Hwy. 44 W, 1½ mi (3 km) north of Oviedo* 🕮 *$3, $65 for tours of Laguna de Oviedo* 🕓 *Daily 8–5.*

NEED A BREAK?

Polo is not only a three-button shirt or horseplay. It's a municipality in the interior known for its "Magnetic Pole." (At one point along the road to Polo, the road appears to be going up, but in fact, it is going down. If you put the vehicle in neutral, it will continue to move, giving the illusion that it's driving itself.) Now its annual organic coffee festival, "Celebrating the Harvest," is making the area popular. Begun in 2007, when it just promoted coffee and other typical regional projects, the early-June festival now also features arts and crafts, international and national artists, and musicians perform. You'll need a four-wheel drive to reach this mountainous, scenic, and biodiverse region. ECO-Tour will take interested parties to the fest.

WHERE TO STAY

If you don't want to get up at dawn to make the drive to Nacional Park Jaragua, there's one simple but decent hotel we can recommend in Pedernales. Owners Marino and Katya are welcoming, and belong to the local ecotourism organization. The simple **Hostal Doña Chava** (⊠ *Calle 2, Barrio Alcoa, Pedernales* 🕮 *809/524–0332* ⊕ *www.donachava.com* ✍ *hostalchava@hotmail.com*) charges about RD$650 per night for a double. The Web site (in English) doesn't always work, but the e-mail usually does.

BEACHES

Bahía de las Águilas. This gorgeous white-sand beach may very well rank among the best you'll ever see, and it's reachable only by boat from the fishing village of Las Cuevas, south of Cabo Rojo, or by a difficult overland route that is not recommended for the inexperienced. Granted, this is not for those who require fancy amenities. This is a pristine, isolated beach with absolutely no facilities and little shade, so bring a cooler of drinks, food, and whatever else you might need. But if you come prepared, you can spend a blissful couple of hours here.

The unnmarked dirt road to Cabo Rojo is approximately 12 km (7.4 mi) east of Pedernales, off the highway to Oviedo. You'll first pass the limestone and cement plant; if you continue about 6 km (3.7 mi), you'll reach the town of Cabo Rojo; after another 10 minutes or so (approximately ½ mi), you'll reach the fishing village of Las Cuevas, and it's here that fishing boats can take you to the beach. Expect to pay US$60 (but try bargaining); agree on a time the fisherman will return to pick you up. Offer to pay one-half on arrival and one-half when he picks you up. Las Cuevas also has a boat-rental operation and a decent seafood restaurant. The beach is also reachable by road if you have a 4x4 vehicle, but be sure to ask a local in Las Cuevas how to get there, and we highly recommend that you do not take this route unless you're experienced driving in the area. There are few gas stations, and if your car breaks down or blows a tire, you're in for a lot of trouble. ECO-Tour Barahona offers organized excursions *(see ⇨ Tours in Planning, above)*. ⊠ *Approx. 6.4 km (4 mi) south of Cabo Robo, 3 km (1.6 mi) south of Las Cuevas.*

Bahía El Cabo Rojo. This is the kind of unspoiled beach that Caribbean dreams are made of, with turquoise water and golden sand, where you can lie back and watch the pelicans dive for their dinner. You'll have to bring yours, for there are no facilities, just mangroves and dry thorn scrubs. If you're into beachcombing, you'll find more conch shells than you can carry. ⊠ *Hwy. 44, 12 km (7 km) east of Pedernales, approximately 2 hrs, from Barahona.*

Playa Los Patos. This beautifully long beach is bisected by a river and well populated with buses full of Dominican and international tourists every weekend. During the week, you may see the ladies of this poor *pueblito* bathing their children and doing their laundry in this, the shortest river in the Caribbean. Bordering the river is a row of colorful cooking shacks with names scrawled on the side. Most sell fried fish on the bone with tostones—sometimes it comes with rice and beans or salad. Some expats prefer the blue shack next to the fried-chicken queen's, to the left of the front entrance. Others say that the ones to the right don't price gouge. When they tell you what they offer, be sure to ask the price. A food plate should range anywhere from RD$150 to RD$400. If they start quoting RD$3,000, keep looking. ⊠ *Hwy. 44, Los Patos ✛ 7 km (4 mi) south of Paraiso.*

Playa Paraiso. Bordering the main *calle* of this town, this is a good long beach, though it can be littered. Modern midrise apartment buildings face the beach, which attracts a fun, young crowd of expats, particularly Habitat for Humanities volunteers. ECO-Tour Barahona has its main headquarters for the region across from the beach. ⊠ *Hwy. 44, Paraiso ✛ 16 km (10 mi) south of San Rafael.*

LAGO ENRIQUILLO

Approx. 129 km (80 mi) west of Baharona; approx. 2½ hours by car

La Descubierta is your gateway to Lago Enriquillo and a good shopping destination for local wares and, if you're lucky, Haiti's Barbancourt Rum. Organized tours to the lake do not stop in the town, but if you're driving, you may want to take a look, though it's hardly a life-changing experience. Although the cold, natural pool of Las Barias Balneario is across the street from the town park, we recommend that you not swim in the water because of the possibility of disease, though Dominicans swim with few worries.

EXPLORING

Lago Enriquillo. The largest lake in the Antilles is on an arid plain outlined by craggy mountains near the Haitian border. The saltwater lake was once the lowest point in the Antilles: 114 feet below sea level. (The lake's depth and size has risen dramatically due to storms and rainfall, and scientists and ecologists are wondering just how much more its ecosystem will change.) It encircles wild, arid, and thorny islands that serve as sanctuaries for such exotic birds and reptiles as flamingos, iguanas, and previously the indigenous American crocodile, which once numbered close to 500 (there are many fewer now). It's an eerie place, where dead trees poke up from the salty water. Your best chance of seeing a croc is at dawn, during the dry season between January and June, but it's rare in the best of times. Flamingo sightings are more likely during their migration season, from April to July; after that, the lake level rises, and the flamingos decamp to the Bahamas.

Isla Cabritos Parque Nacional is a small island within Lago Enriquillo that is the habitat for hundreds of iguanas, and some of their larger cousins, American crocodiles. The word cabritos means little goats, and they roam the island, as do burros (small donkeys). You may see the droppings, but you will rarely see the goats or burros on a visit. Boats to the island leave from the national park dock in the town of Descubierta. The only facility on the island is a little green, wooden casita, where the island's history, the flora, and the wildlife are explained in detail in Spanish and in graphics. For independent travelers, a boat trip to the island is RD$3,500 (about $100), regardless of the size of the group. If you can wait for a sizable group, the price can be reduced to about $10 per person. The trip to the island takes an hour; the best time to pull together a group is in the morning—whatever size the group, be it 2 persons or 15. But you might have to wait some time for a group to come together. ECO-Tour Barahona runs organized trips to the island as well, which will allow you to book ahead *(see ⇨ Tours in Planning, above)*. ■ TIP→ **There is shade and a couple of picnic tables on the island, but the island itself can be monstrously hot. Bring sunglasses, sunscreen, a long-sleeve shirt, insect repellent, and closed-toe shoes (there are a lot of burrs and cacti) for your trip. Neither the national park nor Isla Cabritos has restrooms. Facilities can be found nearby, in the town of Descubierta, but bring your own toilet paper. The Association of Eco-Tourism Guides of Lago Enriquillo offers information on visiting the lake on its Web site.** ✉ *Hwy. 48, 3 km (1.8 mi) east of Descubierta, on northwestern shore of Lago Enriquillo* ☎ *809/816–7441* ⊕ *www.lagoenriquilloguides.com* 💵 *US$3* ⊙ *Daily 8–5.*

WHERE TO STAY

The drive from Barahona to La Descubierta is approximately 2½ hours. If you drive yourself and are too exhausted to make it back to your hotel, there are five very basic places to spend the night in La Descubierta; however, only two are recommendable. Both are simple, Dominican-owned hotels, so don't expect anything fancy. But you'll have a private room, possibly a private bath, a fan (perhaps air-conditioning), and a friendly staff. Both hotels have emergency backup generators to deal with power outages, which are not uncommon. Restaurants also keep it simple, serving rice and beans, empanadas, and fried chicken but little else. The Association of Eco-Tourism Guides of Lago Enriquillo can help you make reservations at one of the local hotels if you don't speak Spanish.

Hotel Iguana (✉ *On main road west of park, La Descubierta* ☎ *809/301–4815*) is the best of the local options, and they can make you lunch or dinner if you notify them in advance. A room (no hot water) costs between RD$300 and RD$500; breakfast, lunch, or dinner is extra.

Mi Pequeño Hotel (✉ *Calle Padre Bellini, next to central park, La Descubierta* ☎ *809/762–6329 or 809/243–1080*) is an acceptable alternative to Hotel Iguana, although it's noisier because it's next to a disco, called Saturday Night Fever. A double room here costs about RD$400, but the hotel serves only breakfast.

The Southeast Coast

BOCA CHICA, JUAN DOLIO,
LA ROMANA, BAYAHIBE

WORD OF MOUTH

"We went to Casa de Campo because my [father-in-law] is an avid golfer and he has been there about two dozen times. Teeth of the Dog is a stunning course."

—Rabbit

"Casa de Campo is a very large, upscale place with a white-sand private beach for swimming and snorkeling and kayaking, three golf courses, a polo field, a gorgeous hotel, clubhouse, shops, and all the amenities. It was very nice and very relaxing to just hang there with my friends. . . . One day we took a little skiff with a guide, going up the Chavón River and fishing as we went."

—PeaceOut

By Eileen Robinson Smith

Las Américas Highway—built by the dictator Trujillo so that his son could race his sports cars—runs east along the coast from Santo Domingo to La Romana, nearly a two-hour drive. Changing names along the way, Las Américas eventually becomes Highway 3 in La Romana. Midway are Santo Domingo's nearest long-established beach resorts, Boca Chica and Juan Dolio.

Juan Dolio has undergone an astounding renaissance, with major beach rejuvenation and new high-end condo developments; it just might become the Caribbean's answer to Miami's South Beach. Boca Chica, on the other hand, has been left to the low-budget travelers looking for cheap, all-inclusive resorts and to sex tourists. Baseball fans may want to make a pilgrimage to Sammy Sosa's hometown, San Pedro de Macorís. Vestiges remain from its heyday in the early 20th century, when it was a thriving port and center of culture.

Sugar was king in the area surrounding the typical Dominican city of La Romana before it was made famous by the mega-golf resort Casa de Campo. To its credit, Casa continues to reinvent itself. In the new millennium, the Casa de Campo Marina was born, and although skeptics thought it would be overkill—that there was not the demand in this area of the Caribbean from either sailboats or motor yachts to warrant such an extravagant facility—it has been so successful that an expansion was necessary. The shops here are the Southeast's best.

Due east of La Romana is Bayahibe Bay, where you can find a handful of all-inclusive resorts, including several on Playa Dominicus, a glorious beach in an area originally settled by Italians, who introduced the locals to tourism. The beaches come as long, unbroken stretches and also as half-moons. This region is more and more becoming a less frenetic and more attractive alternative to the high-density tourist zone of the "Far East," that is, Punta Cana and Bávaro.

ORIENTATION AND PLANNING

GETTING ORIENTED

You can plot your course depending on which area of the Southeast Coast you choose to stay in. One possibility is to break up your stay with half of your days spent in the Juan Dolio area, where you can make easy forays into the capital and tour the Colonial Zone, take lunch at one of the great seafood restaurants on Boca Chica's beach, and dive the sites in the area. If you spend half of your time in La Romana or the Bayahibe/Dominicus area, you can take wonderful excursions, particularly to the islands that are in that region.

TOP REASONS TO GO

"The Teeth of the Dog." The kings' course of Casa de Campo is one of the top golf courses in the Caribbean. Other great courses are at Guavaberry Resort and Metro Country Club.

Altos de Chavón. This re-creation of a 16th-century Italian hill town is filled with restaurants and shops with lots of high-end, often unique merchandise.

Casa de Campo Marina. Resembling the famed marina in Portofino,

Casa de Campo's yacht-filled marina is a great dining and shopping destination, too.

Diving at La Caleta. Close to Juan Dolio, this underwater national park is considered one of the country's best dive sites.

A day trip to Isla Saona. Sail or speed out to this island to enjoy a day of sun and sea and snorkeling energized by a barbecue lunch buffet and rum drinks.

3

PLANNING

WHEN TO GO

This region has some of the best weather in the island, if not the Caribbean, so any time is the right time to visit. During the winter months it does not get as chilly as many other regions. During the rainy season there are periodic, hard-driving showers. They end quickly, and then it's glorious sunshine again.

GETTING HERE AND AROUND

AIR TRAVEL

There are two convenient airports for travel to the Southeast Coast. There are more flights (and often better fares) into Las Américas International Airport, which is about 15 mi (24 km) east of Santo Domingo. This is the most convenient airport if you're staying in Boca Chica or Juan Dolio. If you're staying in La Romana or Bayahibe, then the best airport is La Romana/Casa de Campo International Airport. It's possible to fly into Punta Cana, but then you face a 2-hour drive to La Romana, or 3½-hour drive to Juan Dolio. *For information on specific airlines that fly into these airports, see* ⇨ *Air Travel in Travel Smart Dominican Republic.*

If you have booked a package through a travel agent, your airport transfers will almost certainly be included in the price you pay. Look for your company's sign as you exit baggage claim. If you book independently, you'll probably have to reserve a private driver, take a taxi, or rent a car.

AIRPORT TRANSFERS There are no regular airport shuttle buses in the Dominican Republic, so plan on taking a taxi if you're traveling independently (or arrange airport transfers through your hotel or villa rental agent). Private drivers are also a possibility, but will charge more.

Dré Broders is a reliable licensed tour guide and private driver who speaks English, German, Dutch, Spanish, and French. He will pick up passengers from any of the area airports and bring them to any destination on the Southeast Coast. His late-model car is clean and well maintained, and his driving safe. His prices are often better than regular taxis.

Tropical Tours, the primary tour operator on the Southeast Coast, which has an office in Casa de Campo, also does airport transfers to the resort.

Information Dré Broeders (☎ 809/526–3533; 809/399–5766 cell ✉ peralta162@gmail.com). **Tropical Tours** (☎ 809/556–5801 ⊕ http://tropicaltoursromana.com.do).

Airports Las Américas International Airport (SDQ✉ Santo Domingo ☎ 809/549–0450). **Punta Cana International Airport** (PUJ ☎ 809/686–8790). **La Romana/Casa de Campo International Airport** (LRM ☎ 809/556–5565).

BUS TRAVEL

Privately owned air-conditioned buses are the cheapest way to get around the country. The music on them will be very loud and the air-conditioning, if the bus has it, will be cranked up to the max.

Express Bus provides frequent service from Santo Domingo to the town of La Romana (☎ 809/556–4192 or 809/550–4585). Buses depart from Ravelo Street in front of Enriquillo Park every hour on the hour from 5 AM to 9 PM; the schedule is exactly the same from La Romana, where they leave from Camino Avenue. In Santo Domingo, there's no office and no phone, but a ticket taker will collect your $4 just before departure. There's general chaos, a crazy kind of congestion (allow time in a taxi), horns blowing, and diesel fumes, but it all comes together. Also, keep your eye on your wallet and purse. Travel time is about 1¾ hours, and if luck is with you, the bus may show a first-rate American movie. Once in La Romana, you can take a taxi from the bus stop to Casa de Campo ($25) or Dreams la Romana, in Bayahibe ($40), or Iberostar Dominicus ($45).

CAR TRAVEL

While we generally do not recommend driving in the Dominican Republic, the Southeast Coast, though congested and unnerving around rush hour, is not too bad. But don't drive at night. In the Bayahibe/Dominicus area, the Impagnatiello Rent Car and Yaset Rent a Car are reputable and may be cheaper than the major rental agencies. Budget, with an office at Dreams La Romana, is one of the more reasonable major agencies; you can expect to pay between $45 and $80 a day for a small car; SUVs can be double.

Avis, which has offices in Juan Dolio and La Romana, is a good choice, and it has 24-hour roadside assistance. You can choose a Volkswagen Fox for as low as $32, but a large SUV is $130. All companies deliver cars to the hotels.

Contacts Avis (☎ 809/688–1354 for reservations; 809/526–2344 in Juan Dolio; 809/550–0600 in La Romana). **Budget** (☎ 809/566–6666 in Juan Dolio). **Impagnatiello Rent Car** (☎ 809/906–8387). **Yaset Rent a Car** (☎ 809/258–9340).

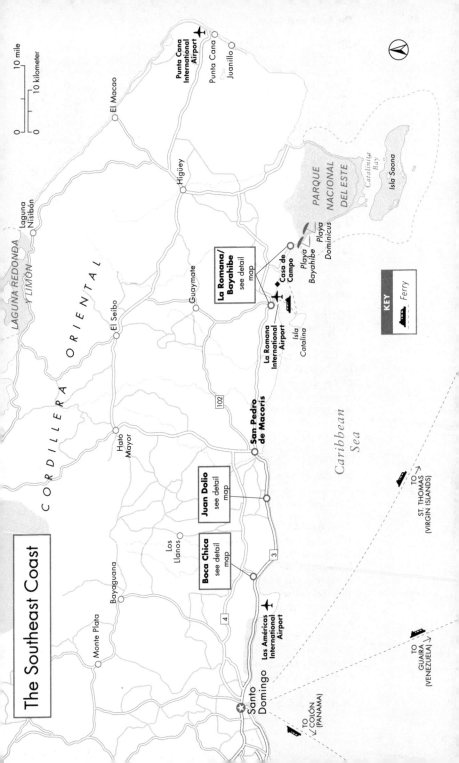

GUAGUA, MOTOCONCHO, AND TAXI TRAVEL

Local buses are called *guaguas*, and although they're not pretty or classy, they'll get you where you're going—not necessarily quickly, but certainly cheaply. You'll marvel at what people bring on the bus; we've seen a musician's kettledrum, a stack of Haitian paintings, and a 25-pound sack of rice. From Playa Juan Dolio near Plaza Oasis, you'll pay about RD$30 to go to San Pedro de Macorís, RD$65–RD$80 to La Romana, and RD$80 for Santo Domingo (be sure to take the express). You'll pay extra for luggage. Though they're crowded and frenetic, using a guagua is doable, and since the typical taxi fare is $60 for less than an hour trip, the guagua will be much easier on your wallet.

Motoconchos (motorcycle taxis) are usually found at the guagua stops. Ride at your own risk.

If you're staying at a hotel, you can arrange a taxi there. If you're an independent traveler, there are a couple of good companies you can call. And if you find a driver you like, get his cell number so you can call him directly.

Taxi Companies Juan Dolio Taxi (✉ *Playa Juan Dolio* ☎ *809/526-2227*). **Santa Rosa Taxi** (✉ *La Romana* ☎ *809/556-5313*).

TOURS

All-inclusive resorts have their own tour desks, and if you're staying in a resort, you can reliably use the company that runs the tour desk. It makes sense to use your hotel's tour operator unless you hear negative comments from other guests or the company doesn't offer the tour you prefer. The primary tour operator on the Southeast Coast is Tropical Tours (with headquarters at Casa de Campo in La Romana), whose prices are even less than some non-pros and some cruise-ship excursions. Their vans are new or nearly new and well maintained. Also, most of their staff speaks English as well as other languages. They can take you on a tour of Santo Domingo, to caves, on outback safaris, zip lining, or even out to a ballgame. The company also operates boat tours to the islands and provides transfers to the three area airports.

Information Tropical Tours (✉ *Casa de Campo, La Romana* ☎ *809/556-5801* ⊕ *tropicaltoursromana.com.do*).

RESTAURANTS

Dining options in the Southeast are as varied as the quality of the accommodations. You can eat like the locals in little side-of-the-road Dominican cafés, where you will always find *moro* (the traditional mixture of rice and beans). There are a good number of international and seafood restaurants on the waterfront in the town of (old) Juan Dolio and nearby Guyacanes.

Some of the region's most sophisticated dining is found at the Casa de Campo resort and in its Altos de Chavón and the Casa de Campo Marina. The village of Bayahibe has a handful of seafood restaurants, some with French and or Italian influences. Of course, much of the food consumption goes on at the all-inclusive resorts. Quality varies among the resorts and even within each individual hotel, from their à la carte restaurants to their buffeterias, where the abundance is legendary.

HOTELS

Juan Dolio is filled with new midrise condominiums for rent, smack on the newly rejuvenated beachfront; a couple of all-inclusives still operate in Juan Dolio, and you can also find a few moderately priced apartments in town. The few inexpensive small hotels quickly fill up with backpackers, European retirees, and sex tourists. With one exception, Boca Chica has lower-end all-inclusives and beach hotels that draw budget and sex tourists. Casa de Campo dominates in La Romana and has just had a glorious makeover. There are nearly a half-dozen all-inclusive resorts in the Bayahibe/Dominicus area, as well as a few smaller basic hotels.

WHAT IT COSTS IN U.S. DOLLARS					
	¢	$	$$	$$$	$$$$
RESTAURANTS	under $8	$8–$12	$12–$20	$20–$30	over $30
HOTELS*	under $80	$80–$150	$150–$250	$250–$350	over $350
HOTELS**	under $125	$125–$250	$250–$350	$350–$450	over $450

*EP, BP, CP **AI, FAP, MAP

Restaurant prices are per person for a main course at dinner and do not include the 16% tax (ITBIS) and 10% service charge (ley). Hotel prices are per night for a double room in high season, excluding 16% tax and 10% service charge.

BOCA CHICA

34 km (21 mi) east of Santo Domingo, 13 km (8 mi) east of Las Américas International Airport.

The Boca Chica resort area is immediately east of Las Américas International Airport. A seasoned destination, Boca Chica is popular mainly with Dominicans and Europeans. Since it's the best beach area near Santo Domingo, it had long been popular with *capitaleños* who considered this a chic place to sun and frolic on the light sand beach, their children splashing safely in the calmest of water. In the 1960s, when all beaches were declared public domain, the tide changed, and the scene went quickly downhill. The crowded, dusty town had become too boisterous and raunchy, the nighttime scene dodgy and dangerous, sex tourism being the primary reason. The good news is that now after 7 PM the city shuts down the main drag, Avenida Duarte, to vehicular traffic. So while there is still some daylight, it can be fun to have a cold beer at one of the makeshift bars, and rows of food stands sell cheap Dominican dishes, the best of which are fried fish (usually bones in), served Boca Chica–style with a criolla onion sauce, and *tostones* (fried green plantains). Just be aware that hygiene is always a question mark at these stands.

WHERE TO EAT

Boca Chica is probably best enjoyed as a day trip from Santo Domingo, a chance to eat lunch and swim in the sea. The trio of seafront restaurants that are the best of Boca Chica seem to be in a universal

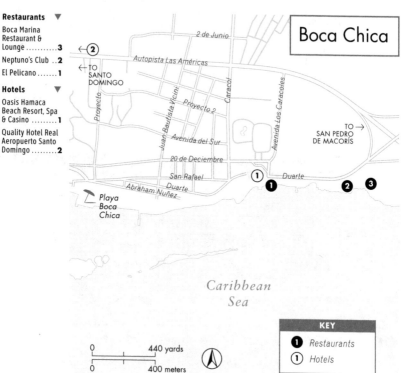

competition. Each vies for a similar clientele of well-heeled *Santo Domingoans* and repeat tourists, all of whom can be fickle in their tastes. If someone does it better—or splashier—they're on to the next place that is even more happening.

■**TIP**→ An alternative to the restaurants recommended here is to buy a day pass at the Oasis Hamaca Beach Resort. For $55 on weekends, $50 during the week, you get food, drinks, and access to the resort facilities and beach for the entire day. You can choose from a bountiful buffet, a seafront restaurant, and a beachside pizzeria. (Although El Pelicano restaurant belongs to the hotel, it's not a part of the resort's all-inclusive package. If you do take lunch there, you can use the beach, too, and the showers in the restrooms.)

$$$ ✕ **Neptuno's Club.** Once a simple seafood spot, beautifully situated at the
SEAFOOD   end of the pier, Neptuno's is now trendy and redecorated. Not only is there draped white fabric but contemporary Euro sofas, a shell motif with shell mobiles. White is the operative color, with rattan-weave furnishings. Glass floor insets give peeks at the green wave action below, while both the outdoor and indoor seating have water views. A ladder goes down to the sea for daytime dips, but there are no chaises like you'll find nearby at Boca Marina restaurant. Most of the food is, of course, from the sea, and the prices are the highest of Boca Chica's trio of good restaurants. The menu includes sushi, a range of pastas,

grilled lobster, and even a few grilled meat offerings, as well as sides that include risottos and grilled vegetables. ⊠ *Calle Duarte 12, Boca Chica* ☎ *809/523–4703* ⊟ *AE, D, DC, MC, V.*

$–$$$
SEAFOOD

✕ **El Pelicano.** A fave over the years, this restaurant has evolved with the times. Now it has an expanded deck and a dozen or more chaise longues; family-sized, cushioned bamboo swings; and even Balinese sun beds both right in the clear water and on the beach. Here hip lounge music plays, but not so loud that it interferes with your fun. Begin with a mango daiquiri and establish your table under a market umbrella. While you wait for your order to arrive, you can sun in a white hammock bed or jump in the shallow water. The best part is that this is the only one of the Boca Chica trio with a beach. (Check the tides, as low tide is only knee-deep and there's a lot of sea grass.) Your food arrives on white geometric plates with linen napkins. Although the cuisine is fairly simple during the day, in order to serve the many clients, the chef is allowed to be his creative self on the night menu. You might want to consider the lobster bisque as a starter. Any fresh fish on the *plancha* (grill) works—most certainly the garlicky lobster. The Boca Chica–style whole red snapper with creole-style onion sauce is excellent here. Fifteen minutes from Las Américas Airport, this is an ideal place to endure a long layover. Enjoy your lunch, swim, sleep in the sun, and then shower in the clean locker rooms. Take a luscious hazelnut piña colada to go and head out. If you come for the pink-layered sunset and dine under moonlight, think conch and scallop risotto or lobster Pelicano in a sauce of yucca and blue cheese. ⊠ *End of Calle Duarte, in front of Hotel Oasis Hamaca Beach Resort, Spa & Casino, Boca Chica* ☎ *809/523–4611 Ext. 830 or 747* ⊟ *AE, MC, V.*

$$
SEAFOOD
Fodor'sChoice
★

✕ **Boca Marina Restaurant & Lounge.** No, this is not a marina, but rather a remarkable seafood restaurant that continues to be the "in" spot for the young, fun, and moneyed locals and hip tourists. With a *nuevo* nautical theme, the whole restaurant is decorated with shells, *palapas* (grass huts), and flowing white sails. Growing popularity has warranted an expansion, which means there are more chaise longues, Balinese sun beds, and space in the dining room. If you want a primo table on the pier, try reserving one. At the end of the pier, an Indonesian threshold, called a joglo, frames the green sea, in a dramatic way. Do bring your beach towel, because you can jump in the water (or descend by a ladder), but there is no beach here. (One consolation: free Wi-Fi.) The brothers Brea, Ricardo, and Eduardo are the effusive hosts and owners. They've invested in some top-of-the-line equipment, including a water purification system and icemakers that make crystalline cubes. Product excellence and hygiene are paramount. Servers are semi-pros, and some are even semibilingual. Start with a baguette drizzled with olive oil and topped by quality Parmesan. The menu is vast, with lots of different preparations of delectable *mariscos* (shellfish), including octopus and lobster, or you can have a perfectly grilled sea bass or red snapper fillet and a side of grilled vegetables. Most of the seafood is 100% fresh and local, with some notable exceptions like the excellent black tiger shrimp; meat is imported from the States. And there's an admirable wine cave. The new chef, Jose Marques, is from Portugal. He's kept on the menu items that have been customer pleasers for 15 years, while also adding his own creations, such as an updated version of *baccalo* (salt cod) and desserts like a panna cotta with prunes marinated in wine and balsamic vinegar, and a drizzle of raspberry coulis. Surprise—breakfast is served here: it's the only high-end restaurant in the area that does. ⊠ *Calle Duarte 12A* ☎ *809/523–6702* ▤ *AE, D, MC, V.*

■TIP→ Women, when you come for lunch, it's a good plan to wear your bathing suit and, say, a pareo. There are spiffy new showers here, in a stylish restroom that's designed around a Japanese-style garden. Men find nearly the same degree of luxury, and there's a modern "waterfall" replacing the normal white fixtures

WHERE TO STAY

Most of the properties in Boca Chica—virtually all one-star all-inclusive resorts—are not recommendable. The Oasis Hamaca is owned by Spain's Globial Group, which has got the property back on track. The region has few, if any, hidden gems. Because the *putas* and their johns frequent the cheapest hotels and resorts, these are not where you want to be. The Quality Hotel is not strictly in Boca Chica (it's next to the airport free-trade zone), and its lack of a beachfront makes it best for business travelers.

$
ALL-INCLUSIVE
☺
Oasis Hamaca Beach Resort, Spa & Casino. A dashing lobby bar with rustic wood slats; Mr. Roger's Bar overlooking the water, a beachside pizzeria, a deluxe, atmospheric spa, an elegant casino, beach pergolas with white fabric, and an Italian restaurant. It's also the only resort in this chain with an Executive Level, and its lounge, terrace, high-end liquors and hors d'oeuvres, and free Internet and terminals just might justify the $70-a-room supplement. The oversized beach rooms are done in a chic, contemporary style, but some garden rooms remain unrenovated—only one building has been updated, and those are the ones you want. The crowd here is primarily European, especially Spanish (with a high volume of rowdy students), but Oasis wants and is courting the American market. If you're staying in the area a day or night pass is just $55 on weekends, $50 during the week. **Pros:** roving trio of musicians serenades nightly in each restaurant; 24-hour service; some international liquors included. **Cons:** low prices can draw a low-class clientele; high volume precludes real luxury or great service; beachside rooms with sea view are $30 to $40 extra. ⊠ *Calle Duarte, Box 2973, Boca Chica* ☎ *809/523–6767 or 809/523–4611* ⊕ *www.oasishotels. com* ⟳ *588 rooms, 1 suite* ⚴ *In-room: a/c, refrigerator. In-hotel: 6 restaurants, bars, tennis courts, pools, gym, spa, beachfront, diving, water sports, children's programs (ages 4–12), laundry service, Internet terminal, parking (free)* ▤ *AE, MC, V* ⭘ *AI.*

$
HOTEL
Quality Hotel Real Aeropuerto Santo Domingo. This modern American chain is the closest hotel to Las Américas Airport and its adjacent Las Américas Free Zone industrial park, drawing both leisure and business travelers. The hotel is a welcoming sight to both expats and businesspeople, sparkly clean and organized, with front desk staff in dark suit jackets over white shirts and ties. The only clue that you're in the

Caribbean is the small outdoor pool and a thatch-roof gazebo. The modest lobby and public spaces are tastefully furnished with large mirrors and plantings. Guest rooms are not as appealing, but are colorful, and have much-appreciated irons and coffeemakers. The restaurant is not bad at all. Ask on arrival if a junior suite is available; you can sometimes get these for just $20 more per night. **Pros:** freestanding spa with reasonable prices; free Internet and local calls and free American breakfast buffet. **Cons:** not a luxury property; though nice has a cookie-cutter feel. ⊠ *Autopista Las Américas, Km 22.5, approximately 35 min east of Santo Domingo by car* ☎ *809/549–2525* ⊕ *www.gruporeal.com* ⇨ *109 rooms, 15 suites* ⌂ *In-room: a/c, refrigerator, Internet, Wi-Fi (some). In-hotel: restaurant, room service, bar, pool, gym, spa, laundry facilities, laundry service, Internet terminal, Wi-Fi hotspot, parking (free)* ⊟ *AE, MC, V* ⚹ *BP.*

NIGHTLIFE

In Boca Chica you should stick to the nightlife in your hotel, because this resort area is the nocturnal haunt of prostitutes, both male and female. This is pretty much ground zero for sex tourism in the Dominican Republic, a form of tourism we strongly discourage, not only because of its illegality but also because of the dangers involved. Although the Politur (tourism police) are quite visible, crime—including even the murders of European expats and tourists—has occurred in the area. If you're here at night, the newly renovated casino at the Hamaca is the closest thing to a safe haven.

BEACHES

Playa Boca Chica. You can walk far out into warm, calm, clear waters protected by coral reefs. The strip with the rest of the midrise resorts is busy, particularly on weekends, drawing mainly Dominican families and some Europeans. But midweek is better, when the beaches are less crowded. One bad thing: if you choose to go to the public beach, you will be pestered and hounded by a parade of roving sellers of cheap jewelry and sunglasses, hair braiders, seafood cookers, ice-cream men, and masseuses (who are usually peddling more than a simple beach massage). Young male prostitutes also roam the beach, and often hook up with older European and Cuban men. The best section of the public beach is in front of Don Emilio's (the blue hotel), which has a restaurant, bar, decent bathrooms, and parking. ⊠ *Autopista Las Américas, 21 mi (34 km) east of Santo Domingo, Boca Chica.*

SPORTS AND THE OUTDOORS

DIVING

Local dive aficionados will tell you that the South Coast, including Boca Chica, Juan Dolio, Isla Catalina, and, most notably, the underwater national park La Caleta, offers the best diving in the country. La Caleta is a half-day trip from Boca Chica, and experienced divers can explore two sunken vessels—the *Limón*, a 115-foot tugboat, or the famous

Hickory, a 130-foot freighter. Both lie in 60 feet of water. Isla Catalina requires a full day, but divers can discover black coral, huge sponges, and sea fans. *(For information on dive shops in the region, see ⇨ Diving under Sports and the Outdoors in Juan Dolio.)*

JUAN DOLIO

18 km (11 mi) east of Boca Chica, 52 km (32 mi) east of Santo Domingo, 78 km (48 mi) west of La Romana.

Like Boca Chica, Juan Dolio is a story of boom and bust. The resort area began life as a pristine beach and developed into *the* place for Santo Domingoans to go on the Southeast Coast for sun and sea. When the Europeans discovered it, the all-inclusive resorts started springing up. In the early 1990s it was a pioneer in the all-inclusive concept, which caught on immediately, and no sooner was the blaze ignited than North Americans started to jump on it as well. But as soon as Punta Cana became the newer hot spot, the *turistas* started to abandon Juan Dolio for its newer, more luxurious AIs and long expanses of palm-studded beach—with white sand, at that.

The resorts dropped their prices to try to stem the flood of tourists heading farther east, but in doing so they had to cut food costs and service staff, the best of whom were already being recruited by Punta Cana. As food went downhill and rooms became shabbier, Juan Dolio entered a years-long cycle of slow decline.

More recently, things are looking much better. Just about every hotel is either new or heavily renovated, and the beach has been revitalized under a new program spearheaded by President Lionel Fernández and the State Secretariat of Tourism. Juan Dolio is now closer to Miami's South Beach than any other place in the Dominican Republic, and is now striving to attract more chic tourists to its shores to supplement the bargain-basement, mass-market tourism of the past decade.

GETTING HERE AND AROUND

Juan Dolio is about 40 minutes from Santo Domingo. It's best to either drive here or be driven, especially when going places after dark.

WHERE TO EAT

$$ ✕ **Café del Sol.** Relax on a partner chaise, swing on a bamboo swing,
SEAFOOD   snooze on a beach bed, or drink something bubbly and cuddle on a hedonistic Balinese sun bed in the clear green sea. And you can also dine on boat-fresh fish and local shellfish (including lobster) from the grill, a garlic sauce, some tostones—life is good. Although not wildly innovative, the menu is better than the usual places (for instance, the Sol seviche has a sauce of passion fruit, orange juice, mango bites, and cilantro). And you can order lobster burritos and red snapper Veracruzana, too. You can also just do a four-cheese pizza with some icy agua verde (slang for Presidente beer, which has a green bottle.) Although this beach cafe was built for the guests of Embassy Suites and the members of Metro Country Club, it is open to the general public on weekdays. Its

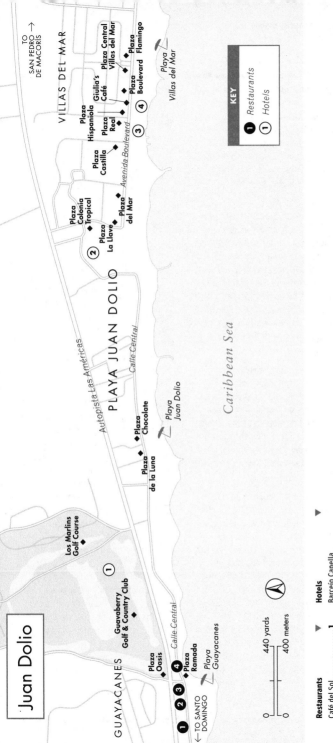

Juan Dolio

GUAYACANES

Los Marlins
Golf Course

Guavaberry
Golf & Country Club

Plaza
Oasis

Plaza
Ramada

Playa
Guayacanes

← TO SANTO
DOMINGO

Calle Central

Autopista Las Américas

PLAYA JUAN DOLIO

Plaza
de la Luna

Plaza
Chocolate

Calle Central

Playa
Juan Dolio

Plaza
Colonia
Tropical

Plaza
La Llave

Plaza
del Mar

Plaza
Castilla

Avenida Boulevard

Plaza
Hispaniola

Plaza
Real

Giulia's
Café

Plaza
Boulevard

Plaza Central
Villas del Mar

Plaza
Flamingo

VILLAS DEL MAR

TO
SAN PEDRO
DE MACORÍS →

Playa
Villas del Mar

Caribbean Sea

440 yards

400 meters

0

0

KEY

● Restaurants

① Hotels

Restaurants ▶

Café del Sol **1**
DeliSwiss **3**
Playa de la Pescador **2**
Tommy's of Austria
at Cacique **4**

Hotels ▶

Barceío Capella
Beach Resort **2**
Costa del Sol **3**
Embassy Suites Los Marlins
Hotel & Golf Resort **1**
Marbella **4**

The Rebirth of Juan Dolio

Children and adults alike were in awe as giant machines spit out tons of sand onto Juan Dolio beach in 2007. The rebirth of the beach, which goes for 2.5 mi, has led to the rebirth of the entire resort area, which has been targeted by the tourism authority as a site for first-class resorts and amenities.

Steven Ankrom, director of sales for Metro Group, a pioneer in upscale development in Juan Dolio, explained: "The beach is breathtaking now, particularly in front of the Costa del Sol condominiums. The government cooperated by marking property lines so that part of the beach is private to each project, meaning [that] guests can sunbathe free of vendors and hair-braiders."

For families, the increase in the number of luxury condominiums has been a big hit. The proximity to Santo Domingo (about 45 minutes away) and Las Américas International Airport (20 minutes away) equals convenience. Retirees are drawn by the good prices and low oceanfront insurance rates.

The Metro Group, headed up by visionary Dr. Luis Jose Asilis, was the first investment team willing to take a chance with major projects here, including the 18-hole Los Marlins Golf Course and adjacent Metro Country Club, which are now surrounded by luxury homes and apartments. Guavaberry Country Club has followed with its own course and country club, positioning the area as a golf destination, and not just for capitaleños. The Embassy Suites, which is adjacent to Metro Country Club, was built in 2003 in part to offer good lodging for visiting golfers, as well as prospective real-estate buyers.

The Costa del Sol condominiums, completed in 2006, now have an extension, Costa del Sol II, next door. Nearby, Club Hemingway's private restaurant is at the end of a pier, offering both quality cuisine and great views.

Other resort/residential structures being built are the final two towers of Marbella; the first of three opened in early 2010. Another burgeoning area is Guayacanes, just west of Juan Dolio, where the trendy beach restaurant Café del Sol opened for Embassy Suites' guests and members of the Metro Country Club. (The public can also go there on weekdays.) Las Olas, Metro Group's newest dream project, with 16 floors and 227 apartments, is being built nearly next door.

Six miles farther east, Costablanca by Metro (⊕ www.costablanca.com. do) is being built. This latest and most ambitious undertaking is a residential/resort community with an 18-hole Greg Norman signature golf course as its major draw. The first nine holes are expected to be ready for play by late 2010, and the back nine by early 2011. The course will have 10 exceptional holes on the water. There is a beach, and a luxury marina is also planned. Metro's 600 acres will also house the Chris Evert Tennis Center. She will be on-site several times a year to play exhibitions. A beach club and golf club will round out the facilities. The first residences, the Founders Club villas, are underway, with other villas, townhouses, and sleek, high-rise condominiums to follow.

weekday hours are 10–6, with lunch starting around 11. On weekends, when it's open until midnight, regular tourists are only admitted with a reservation (ask for Carlos or the manager, Jorge Ventura), and your name will be given to the security guard. Sundays are busy, and they do sometimes fill up. ⊠ *Calle Principal, Playa Guyacanes* ☎ *809/526–1559* ⚑ *Reservations essential on weekends.* ▤ *MC, V.*

$$
CONTINENTAL

✕ **DeliSwiss.** This small beachfront restaurant is owned by a veteran Swiss chef, Walter Kleinerp, who is one of those interesting Caribbean characters you usually only read about. Many diners come for the staggered terraces and the sounds, sight, and smells of the Caribbean just beyond. The interior of the restaurant is dated and unimpressive—except for the framed wine awards. The wine list itself is 22 pages, but oddly there's no menu for the food. Plan on buying a good bottle. The cuisine is simple, with maybe four choices; you can share a plate of European cheeses and meats from the deli counter, including home-made dark bread and a garlic-butter spread. Other options include the daily catch in a perfect garlic sauce, an expensive lobster, or a meat such as pork tenderloin in a creamy peppercorn sauce. If you make it to dessert—and you should—the German pastries are a faraway dream: strawberry pie; stollen; pear cheesecake. Unfortunately, Walter turns in early and the servers are left in charge at dinner. Usually, they are neither gracious nor efficient. ⊠ *Calle Central 38, Guayacanes, Juan Dolio* ☎ *809/526–1226* ▤ *AE, MC, V* ☯ *Closed Mon. and Tues.*

$$
SEAFOOD

✕ **Playa de la Pescador.** This restaurant's Eastern European owner has gained a loyal following among the European expats for his cuisine, which is paired with German and Belgian beers, grappa, cognacs, and good half-bottles of wine. This rustic, two-story palapa offers romantic seating topside, on the sand, or in the open-air dining room. Pumpernickel bread arrives with the well-priced, bilingual menu. Seafood comes off one of the moored boats, so you can order the shellfish seviche with confidence. The mixed grilled shellfish is enough for two and can include a lobster from the tank. Sunday is the big barbecue day, which is best avoided because of the vast number of locals that crowd both the restaurant and the adjacent public beach. Lunch midweek is calm, and you can find a lounge chair and go for a swim. At dinner waiters give the best service, but at breakfast the eggs can come sunny-side up, just like the new day! You might walk in and hear an Italian opera playing. ⊠ *Playa Guayacanes, Guyacanes* ☎ *809/526–2613; 809/862–8547 cell* ▤ *MC, V.*

$–$$
AUSTRIAN

✕ **Tommy's of Austria at Cacique.** This is one surprising find. Who would have guessed that behind an Austrian-owned bar of rather ill repute would be a beachfront restaurant run by another countryman, Tommy Kreuzer, who serves up first-rate specialties. Don't be intimidated by the blackboard specials in German; the menu itself is in five languages. One of the standouts is a humongous portion of baby pork roast with sauerkraut and caraway seeds and bread dumplings floating au jus. Any meat-and-potatoes lover will relish the pounded fillet of beef with peppers, dark brown gravy, and perfect fried potatoes. Other carnivores' dreams include the boiled beef and horseradish sauce and calves' liver and onions. Tommy fixes pasta and the requisite seafood, but aren't

Know Your Juan Dolios

Do you know how to tell one Juan Dolio from the other? Since its resurgence, Juan Dolio is actually made up of two almost completely different places now. Approaching from Santo Domingo, you'll first come across Guyacanes, which is an adjacent small fishing village that has some development. It's at the westernmost end of Juan Dolio's main drag, called Calle Principal, about 3 km (2 mi) before the old town proper. If you're going to Guyacanes, it's faster to travel by the highway.

The original town of Juan Dolio is about 3 km (2 mi) east of here and is sign-posted PLAYA JUAN DOLIO/ GUYACANES. Some call this area Old Juan Dolio, Juan Dolio West, Oasis (pronounced O ah sea), or Oasis Plaza. The beach rejuvenation includes the lovely horseshoe-shape stretch of sand in front of the main waterfront restaurants on the older part of the resort area.

The area characterized by the most condo development is still farther east and is called Villas del Mar, but you may also hear people call it New Juan Dolio. If you're traveling on the highway look for the sign that says CLUB HEMINGWAY or the billboard for BARCELÓ CAPELLA, and you'll know you've found it.

you here for the Wiener schnitzel? ⊠ *Calle Principal, Playa Juan Dolio, Juan Dolio* ☎ 809/848–5306 ▤ *No credit cards* ☉ *Closed Mon. and Tues. No lunch.*

WHERE TO STAY

VILLAS AND CONDOS

When renting an apartment in the Juan Dolio area, be sure to ask about proximity to the beach (it's safer the closer you are), whether an apartment building has an elevator (not all of them do), and whether there are wrought-iron gates on doors and or windows (you want them for security reasons).

Ana-Christina Peralta (⊠ *Residencial Marie Michell 104, Juan Dolio* ☎ *809/526–3533; 809/399–5766 cell* ⊕ *www.guesthouseholland.com* ✎ *peralta162@gmail.com*) along with her husband, manages a roster of 18 apartments and houses that can be rented by the day, week, or month. Prices range from a low of $500 per month for a simple studio to $1,200 per month for an upscale house with private pool and sea views. Prices include water and electricity (normally a hefty expense here). Many clients book online, where they can opt for transfers from the airport, as well as excursions and private tours. Ana-Christina does not ask for a security deposit to hold an apartment or even an advance payment, but credit cards are not accepted.

NEED A BREAK? If you're staying in an apartment in Playa Juan Dolio and don't want to do your own cooking, you can take a break at little **Hotel Fior Loto** (⊠ *Carretera Vieja, Playa Juan Dolio, 2 blocks past taxi stand on opposite side of street, Juan Dolio* ☎ *809/526–1146*) with a tasty breakfast for RD$100.

Mara Sandri, the Italian owner of the *hotelito,* is in love with India, and the decor reflects her love. Later in the day, pull up a chair and have a beer with the backpackers and Italian retirees who make up the interesting mix of guests.

$–$$
ALL-INCLUSIVE

Barceló Capella Beach Resort. This resort has always been the best of the all-inclusives in Juan Dolio, and that much has not changed. After some years in decline, it got better, but now the word on the street is that it is for sale, and maybe that is why it's not being well maintained and no new money is being put into it. That said, the Capella's grounds are nearly palatial, and the mix of Moorish and Spanish colonial architecture works beautifully. Guest rooms are all spacious, particularly in the quietest 1000 building. On the beach, which has been rejuvenated and extended, is the famous disco, a three-story palapa structure that doubles as an à la carte seafood restaurant at lunch and dinner. The principal buffet faces the sea. Food in all the restaurants, including the buffet, can be hit or miss. ■ TIP→ **Non-guests can buy a day or night pass for a mere $45, which gets you either lunch or dinner and all your drinks; by day it's the beach and pools, by night, the show and the disco from 7 to 2 in the morning.** Pros: dive shop under professional German ownership; nightly shows in amphitheater better than most; Aslan Spa quite nice. **Cons:** runs at high occupancy; crowd can be rowdy; the shabby 2000 building is not where you want to be. ⊠ *Blvd. Juan Dolio, Box 4750, Villas del Mar, Juan Dolio* ☎ *809/526–1080, 809/221–0564, or 800/924–5044* ⊕ *www.barcelohotels.com* ➬ *491 rooms, 6 suites* ⌂ *In-room: a/c, safe, refrigerator. In-hotel: 5 restaurants, room service, bars, tennis court, pools, spa, beachfront, diving, water sports, children's programs (ages 4–12), laundry service, Internet terminal, parking (free)* ⊟ *AE, D, MC, V* �101 *AI.*

$$$
VACATION
CONDO

Costa Del Sol I and II. This condo complex is symbolic of the new Juan Dolio Beach. Architecturally speaking, it has a simplicity that flows, an undulation of off-white stucco that mimics the 2.5 mi of new beachfront. When standing on a balcony, you feel as if you could reach the coco palms when they sway. The white-on-white lobby calms; the owners' lounge (which renters sometimes use) is even more attractive, with comfy salon furnishings, Wi-Fi, and a wide-screen TV. Costa I debuted in 2006 as a six-story tower with 142 condos; its mirror-image Costa II followed in 2008, with 47 apartments. Go for the newer building. Condos are long and narrow with a balcony as their focal point. Kitchens are small but adequate and well equipped. The classy, sleek furnishings around the pool below complete the idyllic Caribbean picture. The Texas Rangers baseball team rented a couple of penthouses a few years back and loved them. **Pros:** incredible sea views; good value for the money (particularly for families); taxes are included in prices quoted. **Cons:** rentals don't have standardized decor, so you get what you get; restaurant on-site is very limited; some staff need more training. ⊠ *Blvd. Juan Dolio, Villas del Mar, Juan Dolio* ☎ *809/526–2236 or 809/526–2131* ⊕ *www.rentalmetrocountry.com* ➬ *284 2-bedroom condos, 38 3-bedroom condos* ⌂ *In-room: a/c, no phone (some), safe (some), kitchen, refrigerator, DVD (some). In-hotel: restaurant, bar,* *pool, beachfront, Wi-Fi hotspot, laundry facilities, parking (free)* ▭ *AE, MC, V* 🍽 *EP.*

$ HOTEL **Embassy Suites Los Marlins Hotel & Golf Resort.** Guests are impressed by the atrium lobby and subtropical plantings splashed by the waterfall in this all-suites hotel—it's like getting two rooms for the price of one (families especially love having two TVs)—and businesspeople can make an office in the living room, where there's a desk. Although there is a large contingent of businesspeople here—you'll see laptops open to Wi-Fi in all the public spaces—that doesn't mean that there isn't a fun quotient. Guests make conversation at the complimentary hot breakfast in the morning (there's an omelet station) and make new friends at the nightly manager's cocktail hour, which is also included. The Embassy offers a taste of home for its diverse mix of guests, which includes baseball's major-league players, scouts, and managers; golf buddies, business folks, tourists, even missionaries. The freestanding spa can sooth golfing muscles; its beauty salon can give ladies a Dominican glamour makeover. There's a free shuttle to the beach and the trendy new Café del Sol restaurant. **Pros:** balconies overlook the pool and palapa bar; super management and staff; an AI plan available. **Cons:** no free in-room Wi-Fi; living rooms very utilitarian, with little style; free snacks at happy hour not good for the waistline. ✉ *Metro Country Club, Autovia del Este, Km 55, Juan Dolio* ☎ *809/688–9999 or 800/362–2779* 🌐 *www.losmarlins.embassysuites.com* *125 suites* *In-room: a/c, safe, refrigerator. In-hotel: 3 restaurants, room service, bars, golf course, tennis courts, pool, gym, laundry service, Internet terminal, Wi-Fi hotspot, parking (free)* ▭ *AE, MC, V* 🍽 *BP.*

$$$$ VACATION CONDO **Marbella.** These stunning new condominium towers have just brought this beach's offerings to the next luxury level, and roughly 40% of these two and three-bedroom beachfront apartments will be available for rent. What differentiates rooms at the Marbella from the others on the "new" Juan Dolio Beach are Italian designer kitchens; high-end fixtures, lighting, and bathrooms; doors paneled in precious woods; and large sea-view terraces with space for a large dining-room table. The first phase of this resort/residential complex was completed in early 2010. Guests are also drawn by the amenities, which include a gorgeous seafront infinity pool, Jacuzzis, a children's playground, an on-site concierge, and 24-hour reception; and a kid-friendly beachfront restaurant with international, seafood, and Dominican specialties. When completed, Marbella will have five towers and a total of 465 apartments. **Pros:** panoramic sea views; the ideal white-sand beach. **Cons:** children's playground interferes with the water view in some of the units; long and narrow condo layouts, with no water views from the bedrooms. ✉ *Blvd. Juan Dolio, Villas del Mar* ☎ *809/566-8645* 🌐 *www.groupmetro.com* *299 rooms* *In-room: a/c, no phone, kitchen, refrigerator, DVD (some), Wi-Fi. In-hotel: restaurant, bar, pool, gym, beachfront, water sports, bicycles, laundry facilities, laundry service, Wi-Fi hotspot, parking (free), some small pets allowed* ▭ *AE, MC, V.* 🍽 *EP.*

NEED A BREAK?

Giulia's Café (✉ *Plaza Hispaniola, Blvd. Juan Dolio, across from Marbella condos, Villas del Mar, Juan Dolio* ☎ *809/526–1492*) is a sports bar and café where you can grab a grilled sandwich and beer while using the free

Wi-Fi or watching baseball or boxing on satellite TV. You can also have a leisurely breakfast here with "natural" (meaning fresh-squeezed) juices, house-baked croissants, and apple tarts. They have full meals at this cash-only spot, but prices are nearly as high as at the better restaurants (the fact that there's no separate 26% charge for service or tax helps a lot). Giulia, the charismatic owner who is half Welsh, half Italian, makes real french fries and is famous for her lasagna. You'll want to get on down Mondays for the dancing and live music.

NIGHTLIFE

There's not a great deal of nightlife in Juan Dolio. Often people simply continue their night where they had dinner, particularly if it's on the water. Some of these places have DJs on weekends. Those staying at resorts almost always dance the night away on-site. The American Casino is another popular option.

The American Casino (⊠ *Calle Principal, across from Coral Costa Caribe Hotel, Playa Juan Dolio, Juan Dolio* ☎ *809/526–3318*) is a particularly fun place that's innovative in its offerings, from Friday-night blackjack tournaments to inexpensive Wednesday slot tournaments. There are tables for roulette, craps, and Caribbean stud, and free drinks and sandwiches are handed out to players. Saturday night brings live local bands. The casino is open from 8 PM to 4 AM, and has free shuttles from area hotels and restaurants.

⚠ An ATM outside the American Casino comes in handy, but often runs out of cash. Remember that you get pesos, not dollars, and don't forget to retrieve your card as soon as the machine spits it out; otherwise, it may take it back. Across the street is another bank ATM. It's guarded, but take the same precautions.

El Popeye's (⊠ *Calle Principal, Playa Juan Dolio*) is a fun hangout, both indoors and particularly out on the terrace or under the white beach tents in the sand, as on the set for Lawrence of Arabia. Once the Casa Blanca restaurant/bar, Popeye's has far more food now, but you'll find no spinach on the predominately seafood menu. The new Czech owner has done a substantial redecoration, with handsome wicker furnishings and a handsome wine rack filled with handsome bottles, and he employs professional servers. Still expats seem to be concentrating on the well-priced cocktails more than the lambi (conch) in garlic sauce or penne in a sauce made with Middle Eastern spices. Fresh OJ is a must for breakfast, and joining the requisite eggs are also crepes and even hamburgers.

BEACHES

The coral reef off Playa Juan Dolio protects the natural marine habitat. The water here is relatively shallow, with gentle currents to keep things clean and clear. It's safe for kids and easy to snorkel.

Playa Juan Dolio (⊠ *Blvd. Playa Juan Dolio, Playa Juan Dolio, Juan Dolio*) is now glorious, especially in the Villas Del Mar area. Its regeneration, which goes for 2.5 mi, included the relocation of more than 14 million cubic feet of nearly white sand. It has led to the town's rebirth, and the tourism authority's goal is to turn Juan Dolio into a major Caribbean destination—the next South Beach—with condominium projects that demonstrate style and first-class amenities fit for the international tourists. The beach rejuvenation continued to the horseshoe-shape public beach in Playa (Old) Juan Dolio, starting in front of El Popeye's Restaurant and going out in either direction

SPORTS AND THE OUTDOORS

DIVING

Local dive aficionados will tell you that the South Coast, which includes Boca Chica, Juan Dolio, Isla Catalina, and, most notably, the underwater national park La Caleta, has the best diving in the country. La Caleta is a half-day trip from Juan Dolio (about $70 for excursion plus $35 for a dive), and divers can explore two sunken vessels: the *Limón,* a 115-foot tug boat, and the *Hickory,* a 130-foot freighter that once functioned as a treasure-hunting vessel. Both lie in 60 feet of water. Isla Catalina is just another day in Paradise ($75 for transportation plus $35 a dive); divers can discover black coral, huge sponges, and beautiful sea fans. Cave diving in Cueva Taina is another possibility ($70 for the transportation plus $35 per dive). If you prefer snorkeling, you can find the viewing good near the coral reef that rims the regenerated Playa Juan Dolio.

Neptuno Dive (✉ *Barceló Capella Beach Resort, Villas del Mar, Juan Dolio* ☎ *809/526–2005* ⊕ *www.neptunodive.com*), the SSI dive shop at the Barceló hotel, is run by a professional German team. (Formerly a PADI 5-star center, they can still teach their system, but PADI apparently offers no cave courses, so they went with the equivalent European designation SSI.) Dive instructors and dive masters speak German, English, Spanish, French, and Italian. In addition to simple dives, you can also arrange certification or refresher courses. Among other options, Neptuno Dive does a half-day trip to La Caleta as well as an all-day excursion to Isla Catalina, which is great for the whole family, even if you aren't divers. That price includes food, drink, and the possibility of two tank dives. The Neptuno team has also explored Cueva Taina, a cave system near Santo Domingo, and offers dives there. They have discovered more sites and caves, as far afield as Bayahibe—some with stalactites. Additionally, they offer the option and sometime insist that those who want to explore the more elusive caves take their special instructions/classes for cave diving. Open to nonguests, Neptuno can often pick students up at other hotels by boat.

GOLF

The 7,156-yard, par 72, 21-hole course at **Guavaberry Golf & Country Club** (✉ *Autovia del Este, Km 55, Juan Dolio* ☎ *809/333–4653* ⊕ *www. guavaberrygolf.com*), designed by Gary Player, has earned a reputation as one of the top courses in the country. Player designed it with an island hole and a wide putting area, beautifying it with bougainvillea and coral stone. Intimidating at first glance, it's a challenging but fair course with

EX

long fairways. Play costs $100, including a cart. The golf director is a PGA pro. A branch of the Montréal-based Golfologist Academy, which gives audiovisual analysis of your golf swing, opened in 2006.

Los Marlins Championship Golf Course (⊠ *Autovia del Este, Km 55, Juan Dolio* ☎ *809/526–1359*) is an 18-hole, 6,400-yard, par-72 course designed by Charles Ankrom. Guests of the adjacent Embassy Suites pay $45 for 18 holes including cart, $22 for 9 holes; nonguests pay $70 for 18 holes, $40 for 9. Golfers get 10% off at the Metro Country Club. A Fuentes Cigar Club, one of the few such clubs in the country, is on the second floor. Kids and moms can be seen on the 18-hole miniature golf range when the dads are playing the 18-hole course. The tennis courts are lit at night. ■ TIP➡ **If you're playing golf at Los Marlins, plan on taking your lunch at the adjacent Metro Country Club. You can sit in the air-conditioned dining room or outside on the terrace. Some of the menu items, particularly the starters, are especially good, and the mains are reasonably priced.**

HORSEBACK RIDING

Guavaberry Equestrian Center (⊠ *Guavaberry Golf & Country Club, Autovía del Este, Km 55, Juan Dolio* ☎ *809/333–4653*) has a clean stable, good stock, and English and Western saddles. Delightful hour-plus trail rides throughout the extensive grounds of the resort cost $25; free transportation is provided from all Juan Dolio hotels.

SAN PEDRO DE MACORÍS

24 km (15 mi) east of Juan Dolio.

The national sport and the national drink are both well represented in this city, an hour or so east of Santo Domingo. Some of the country's best baseball games are played in **Tetelo Vargas Stadium.** Many Dominican baseball stars have their roots here, including George Bell, Tony Fernández, Jose Rijo, and Sammy Sosa. The **Macorís Rum** distillery is on the eastern edge of the city. From 1913 to the 1920s this was a very important town—a true cultural center—and mansions from that era are being restored by the Office of Cultural Patrimony, as are some remaining vestiges of 16th-century architecture and the town's cathedral, which has a pretense to the Gothic style, even gargoyles. There's a **Malecón,** a nice promenade along the port, and by night the beer and rum kiosks come alive. The Dominicans, Europeans, and North Americans staying in Juan Dolio head to San Pedro for its stores, including its *supermercados,* which are Jumbo, Iberia (it also has a big pharmacy), and Zaglul. *For information on baseball in San Pedro, see* ➪ *Baseball in Sports and the Outdoors in Chapter 1, Santo Domingo.*

EXPLORING SAN PEDRO DE MACORÍS

Some of the caves in the Dominican Republic are well worth exploring, even for nonaficionados. **Cueva Las Marvillas** is an incredible cave with the requisite stalactites and stalagmites, but its true highlight is a series of primitive Taino cave paintings. Concrete walkway steps and ramps make exploration easy, and the ramp can accommodate visitors

casinosdiamante.com/bayahibe), across from the Iberostar, opened after a couple of bumpy years in early 2010. This brightly lit hotspot in Bayahibe has high, arched ceilings. Gamblers can try their luck at one of 23 table games, 60 slots, or at the sports book. There's Bubaraba, a sensual disco; a classy sports bar with a hand-painted mural; and an inexpensive, casual restaurant that looks expensive. (It's open daily from 9 PM to 5 AM.) A nightly, continuous shuttle service (using both a bus and golf carts) runs from all major Dominicus- and Bayahibe-area resorts. The casino is open daily, from 6 PM to 4 AM.

Punta Cana

WORD OF MOUTH

"In Punta Cana, walking on the beach with the only goal of 'let's just walk until we get to that point over there' is a daily routine."

—kep

"My boyfriend and I went to Punta Cana, and let me just say you are in for [an] awesome time. The beach is AMAZING. No words can describe what I was feeling when we got to our hotel."

— tinkernut

By Elise Rosen   As the sun rises on Hispaniola, Punta Cana awakens to the lapping ocean, its clear, unspoiled blue brushing up against the pristine stretches of sugar-white sand, with swaying coco palms in the backdrop. A thriving tourism industry fuels the region, and with such ripe ingredients as sun (the average daily temperature is 82°F; any downpours tend to be short bursts that give way to more sunshine), sand (35 mi of uninterrupted powder), and sea (opportunities for water sports abound)it's no wonder.

For Punta Cana, it was only a matter of time. In 1969, when the terrain was covered in jungle, a group of North American investors bought some land along the eastern coast. They put up a small hotel and an airstrip (which spawned an international airport) and—voila!—tourism in Punta Cana was born. Their visionary project, now the PuntaCana Resort & Club, spreads out across 15,000 verdant acres (23.4 square miles). Club Med opened its doors as the first all-inclusive in the area, and following its lead dozens of others popped up within their own spacious enclaves along the coast. More recently, a fresh crop of boutique hotels has sprung up. Many resorts, including those on beaches as far north as Uvero Alto and as far south as Juanillo (Cap Cana), tag on the moniker "Punta Cana" although they're in their own distinct geographical areas. But the name "Punta Cana" is now a recognized draw for the swarms of visitors who arrive through Punta Cana International Airport. Indeed, the privately owned and operated airport is the second most heavily trafficked in the Caribbean, behind only Cancún, and 51% of all visitors to the Dominican Republic now pass through its gates.

A hot destination for golf, Punta Cana lures players with its abundance of spectacular courses—crafted by renowned designers—and posh clubhouses. The area's growth shows no signs of slowing. Major new development projects include Cap Cana and Rōco Ki, and a handful of other megaresorts peppering the coastline. With more than 60 hotels, the region already accounts for nearly half the total lodging in the Dominican Republic. Tourism officials estimate that Punta Cana and Bávaro will have more than 50,000 rooms by the end of 2010.

Higüey, capital of Altagracia Province (which includes Punta Cana) sits 21 mi (34 km) to the west. The site of three visits by Pope John Paul II, Higüey is notable for its towering, arched concrete cathedral. Its open-air market bustles in the morning when local shoppers flock in to buy produce and meat. The city is a thriving commercial center for the entire province. Higüey is the site of the only post office that services Punta Cana and the east-coast region, and is a transit hub for buses bound for Santo Domingo and elsewhere. It's also home to a large segment of the support staff at the resorts, about an hour's commute away.

TOP REASONS TO GO

All-Inclusive Resorts. If you want everything in one package, Punta Cana is one of the top destinations in the Caribbean for the AI concept. If you don't leave the resort or avail yourself of spa treatments (and many guests do not), aside from your tourist card, a souvenir, and a few extra tips, you'll likely spend very little beyond the upfront costs. Drinks, food, activities, entertainment: it's all included.

Sun, sand, and sea. Sink your toes in the cool sand at water's edge and soak up the sun as you watch the white-capped tide roll in. Punta Cana has some of the best beaches in the Caribbean.

Great golf. It's a destination of choice for serious golfers, who come to play at the area's many renowned golf courses—for example, Punta Espada or the Faldo Legacy Course.

Vibrant music and dance. Take a merengue or bachata lesson and hit the dance floor. The nightlife doesn't get any better than at Imagine, built into a cave, or Mangú, at the Occidental Grand resort.

Natural landscape. Exploring the local life, the sugarcane fields, and the countryside on any of the popular guided safari jeep tours makes a fun day.

Everywhere you turn, you are likely to encounter friendly, smiling people. English is widely spoken by guest relations staff in the hotels. Though it's not essential, knowing a few phrases of Spanish to communicate with support staffers—for example, housekeeping and maintenance—goes a long way.

ORIENTATION AND PLANNING

GETTING ORIENTED

Nestled along a 35-mi contiguous stretch of sand along the East Coast, Punta Cana and its tentacles extend from the south at Juanillo (Cap Cana) to the north at Uvero Alto, encompassing the beaches and villages of Punta Cana, Bávaro, Cabeza de Toro, El Cortecito, Arena Gorda, and Macao in between. Within the alluvial plains that reach from the eastern coast inland toward Santo Domingo, the terrain is characterized by lush, green countryside, mostly flatlands with mangroves and some swampy areas.

Punta Cana. Any of the distinct geographical locations within the entire East Coast region serviced by Punta Cana International Airport are often loosely called Punta Cana. Punta Cana proper is home to the PuntaCana Resort & Club and PuntaCana Village, about a 10-minute drive from the airport.

Bávaro. This long stretch of eastern coastline includes the further subdivisions of Cabeza de Toro, El Cortecito, and Arena Gorda. It's all a hub of development, shopping, commercial activity, and nightlife.

Macao. Just north of Bávaro Beach, but along the same stretch of coastline, this rural village is much less bustling than Bávaro. Beachgoers, golfers, and real-estate developers all find its natural beauty alluring.

Playa Uvero Alto. This remote coastal village is about an hour's drive from the airport. It's the northernmost part of the great Punta Cana region to have attracted some luxury resorts.

Higüey. The capital city of La Altagracia, the province that includes all of Punta Cana and the rest of the East Coast areas covered in this chapter. It's about an hour west of Punta Cana by car or bus.

PLANNING

WHEN TO GO

Punta Cana's climate is generally inviting to beach lovers and outdoors enthusiasts year-round, with temperatures averaging in the 80s during the day and dipping into the 70s in the evening. Although an abundance of sunshine prevails most days, tropical downpours are not uncommon at any time, but they usually last no more than 15 minutes. Longer tropical storms are possible at any time of the year, too, but they are more prevalent in September and October, during the typical Caribbean hurricane season, which spans from June through November. Many North Americans head to Punta Cana from mid-November through March, which encompasses the high season from December through February. Whenever you go, book early, as Punta Cana resorts run at high occupancy, particularly in high season.

GETTING HERE AND AROUND

AIR TRAVEL

The following airlines provide service from the United States (or connections through San Juan): American Airlines/American Eagle, Continental, Delta, United, and US Airways. Many visitors fly nonstop on charter flights to the Dominican Republic direct from the East Coast, the Midwest, and Canada—particularly into Punta Cana. These charters are part of a package, and can only be booked through a travel agent.

When you arrive at Punta Cana International Airport, greeters in traditional Dominican dress will welcome you and take your photograph for optional purchase as a souvenir when you depart. There is otherwise no charge for this service. Immediately behind the greeters is the Immigration Desk, where every visitor must purchase a "tourist card" for $10 (U.S. currency only). American citizens do not require a visa to enter the country, only a valid passport.

If you book a package through a travel agent, your airport transfers will almost certainly be included in the price you pay. Look for your company's sign as you exit baggage claim. If you book independently, you may have to take a taxi or rent a car.

When you leave the Dominican Republic, anticipate long, slow-moving lines, and be sure to give yourself a full two hours for international check-in.

Contact Punta Cana International Airport (PUJ) ☎ 809/686–8790 ⊕ www.punta-cana-airport.com.

BUS TRAVEL

Public buses (known as guaguas) service Punta Cana and Bávaro, but it's not easy to coordinate travel from point to point. Schedules are sporadic, with buses about once every half-hour, and stops are not always clearly marked (it's best to tell the driver where you want to get off). But for 35 pesos (about $1) it is possible to get from the hotels to stops within walking distance of popular shopping centers and restaurants. Note that it may be a long walk from your room to your resort's main entrance, along the road where the buses stop.

Traumabapu buses (playeros) run along the beaches where the resorts are located until about 7 PM. Sitrabapu buses run on the Punta Cana/Bávaro–Higüey routes until 10:30 PM; from Friusa/Bávaro, you can travel to Higüey for 110 pesos (about $3).

> ### PUNTA CANA INTERNATIONAL AIRPORT
>
> With its thatched-roof hangars blending seamlessly into the tropical landscape, the Punta Cana International Airport has grown from its origin as a humble private airstrip. The airport, which opened in 1984, is now one of the largest and busiest in the Caribbean, and is the port of entry for more than half of all passengers arriving by air to the Dominican Republic. It handles about 1.5 million passengers a year. During the winter months about 250 international flights arrive here weekly; in summer about 100 flights arrive per week.

To get to Punta Cana from Santo Domingo, Expreso Bávaro buses depart from the Sitrabapu-Sichoprola terminal on Calle Juan Sanchez Ramirez, near the intersection with Avenida Máximo Gómez. The buses have air-conditioning and the price is right (325 pesos, about $9, for a four-hour trip). If you're going to one of the Punta Cana resorts, you get off at the Friusa/Bávaro stop and take a cab from the taxi stand.

Bus Contacts Expreso Bávaro (☎ 809/682–9670 [Santo Domingo] or 809/552-1678 [Sitrabapu station, Carretera Coco Loco-Riu, Friusa/Bávaro]). **Sitrabapu/Traumabapu** (☎ 809/552-0771).

CAR TRAVEL

If you're visiting or flying into another region of the country, it's possible but difficult to drive to Punta Cana. Throughout the region, main roads (*carreteras*) are mostly paved country roads with two-way traffic, but few dividing lines. Potholes pose a hazard, although there have been some notable improvements in recent years, as some long stretches, notably in Uvero Alto, have been paved over by the government. A 20-mile network of privately funded new roads built within the vast Cap Cana development is impeccably smooth and well lit, as are some nearby roads constructed privately by the PuntaCana Resort & Club. Elsewhere, be alert for potholes, which are particularly hazardous after heavy rains, when the larger ones fill up with water and drivers have to avoid—or slog through—the big puddles. It's extra tough around the bends, but drivers adhere to a set of commonsense unwritten rules of the road—basically, choose the path of least resistance, dodge potholes, and get out of the way when facing an oncoming vehicle. Night driving is not a good idea.

Traffic signs and road-name labels are scarce throughout the region; resort billboards at junctions and landmarks give clues to point you in the right direction, but detailed road maps of the area are nonexistent, and driving can be confusing. However, it seems that better driving conditions in some areas aren't too far down the road. New pavement was being laid down in some spots, and a signage deal was in the works—look for street labels, lane markings, traffic lights, and road maps to follow in the next few years.

A new highway—the so-called "Tourist Boulevard"—is being constructed from the airport to Uvero Alto, and should significantly reduce the traveling time along that stretch, from about one hour to 25 minutes, as well as improve driving safety conditions. Actual work on the boulevard, however, happens in fits and starts, often coinciding with election periods, according to observations made by local hotel managers. And the targeted completion date of the project has been set back for several years by additional obstacles, including negotiations with owners of existing properties that lie in the path of the road.

Few vacationers choose to rent cars in Punta Cana, but rental cars are an economical choice, given the expense of taxis in the area. Several major car-rental companies have outlets at the Punta Cana airport, as well as in Bávaro. Most will deliver cars to area hotels (in some cases, they will complete the paperwork at your hotel; in others, they will bring you back to the office to complete the paperwork).

Free parking is available at all the resorts. When you venture out, free parking is also common, including at the shopping plazas and local restaurants—and generally easy to find, except perhaps on the cluttered streets of Higüey.

Car Rental Avis (⊠ *Punta Cana International Airport, Punta Cana* ☎ *809/688-1354* ⊠ *Carretera Arena Gorda, Plaza Caney, Bávaro* ☎ *809/688-1354*). **Budget** (⊠ *Carretera Verón–Bávaro, Bávaro* ☎ *809/696-6401*). **Europcar** (⊠ *Punta Cana International Airport, Punta Cana* ☎ *809/686-2861* ⊠ *Carretera Friusa-Melia, Friusa, Bávaro* ☎ *809/686-2861* ⊕ *www.europcar.com.do*). **National** (⊠ *Carretera Verón–Bávaro, Bávaro* ☎ *809/466-1083*).

Gasoline Shell (⊠ *Carretera Verón–Punta Cana, Verón*). **Texaco** (⊠ *Intersection of Carretera Friusa and Carretera Riu–Arena Gorda, Friusa, Bávaro*). **Texaco** (⊠ *Carretera Bávaro–Macao, east side of road, Macao*).

TAXI TRAVEL

Fares in Punta Cana are high, and there are set fares between resorts and the airport or other popular destinations. It's not uncommon to be charged US$40 for a 20-minute ride if you book through your resort's concierge. At Plaza Bávaro shopping center, where many taxis are standing around—and especially if you can negotiate in Spanish—you can get one for a fraction of that price. There are no meters, so confirm the rate with the driver before beginning your trip.

Information Arena Gorda Taxi (☎ *809/552-0711* ⊠ *Arena Gorda*). **Asotatupal 24-Hour Taxi Service** (☎ *809/688-8978* ⊠ *Uvero Alto*). **Siutratural Taxi**

Service (☎ 809/552–0617 ✉ *Plaza Meliá, Bávaro* ☎ 809/221–2741 ✉ *Carretera Friusa, Bávaro*). **Taxi Verón** (☎ 809/455–1222 or 809/466–1133 ✉ *Carretera Bávaro-Punta Cana, cruce de Verón, Verón*).

INTERNET

Internet access is generally available in the resorts, typically at an Internet café or business center, and less frequently in the guest rooms. Public Wi-Fi is becoming more commonly available in the lobby or in communal spaces. Often you must purchase an access code. Upgraded packages, however, sometimes include free wireless. In the hotels, service is expensive, and Internet cafés tend to charge US$3 to $4 for 15 minutes, or anywhere from US$10 to $25 for 24 hours of Wi-Fi access, with some multiday or weekly discounts available.

MONEY MATTERS

You may need to change some money, particularly if you're not staying in an all-inclusive resort, where dollars are usually accepted. Most resorts will exchange money at the front desk (from U.S. dollars or euros to pesos, but not the other way). Some will break a US$20 or US$10 into smaller U.S. dollar bills. There are also money-exchange storefronts at all the main shopping plazas. ATMs, which dispense only pesos, can be found on the grounds of many resorts and at the shopping plazas.

PROSTITUTION

If you're looking for prostitution in Punta Cana, you can find it, but it's not a problem that surfaces—at least not blatantly—at the resorts. Although officials have made strides at curbing the Dominican Republic's reputation as a destination for sex tourism, if you venture off resort grounds onto local streets, you might encounter "gentlemen's clubs," where it's no secret that sex services are available.

SAFETY

Violent crime against tourists in the Dominican Republic is rare, and the destination has a history of being safe. Punta Cana remains one of the safest regions, Uvero Alto even more so. However, poverty is everywhere in the country, and petty theft (particularly of cell phones), pickpocketing, and purse snatching do happen, particularly in Higüey.

Security at the resorts is very good, but it's important to take precautions against petty theft. As everywhere, common sense rules apply. Leave your valuables in the hotel when you walk along the beach. Use the safe in your hotel room or at the front desk; hide your laptop if it doesn't fit in the safe. It's safe to rent a car and drive yourself around the Punta Cana area, but when driving, always lock your car and don't leave valuables inside. Take hotel-recommended taxis at night. Don't buy or bring drugs: the penalties in this country are extremely tough—jail (not pretty), fines, and no parole.

Politur is a special branch of the police department dedicated to protecting the safety of tourists, with branches in Friusa and Uvero Alto. Its officers maintain a presence in the hotel areas and also monitor excursions. For emergencies, dial 911.

Information Politur (✉ *Carretera Friusa–Arena Gorda, near Sitrabapu Bus Terminal, Friusa, Bávaro* ☏ *809/688–8727 or 809/754–3073*). **Politur** (✉ *Plaza Uvero Alto Shopping Center, Uvero Alto* ☏ *809/754–3044 or 809/754–2985*).

TOURS

Visitors to Punta Cana have a plethora of excursions to choose from, with many tour companies offering similar packages. Clients traveling on a tour-company package tend to book excursions with the same company, or through the company affiliated with their resort (e.g., Vacaciones Barceló). Amstar is well managed and reliable, and is associated with Apple Vacations. Go Golf has services tailored to clients seeking to make golf part of

> ### PUNTA CANA: ORIGIN OF THE NAME
>
> The easternmost tip of the island was originally dubbed "Punta Borrachón," that is, Drunken Point. But with its blatant negative connotations, Frank Rainieri, the visionary cofounder of PuntaCana Resort & Club, believed that simply wouldn't work to reel in the jet-setting crowd. So, inspired by the *Palma Cana*—the Dominican Republic's national tree that grows abundantly in the region—he coined the much more pacifying name "Punta Cana," thereby setting the stage for the burgeoning tourism industry here.

their getaway—whether it's the primary focus or just a one-time outing; the company will help arrange tee times, golf instruction, and transport to courses.

Contacts Amstar DMC–Apple Vacations (✉ *Carretera Bávaro, Bávaro* ☏ *809/221–6626* ⊕ *www.amstardominicana.com or www.applevacations. com*). **Colonial Tours & Travel** (✉ *Plaza Brisas de Bávaro, Bávaro* ☏ *809/687–2203* ⊕ *www.colonialtours.com.do*). **Go Golf Tours (GGT)** (✉ *Cocotal Golf & Country Club, Bávaro* ☏ *809/687–4653* ⊕ *www.tee-off-times.info or golfreservationcenter.com*). **Takeoff Destination Service** (✉ *Plaza Brisas de Bávaro 8, Bávaro* ☏ *809/552–1333* ⊕ *www.takeoffweb.com*). **Vacaciones Barceló** (✉ *Barceló Bávaro, Plaza Dominicana, Bávaro* ☏ *809/686–5658 Ext. 1608* ⊕ *www.vacacionesbarcelo.com*). **VIP Travel Services** (✉ *Plaza Cueva Taina, Carretera Bávaro–Arena Gorda, Bávaro* ☏ *809/566–7737 or 809/466–1002* ⊕ *www. viptravelservices.com*).

PUNTA CANA

5 mi (8 km) east of Punta Cana International Airport.

Playa Punta Cana is where the tourism in the entire region began, with the opening of the first hotel in the 1970s. Nowadays development continues in Punta Cana Village, which is a draw for visitors from around the area, with its quaint stores and restaurants. There's plenty to do, too, on the grounds of the PuntaCana Resort & Club, including fine dining, golf, a Metamorphosis Spa, a tennis club, riding stables, an ecological park, and a marina, making it an appealing day-trip (or evening) destination for anyone not staying here, but the resort does not offer any kind of a day or night pass to nonguests, so in order to

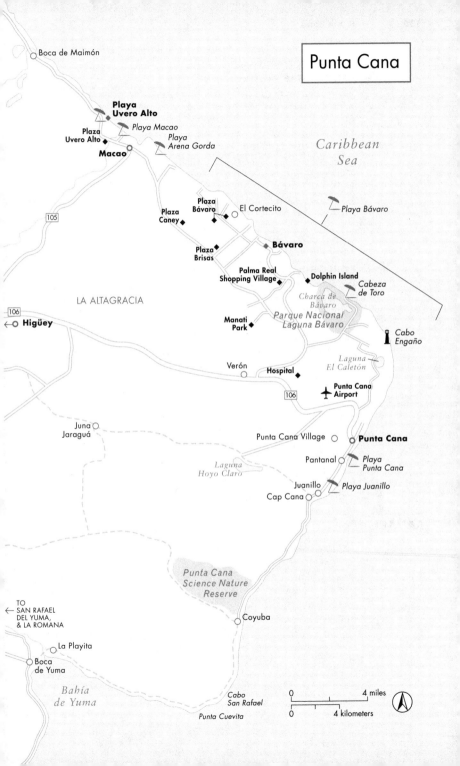

Punta Cana

Boca de Maimón

Playa Uvero Alto

Plaza Uvero Alto

Playa Macao

Macao

Playa Arena Gorda

Caribbean Sea

105

Plaza Caney

Plaza Bávaro

El Cortecito

Playa Bávaro

Plaza Brisas

Bávaro

Palma Real Shopping Village

Dolphin Island

Cabeza de Toro

Charca de Bávaro

LA ALTAGRACIA

Parque Nacional Laguna Bávaro

106

← **Higüey**

Manati Park

Cabo Engaño

Laguna El Caletón

Verón

Hospital

106

Punta Cana Airport

Juna Jaraguá

Punta Cana Village

Punta Cana

Pantanal

Playa Punta Cana

Laguna Hoyo Claro

Juanillo

Playa Juanillo

Cap Cana

Punta Cana Science Nature Reserve

TO
← SAN RAFAEL DEL YUMA, & LA ROMANA

Coyuba

La Playita

Boca de Yuma

Bahía de Yuma

Cabo San Rafael

Punta Cuevita

0   4 miles

0   4 kilometers

take part in an activity here, you must make prior arrangements to get access to the resort grounds.

GETTING HERE AND AROUND

Many resorts offer transfers from the airport; these can be arranged in advance. There are also taxis waiting to carry arriving passengers to their final destinations. Once you've collected your luggage at the airport, head for the exit, where shuttle vans and taxis will be waiting. If you have arranged for a ride ahead of time, look for the line of drivers holding placards with names on them, or seek out the kiosk for your rental-car company. Most resorts in Punta Cana, Cap Cana (Juanillo), and Bávaro are a 15- to 30-minute drive away. Those in Macao and Uvero Alto are 40 minutes to an hour away. If you're driving a rental car, note that road maps for the entire region are poorly designed and incomplete. Factor in limited street signs, and it becomes difficult to get around when you are unfamiliar with the area. Be sure to get detailed directions. It also helps to carry a cell phone activated for local use.

EXPLORING

PuntaCana Ecological Foundation. This eco-reserve is on a 1,500-acre private tract in PuntaCana Resort that encompasses tropical forest, natural lagoons, cold water springs, gardens, a petting zoo, and an iguana habitat, this foundation has Its mission is to promote sustainable development throughout the country by fostering cooperation between economic development and environmental protection, as well as involving the community. The foundation works with various research institutions to document all of the island's biodiversity and to inform management practices regarding sustainable tourism. It also maintains an organic vegetable garden, which started as an experiment; now its produce—for example, arugula, tomatoes, peppers, basil, chives, melons, and *auyama* (Dominican pumpkin)—is sold locally, including to some area restaurants. Entomology exhibits—butterflies, moths, and beetles—are drawn from species in the area. Guided tours of the reserve are available by appointment. Proceeds benefit the nonprofit foundation. ⊠ *PuntaCana Resort & Club* ☎ 809/959-9221 ⊕ *www.puntacana.org* ✆ *$10 for non-hotel guests* ☉ *Daily 8:30–5.*

BÁVARO

15 mi (24 km) northeast of Punta Cana International Airport.

Bávaro is centrally located along the eastern coast and is a hub of tourist activity. Many of the region's all-inclusive resorts are on Playa Bávaro, and shopping plazas, restaurants, nightlife, and services have sprung up to accommodate the burgeoning number of visitors.

El Cortecito is a colorful fishing village within Bávaro. It's home to a vibrant artisans' market, where you can browse for souvenirs in the open-air stalls, as well as waterfront bars, snack stands, restaurants, and vacation apartments. Also within Bávaro, farther north along the coast is a stretch of beach known as **Arena Gorda**, literally "fat sand." About 20 mi (32 km) from Punta Cana International Airport, it's an area brimming with coconut groves and the location of several resorts.

GETTING HERE AND AROUND

Bávaro resorts are about 20 to 30 minutes from the airport. Taxi rates to specific resorts are fixed according to distance. Once in Bávaro, you can take taxis from your hotel to restaurants, shopping, or other popular destinations for fixed rates.

EXPLORING

Dolphin Island Park. The adventure starts with a short boat ride as you leave the beautiful shore of Bávaro in the background, where you can spend some of your day lingering on the beach if you choose, before or after a swim with the dolphins or sea lions. The main program includes instruction, a show, and a 25-minute swim in calm, protected waters with the adorable dolphins or sea lions. An encounter with sharks and stingrays is an optional feature at no extra charge. You must be eight or older to swim, and no pregnant women are allowed, but no special skills are required. Snorkeling gear and a flotation vest are provided. A DVD capturing your experience will be available to buy as a souvenir. Sessions are at 9 AM and 2 PM daily; in high season there's an additional session at 4 PM. Reservations must be made at least one day in advance. Free shuttles depart from the hotels. ⊠ *Carretera Manatí, Bávaro* ☎ *809/221–9444* ⊕ *www.dolphinislandpark.com* ⊠ *$120 for dolphin swim; $75 for sea lion swim; $25 for accompanying visitors* ⊗ *Daily 9–5:30.*

Manatí Park. This zoo and cultural park showcases local animals, ★ which include iguanas, crocodiles, and tropical birds. A half-day tour (9 AM–1:30 PM or 1 PM–5:30 PM) includes a Taino cultural show, a horse show, and a dolphin and sea lion show. Ducks roam the gardens, where there's Dominican art on display. A brief swim or encounter with the dolphins is an option; bring your swimsuit and a towel (Dolphin Island, run by the same owner, offers a more extended swim program). Free shuttles depart from the hotels. ⊠ *Carretera Manatí, Bávaro* ☎ *809/221–9444 or 809/552–6100* ⊕ *www.manatipark.com* ⊠ *$30; $95 for admission and dolphin swim* ⊗ *Daily 9–6.*

> **ABOUT DOLPHIN SWIM PROGRAMS**
>
> Several organizations, including Greenpeace, have spoken out against captive dolphin encounters, asserting that some water parks get dolphins from restricted areas and that the confined conditions at some parks put the dolphins' health and safety at risk. Only you can decide whether you want to pay the $100-plus fee toward interacting with a dolphin. For some it's a positive, life-changing experience; for others, it's traumatic.

NEED A BREAK? Drop in for tapas and wine tastings at **Latasca Wine & Food Sensations** (⊠ *Palma Real Shopping Village, Bávaro* ☎ *809/552–9000*) whenever you need a break from the sun, from shopping, or from the same old routine at your resort. It's open daily from 10 AM to midnight.

MACAO

20 mi (32 km) north of Punta Cana.

Macao is a pastoral village full of pastures and ranches. Its striking beach, with dramatic headlands, inspired one of the most ambitious resort development projects on the East Coast, Rôco Ki, where construction is ongoing. Hard Rock Hotel & Casino is also staking a claim here, with the brand's first all-inclusive property anywhere in the world opening in summer 2010.

GETTING HERE AND AROUND

Macao is about a 40-minute drive from the airport. A taxi ride to resorts here could cost upwards of US$50. For cost effectiveness, it's best if you arrange a shuttle transfer to your hotel in advance. This ride may be shared with other guests arriving at the same time. If you're leaving the resort for shopping or dinner or nightlife in Bávaro, expect expensive taxi rides. Some resorts have round-trip shuttles to popular shopping centers and nightclubs that can cut down on transportation costs.

PLAYA UVERO ALTO

7 mi (12 km) north of Macao, 24 mi (39 km) north of Punta Cana.

Ranches and rustic living characterize this beach village, which has coconut groves and a stunning beach where development continues to press north of Macao. It's home to several high-end resorts.

GETTING HERE AND AROUND

It takes about an hour to get to Playa Uvero Alto from the airport. Newly paved sections of the road have made the trip less bumpy than in years past. To the most exclusive outposts, there's always the option of going by helicopter, landing directly on the beach of your resort.

HIGÜEY

37 mi (60 km) west of Punta Cana.

Meaning "place where the sun rises" in the language of the indigenous Taino Indians, Higüey was one of the first areas to be settled by the Spanish conquistadors in 1502. Capital of Altagracia Province (which encompasses Punta Cana), the city is considered holy by Catholics because of a vision of the Virgin Mary that was seen there, as well as many reported miracles in the area. Higüey was the site of three visits by Pope John Paul II (in 1979, 1984, and 1992), and nowadays the cathedral near the central square is the main draw for tourists. An open-air market within walking distance reveals a not-so-pretty slice of life, and is a point of interest rather than a shopping destination. On the cluttered city streets motorcycles are a heavy presence and zip around from every which way, so be alert whether driving or on foot. The Expreso Bávaro Bus Terminal, a hub of transit between the region, Santo Domingo, and elsewhere in the country, is here, as is the Altagracia Province post office, which services Punta Cana and the surrounding areas. Many people employed by the hotels along the East Coast beaches are residents of Higüey, with a commute of about an hour each way.

Saona Island

This scenic, secluded island known for its exquisite beach is off the southeastern coast of the Dominican Republic, near Bayahibe *(see* ⇨ *Chapter 3, The Southeast Coast, for more information).* Saona is part of a government-protected nature reserve, with tropical wildlife and exotic birds in their natural habitat. The island's blue waters teem with various species of marine life, most notably the area's indigenous starfish. Protective sandbars keep the sand sparkling white. The beach is a popular day-trip destination for tourists from the resorts in Punta Cana and La Romana. Most tours sail here by catamaran from Bayahibe (about 90 minutes from Punta Cana by a tour bus, which will pick you up and drop you off at your hotel), and you can spend the day kicking back on the beach or swimming. Extra features, like a stop at a natural pool, are included with some tours, which cost about $90 to $95 for a full day, including, lunch and beverages. Bring suntan lotion, towels, a swimsuit, a camera, and some cash for souvenirs or extra drinks.

GETTING HERE AND AROUND

Higüey is about 45 minutes west of the airport. To reach the resorts, a round-trip taxi ride to the city will be about US$90–$100, but make sure to discuss any extra costs for waiting time. From the Sitrabapu station in Friusa/Bávaro, you can take a cheap bus ride to Higüey.

EXPLORING

Basilica de Higüey Nuestra Señora de la Altagracia. Higüey's concrete basilica was built in 1972, and is characterized by its representations of oranges, symbolic of the nearby orange grove where a vision of the Virgin Mary has become legend. There's a shrine depicting an orange tree and stained-glass windows with cutouts shaped like oranges inside the cathedral, where you can climb the stairs of the sanctuary and touch the encased icon of the Virgen de la Altagracia, patron saint of the Dominican Republic. Outside, you can light a candle or purchase religious mementos. The pinched arches of the facade stretch 250 feet (75 meters) high. The basilica is the site of annual pilgrimages on January 21 and August 16. ⌂ *Agustin Guerrero 66* ☎ *809/554-4541* ✉ *Free* ⊙ *Daily 5 AM–7 PM; masses daily at 5, 8, and 10 AM, and noon; also Sat. at 6 PM and Sun. at 5 PM.*

Mercado Publico de Higüey. Produce and meat are laid out for display at dozens of stalls at this open-air market. With dogs roaming around, flies abuzz, and slabs of freshly butchered meat strung up or strewn about in wheelbarrows—this market is perhaps not the best place to seek out a snack, but nonetheless it's captivating to see while you're in the area. If you want to purchase anything, nonperishables are the safest; if you do buy produce, make sure you wash it before eating. ⌂ *Plaza Central, Av. Libertad* ⊙ *Mon.–Sat. 8–5.*

Plaza Higüeyana. On the outskirts of Higüey, as you head into town along Carretera Higüey–La Otra Banda, you can find this artisans' market that draws busloads of tourists—on the right-hand side of the road. Here you can browse through racks and shelves full of souvenirs, like the herbal mamajuana liqueur, rum, T-shirts, amber and larimar jewelry, crafts, and ceramics.

Inside the Plaza Higüeyana, you can take a free tour (in English) of the Museo Vivo Del Tabaco, where you can see how tobacco is planted, harvested, and rolled into cigars and learn about the history of tobacco cultivation in the country. Near the entrance to the museum, you can also purchase hand-rolled cigars. Personalized cigars or cigar boxes are available with 24-hours notice. Free transportation from your hotel can be arranged, and you can also have purchases delivered. Private tours are also an option by prior arrangement. ⊠ *Carretera Higüey–La Otra Banda, at east end of Higüey* ☎ *809/551–1128 for museum* ⊕ *www. museedutabac.com* ⊗ *Daily 9* AM–7 PM.

EN ROUTE

Along the drive between Higüey and Punta Cana, the town of La Otra Banda is notable for its colorful, traditional homes. With its local flavor and picturesque setting 30 to 40 minutes inland from the beachside resorts at Punta Cana and Cap Cana, the area is poised for growth once the real-estate market emerges from its slump.

WHERE TO EAT

Punta Cana's mushrooming growth has spawned a smattering of non-resort restaurants that might entice you to venture off the grounds of your all-inclusive resort and eat at least some meals elsewhere. Although the options are still limited outside the resorts, there are now options that include familiar American chains like Hard Rock Cafe, oceanfront cafés, and top-notch restaurants on the grounds of boutique hotels. However, even the more remote areas have at least a few local restaurants beyond those listed here that are worth seeking out if you are adventurous. You might find good food, good value, and friendly service, but keep in mind that the farther you go off the beaten track, the more unlikely it is that English will be spoken.

The majority of visitors to the region are guests at all-inclusives, and eat most—if not all—of their meals at the resort where they are staying, for reasons of convenience as well as budget. Generally, a variety of options are included in all price plans at any given resort, typically including a main buffet open for all daily meals. In addition, most all-inclusive resorts offer at least one or two à la carte restaurants with the standard package; the largest resorts may have five or more. In cases where a "VIP" package is offered, there's usually at least one exclusive restaurant for guests on this plan. For the à la carte restaurants in most resorts, dinner reservations are usually necessary, especially in high season.

A dinner dress code barring shorts, tank tops, and beachwear is fairly standard at the à la carte restaurants. Although jackets are not typically expected, some restaurants require long pants, closed shoes, and collared shirts for men. Check ahead at your resort if you're looking for more casual options.

WHAT IT COSTS IN U.S. DOLLARS					
	¢	$	$$	$$$	$$$$
RESTAURANTS	Under $8	$8–$12	$12–$20	$20–$30	over $30

Restaurant prices are per person for a main course at dinner and do not include the 16% tax and 10% service charge.

$$$
SEAFOOD
Fodor'sChoice
★
✕ Blue Marlin. The setting here is reminiscent of a fantasy island in the South Pacific, with dining beneath a *palapa* (an open-sided grass hut) on a pier that sits over the Caribbean's gentle waters at the Secrets Sanctuary Cap Cana (⇨ *Where to Stay*). The Blue Marlin's own small fleet of fishing boats harvests the waters daily for fresh catch, which are among the most popular menu items and are prepared as you like (e.g., steamed with ginger and soy or baked in spiced banana leaves), with sauce options such as Caribbean pineapple vinaigrette. Fish specialties come from around the world—Mexico, Peru, Spain, and New Orleans, with many dishes from the Pacific Rim. Grilled Caribbean lobster flanked by spicy Dominican *tostones* (fried green plantains) is a treasured delicacy. Salads are creative and clear the palate. Sandwiches, burgers, sushi, and pizzas—some in the gourmet genre—are lunch favorites, but are available on the dinner menu, too. (Non-hotel guests are welcome, but must make reservations to pass through the security gates.) ✉ *Secrets Sanctuary Cap Cana Golf & Spa, Cap Cana, Playa Juanillo* ☎ *809/562–9191* ⚑ *Reservations essential* 🖃 *AE, D, DC, MC, V.*

$$$
SEAFOOD
✕ Capitán Cook's. Lobster, king crab legs, and lots of fish are what's cooking at this seafood specialty house on the sand, where the fresh catch is stashed on ice in a fiberglass vault and grilled before your eyes. The menu is hand-scrawled on a jumbo chalkboard, with prices given in pesos, but U.S. dollars are accepted, too. Despite naysayers who object that the quality of the food has gone downhill, the bazaar-like atmosphere on the waterfront keeps reeling in the tourists. The restaurant, open from 11 AM to 11 PM, offers free round-trip transportation by water taxi from the area hotels (daylight only). The prix-fixe special (about $40 per person) includes national drinks and the signature dish parrillada mixta (mixed grilled seafood) with fries and salad, followed by coffee, fruit, and shots of fiery *mamajuana*. Sit in the sand at the water's edge and watch as the fishermen hang their catch up by the tail. It's boisterous fun as mariachis play live music, vendors hawk souvenirs, and waiters sprint to the beach tables delivering sizzling cauldrons of food. ✉ *El Cortecito, Bávaro* ☎ *809/552–0645* ⚑ *Reservations essential* 🖃 *MC, V.*

$$$
ITALIAN/
MEDITERRANEAN
★
✕ Il Cappuccino. Enchanting views of the Cap Cana Marina enhance the experience of a meal at this Mediterranean-style eatery with an alfresco deck well suited for a romantic waterfront dinner or lively conversation with friends. It's not uncommon to see the owner making the rounds and chatting with guests. Wine aplenty (with knowledgeable guidance from the maitre d') can accompany the savory, hearty plates of pasta (like the delectable black fettuccini with lobster and shrimp) or meat and seafood entrées, such as the baked fish almondine. Polish it all off with a sweet and tart homemade limoncello. If you're

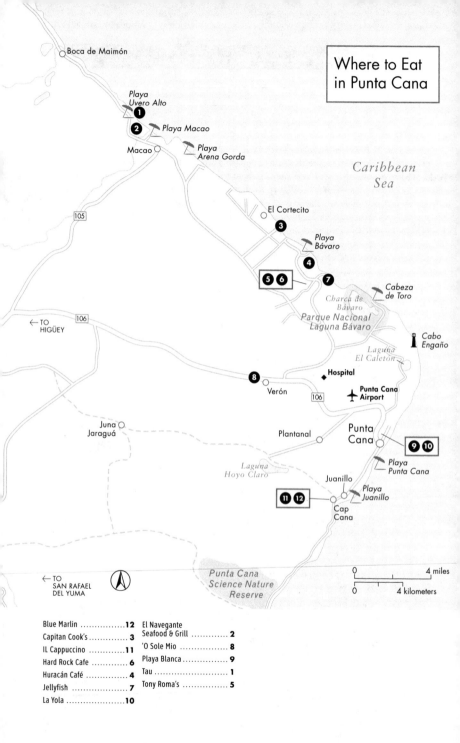

Where to Eat in Punta Cana

Boca de Maimón

Playa Uvero Alto ❶

❷ Playa Macao

Macao

Playa Arena Gorda

Caribbean Sea

105

El Cortecito ❸

Playa Bávaro ❹

❺ ❻ ❼ Cabeza de Toro

Charca de Bávaro

Parque Nacional Laguna Bávaro

← TO HIGÜEY

106

Laguna El Caletón

Cabo Engaño

◆ **Hospital**

❽ Verón

✈ **Punta Cana Airport**

106

Juna Jaraguá

Plantanal

Punta Cana ❾ ❿

Playa Punta Cana

Laguna Hoyo Claro

Juanillo

Playa Juanillo

⓫ ⓬ Cap Cana

← TO SAN RAFAEL DEL YUMA

Punta Cana Science Nature Reserve

0   4 miles
0   4 kilometers

farther north along the East Coast, you might opt for Cappuccino's sister location, with the same owners, that's near the Riu complex. And the original restaurant, in Santo Domingo, still thrives there. ⊠ *Marina Cap Cana, Cap Cana* ☎ *809/469–7095* ⚞ *Reservations essential* 🖃 *AE, MC, V* ⊠ *Carretera Riu–Friusa, Arena Gorda, Bávaro* ☎ *809/468-4116*

$$–$$$
AMERICAN–
CASUAL
☺
✕**Hard Rock Cafe.** There's nothing that takes a bite out of the blues like this familiar American standby, with all the namesake rock-and-roll memorabilia adorning the walls and the café's standard fare: 10-ounce certified Angus beef burgers, hickory-smoked chicken wings, white-cheddar smashed potatoes, "twisted" mac and cheese, sandwiches, salads, and the like. Memorabilia on display here includes Madonna's black teddy with pink feather trim from her "Blonde Ambition" tour and original Jimi Hendrix drawings and lyrics scrawled on a 1968 copy of the *New York Times*. Top off your meal with a visit to the gift shop, and take out a souvenir HARD ROCK PUNTA CANA T-shirt or glass. Free shuttles are available from many Punta Cana hotels. ⊠ *Plaza Palma Real, Carretera El Cortecito 57, Bávaro* ☎ *809/552–0594* 🖃 *AE, MC, V.*

$$
ITALIAN
✕**Huracán Café.** A thatched-roof palapa over a wooden deck in the sand shelters diners from the elements at this tony outdoor eatery set back a few paces from the ocean on a prime stretch of beach. Pastas and other Italian dishes dominate the menu, but a few Tex-Mex options are also available. A prix-fixe dinner is a popular choice; for about $25 you get an appetizer, main course, mixed grill, wine, and coffee. By prior arrangement, the chef will also prepare special dishes according to your tastes. After dinner, kick back with a Cuba libre and enjoy the starlight. The place turns lively on Saturday nights, with weekly theme parties and a DJ spinning jams. If your timing's right, the full-moon parties are rollicking. ⊠ *Playa El Cortecito, Bávaro* ☎ *809/221–6643* 🖃 *MC, V.*

$$$
SEAFOOD
Fodor's Choice
★
✕**Jellyfish.** With round edges evoking the shape of its namesake, and double decks reminiscent of a yacht, this open-air restaurant on the sand puts the accent on maritime, and gets it right in both food as well as form. Main dining-room tables are on light wooden platforms, sheltered by thatched roofing but not fully enclosed. When weather demands it, sheer white linens are secured to the wooden railings to protect against sun, wind, or rain without obstructing the exquisite beachfront views. Other tables are under palapas right on the beach. At night, soft lighting creates a romantic effect, and lounge music enhances the ambience.

BIRDS OF PUNTA CANA

Within the diverse natural habitats of the area—beaches, fields, forests, and mangroves—more than 100 species of birds have been spotted. Among them are nectar-slurping hummingbirds, gliding frigate birds, plunge-diving royal terns, fish-engulfing brown pelicans, mockingbirds, and wintering Cape May warblers. Hiking through a nature preserve or walking along Madre de los Aves Beach, you might see or hear 20 to 30 species in a single day. The Cornell Biodiversity Laboratory at the PuntaCana Ecological Foundation studies the region's unique birds and microclimates to help protect and conserve them.

4

Fresh seafood caught by local fishermen is the focus of the menu, but chicken and beef dishes are also available, as is a special children's menu. Lobster lovers can look forward to sinking their claws into the oven-baked *langosta de la casa* (house lobster). For a more diverse shellfish meal, try the seafood grill for two, which included crawfish, lobster, shrimp, conch, and octopus. If you spend a minimum of $100, the restaurant includes free transportation back to your hotel (though not free transportation *to* the restaurant). Some resorts, like Paradisus Palma Real and the Barceló Bávaro complex, are within walking distance. The space is sometimes closed for private parties and weddings, so it's best to call ahead for reservations. ⌧ *On the beach, between Meliá Caribe Tropical and IFA Villas, Playa Bávaro* ☎ *809/840–7684 or 809/868–3040* ⚲ *Reservations essential* ▤ *AE, MC, V.*

$$$
MEDITERRANEAN
★

✕ **La Yola.** Dining on a deck, gentle breeze blowing, over the PuntaCana Marina, you feel as if you were actually aboard a *yola* (a small fishing boat). Using thatched cane for overhead shelter, and the sea as a backdrop, this restaurant has a gratifying, open-air dining ambience. The cuisine has Mediterranean and Caribbean influences, and attentive service enhances the experience. Seafood and fish dominate the creative menu (you'll also find beef and chicken selections). For an appetizer, the spicy tuna tartare with guacamole relish starts you off with a pleasing burst of flavor and satisfying texture. Main plates, including the catch of the day—usually red snapper, grouper, or *dorado* (mahimahi)—are artfully prepared and presented. Baked Chilean sea bass with clam-and-cherry-tomato risotto is a savory special, but costs as much as the lobster—$45. For a more frugal alternative, have a side of lobster risotto for $7 and an ample appetizer. ⌧ *PuntaCana Resort & Club, Punta Cana* ☎ *809/959–2262 Ext. 8002* ⚲ *Reservations essential* ▤ *AE, MC, V* ☾ *Closed Tues.*

$$
SEAFOOD

✕ **El Navegante Seafood & Grill.** Dig your toes in the sand or dine on the sheltered wooden porch as you savor your seafood at this local beachfront favorite. A tasty *parillada* (mixed grill) for two ($55) includes baby lobster, shrimp, octopus, conch, and fillets of fish. The catch is always fresh, and now and then selections include fish reeled in by the owner himself that day. For those favoring turf over surf, there's also steak and chicken. To get here, from Carretera Uvero Alto, turn on the unpaved beach access road at the billboard south of Excellence Resort and drive about ¾ mi (1 km) to the end. ⌧ *Playa Uvero Alto* ☎ *809/552–6166* ▤ *AE, MC, V.* ☾ Closed Tues.

$$
ITALIAN
★

✕ **'O Sole Mio.** Tucked away on a nondescript street, with no sign posted outside, this delicious secret of a restaurant looks like any ordinary house; you really have to know where you're going to find it. Once you do, you'll likely encounter the owner, Nino, who's catered to an exclusive set of Punta Cana admirers (including Oscar de la Renta) with scrumptious Italian cooking since the early 1990s. There's seating for 50 people on an outdoor sheltered patio. Diners return time and again for the homemade pastas and savory sauces. Many vegetables and herbs used here, including arugula, spinach, onion, and basil, come straight from the garden of the PuntaCana Ecological Foundation. Meat is imported from the United States. There's a small menu, including highlights like baby lobster in wine sauce, plus daily specials. Foods are prepared simply—boiled or grilled rather than sautéed—and the chef will address any special dietary needs. Choose from an extensive list of imported wines to complement your meal. Sometimes organic homemade ice cream is available for dessert. To get here from Punta Cana, take Carretera Punta Cana–Bávaro to Carretera Verón–Punta Cana; drive west along Carretera Verón-Punta Cana toward Higüey. In about 3 mi (5 km) you will come to a traffic light (not necessarily working); the junction is the turnoff toward Bávaro to your right. There will be a Shell gas station on your left. Go past the light; the first gated entrance on your right is the restaurant. ⊠ *Carretera Verón–Punta Cana, Verón* ☎ *809/455–1143* ⌦ *Reservations essential* ▭ *AE, D, DC, MC, V* ☾ *Closed Sun.*

SEGWAY TOUR

When a parade of people on motorized two-wheelers rolls past you over grass, beach, and pavement, you might do a bemused double take. And you might do so even if you already know it's part of a three-hour ride by Segway Tours, which departs from the Playa Blanca Restaurant and takes you on the beach, past the golf course, and all the way to the ecological reserve (US$40).

4

$$–$$$
SEAFOOD

✕**Playa Blanca.** On a white-sand beach shaded by coco palms, the dining area is sheltered by a large palapa. Understated coolness comes in shades of white on white—the gauzy fabric, the contemporary tableware, the modern chairs. Background chill-out music with a quickened pace completes the mood. Hedonistic detail emerges in the Balinese sun beds in the sand. Start with a perfectly executed cocktail—like a lime or mango daiquiri. The food is savvy but simple—fresh fish is a staple; opt for fried or grilled and choose a sauce. The orange-ginger glaze is lovely, as is the house-made salsa. A mixed grill could include calamari, mussels, shrimp, and fish. There's Caribbean lobster and on special occasions, sancocho, a traditional, hearty meat and vegetable stew. On alternate Thursdays and Sundays the DJ makes it a party. ⊠ *Playa Blanca, Punta Cana* ☎ *809/959–2714, Ext. 2233* ▭ *AE, MC, V.*

$$$
ASIAN FUSION

✕**Tau.** The highly attentive service and well-thought-out plates incorporating savory Asian fusion influences make this eight-table restaurant at the Sivory resort worth venturing out for, especially if you're staying in northern areas of the region, like Uvero Alto or Macao. The tuna tartare appetizer is consistently popular. You might opt for the chef's surprise selections, or go with the tasty Caribbean lobster tail for your main dish. A ginger-infused chocolate confection makes for a perfect closer. ⊠ *Sivory Resort & Spa, Uvero Alto* ☎ *809/333–0500* ⊕ *www.sivory-puntacana.com* ⌦ *Reservations essential* ▭ *AE, MC, V* ☾ *closed Mon.*

$$
STEAK

✕**Tony Roma's.** Sink your teeth into succulent ribs—imported from the United States—at this internationally renowned place for meat. Juicy baby backs and other types of ribs smothered in your choice of signature sauce (e.g., original, honey, smoke, and hot) head up the menu, which also includes steaks, seafood, chicken, burgers, and salads. For starters, the onion loaf—a giant conglomeration of onion rings deep-fried to a golden crisp—is another favorite. ⊠ *Palma Real Shopping Village, Suite 31, Bávaro* ☎ *809/552–8880* ▤ *AE, MC, V.*

WHERE TO STAY

With its sweet trifecta of pearl-sand beaches, pleasant climate, and palm trees, Punta Cana has no trouble enticing visitors. It has become the so-called Cancún of the Dominican Republic, and despite having more than 40,000 hotel rooms, the region's resorts are often filled to the brim. Even in the heart of hurricane season (late August through October), when you can usually get a room somewhere, booking far in advance is advisable for the best properties.

Most hotels in the region are clustered around Punta Cana and Bávaro, where more than 90% of the existing properties are all-inclusive. But development continues to press outward—northward to the more remote locations of Macao and Uvero Alto, and southward to the nearby Juanillo—and several of the newer offerings are ultraluxury resorts, not all-inclusives. Other high-end resorts have all-inclusive options designed for guests who might prefer the convenience of paying for everything at once, but who are not necessarily concerned with cost savings.

Playa Uvero Alto, the northernmost developed area of the region, has five resorts along its idyllic beach shaded by coconut groves. In its more remote setting, about 24 mi (39 km) from the airport, the area is less crowded than Punta Cana/Bávaro, but hotels still fill up quickly despite the longer trip to the airport. Traveling time to and from this area should improve markedly once the new "Tourist Boulevard" is completed; for now, newly paved roads shave some time off the trip and make traversing the area a much less bumpy endeavor.

Macao, which lies between Bávaro and Uvero Alto, is another charmed spot, and is the site of phased luxury residential and resort development along the beachfront at Rōco Ki. Although the acclaimed Nick Faldo-designed "Faldo Legacy" golf course has been open here since 2008, completion of the Westin Rōco Ki Beach & Golf Resort, the first of several hotels planned here, has been delayed repeatedly; the resort is now slated to open in 2011. Ownership of the entire complex is in flux at this writing.

All the resorts listed in this chapter are along the beachfront; however, not all rooms are right on the beach (a feature factored into the price). In many resorts you might face a several-minute walk or shuttle ride to the ocean, so choose your accommodations accordingly. Many resorts have spas attached.

FUTURE DEVELOPMENTS

With development mushrooming in and around Punta Cana, several resorts were still under construction or rebranding as this book was being written. At this writing, the Westin Rōco Ki Beach & Golf Resort is expected to open in fall 2011, after repeated delays. Moon Palace in Macao is expected to complete its transformation into a Hard Rock Hotel & Casino (1,800 rooms) sometime in late summer 2010.

A boutique-style hotel from NH Hoteles, a Spanish lodging brand, is under construction at Cap Cana, with an unspecified targeted completion date. All these hotels are expected to be major players in the area.

WHAT IT COSTS IN U.S. DOLLARS					
	¢	$	$$	$$$	$$$$
HOTELS*	under $80	$80–$150	$150–$250	$250–$350	over $350
HOTELS**	under $125	$125–$250	$250–$350	$350–$450	over $450

*EP, BP, CP **AI, FAP, MAP

Hotel prices are per night for a double room in high season, excluding 16% tax and 10% service charge. All-inclusive rates include tax.

4

PRIVATE VILLAS AND CONDOS

With its allure as a residential area growing, Punta Cana and the surrounding region have seen an ever-increasing number of villa and apartment enclaves marketed as second homes, vacation residences, or investments. Most of these enclaves have units for rent when the owners are not in residence.

Caletón Villas (⌂ *Cap Cana, Caletón Beach, Juanillo* ☎ *809/562-6725* ⊕ *www.capcana.com*). Nineteen elegant bungalows and villas, each uniquely appointed, comprise this luxury boutique rental complex within Cap Cana. Each dwelling has its own private terrace, with stunning views of the ocean at Caletón Beach and the Punta Espada golf course, and a full kitchen. Visitors have access to the exclusive Caletón Beach Club.

Palma Real Villas Golf & Country Club (⌂ *Cocotal Golf & Country Club, Bávaro* ☎ *809/730–6767, 809/221–1290 Ext. 5555, or 877/213–5002* ⊕ *www.palmarealvillas.com*), by Sol Meliá, is an upscale ownership community with several different styles of two- to four-bedroom villas and condominiums, all with membership privileges at the Cocotal Golf Course—including discounted greens fees and access to the clubhouse and golf academy. Also in the package are discounts and benefits at the Meliá Caribe Tropical Hotel and 24-hour security. The complex is a 20-minute drive from the airport and close to the Palma Real Shopping Village. A managed property-rental program is offered.

The **PuntaCana Estates** (⌂ *PuntaCana Resort & Club, Punta Cana* ☎ *809/959–7325* ⊕ *www.puntacana.com*) are composed of the Corales, Hacienda, and Arrecife enclaves, privately-owned, Dominican-style estates that blend elegant architecture with the inherent beauty of the natural environment. Within sublime surroundings that include a 5-mi stretch of pearly beach and skyscraping palm trees, homeowners in these private retreats enjoy top-notch amenities and services, including a private terminal at the Punta Cana International Airport, access to highly acclaimed golf courses designed by P. B. Dye and Tom Fazio, elite clubhouses, the mesmerizing Six Senses Spa, an ecological preserve with natural springs, a full-service marina, tennis courts, housekeeping and nanny services, and all of PuntaCana Resort's restaurants and facilities. Owners can rent out their homes through a managed property-rental

All-Inclusive: The Concept

All-inclusive resorts are the most common type of accommodations you'll find in Punta Cana. Here's a primer for anyone unfamiliar with this style of lodging.

Meals: At least one buffet restaurant serves breakfast, lunch, and dinner. Often, at least one, and usually more, à la carte specialty restaurant is included (e.g., Mexican, Italian, Japanese, Asian Fusion, and Dominican). A few restaurants such as premium steak houses might carry an extra charge. Snack bars will get you through the interim periods.

Beverages: Soft drinks, bottled water, alcoholic beverages (generally non-premium brands, whether domestic or international), and domestic beer are included, as well as a stocked minibar in all guest rooms. Some resorts even have liquor dispensers in the rooms.

Room Service: Policies vary. Where available, it may cost extra, have limited hours, or be an option only on upgraded packages.

Kids' Clubs: Most resorts have special kids' programs, and they are typically geared to ages 4–12; a few hotels stand out with offerings in an extended (or more limited) range. Babysitters cost extra.

Activities: Nonmotorized water sports are generally included. Some resorts include one diving lesson in the pool. Diving and motorized sports are extra. There's always a slew of arranged activities going on—usually by the pool or in a games area. These might include dance lessons, Spanish lessons, stretching, yoga, water aerobics, volleyball, or pool tournaments. Some places have extras like bowling, rock climbing, or a trapeze.

Animation Teams: These are the folks who enthusiastically run the activities and try to generate a buzz among guests.

Tips: Though usually included, additional tipping for good service is not uncommon and is highly appreciated. Carrying extra $1 bills comes in handy.

Gym & Spa: Use of the gym is included; personal trainers cost extra. Most resorts have a spa. Sometimes use of steam rooms, saunas, and hot tubs is included. Massages and other treatments cost extra.

Nightlife: Some resorts are renowned for a show that stands out; generally, non-esort guests can attend by purchasing a night pass. Entertainment usually rotates on a 7-day or 14-day cycle. Discos are standard; a few of the better ones are open to nonguests.

Casino: Many resorts have casinos with slot machines; some offer roulette and a few card tables with blackjack and assorted poker games. Texas Hold 'em tables are not in abundance.

Excursions: Off-site excursions are not included.

Medical Care: Care is available 24 hours at onsite clinics. Charges for doctor services and medications are not included. International health insurance is accepted, but you must have the appropriate coverage.

Bracelets: When you arrive, most resorts will band you with a bracelet that identifies you as a guest and indicates your package level.

Rōco Ki

Translated from the Taino language as "honoring the land," the multibillion-dollar development at Rōco Ki is a heavenly world set on the charmed Macao Beach. Its 2,700 acres on the East Coast enchant with dramatic cliffs, palm trees, mangroves, and jungle. The backdrop is like nature's equivalent of a laser light show: green vegetation, a turquoise sea, fuchsia flowers, blue sky, white sand. The blueprint for the 15-year phased development project maps out plans for posh hotels (seven to nine total), golf courses, a marina, a sports training complex, and various luxury housing, all exuding an easygoing affluence in an environment at peace with nature. The magnificent undertaking strives to achieve the perfect balance between low-density, low-environmental-impact design and high-end comfort. With buildings and villas spread out among lagoons, mangroves and coastline, and weaved around ample conservation areas teeming with wildlife, the development is conceived with respect toward preserving the natural habitat without stinting on the opulence.

First to go up was the championship 18-hole, Nick Faldo–designed course, with its striking 17th hole on a sculpted cliff, which opened in 2008. Also part of phase one are the Westin Rōco Ki hotel and branded villas, although their opening has been pushed back to 2011. The developers are working in cooperation with the government to preserve Taino artifacts unearthed during excavation at the Rōco Ki site. They will be displayed at a museum near the complex entrance; for now the artifacts are in storage in Santo Domingo.

program. Oscar de la Renta and Julio Iglesias, two of the three partners in the PuntaCana Resort & Club, as well as Mikhail Baryshnikov, have vacation homes in the Corales section.

Rōco Ki (✉ *Macao* ☏ *809/731–2800 or 888/476–2654* ⊕ *www.rocoki. com*) is a huge development project that includes villas, bungalows, and gigantic luxury estates, with either beach or jungle views. Some Westin-branded condos and villas, from studios to three-bedrooms, and in various stages of construction, are between the striking Nick Faldo–designed golf course and the Westin Rōco Ki Beach & Golf Resort. The project as a whole is targeted for completion in 2011. The architectural styles draw inspiration from Taino culture. The amenities, designed to meet the needs and desires of the most discerning residents, include room service, a concierge, and housekeeping. Rental plans will be available.

$$–$$$
ALL-INCLUSIVE
♻
🍴 **Barceló Bávaro Beach Resort.** On verdant grounds brushing up against a luscious beach, this expansive, always bustling complex is undergoing a major face-lift and redesign that will include the construction of a new clubhouse, meant to be the resort's dining and social hub. When complete by early 2011, the centerpiece Casa Club will showcase 10 restaurants, a new casino, a new disco, a spa, shops, a piano bar, a theater to seat 1,300 people, two large swimming pools, two lobbies, a game room, an Internet café, and a kids' club. There are now three distinct

New and Noteworthy Resorts

CLOSE UP

Two major resorts were in various stages of completion as this book was being written.

Hard Rock Hotel & Casino Punta Cana. The former Moon Palace, Hard Rock's first all-inclusive property, will be set on the spectacular Macao beach, pairing its famous brand with the latest hospitality trend in Punta Cana: delivering superior luxury in an all-inclusive. The 121-acre property will showcase the resort's main features, all composed to grand scale: one of the largest casinos in the Caribbean, with a high-stakes poker room, table games and slots, a VIP lounge, race and sports book; 65,000 square feet of meeting and conference facilities to accommodate groups of up to 2,800 people with various indoor and outdoor meeting options; the Rock Spa, a 68,000-square-foot facility with 48 spa treatment rooms; a 15,000-square-foot Body Rock fitness center; an Xtreme center with rock-climbing wall; a nightclub and 12 bars and lounges. And it wouldn't be a Hard Rock without the hallmark collection of music memorabilia on display. ⊠ Blvd. Turístico del Este 74, Km 28, Playa Macao ☎ 809/687–0000 ⊕ www.hardrockhotels.com ↝ 1,800 rooms ⚴ In-room: a/c, safe, refrigerator, DVD, Wi-Fi. In-hotel: 11 restaurants, room service, bars, golf course, tennis courts, pools, gym,

spa, beachfront, diving, water sports, bicycles, children's programs (ages 4–12), laundry facilities, laundry service, Internet terminal, Wi-Fi hotspot. ⊟ AE, D, DC, MC, V ⚏ AI.

Westin Rōco Ki Beach & Golf Resort. Rising up dramatically at the edge of a cliff that juts out into the sea, this grand Spanish Renaissance–style resort is visible from some beaches many miles farther south along the coast. At this writing, the resort was expected to open in 2011, the first instance of a true luxury hotel in Macao that's also not all-inclusive. Plans for the complex include not only the hotel but also Westin-branded condominiums and villas, seven restaurants, 24-hour room service, bars, a spa, tennis courts, a wedding gazebo, a marina, a gourmet market, and a conference center. The spectacular Nick Faldo–designed golf course, which already opened, is steps away, and guests here have special privileges. ⊠ Macao ☎ 954/624–1771 or 800/937–8461 ⊕ www.westin.com ⚴ In-room: safe, kitchen (some), refrigerator (some), Wi-Fi. In-hotel: 7 restaurants, room service, bars, golf course, tennis courts, pool, gym, spa, beachfront, water sports, children's programs (ages 3–12), laundry service, Internet terminal, Wi-Fi hotspot. ⊟ AE, D, DC, MC, V.

resorts to meet various budgets and preferences. The family-friendly **Barceló Bávaro Palace Deluxe**, with 1,119 rooms and 47 suites, is the top of the line. The **Barceló Bávaro Beach and Convention Center** is adults-only, and in addition to the dining options at the clubhouse, has its own buffet and a French restaurant, both of them only for its guests. The most economical option, the **Barceló Bávaro Casino** hotel, does not face the beach, and has no ocean views. It has 236 rooms. All resort guests get a half-price discount on greens fees at the 18-hole golf course, which sits amid lush vegetation. Among the diversions are minigolf,

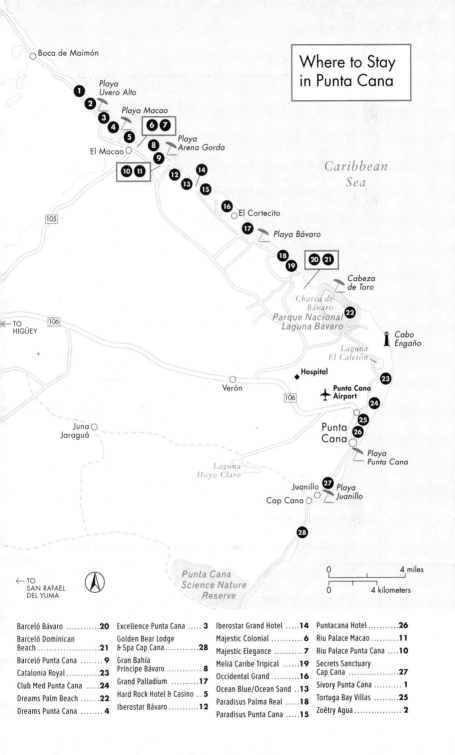

Where to Stay in Punta Cana

Playa Uvero Alto

Playa Macao

El Macao

Playa Arena Gorda

Caribbean Sea

105

El Cortecito

Playa Bávaro

Cabeza de Toro

Charca de Bávaro

Parque Nacional Laguna Bávaro

← TO HIGÜEY

106

Cabo Engaño

Lagunia El Caletón

◆ **Hospital**

Verón

Punta Cana Airport

106

Juna Jaraguá

Punta Cana

Playa Punta Cana

Laguna Hoyo Claro

Juanillo

Cap Cana

Playa Juanillo

← TO SAN RAFAEL DEL YUMA

Punta Cana Science Nature Reserve

| 0 | | 4 miles |
| 0 | | 4 kilometers |

Other Hotel Choices

Punta Cana is awash in hotels. Those recommended in this chapter are our favorites, but there are others worth considering, such as:

$ Bávaro Princess All Suites Resort, Spa & Casino (⊠ *Bávaro* ☎ *809/221–2311* ⊕ *www. princessbavaroresort.com*). Some aspects of this Princess (one of four hotels within this kingdom, with one adults-only) make you feel as if you're in a fairy tale. Take the infinity pool, for instance, with its palm-studded islets and swim-up bar; the graceful lobby with lush tropical plants and white pillars is another wonder. Upgrading to a higher-level package is worth the charge here. Be Queen for the Day and marry in the white-domed rotunda with the azure sea as your photographic backdrop—it's included in some packages. The Chopin international restaurant is a favorite among diners; there are also six others. There's a casino on the complex, as well as a popular disco.

$$ Hotel Grand Oasis Punta Cana (⊠ *Cabeza de Toro,Bávaro* ☎ *809/686–9898* ⊕ *www. hotelesoasis.com*) is a handsome, British-Caribbean style all-inclusive resort with 450 rooms along Cabeza de Toro beach. The lobby is bright and inviting,

with an ivory-toned, marbleized floor, buttercup-yellow walls and elegant, spiral staircases with iron railings. A similar palette is used in the guest rooms, which have four-poster beds, Jacuzzi tubs, and a balcony or terrace. There's a pretty pool, and the beach is fetching, with white sand and palm trees sprouting up everywhere. The Metamorphosis Spa, with a meditation garden, offers a sleek sanctuary; conversely, there's a fun casino and a disco. There's also a gym, tennis courts, and activities for the kids.

$$– $$$ NH Royal (⊠ *Avenida Alemania, El Cortecito,Bávaro* ☎ *809/285–6517* ⊕ *www.nh-hotels. com*). One of the newcomers to the all-inclusive scene in Bávaro, this adults-only resort has attractive, contemporary design elements, pretty grounds, and a dazzling beachfront. Where some guests say it falls short is in the two à la carte restaurants and buffet that are exclusively for guests here; there's also the option of six other restaurants at the neighboring sister resort, the family-friendly NH Real Arena, where Royal guests have access to all facilities. Within walking distance from shopping centers, restaurants, beach cafes, and golf, the location is tough to beat.

horseback riding, baseball and soccer fields, and a weekly movie night. A free shuttle transports guests around the complex. **Pros:** beautiful golf course; enormous range of entertainment and activities; fun production show. **Cons:** limited room-service hours; pool gets crowded and noisy; resort draws large conventions and groups. ⊠ *Carretera Bávaro, Bávaro* ☎ *809/686–5797* 🖷 *809/685–2590* ⊕ *www.barcelo. com* 🛏 *1,990 rooms, 941 junior suites, 55 suites* 🛎 *In-room: a/c, safe, refrigerator, Internet. In-hotel: 11 restaurants, bars, golf course, tennis courts, pools, gym, spa, beachfront, diving, water sports, children's programs (ages 4–12), laundry service, Internet terminal, Wi-Fi hotspot* 🖃 *AE, MC, V* ⏺*AI.*

$ ⬚ **Barceló Dominican Beach.** An exceptional value, this well managed
ALL-INCLUSIVE resort exudes appeal that rivals the higher-tier Barceló properties. Many
★ guest rooms are outfitted with pillow-top mattresses; all rooms have
balconies, cable TVs, irons and boards, safes, alarm clocks, and coffeemakers, and the minibar is restocked daily. The gym has all the
standard machines—treadmills, stair steppers, and stationary bikes—
and free weights to get (or keep) you in top form. The wonderful spa
looks out over the ocean, adding another dose of soothing to the mix
of treatments. The Japanese restaurant is often cited as a guest favorite,
and the Brazilian rodizio (rotisserie-grilled meat) restaurant also gets
praise. For a pick-me-up in the afternoon, the coffee bar is an ever-
popular retreat. Basketball, archery, dance lessons, and Spanish lessons
are among the full plate of daytime activities, and there's an Internet
center in case you want to keep in touch with the world beyond. For
nightly fun, three theaters feature a schedule of entertainment on a
14-day rotation; weekly beach parties, a casino, and a disco round
out the entertainment options. Wi-Fi is available in all rooms (still
uncommon in Punta Cana), although there is an extra charge. Discount golf rates are available for the Barceló Golf Bávaro course. Elite
Club packages are an option, with upgrades including private check-in
and checkout, 24-hour room service, free Internet access, and nightly
turndown. **Pros:** attention to detail; Wi-Fi throughout; great coffee bar.
Cons: beach parties can get loud; extra cost for Wi-Fi. ⊠ *P.O. Box
A-B 108, Bávaro* ☎ *809/221–0714 Ext. 1801* 🖷 *809/221–6991* ⊕ *www.
barcelo.com* 🖝 *732 rooms, 96 suites* ⚿ *In-room: a/c, safe, refrigerator,
Wi-Fi. In-hotel: 9 restaurants, room service (some), bars, tennis courts,
pools, gym, spa, beachfront, diving, water sports, bicycles, children's
programs (ages 4–12), laundry service, Internet terminal, Wi-Fi hotspot*
⊟ *AE, DC, MC, V* ⃝I *AI.*

$–$$ ⬚ **Barceló Punta Cana.** White Spanish-style buildings with large pillars
ALL-INCLUSIVE and red-tile roofs add to the spectacular vistas at this resort, where
🕭 from ocean-facing balconies you can see towering palms swaying in the
breeze on the sand. You might even spot acrobatic performances on the
trapeze near the beach, among the activities that make this resort fun
for the whole family. A rock-climbing wall, and, for the kids, a water
slide and trampoline are some others. If you choose the standard package, it's worth it to pay extra for the deluxe rooms in Buildings 1, 2,
and 3, which have sophisticated decor and are now nicer than some of
the costlier, but older, suites. But the Premium Club suites also include
upgraded amenities, such as a club room with bar and snacks, free
Internet access, and preferred restaurant reservations. The Japanese
and Dominican restaurants are top choices among the varied à la carte
options, and the Tex-Mex venue, on a veranda overlooking the beach,
deserves a blue ribbon for the good food and service. Golf packages
are available at nearby courses. One swimming pool caters to activity
seekers; a second is quiet. Two theaters and a large casino offer nighttime diversions, and the sports bar, with pool tables, backgammon,
chess, and other games, can keep you busy til 4 am. There's a separate game room devoted to teens. A basic wedding ceremony—with
cake, sparkling wine, and flowers—is included (upgrades are available).

Pros: separate "quiet" pool; helpful staff; trapeze. **Cons:** unrenovated room interiors are tired; uninspiring hallways; extra charge for room service. ⊠ *Carretera Macao, Playa Arena Gorda, Bávaro* 🕾 *809/476–7777* 🖷 *809/412–2288* ⊕ *www.barcelopuntacana.com* 🖙 *751 room, 47 suites* ⚙ *In-room: a/c, safe, refrigerator, Internet. In-hotel: 7 restaurants, room service, bars, tennis courts, pools, gym, spa, beachfront, diving, water sports, bicycles, children's programs (ages 4–12), Internet terminal, Wi-Fi hotspot* ⊟ *AE, DC, MC, V* ⭑◎⭑ *AI.*

$$$
ALL-INCLUSIVE
Fodor'sChoice
★

Catalonia Royal Resort. This adults-only haven is a perfect example of the trend toward including top-tier hospitality offerings in an all-inclusive package. The beautiful grounds set the tone, and are particularly stunning at night, when fountains dance in the sparkling pool against the glimmering lights of the surrounding buildings. In all rooms the amenities include a pillow menu, turndown service, 24-hour room service, and 26-inch flat-screen TVs. Duplex executive suites have floor-to-ceiling windows (with remote-controlled curtains) that open out onto a terrace with your own infinity plunge pool. At the main pool, you can lounge on land, or chill out at the swim-up bar with a piña colada or cold Presidente. Or get energized at the juice bar on the beach, where you can sip fresh-fruit concoctions on rope swings anchored in the sand. Besides the exclusive offerings at the Royal, guests here have access to all the restaurants and other facilities of its sister property, the family-friendly and more economical **Catalonia Bávaro Resort**, with 711 rooms and 7 suites (note: it's not a reciprocal privilege). Activity seekers might let go with crazy games on the beach or merengue or painting lessons. To get some quiet, there's a special zone along the pristine beach where no water sports are allowed. Outdoor hot and cold tubs near the spa are inviting for a quick dip. No reservations are needed for the restaurants, including the wonderful Cata Tapa, where magnificent sealife sculptures, funky lamps, and black marbleized tabletops accompany the Spanish food. Steps away are a 9-hole golf course run by the resort, plus a putting green. There's also an 18-hole course nearby, where guests get discount rates. Finally, the nightly entertainment, including a casino, disco, and an all-night pizzeria, ensure there's never a dull moment. **Pros:** all rooms have hammocks on terraces; 24-hour room service and turndown included. **Cons:** in-hotel sundries shop could be better stocked; loose fliers (rather than a printed pamphlet or booklet) to list hotel facilities and services seem sub-par. ⊠ *P.O. Box 8, Playa Bávaro* 🕾 *809/412-0011* ⊕ *www.hoteles-catalonia.com* 🖙 *247 rooms* ⚙ *In-room: a/c, safe, kitchen (some), refrigerator, DVD, Wi-Fi. In-hotel: 11 restaurants, room service, bars, golf course, tennis courts, pool, gym, spa, beachfront, diving, water sports, bicycles, laundry service, Internet terminal, Wi-Fi hotspot, parking (free), no kids under 18.* ⊟ *AE, D, DC, MC, V* ⭑◎⭑ *AI.*

$$–$$$
ALL-INCLUSIVE
★

Club Med Punta Cana. Whimsy and camaraderie are characteristic of this family-friendly resort, Punta Cana's original all-inclusive, which continues to attract many return visitors. Interactive parent-and-infant learning workshops are among the offerings at the Baby Club, one of only a few in the region catering to kids under four. At the teen center, a create-your-own-soda bar is a bubbling hit, and a skate park gives boarders a venue to show off those ollies and slides. The lively beach bar is a hotbed, by day and late night, with light fare served 'til 2 AM. The deluxe spa has 10 treatment rooms and oceanfront palapas for beach massages. The 200-person convention center is also on the seafront. As always, cheery staffers (called G.O.s, or "gracious organizers") do their best to spark things up, encouraging participation in everything from merengue lessons to circus programs to water aerobics. They go off-site too, accompanying guests on jungle excursions with zip lining. Day passes are available for $99, $103 by night, $125 for Friday's gala. **Pros:** inspiring, animated staff; themed weeks for music, dance, and sports; special events like Wine & Food Festival. **Cons:** limited dining options; Wi-Fi is expensive and only in public spaces; in-room Internet cables (free) in Tiara suites only. ⊠ *Provincia La Altagracia, apartado postal 106, Punta Cana* ☎ *809/686–5500 or 800/258–2633* ⊕ *www.clubmed. com* ➾ *553 rooms, 32 family suites* ⚭ *In-room: a/c, safe, refrigerator, Internet. In-hotel: 3 restaurants, bars, tennis courts, pools, gym, spa, beachfront, diving, water sports, children's programs (ages infant–17), laundry service, Internet terminal, Wi-Fi hotspot* ▭ *AE, MC, V* ⦿ *AI.*

$$$$ 🖭 **Dreams Palm Beach.** This glorious Dreams—a luxurious brand that's
ALL-INCLUSIVE   also family- and American-friendly, is perched on a gorgeous stretch of
   ⚙   beach with white-sugar sand. Despite all the water sports, it's active but not plagued by whistle-blowing animation boys. Two other highlights are that there are no mandatory wristbands and that no reservations are needed for à la carte restaurants. Supervised activities allow the kids to explore, and there are beepers to keep you in touch, especially handy with the teenagers, who hang out in their own Core Zone. Adults are freed up to indulge in the full-service spa. For a few pesos more you can be housed in the impressive oceanfront Preferred Club. **Pros:** excellent meeting group incentives; great fitness room with cardio training; no wristbands to identify guests. **Cons:** singles may feel left out with all the families; romantic couples may prefer an adults-only resort. ⊠ *P.O. Box 68, Cabeza de Toro, Bávaro* ☎ *809/552–6000; 866/237–3267* ⊕ *www. dreamsresorts.com* ➾ *325 rooms* ⚭ *In-room: a/c, safe, refrigerator, DVD, Internet (some), Wi-Fi (some). In-Hotel: 8 restaurants, tennis courts, pools, gym, spa, water sports, bicycles, children's programs (ages 3–17), laundry service, Internet, Wi-Fi hotspot* ▭ *AE, MC, V* ⦿ *AI.*

$$$ 🖭 **Dreams Punta Cana Resort & Spa.** The fun quotient runs high at this
ALL-INCLUSIVE   resort, which is especially good for families traveling with kids. In
   ⚙   the remote, pastoral setting vacationers can find everything under the
   ★   Caribbean sun, including a plethora of good à la carte restaurants, an exceptional buffet, 10 bars, and a large pool that winds around the grounds. Guests spend hours bopping around on rafts in the lazy-river pool, breaking to jump up to aqua aerobics, and rewarding themselves with a frosty piña colada at the adjacent beach bar. A deluxe swim-out room is really the high life. The Explorers Club (for kids ages 3–12) has activities that include sandcastle building, arts and crafts, and rock climbing. At their own Core Zone, teens have a good time. The all-around camaraderie appeals to wedding groups, singles, and friends, too. Dreams runs high-occupancy, but you'll find tranquillity in the lavish spa complex with its full water-therapy course of icy-cold to hot

pools, whirlpools, and showers. If you win big at the casino you may want to bump up to the Preferred Club. **Pros:** a beautiful, friendly, feel-good place; nightly entertainment is a cut above the others. **Cons:** you have to be early (or clever) to be guaranteed a raft in the pool; some service lapses; expensive Wi-Fi. ⊠ *Playa Uvero Alto* ☎ *809/682–0404 or 866/237–3267* ⊕ *www.dreamspuntacana.com.do* ⤣ *592 rooms, 28 suites* ♿ *In-room: a/c, safe, refrigerator, DVD, Wi-Fi. In-hotel: 7 restaurants, room service, bars, tennis courts, pool, gym, spa, beachfront, diving, water sports, bicycles, children's programs (ages 3–17), laundry service, Internet terminal, Wi-Fi hotspot.* ⊟ *AE, MC, V* ◎ *AI.*

\$\$\$\$
ALL-INCLUSIVE
Fodor's Choice
★

🏨 **Excellence Punta Cana.** A sumptuous lovers' lair, this adults-only all-inclusive is particularly appealing to honeymooners', wedding parties, and couples celebrating anniversaries. With romance emanating from every corner, the resort attracts a clientele that's mostly over 30, and quite a few couples well into their 70s and beyond. The name "Excellence" fits as well as a groom's tuxedo. The open-air, tropical lobby looks onto grounds enveloped by a palm grove, where wedding ceremonies (more than 250 each year) are held at the dainty gazebo or on the heavenly beach. A gorgeous spa—with a Zen fountain, indulgent massages and other well-given treatments, plus hot-and-cold water tubs—attends to soothing body and mind. Adorned with light pink–painted wood furnishings, all the spacious suites have double Jacuzzis (some with a second outdoors); most have four-poster king beds with a choice of pillows, robes and slippers, turndown service, a coffeemaker, scale, and DVD player. Excellence Club rooms have perks such as concierge service and Bulgari amenities; swim-out suites open directly onto the lazy-river pool that snakes around the grounds. Honeymooners may appreciate round-the-clock room service, but if you're inclined to step out, there's a full range of water sports and other activities to choose from, including guided horseback rides (moonlight tours cost extra). No reservations are required at any of the restaurants, so walk in for dinner where you want—good options include the French and Asian fusion restaurants. Afterwards, check out the nightly entertainment (the Michael Jackson Show is very popular), then dance the night away at the disco or try your luck at the casino, which is open only to hotel guests. **Pros:** adults-only getaway; gorgeous setting for weddings; waiter service at pool and beach. **Cons:** distant from shopping, other restaurants, and nightlife; isolating for singles. ⊠ *Playa Uvero Alto* ☎ *809/685–9880* ⊕ *www.excellence-resorts.com* ⤣ *452 suites* ♿ *In-room: a/c, safe, refrigerator, DVD. In-hotel: 8 restaurants, bars, tennis courts, pools, gym, spa, beachfront, diving, water sports, bicycles, laundry service, Internet terminal, Wi-Fi hotspot* ⊟ *AE, DC, MC, V* ◎ *AI.*

\$\$\$\$
RESORT

🏨 **Golden Bear Lodge & Spa Cap Cana.** A haven for golf enthusiasts, this new resort affords panoramic views of Las Iguanas, the second Jack Nicklaus-designed golf course at Cap Cana, and the dazzling Caribbean in the background. Large 1- or 2-bedroom villas with dining rooms and kitchens (with dishwasher, microwave, and tableware) are suitable for relaxing with family or entertaining. Other niceties include robes and slippers, nightly turndown service, flat-screen TVs, and a washer/dryer. Two porches, one with patio furniture and the other with an outdoor

Jacuzzi, are enticing spots to relax. There's also an indoor Jacuzzi, so an evening chill or rain is never a deterrent. Although there's a pool on the grounds, the beach itself is a 10-minute drive away, within the Cap Cana grounds. The restaurants, shops, and facilities of the Cap Cana marina are also a hike, but a free shuttle takes guests anywhere within the complex. Guests can count on attentive service from a staff that is eager to be helpful. The two on-site restaurants do a commendable job with the food and service. In addition, there are a variety of fine-dining options throughout the Cap Cana complex, including the acclaimed Blue Marlin *(see above)* seafood restaurant, a steak house on the grounds of Secrets Sanctuary, and Il Cappuccino (also above) at the marina. The lodge's grounds are meticulously kept, but some guests say noise from ongoing construction at Cap Cana is a problem. There's also a beauty salon on-site, a full-service spa, and a golf library. Discounted golf rates are available to guests, for now at Punta Espada, and soon, too, at Las Iguanas, which is slated to open by early 2011. **Pros:** highly attentive service; exceptional golf; palatial villas with indoor and outdoor Jacuzzis. **Cons:** sundries shop, golf course, and some services not yet finished; beach not in walking distance. ☒ *Cap Cana, Playa Juanillo* ☎ *809/469–7425* ⊕ *www.ZoetryResorts.com* ↷ *85 villas managed by AMResorts (140 apartments total)* ☖ *In-room: a/c, safe, kitchen, refrigerator, DVD, Internet. In-hotel: 2 restaurants, room service, bar, golf course, tennis courts, pool, gym, spa, bicycles, laundry facilities, laundry service, Internet terminal, Wi-Fi hotspot, parking (free).* ▭ *AE, D, DC, MC, V* ⦿⧉ *EP.*

$$
ALL-INCLUSIVE
★
♻

⌸ **Gran Bahía Príncipe Resort.** The four hotels within this sprawling complex each have their own reception, well-appointed lobby, and buffet restaurants, but what they have in common are the superb, dependable, multilingual staff, meticulous grounds, and a simulated Caribbean village that's the social and commercial hub. There you'll find shops, à la carte restaurants, a karaoke/piano bar, a casino, pool tables, and a disco. On this huge property, which has a capacity of 6,500 guests, most visitors have to be shuttled to the beach and the buffet. Standard options are **Bahía Príncipe Punta Cana**, with 780 junior suites, and the **Bahía Príncipe Bávaro**, with 792 junior suites. Pricier options, part of the high-end "Don Pablo Collection," are the newest hotel, **Bahía Príncipe Esmeralda**, where guests have access to its own pool, restaurant, and other amenities; or the adults-only **Bahía Príncipe Ambar**, which opened in 2009, also with exclusive restaurants and a pool and other amenities, such as butler service on request, free Wi-Fi on the property, and robes and slippers in your room. Wherever you lay your head to rest (and pillow menus are available), there are plenty of choices for food and fun to satisfy the whole family, as well as for couples. All rooms are outfitted with Jacuzzi tubs, satellite TV, and a balcony or terrace. You can request a sea view if you opt for any of the premium club packages, which also offer perks such as a concierge, private check-in, 24-hour room service, and upgraded amenities. Discounted rates for golf are available at the Punta Blanca course next door. Or pamper yourself at the spa, which sometimes employs ingredients like mango or chocolate. **Pros:** polished, multilingual staff; golf nearby;

good upgrade packages. **Cons:** two of the four hotels require a shuttle to reach the beach; limited access to à la carte restaurants, no in-room Internet access, extra charge for use of in-room safe in the standard hotels. *Carretera Arena Gorda–Macao* ⊠ *Playa Arena Gorda, Bávaro* ☎ *809/552–1444* ⊕ *www.bahia-principe.com* ⇥ *2,844 junior suites, 4 hotels* ⟳ *In-room: a/c, safe, refrigerator. In-hotel: 12 restaurants, bars, pools, gym, spa, beachfront, water sports, children's programs (ages 4–12, except in adults-only Ambar), laundry service, Internet terminal, Wi-Fi hotspot* ⊟ *AE, MC, V* ⵜⵀⵍ *AI./></R>*

$$$–$$$$
ALL-INCLUSIVE
☾
★

⌗ **Grand Palladium Resort Spa & Casino.** Holding four resorts laid out in clusters of buildings amid tropical palm and coconut trees, with restaurants, bars and shops scattered throughout, the well-kept grounds feel like a beachside village. In a concession to the sprawl, there's even a train that makes the rounds throughout the property until 2 AM. (Fortunately, everything is well marked, and there are maps in key spots to keep you on track.) Three of the sister hotels, **Grand Palladium Bávaro** (636 rooms), **Grand Palladium Punta Cana** (451 rooms), and **Grand Palladium Palace** (364 rooms) share each other's facilities. Guests at the top-tier, adults-only **Royal Suites Turquesa** (372 suites) have access to all the main complex facilities, as well as to their own exclusive restaurant and other offerings. The Royal Suites are closest to the ocean, with two clusters of villas, each with its own private pool and some swim-out suites. All rooms in the four resorts have hydromassage tubs, coffeemakers, alarm clocks with MP3 stations, and irons with ironing boards; pillow menus are available for an extra charge. Bilevel loft suites are an option at the Palace. Around-the-clock, there's something to eat or drink. The sports bar near the disco serves pizza and snacks all night long. Also noteworthy are the friendly and attentive staff and management. At the popular Japanese restaurant, diners can opt for a communal table and watch a chef prepare their meal. The Brazilian rotisserie-grilled-meat restaurant is a favorite among carnivores. After dinner, nightly entertainment (the Michael Jackson tribute performance is especially popular) at one of two theaters on-site is the typical stopover before hitting the disco or casino. A coral reef near the shore makes for exceptional snorkeling and diving. There's also a minigolf course, soccer fields, and a full plate of organized activities. The kids' club includes a dining room and video game room, and a separate teens' club has specialized activities and a sports program. The soothing spa is a top-notch operation. A brand-new convention center in the works is sure to attract a larger segment of the business meetings and conference market. The clientele is predominantly European, with Canadians close behind. But the resort is poised for the U.S. market to grow with the addition of the conference facilities and the latest upgraded options. **Pros:** excellent offshore snorkeling; rooms are quiet, because far removed from disco and other activity centers; good specialty restaurants; nice spa. **Cons:** few rooms have ocean view; no room service or Internet access available in standard rooms, minibar restocked three times per week. ⊠ *Carretera El Cortecito,El Cortecito, Bávaro* ☎ *809/221–8149 (Bávaro); 221-0719 (Punta Cana, Palace & Royal Suites Turquesa)* 🖨 *809/221–8150 (Bávaro); 809/221-0819*

(Palace & Royal Suites Turquesa) ⊕ *www.fiesta-hotels.com* ⇋ *1,823 rooms* ⚫ *In-room: a/c, safe, refrigerator Wi-Fi (some). In-hotel: 13 restaurants, bars, tennis courts, pools, gym, spa, beachfront, diving, water sports, children's programs (ages 4–12; 13–17), laundry service, Internet terminals, Wi-Fi hotspot* ▤ *AE, DC, MC, V* ⏇ *AI.*

$$
ALL-INCLUSIVE
☾

▦ **Iberostar Bávaro Resort.** Like its two sister resorts, this Spanish entry has panache, evidenced in its lobby, an artistic showpiece. It's one of the more desirable Punta Cana properties, though not one of the newest, and a good value. The dramatic public spaces lead into grounds crisscrossed with lagoons and then broad, beautifully maintained whitesand beach. Although rooms don't compare with the public spaces of the three hotels in the complex, the Bávaro's are the sweetest (and most expensive), with a separate sitting area. True to Iberostar's emphasis on quality food and beverages, there are 11 restaurants, with a variety of cuisines, including Cajun and high-end gourmet. The shows are better than average, with house dancers, a band, and vocalists. The Iberostar Punta Cana and Iberostar Dominicana share facilities in the complex, but only guests at the more expensiveBávaro can dine at restaurants there. **Pros:** variety of good dining options; fun entertainment; dramatic lobby and grounds. **Cons:** not good for couples; no Internet access in rooms. ✉ *Bávaro* ☏ *809/221–6500 or 888/923–2722* 🖷 *809/688–6186* ⊕ *www.iberostar.com* ⇋ *590 rooms, 8 apartments* ⚫ *In-room: a/c, safe, refrigerator. In-hotel: 11 restaurants, room service, bars, tennis courts, pool, gym, spa, beachfront, diving, water sports, children's programs (ages 4–12), laundry service, Internet terminal, Wi-Fi* ▤ *AE, MC, V* ⏇ *AI.*

$$$$
ALL-INCLUSIVE
★

▦ **Iberostar Grand Hotel.** Iberostar's first resort just for those 18 and over is a knockout. The jaw dropping begins in the glamorous lobby. The suites are elegant, with contemporary lighting, island photos hanging on the walls, and juices and premium liquor in the minibar; the Club suites offer whirlpools on the balconies and vistas of the Caribbean. But what you won't forget are the dance club, housed in a replica of a Spanish galleon; the glorious two-story spa with a gym and beauty salon; the sea views; the pool complex at the stunning beach with Balinese beds for all; and La Scala Theater with crimson velvet, classy glitz, and deep cushy seats. **Pros:** impressive collection of designer restaurants with outstanding cuisine; great for honeymoons. **Cons:** no in-room Internet, and connection in public areas is spotty. *Playa Bávaro* ☏ *809/221–6500, 888/774–0040* ⊕ *iberostar.com* ⇋ *260 suites, 13 grand suites, 1 presidential* ⚫ *In-room: a/c, safe, refrigerator, DVD. In-hotel: 5 restaurants, golf course, tennis courts, pools, gym, spa, bicycle, laundry service, Internet, Wi-Fi hotspot, parking free, no kids under 18.* ▤ *AE, MC, V* ⏇ *AI.*

$$–$$$
ALL-INCLUSIVE
☾

▦ **Majestic Colonial.** In the roomy quarters here the special touches include jetted tubs, bathrobes and slippers, a furnished balcony or terrace, and satellite TV. A special room-service closet ensures your privacy when you order in (room service, however, costs extra). But with so many choices outside your room, you might not spend much time there. The grounds are punctuated with red and pink *coralillo doble* flowers lining cobblestone walkways. Nine bars, including a sports bar, pool, and beach bars, and a piano bar, accommodate drastic mood swings and engender bonhomie among guests. You'll find premium liquors in the mix of what's served at the lower lobby bar. Caribbean Street, the commercial center shared with the Majestic Elegance resort, is where you can get fitted out with a new look at the tattoo or hair-braiding parlors before hitting the nightly show (the Michael Jackson show gets raves), the disco, or the casino. By day, you can take aerobics or dance lessons, or play basketball, pool, or Ping-Pong. For the kids, there's a 9-to-5 club with plenty to keep them occupied, whether outdoor activities or indoor games, including Nintendo. Golfers get special rates at the nearby Punta Blanca course. Free wedding packages are available. **Pros:** room-service closet for privacy; some suites have outdoor Jacuzzis; great Michael Jackson show. **Cons:** two-beer daily limit in minibar; no coffeemaker in standard rooms. ⊠ *Arena Gorda, Bávaro* ☎ *809/221–9898* 🖷 *809/552–9995* ⊕ *www.majesticcolonial.com* 🛏 *641 rooms, 17 suites* ⚴ *In-room: a/c, safe, DVD (some), Internet. In-hotel: 8 restaurants, room service, bars, tennis courts, pool, gym, spa, beachfront, diving, water sports, children's programs (ages 3–14), laundry service, Internet terminal, Wi-Fi hotspot* ▭ *AE, D, MC, V* ⦿ *AI.*

$$$
ALL-INCLUSIVE
★

🖭 **Majestic Elegance.** This regal resort's grandeur is well suited to the wedding market, which it serves with both a white wedding gazebo and a Catholic church on-site; ask about free honeymoon packages. The property also targets meetings and conventions. Its smallest room is a junior suite; there's also a premium, adults-only option, the Elegance Club, which comes with free Wi-Fi, private pools, and lounges. At the fitness center there's spinning, Pilates, yoga, and cardio. Musicians perform in the plaza, and by night there are professional shows in the theater. The Asian restaurant features a full sushi bar; the Italian restaurant hosts wine tastings ($30). There's a splendid new spa, with Turkish baths, hydrotherapy, and a full menu of massage treatments. Guests get one round of complimentary golf. **Pros:** animation staff is nonintrusive; premium liquors at all bars and à la carte restaurants **Cons:** large size can make it impersonal; buffeteria lacks personality. ⊠ *Arena Gorda, Bávaro* ☎ *809/221–9898* ⊕ *www.majestic-resorts.com* 🛏 *537 junior suites, 59 suites* ⚴ *In-room: a/c, safe, refrigerator, Internet. In-hotel: 6 restaurants, tennis courts, pools, gym, spa, children's programs (ages 3–14), laundry service. Internet, Wi-Fi hotspot, parking (free)* ▭ *AE, MC, V* ⦿ *AI.*

$–$$
ALL-INCLUSIVE
☾
★

🖭 **Meliá Caribe Tropical.** Impressive grounds, inviting lobbies in the twin hotels that make up the complex, and eye-catching adornments are hallmarks of this enormously popular, American-friendly resort. First-rate meeting and banquet facilities make this an ideal choice for conventions and weddings, which account for most of the business here. Because it's a long walk to the beach from many rooms, most guests choose to hop a ride on the train that circles the complex to get to the beach. For an extra $70 per night you can bump up to the VIP Royal Service, which gets you a master suite with butler service, a pillow menu, room service, beer added to the minibar selections (booze isn't stocked in the standard rooms), a stunning pool with a "Grecian ruin," and a private beach area with Balinese sun beds. The so-called Roman Suites near the beach have terraces with outdoor Jacuzzis and are the best option for those who don't want to ride the shuttle to get to the ocean. Guests often cite the Japanese restaurant as a favorite among the many restaurants, but the Market Place buffet is also a standout. At least one round of golf is included at the adjacent Cocotal Golf Club, and you get preferred tee times. The Flintstone-themed kids' clubs are a hit, with an adventure park and programs for infants to tweens. One extra-special activity for the kids is overnight camping on the lawn, complete with tents, bonfires, hot dogs, and ghost stories. A unique program in which guests can plant coconut, cacao, and other trees throughout the grounds is one feature contributing to the resort's green designation. Teens have their own stuff to do, including graffiti workshops and off-site excursions. **Pros:** adjacent to Palma Real Shopping Village; outstanding meeting and banquet facilities; close to golf course. **Cons:** most rooms far from the beach; extra charge for use of in-room safe; no booze in the minibar of standard rooms. ⊠ *Bávaro* ☎ *809/221–1290 or 800/336–3542* ⊕ *www.solmelia.com* ⇴ *1,200 junior suites* ⌂ *In-room: a/c, safe, refrigerator, Internet, Wi-Fi (some). In-hotel: 13 restaurants (including one only for Royal Service), room service, bars, golf course, tennis courts, pools, gym, spa, beachfront, water sports, children's programs (ages 4 months–17), laundry service, Internet terminal, Wi-Fi hotspot* ▭ *AE, MC, V* ⵏⵎⵍ *AI.*

$$$–$$$$
ALL-INCLUSIVE
☾
★

🏨 **Occidental Grand Punta Cana.** Plenty of choices for food and fun at this gigantic resort are likely to impress both families and night owls. Most of the tastefully designed, spacious rooms (all of which have a balcony or terrace) got brand-new furnishings in 2008. A graduated pool—one of the largest in Punta Cana—winds through the handsome grounds, with a swim-up bar that's a hub of activity; a separate "quiet" pool has no activities nearby, and with so many things going on all day, you may want to escape from time to time. The activity-packed children's programs include a minidisco every evening, special entertainment for the kids, painting, family games, and theme parties. An ever-popular steak house, a Chinese restaurant, and a sports bar serving fast food are among the dining options. The disco, Mangú, open to nonguests, draws crowds until the early hours. The nightly show rotates on a seven-day cycle. Royal Club guests have their own section of beach, private check-in, a private lounge, free Internet access, and an exclusive à la carte restaurant in a air-conditioned space overlooking the beach. **Pros:** excellent nightlife; late-night pizzeria; fun for whole family. **Cons:** no wheelchair-accessible rooms; no room service for standard rooms. ⊠ *Calle Friusa, Bávaro* ☎ *809/221–8787* ⊕ *www.occidentalhotels.com* ⇴ *840 rooms, 25 suites* ⌂ *In-room: a/c, safe, refrigerator. In-hotel: 9 restaurants, room service (some), bars, tennis courts, pools, gym, spa, beachfront, diving, water sports, children's programs (ages 4–12), laundry service, Internet terminal, Wi-Fi hotspot* ▭ *AE, D, MC, V* ⵏⵎⵍ *AI.*

$$
ALL-INCLUSIVE
★

🏨 **Ocean Blue/Ocean Sand Golf & Beach Resort.** Designed like a small town, with restaurants, shops, and nightlife concentrated near a central public square, this charming resort exceeds expectations on many fronts, making it a great value in its moderate price range. A free trolley crosses the lovely, expansive grounds, which are especially pretty at night. All rooms have a balcony or patio, but you pay extra to be near the exquisite beach; some room interiors could use a face-lift. Upgrades to premium suites, which have oversize marble bathrooms, Jacuzzi tubs, 24-hour room service, free in-room Wi-Fi, and a VIP lounge, are worth the extra cost of about $25 per person/per night in high season. Honeymoon suites are delightful, with their breezy, romantic decor, second-level Jacuzzi and outdoor shower (private, but with a view of the beach). The pool is divided into two sections, one designated for activities and the other for relaxation. The food and number of options at the main buffet are exceptional, compared with others in the region. The resort's authentic Dominican restaurant is modeled after a traditional local home, but if you're craving Americana with a side of fries, try the retro Route 66 diner. Mike's Coffee Shop serves made-to-order frozen coffees and other hot and cold java drinks and herbal teas. An outstanding new club for teens will keep them occupied for hours on end with six Wii stations, pool, board games, movies, and their own disco. Guests pay reduced rates at the White Sands Golf Course; the resort itself has a bowling alley and casino. Service everywhere is prompt and friendly, and there's free Wi-Fi for all guests in the lobby. Good conference facilities have attracted big companies like Coca-Cola and Sprint. The resort is transitioning to become an almost entirely no-smoking property, with only a few smoking rooms allowed. **Pros:** noteworthy buffet; Mike's Coffee Shop; bowling alley; teen center. **Cons:** expensive extra charges for in-room Wi-Fi; some drab interiors. ⊠ *Playa Arena Gorda, Bávaro* ☎ *809/476–2326* ⊕ *www.oceanhotels.net* ⇱ *708 junior suites* ⚫ *In-room: a/c, safe, refrigerator, Wi-Fi. In-hotel: 9 restaurants, bars, golf, tennis courts, pools, gym, spa, beachfront, diving, water sports, bicycles, children's programs (ages 4–12; teen center, 13–17), laundry service, Internet terminals, Wi-Fi hotspot* ⊟ *AE, MC, V* ¶⊙¶ *AI.*

$$$$
ALL-INCLUSIVE
☾
Fodor's Choice
★

☷ **Paradisus Palma Real Resort.** A member of the Leading Hotels of the World, this luxury all-inclusive is a visual showstopper. The average suite, with flat-screen TV, CD player, balcony or terrace, and semi-open marble bathroom with jet showers and a Jacuzzi for two, is extraordinary. You won't need to upgrade, but if you choose the adults-only Royal Service, you'll get a personal butler, private check-in, a lounge with daytime snacks and evening cocktails (with premium liquors), and customized turndown service. Balinese sun beds—some with thatched roofs—are cozy for lounging beside the glorious pool. There's also the Reserve, a private self-contained group of 190 luxurious suites in the interior of the property. Staying here comes with even more resort amenities, including exclusive pools, separate check-in and checkout, and dedicated concierge service. The optional, signature family-concierge plan, only at The Reserve, includes lavish attention for kids, who get their own check-in, welcome backpacks full of kids' amenities and treats, and mini-size robes and slippers. A remarkable Kid's Zone at The Reserve is for those 13 and under. The only drawback of the luxury enclave is that you must take a shuttle to the private beach. The resort's restaurants are situated around a central plaza and are opulently decorated, though in some cases the decor may outshine the food, as with the Mediterranean room. Gabi Beach restaurant, only for guests of the assorted VIP options, with its international fusion cuisine and impressive contemporary presentation, is exceptional. The Asian-inspired YHI Spa has lagoons, boardwalks, and a hushed serenity. Its staff is to be applauded for service, professionalism, and skill. Greens fees at the nearby Cocotal Golf Course are included (though charges apply for carts, etc.), but nongolfers may be won over by horseback-riding or biking excursions. **Pros:** personalized attention; enticing and professional spa; free golf. **Cons:** Internet access costs extra; service can be sketchy even within the Royal level; the restaurants and nightlife are far from the rooms and there is no shuttle service; no beachfront or sea views at The Reserve. ⊠ *Bávaro* ☎ *809/688–5000 or 800/688–5000* ⊕ *www. paradisuspalmareal.travel or www.paradisuspalmareal.solmelia.com* ⤳ *554 suites* ⚹ *In-room: a/c, safe, refrigerator, DVD, Internet. In-hotel: 7 restaurants, room service, bars, tennis courts, pools, gym, spa, beachfront, diving, water sports, bicycles, children's programs (ages 5–12 or 1–12 in The Reserve), Wi-Fi hotspot* ⊟ *AE, D, DC, MC, V* ⑩ *AI.*

$$$
ALL-INCLUSIVE
☾

⛨ **Paradisus Punta Cana.** Big-league improvements have been made in recent years at this seasoned tropical getaway, as it has struggled to keep pace with the newer competition. One addition is The Reserve, a family-friendly resort within the resort, with 174 suites, separate pools, and first-rate amenities that include an exclusive lounge and private concierge service. Within the main resort there's an adults-only Royal suites option for upgraded privileges, including access to the exclusive Gabi Club restaurant, which looks as good as the fusion food served here. On the main grounds, the pool complex is like a Hollywood set, with Balinese sun beds and sculptures spouting water; the beach is alluring. An full dozen restaurants—few all-inclusives in Punta Cana offer so many—mean that you'll never tire of the options. You can show your more gregarious side at the karaoke bar—one of the more convivial spots to mingle—before retreating to your room, where 24-hour room service is available. There's a nightly show and a casino. A batting cage, a rock-climbing wall, and an archery range make up an action park. Or you can head for the links: unlimited greens fees are included at the Cocotal Golf Course. **Pros:** some impressive architecture and décor; management has service down pat; The Reserve provides ultra-luxury, family-style. **Cons:** not for solo travelers; older rooms show signs of wear; dining room can be noisy. ⊠ *Bávaro* ☎ *809/687–9923* ⊕ *www.paradisuspuntacana.solmelia.com* ⤳ *509 suites, 80 Royal Service suites, 174 Reserve suites* ⚹ *In-room: a/c, safe, refrigerator, Wi-Fi. In-hotel: 12 restaurants, room service, bars, golf course, tennis courts, pool, gym, spa, beachfront, diving, water sports, bicycles, children's programs (ages 5–12), laundry service, Internet terminal, Wi-Fi hotspot* ⊟ *AE, D, DC, MC, V* ⑩ *AI.*

$–$$
ALL-INCLUSIVE
☾
★

⛨ **Puntacana Hotel.** A plethora of amenities—not to mention meticulously kept grounds and world-class golf—await guests at this charismatic resort, which spearheaded the area's tourism industry and has since kept pace with the times. Innovations and renovations consistently delight the clientele, who can rely on caring service from the attentive staff (many long-term). All rooms, with dark-wood furnishings and Frette linens, have a balcony or terrace. Though guest rooms here are more simply decked out than at its high-end sister, Tortuga Bay Villas (and priced that way), the shared access to all facilities of PuntaCana Resort & Club make the Puntacana Hotel a good value. Specialty restaurants are decorated with chic detail, as in Cocoloba, with the incomparable touch of Oscar de la Renta; La Yola, at the marina, where you can eat sophisticated seafood options; and La Choza, the feet-in-the-sand beach restaurant, dressed up in white draped fabric and Bali beds for a casually elegant lunch. At the Six Senses Spa the treatments might use lemongrass, aloe vera, or locally grown tropical fruit. Zipping along the shore paths in a rented golf cart is an enjoyable way to get where you're going on the grounds, where you can explore hiking trails, swim at a freshwater spring, or visit the petting zoo. There is also a shuttle that can take you throughout the resort. Kids' club activities include stretching classes, crafts, minibowling, Nintendo, Spanish lessons, and pony rides. Full trail rides, for kids and adults, are also available at the stables. Beachfront family casitas are equipped with video baby monitors. In the nearby Punta Cana Village you'll find a Portuguese restaurant, a much-adored bar, an art gallery, bowling lanes, and more shops. Meal plans are available. **Pros:** expansive and beautiful grounds; spectacular golf and spa; one of the area's most gorgeous beaches. **Cons:** limited nightlife on-site; alienating for solo travelers. ⊠ *Punta-Cana Resort & Club, Punta Cana* ☎ *809/959–2262 or 888/442–2262* ⊕ *www.puntacana.com* ➱ *175 rooms, 16 junior suites, 11 suites, 38 casitas* ⌂ *In-room: a/c, safe, refrigerator (some). In-hotel: 9 restaurants, bars, golf courses, tennis courts, pools, gym, spa, beachfront, diving, water sports, bicycles, children's programs (ages 4–12), laundry service, Internet terminal, Wi-Fi hotspot* ⊟ *AE, MC, V* ⊺⊙⏐ *BP.*

$$–$$$
ALL-INCLUSIVE

⛱ **Riu Palace Macao.** A beautiful fountain beckons you into the pool at the heart of this resort, one of the prettiest spots in the sprawling Riu complex of five hotels. Victorian architecture with Caribbean touches sets a sophisticated tone for this three-story building, matched by the room decor of elegant dark-wood furnishings and crisp white walls. Nightly turn-down, 24-hour room service, and premium liquors in the in-room dispensers set this hotel apart from the three more basic sister properties with which it shares facilities, and bring it closer to the top-of-the-line Riu Palace Punta Cana. (The Riu ClubHotel Bambu reopened in June 2010 after major renovations; the Bambu hosts the main kids' club for the complex. The Riu Taino remains closed at this writing for a complete makeover, with no reopening date yet scheduled.) Waiter service is an option at the beach and the pool, so you can kick back and keep the Banana Mamas coming. The Jacuzzi suites are roomy and comfy, giving extra living space, two satellite TVs, and two balconies, plus a view of the beach and its towering palms. Splurge for a third-floor suite, with its indulgent rooftop Jacuzzi enclosed in a white cupola. Sometimes the resort's gardeners will come around with fresh coconuts and offer to prepare them for guests on the spot. There's a personal touch to buffet dining at the resort: the same table will be reserved for your party throughout your stay, so you never have to scrounge for a place to sit. À la carte options were recently elevated to a higher level with the addition of the chic Cristal restaurant, which sits on a wooden pier over the ocean and has an international fusion menu. The casino is in this hotel, and is open only to guests of the Riu resorts. It's a short stroll to the complex's shops on Caribbean Street and the popular Pacha disco. **Pros:** great Jacuzzi suites; lovely waterfront Cristal restaurant; near casino. **Cons:** limited beach views; dull hallways; only ATM is at main security gate, a long walk from the resort. ✉ *Playa Arena Gorda, Bávaro* ☎ *809/221–7171* 📠 *809/468-4645* ⊕ *www.riu.com* 🛏 *328 rooms, 36 suites* ♿ *In-room: a/c, safe, refrigerator. In-hotel: 5 restaurants, bars, tennis courts, pools, gym, spa, beachfront, water sports, laundry service, Internet terminal, Wi-Fi hotspot* ▭ *AE, MC, V* ⧠⊙⧠ *AI.*

$$–$$$
ALL-INCLUSIVE
★

⧠ **Riu Palace Punta Cana.** On a moonlit night this megaresort decorated with Arabian-style domes looks like a fairy-tale palace. A grand staircase winds up to the vast, dazzling lobby, which aspires to opulence with a crystal chandelier, replicas of Rubens paintings, and faux-gold everything. The wrought-iron lobby bar with its occasional piano player are both admirable. Another plus is the Wi-Fi there; the only other area with it is the noisy sports bar. The long-and-wide junior suites are simple but attractive: with dark wood against sunny yellow walls, it's shades of Old Havana. Each has a jetted bath and a terrace (but not necessarily a sea view), flat-screen TV, coffeemaker, and lots of liquor. At the buffeteria, where the options are flavorful and wide-ranging, the same table will be reserved for your party for the length of your stay, lending a personal touch. Don't be surprised if the managers know who you are. The buffet outshines some of the à la carte options, among which the Brazilian restaurant is a standout. In the pool a lively swim-up bar, four Jacuzzis and semisubmerged lounge chairs add panache; here or at the beach you can have your Coco Locos or other refreshments delivered by a waiter. Guests here, who tend to be over 40, and often in their 50s and 60s, have access to all facilities within the Riu complex, including free admission to the casino at Riu Palace Macao (where the alcoholic beverages are included, and there's a free nightly shuttle to get there). Riu guests also get discounts at the nearby Cocotal Golf Course. **Pros:** the 24-hour room service; the grand hotel elements. **Cons:** not good for solo travelers; only ATM is at the main security gate, which is a long walk from the resort. ✉ *Playa Arena Gorda, Bávaro* ☎ *809/687–4242* 📠 *809/687–7878* ⊕ *www.riu.com* 🛏 *584 junior suites, 28 suites* ♿ *In-room: a/c, safe, refrigerator. In-hotel: 6 restaurants, bars, tennis courts, pools, gym, spa, beachfront, water sports, children's programs (ages 4–12), laundry service, Internet terminal, Wi-Fi hotspot* ▭ *AE, MC, V* ⧠⊙⧠ *AI.*

$$$$
ALL-INCLUSIVE
Fodor's Choice
★

⧠ **Secrets Sanctuary Cap Cana Golf & Spa.** The first hotel to be built within the gates of Cap Cana, Secrets is now an all-inclusive for adults only. Its gorgeous stone facade is reminiscent of the 16th-century Alcázar de Colón in Santo Domingo, and the interior, influenced by Dominican colonial-style mansions, has a stained-glass ceiling and enormous stone columns stretching up to the second floor, which is bedecked with intricate iron balconies and keystone arches. In the spacious main hall you can find upscale shops and a stone fountain. Near the suitably awe-inspiring lobby, peach-toned villas spread out along the beachfront, some with a Jacuzzi that opens onto the water. One- and two-bedroom suites offer balconies or terraces looking onto the white-sand stretch of Juanillo Beach, an exquisite feature that is tough to surpass. A lavish, 5,550-square-foot suite set on a private isle is $1,800 a night. Though you can get a suite with your very own plunge pool, there are three large swimming pools available to all hotel guests. Bonfire night and karaoke night are both good ways bring out your more gregarious side. Or you might try your hand at cocktail classes, dance lessons, or the casino. Throughout the resort, the decor is chic and contemporary. An underground tunnel throughout the grounds for use by employees contributes to guests' sense of privacy. A new spa was expected to open by the end of 2010. At every turn, gorgeous vistas seem the perfect backdrop for weddings, and indeed lots of couples exchange vows here. World-class golf is a stone's throw away at Punta Espada, and another Jack Nicklaus-designed course within the Cap Cana complex was nearing completion at this writing. Easy access to the Marina Cap Cana increases the number of good restaurants, and there's always 24-hour room service if you just want to stay put. **Pros:** gorgeous beach; top-notch golf; ultraposh accommodations. **Cons:** continuing development all around at Cap Cana; some facilities, like the spa, aren't ready yet. ⊠ *Playa Juanillo, Cap Cana* ☎ *809/562–9191 or 800/836–9618* ⊕ *http://secretsresorts.com/sanctuary* ➾ *115 junior suites, 27 suites, 33 villas* △ *In-room: a/c, safe, kitchen (some), refrigerator (some), Internet. In-hotel: 5 restaurants, room service, bars, golf courses, tennis courts, pools, gym, spa, beachfront, water sports, laundry service, Wi-Fi hotspot* ⊟ *AE, MC, V* ⏸ *AI.*

$$$$
RESORT
Fodor'sChoice
★

Sivory Punta Cana. The best things really do come in small packages at this enchanting, 55-suite boutique resort, which delivers on its promise of expressly personal service and top-shelf details in an environment of utter tranquillity. Guests at this non-all-inclusive (Sivory pioneered this style of hospitality in the region) are seeking indulgences and relaxation far from the crowds. Zen elements in the architecture, design, and mood of this secluded retreat work well in the exquisite natural setting, with indigenous vegetation used in the landscaping throughout the grounds. Although a do-nothing itinerary is possible here, there are some pleasurable options to keep guests occupied, among them special golf packages at the nearby Faldo Legacy Course, or an ecowalk through neighboring gardens. Alluring treatments performed by qualified hands at the spa might tempt you to venture out of the handsome suites, where a tone of laid-back luxury is achieved with East Asian and Caribbean adornments. All rooms have satellite plasma TVs, DVD/CD players, robes and slippers, stocked wine coolers, and minibars with soft drinks; the 950-square-foot oceanfront Ysla Bonita suites have private plunge pools, a Jacuzzi on the terrace, an outdoor shower (in addition to the double-headed indoor one), and a private club area on the beach. Free coffee, juice, and pastries are dropped off at your door each morning. At the communal infinity pool, chaise longues are outfitted with comfortable cushions; waiter service is available. Two of the resort's acclaimed restaurants, Tau for Asian fusion and the fancier Gourmond for French bistro fare, are open to nonguests; an 8,000-bottle wine cellar and a knowledgeable sommelier bestow a worldly touch. Once a week, guests can prepare their own delightful meal in a cooking class with the resort's personable and highly skilled head chef, Fernando. At night a bar with live entertainment offers a spot to savor a cocktail under the stars. There's also a separate cigar lounge. An all-inclusive plan (with amenities like unlimited select wine bottles and 24-hour room service) is available for an extra charge. **Pros:** relaxing surroundings; extensive wine cellar; free Wi-Fi throughout; gay-friendly. **Cons:** far from off-resort nightlife and shopping; limited on-site dining options. ⌧ *Uvero Alto* ☎ *809/333–0500* 🖷 *809/334–0500* ⊕ *www.sivorypuntacana.com* ↩ *55 suites* ⌂ *In-room: a/c, safe, refrigerator, kitchen (some), DVD, Internet, Wi-Fi. In-hotel: 3 restaurants, room service, bars, tennis court, pool, gym, spa, beachfront, water sports, laundry service, Wi-Fi hotspot* ⊟ *AE, MC, V* ⎢◎⎜ *EP.*

$$$$
VACATION VILLAS
Fodor's Choice
★

Tortuga Bay Villas. Shuttered French windows that open to grand vistas of the sea and a cotton-white private beach are hallmarks of this luxury-villa enclave within the grounds of PuntaCana Resort & Club. Personal attention is big here; your own villa manager, who can be reached by a cell phone given you on arrival, will grant your every desire. Although privacy is paramount here, there's also a sense of community. Oscar de la Renta designed the classy colonial-Caribbean rooms, which exude contemporary, understated elegance with a soft palette of colors and plush bed linens. The breathtaking bathrooms, made in stone, have a Jacuzzi for two; other amenities include robes, slippers, and Gilchrist & Soames toiletries. The minibar is stocked with premium liquors, and there's a huge flat-screen TV. A golf cart is included to help you get around, and you can rent a laptop. Villa guests have an exclusive restaurant plus access to all the facilities of the main resort, including the impeccable La Cana Golf Course, designed by P. B. Dye, and the glorious Six Senses Spa. **Pros:** exceptional, personal attention; gorgeous sprawling grounds; outstanding golf; VIP check-in at airport. **Cons:** little nightlife; too isolated for singles. ⌧ *PuntaCana Resort & Club, Punta Cana* ☎ *809/959–8229 or 888/442–2262* ⊕ *www.puntacana. com* ↩ *15 1- to 4-bedroom villas* ⌂ *In-room: a/c, safe, kitchen, refrigerator, DVD, Internet. In-hotel: 9 restaurants, room service, bars, golf courses, tennis courts, pools, gym, spa, beachfront, diving, water sports, bicycles, children's programs (ages 4–12), laundry service, Internet terminal, Wi-Fi hotspot* ⊟ *AE, D, MC, V* ⎢◎⎜ *BP.*

$$$$
RESORT
★

Zoëtry Agua Resort & Spa. No stone is left unturned when it comes to ensuring satisfaction for guests at this serene all-inclusive oceanfront resort, where rustic natural beauty and high architectural style blend seamlessly. An impressive list of amenities, available for all guests and called "endless privileges," includes a complimentary 20-minute massage, 20-minute session with a wellness guru, a welcome bottle of rum, a daily bottle of champagne and fruit basket, unlimited worldwide calling, rides to and from the airport, 24-hour room service, 24-hour laundry service, and a pillow menu. You can also check in or check out whatever time suits you best. A thatched-roof, open-air lobby welcomes you to the resort, where the design shows Dominican and Balinese influences throughout, utilizing materials like limestone, cane, wicker, and wood. All rooms have four-poster beds with Frette linens, a furnished terrace, and a large flat-screen TV; some have dramatic ocean views. The remarkable stone bathrooms have porcelain basins and Bulgari bath amenities. Second-level villas are enormous, with soaring cane-thatched roofs. The pool snakes through the grounds, making swim-out suites an alluring option, but the impeccable beach is a winner, too. Beyond the shore is an amazing barrier reef, so the waves are never too strong for swimming. Wine tastings, rum tastings, cigar-rolling classes, and cooking classes are some of the more unusual options among the large array of included activities and water sports. Service is superattentive, and the resort can organize horseback riding or helicopter tours, or simply lend you a DVD. There's no buffet dining here, in keeping with efforts to avoid any association to all-inclusive with low budget. This is an adult-oriented resort, but organized kids' programs serve ages five to nine. **Pros:** unsurpassed luxury details; serene, rustic location; attentive staff. **Cons:** mosquitoes; limited nightlife. ⊠ *Playa Uvero Alto* ☎ *809/468–0000* ⊕ *www.aguaresort.com* ⤳ *53 suites, 5 2- or 3-bedroom villas* ⚭ *In-room: a/c, safe, DVD, Wi-Fi. In-hotel: 3 restaurants, room service, bars, tennis court, pools, gym, spa, beachfront, water sports, children's programs (ages 5–9), laundry service, Internet terminal, Wi-Fi hotspot* ⊟ *AE, MC, V* ⦿⊧ *EP.*

NIGHTLIFE

With the predominance of all-inclusive hotels, nightlife in Punta Cana tends to center on whatever resort you are staying at. But there's more out there than first meets the eye. Some clubs, casinos, and shows at other resorts have very good reputations and are open to outsiders. Cover charges at the discos vary, ranging from none when it's early on an ordinary night to US$10 or $20 during peak hours, especially when there's live entertainment. Don't forget your ID; when nonguests are allowed into the disco on a resort's grounds, security keeps a close eye on who is coming and going. Some resorts offer nighttime excursions to a local disco, where you can go with a group and return at a scheduled hour.

An atmospheric lounge with big-screen TVs, **High Wave Café** (⊠ *Plaza Bávaro Shopping Center, Bávaro* ☎ *809/552–0172*) is a pleasant spot to drop by for cocktails after dinner and is easily accessible from the hotels on Bávaro. Early birds can grab a swinging love seat on the front porch.

★ Even if their night begins elsewhere, many party-scene insiders wind up sooner or later at **Mangú** (⊠ *Occidental Grand Punta Cana, Bávaro* ☎ *809/221–8787*), with two floors of pulsating rhythms to keep club goers charged. Upstairs, techno is pumped nonstop, while the downstairs dance floor tends toward reggaeton, hip-hop, and urban music mixed up with salsa, merengue, and bachata. The dance club, on the grounds of the Occidental complex, allows guests from off-property, and you'll find a mix of tourists and locals at all hours of the night. Things don't get hot here until after midnight, and they keep on going all night long, until it's time to wrap up with an after-hours bite at the resort's pizzeria, open until 6:30 AM. One draw before things heat up

Punta Cana: Then and Now

In 1972 the area that became Punta Cana was nothing but wilderness. Through the jungle, a trip by four-wheel-drive vehicle would take six to eight hours from Higüey, the nearest city (now the route takes about an hour by regular car). "When we arrived, the country did not believe in tourism," says Frank Rainieri, a cofounder of PuntaCana Resort & Club. At the time, there were only 962 hotel rooms in the entire Dominican Republic. Partnering with Club Med, the pioneer developers built the first hotel in the region, with a mere 20 rooms, followed shortly thereafter by an airstrip, thereby opening a window to the world beyond and planting the seeds of Punta Cana's emergence

as the major vacation destination that it has become. In 1999 Grupo PuntaCana teamed up with Cornell University to form a biodiversity laboratory with an ecological reserve on its grounds; now it's not only a hub of research on the area's ecosystems and sustainability but also an indicator of the founders' ongoing commitment to these causes. Grupo PuntaCana also established a polytechnic institute to help teach the area's potential workforce the skills necessary to do the jobs related to the tourist industry. "It is not simply a resort, it is a community," says PuntaCana cofounder Ted Kheel. Indeed he, along with partners Rainieri, Oscar de la Renta, and Julio Iglesias, all have homes at PuntaCana.

on the dance floor: the club's big-screen TV is good for watching sporting events. There's usually a cover charge, ranging from US$10 to $20 depending on whether there's live music.

The name says it all at **Areito** (⊠ *Bávaro Princess Resort, Bávaro* ☎ *809/687–7788*), which means "party" in Taino, and regulars have shunned attempts to call it anything else. It's among the best resort-based dance clubs in Punta Cana. Open to the public, Areito attracts tourists and locals who let everything go on the dance floor, as the DJ spins international club beats.

Fodor's Choice ★ **Imagine** (⊠ *Carretera Cocoloco–Riu, Coco Loco/Friusa, Bávaro* ☎ *809/466–1049* ⊕ *www.imaginepuntacana.com* ⊟ *$35 includes cover, transportation, and 2 drinks* ⊙ *11 PM–after 4 AM*) you were dancing the night away in a natural cave, with earth-rocking acoustics. You can bounce back and forth between two separate, but equally hot dance floors, one featuring house/club jams, the other merengue/salsa/world beats. At Punta Cana's thriving hotspot, locals and tourists alike pack the various salas adorned with stalactites and stalagmites. Come late and stay early: things start getting steamy well after midnight, when many club crawlers descend via shuttle (round-trip) from the local resorts. Special rates are offered for a weekly, multiple-entrance pass, with one night including an open bar. One massive chamber is reserved for concerts and private events.

A favorite among locals and still one of the best resort-based dance spots, **Pacha** (⊠ *Av. Estados Unidos, at Riu complex, Bávaro* ☎ *809/221–7575*) plays more merengue and bachata than most of the other clubs. Drinks here are cheaper, too. For a beer, expect to pay about 80 pesos (or about $2.50); the price can be double in some of the other clubs. Cover charges apply when live bands perform; otherwise it's free to enter, and non-resort guests are welcome.

SPORTS AND THE OUTDOORS

FISHING

Big-game fishing is big in Punta Cana, with blue and white marlin, wahoo (a kind of mackerel), sailfish, and mahimahi among the most common catches in these waters. Several fishing tournaments are held every summer. Marina Cap Cana hosts three big-game tournaments during the summer, including Blue Marlin and White Marlin Invitationals and a Dorado Open. The PuntaCana Resort & Club has hosted the ESPN Xtreme Billfishing Tournament every year since 2003. Blue marlin tournaments are also held annually on the La Mona Channel originating out of Cabeza de Toro. Several tour operators offer organized deep-sea fishing excursions.

At **PuntaCana Marina** ($\boxtimes$ *PuntaCana Resort & Club, Punta Cana* $\textcircled{a}$ *809/959–2262 Ext. 8004* $\oplus$ *www.puntacana.com*), on the southern end of the resort, half-day, deep-sea fishing excursions are available for US$95 per person, with a minimum of two people, $70 for observers. For a Bertram 33-footer to go after tuna, marlin, dorado, and wahoo, it's $575 for four hours. It costs the same to charter a 45-foot Sportfisherman. Also, ask about the *yolas*, simple fishing boats with outboards.

Marina Cap Cana ($\boxtimes$ *Cap Cana, Juanillo* $\textcircled{a}$ *809/695–5539* $\oplus$ *www. capcana.com/site/index.php/en/activity/marina*) on the Mona Passage on the southeastern edge of the Dominican Republic, offers a superb port for sportfishing during the summer season, when the grounds are renowned for an abundance of blue marlin and white marlin. Currently, 89 wet slips are available for vessels of 30 feet to 130 feet. All have cable TV, water, and Wi-Fi. A thousand slips are planned, some with capacity for yachts over 150 feet long. Slip rentals are available; anglers participating in any of three seasonal fishing tournaments get discount dockage rates. For deep-sea fishing, 48' and 51' Riviera Sportfish may be chartered (4- or 8-hour excursions for marlin, wahoo, tuna, snapper, grouper, etc.). There's also a designated fishing area for snook, tarpon, barracuda, and jack, with guides and equipment available. The marina hosts festivities and cocktail parties during the height of the fishing season.

GOLF

With a comfortable climate year-round, abundant greenery, and stunning natural backdrops, Punta Cana is a highly desirable location for golf. Indeed, the region has some of the best golf courses in the Caribbean, designed by top golf architects including Nick Faldo, P. B. Dye, Tom Fazio, Jack Nicklaus, Jose "Pepe" Gancedo, Nick Price, and Alberto Sola. The region's reputation as a golf hot spot shows no

Cap Cana

Cap Cana is a resort and villa complex spread out over 30,000 acres along 3.4 miles of precious beach on bluffs 270 feet above sea level, and about 10 minutes south of the Punta Cana airport. In time it will have at least four luxury hotels with 3,000 rooms, 5,000 residential units, 5 golf courses, a 5,000-seat amphitheater, casinos, a marina with yacht clubs and deep-sea fishing fleet, beach clubs, polo grounds, spas, and tennis and squash courts.

The flagship hotel, the Sanctuary Cap Cana Golf & Spa, opened in 2008 but has since become Secrets, an adults-only, all-inclusive resort. The pioneer of the golf courses, Punta Espada—one of three Jack Nicklaus signature courses planned for the complex—opened in 2006 and is the site of an annual PGA Champions Tour event. The second course, Las Iguanas, was preparing to open in 2010, with meticulous links snaking alongside the Golden Bear Lodge Golf & Spa, which opened in December 2009. (Golden Bear Lodge is made up of luxury villas, many of which are managed together under the AMResorts umbrella, with the rest independently operated.) Also up and running is the exclusive Caletón Beach Club, with its palapa roof and spectacular pool carved into a coral base, and the Juanillo Beach Club. Marina Cap Cana is being built in three phases, over the

next 10–15 years; it's destined to be the Caribbean's largest marina. So far, as part of phase one, there are nearly 90 wet slips. Just off the treasured fishing grounds of the Mona Passage between the Dominican Republic and Puerto Rico, the marina will have a port authority and customs, restaurants (four are up and running), shops, and nightclubs.

Other projects in various stages of development are an NH resort and residences on Juanillo Beach, and the Ritz-Carlton, a billion-dollar mixed-use complex with a 220-room hotel, residences, a spa, private beach club, five restaurants, and lounges. Also underway is Donald Trump's $2-billion real-estate project, Trump at Cap Cana, which when complete will have a luxury resort, golf course, golf villas, estate lots, a beach club, condo hotel, and residences. The Trump Farallon Estates at Cap Cana generated record sales of its lot sites in 2007, though little construction has been accomplished so far.

Among the real treasures of Cap Cana is the biodiversity represented in its flora and fauna, some of which can be observed along the so-called Great Ecological Trail. A 15-km hike begins where an endangered Cotoperí fruit tree, endemic to the area, marks the trailhead, which leads to grottos, wet forests, and a pond of shimmering blue water.

signs of slowing, with the major resort community developments at Rōco Ki, Punta Cana, and Cap Cana each planning to add new links in the next few years.

The prices below are all given in U.S. dollars.

Barceló Bávaro Golf (✉ *Bávaro* ☎ *809/686–5797*) is an 18-hole, par-72 course integrated within the Barceló Bávaro Beach Golf & Casino Resort complex, which is open to its own guests and those of other hotels. The course, with numerous water obstacles, was designed by Juan Manuel Gordillo, and was the first in the Bávaro area. The rate for those not staying at Bávaro is $130, which includes greens fees, golf cart, and a day pass to the resort, where you can get food and beverages for the day. Complete renovations have been undertaken by designer P. B. Dye; the back nine opened in early 2010, and work on the front nine was expected to be finished by the end of 2010.

Cabeza de Toro (⊠ *Catalonia Bávaro Resort, Cabeza de Toro, Bávaro* ☎ *809/321–7058* ⊕ *www.cataloniabavaro.com*), a 9-hole, par-35 resort course, was designed by Alberto Sola. Greens fees are $65 for 18 holes, $45 for 9 holes.

Cana Bay Palace Golf Club (*Arena Gorda, Macao* ☎ *809/635–1836*) preserves the indigenous flora and fauna in its immaculate landscaping designed by Jack Nicklaus and Mark Meijer.

Challenging and reasonably priced, **Catalonia Caribe Golf Club** (⊠ *Catalonia Bávaro Resort, Cabeza de Toro, Bávaro* ☎ *809/321–7058* ⊕ *www.cataloniabavaro.com*) is an 18-hole, par-72 course spread out on greens surrounded by five lakes and an abundance of shady palms. Alberto Sola was the designer. Greens fees are $120, including golf cart.

Named for the coconut plantation on which it was built, **Cocotal Golf Course** (⊠ *Bávaro* ☎ *809/687–4653* ⊕ *www.cocotalgolf.com*), designed by Spaniard José "Pepe" Gancedo, has 18 championship holes and 9 regular holes. It's a challenging par-72 course in a residential community dotted with palm trees and lakes. There's also a driving range, clubhouse, pro shop and golf academy. Greens fees are $149 for 18 holes if you come from the "outside," including the cart. The cost is $65 for 9 holes, excluding cart. Guests at the Sol Meliá properties play for free.

Corales Golf Course (⊠ *PuntaCana Resort & Club, Punta Cana* ☎ *809/ 959–4653* ⊕ *www.puntacana.com*), designed by Tom Fazio, is a dramatic 18-hole course (open only to members and some resort guests) that opened in 2009. Laid out along cliffs and coves within a private enclave of luxurious homes, these links are on the grounds of the PuntaCana Resort & Club. Since the resort owns and operates the Punta Cana International Airport, flight paths were detoured so as not to disturb the peace for golfers here.

Fodor's Choice ★ **The Faldo Legacy Course** (⊠ Rōco Ki, Macao ☎ 809/688–9898 ⊕ *www. troongolf.com*) is Nick Faldo's championship course (18-hole, par-72), with challenging tees spread out over 7,000 yards of green. It winds along the beach, through a tropical mangrove forest, and stretches across the headland, with stunning cliff-top views of the sea. The spectacular, much-photographed 17th hole sits on a cliff with the ocean waves spraying up against the rocks. Faldo called this area of the course Los Dos Rezos ("The Two Prayers"), because even the greatest golfers might need more than finesse to get through it. The eco-friendly course sits on the grounds of the Westin Rōco Ki Beach & Golf Resort, due to open in 2011. Because of beach erosion, some bunkers fell into the ocean and are expected to be permanently relocated; the affected land areas are being refilled and regrassed. For now, greens fees top out at about $275, though reduced rates kick in during slow times, and prices

Popular Excursions

Beyond the gates of your resort there are many opportunities to leave your chaise longue behind and explore the surrounding area. The following excursions are all extremely popular, and several different tour companies generally offer similar trips (prices cited, in U.S. dollars, are just examples, and most charge tax on top of the fee):

Aquatic Speedboat Tour: Cruise along the coast in a speedboat to a magnificent snorkeling spot (Apple, $75).

ATV Tour: Get off the beaten path in a four-wheeler for an insider's view of the local countryside for half a day (VIP Travel, US$65 [shared ATV]–$90 [individual]).

Bávaro Runners: Tour the local countryside for the full day, with stops at sugarcane fields, cocoa plantations, and a typical Dominican home, and eat an authentic Dominican lunch (Apple, $90; Vacaciones Barceló, $90; VIP, $90).

Catalina Island: Sail to this unin-habited, pristine 6-square-mi island off the coast of La Romana. It's a secluded spot that's fabulous for snorkeling and diving. The all-day tour (9 hours) starts by bus from the hotels to Bayahibe (90 minutes); from there, you take a boat to the island. There's also a stop along the way to tour Altos de Chavón. (Colonial, $105, with lobster lunch buffet, water, and soft drinks).

Manatí Park: Exploring the park (see ⇨ Manatí Park in Exploring Bávaro, above).

Marinarium: Snorkeling among nurse sharks and sun rays on a coral reef (Apple, $87).

Outback Safari: A half-day or full-day adventure takes you through the back roads to visit a cocoa plantation, local craft stores, a typical Dominican home, a cigar factory, and a secluded beach for some Boogie boarding (Apple, $70–$90; full-day includes lunch).

Samaná Whale Watching: From January through March, head out to watch the wintering humpback whales that return to Samaná in droves for their mating and birthing season (Colonial, $150, 9-hour tour includes flight and buffet lunch).

Santo Domingo: Full-day tour of the colonial capital, visiting the first cathedral in the New World and other architectural, historical, and cultural points of interest (VIP, $95, includes lunch at Hard Rock Cafe; Apple, $84, includes buffet lunch; Vacaciones Barceló, $75).

Saona Island: See ⇨ Saona Island box under Higüey, above (about $90 to $95 for a full day, including fuel surcharge, lunch, and beverages).

Zip Lining: A half-day canopy tour that will have you swinging across Anamuya Pond on 10 different steel cables (the longest of which is 820 feet) from platforms spaced across a one-mile stretch of Taino Mountain. A 45-minute drive aboard a safari truck brings you to the welcome center, where qualified guides provide instruction and safety training. (VIP, $89, includes instruction, soft drinks, and fruit).

4

could climb as development progresses at the complex. An experienced caddy is an extra $25.

At this writing, **Hacienda Golf Course** (⊠ *PuntaCana Resort & Club, Punta Cana* ☎ *809/959–4653* ⊕ *www.puntacana.com*), designed by P. B. Dye and scheduled to open in 2011, is expected to be a challenging addition to the spectacular courses at PuntaCana Resort & Club.

Iberostate Bávaro Golf Club (⊠ *Iberostar Bávaro ResortArena Gorda, Bávaro* ☎ *809/221–6500*), with its P. B. Dye-designed fairways set along the coast, opened in late 2009. The beauty of the natural setting shines in the layout of the links at this 18-hole, par 72 course. Greens fees of $175 include cart, snacks, and non-alcoholic beverages.

★ **La Cana Golf Course** (⊠ *PuntaCana Resort & Club, PuntaCana* ☎ *809/959–4653* ⊕ *www.puntacana.com*) is a breathtaking 18-hole championship course designed by P. B. Dye, with spectacular ocean views—four holes play right along the water. For resort guests, greens fees are $75 for 9 holes, $125 for 18 holes, with cart included; for nonguests, fees are $102 for 9 holes, $165 for 18 holes, and that includes a golf cart, water, and tees, but not the caddie ($20–$30). Reserve two weeks in advance from November through April. Lessons and clinics are offered at the resort.

Punta Blanca Golf Course (⊠ *Carretera Arena Gorda, near Majestic Colonial Resort, Bávaro* ☎ *809/257–7360*) is a beautiful 18-hole, par-72 course designed by Nick Price. Greens fees are $175, including cart and nonalcoholic beverages.

Fodor's Choice ★ **Punta Espada Golf Course** (⊠ *Cap Cana, Carretera Juanillo, Playa Juanillo* ☎ *809/688–5587*) is a par-72 Jack Nicklaus signature golf course with striking bluffs, lush foliage, and winding waterways. There's a Caribbean view from all the holes, and eight of them play right along the ocean. It's the first of three Jack Nicklaus signature courses planned at Cap Cana, and the site of an annual, internationally televised PGA Champions Tour event. The top-notch golf club has concierge services, a restaurant, the Hole 19 bar, a pro shop, a members' trophy gallery, a library, lockers, an equipment repair shop, and a meeting room. Greens fees are $395, which includes golf cart, caddy, tees, water, and practice on the driving range. The course is closed Tuesdays for maintenance.

Las Iguanas Golf Course (*Cap Cana, Juanillo* ☎ *809/227–2262*) is the second of three Jack Nicklaus courses planned for Cap Cana, and the $26-million-dollar spectacular was readying to open by the end of 2010. Some of the holes play along the backdrop of the Caribbean, and others wind inland amid tropical vegetation.

White Sands Golf Course (⊠ *Near Ocean Blue Golf & Beach Resort, Bávaro* ☎ *809/552–6750* ⊕ *www.oceanhotels.net*), designed by Spanish champion Jose "Pepe" Gancedo—nicknamed the "Picasso of Golf"—is a handsome and challenging addition to the golf spectrum. After an addition in 2007, it's now an 18-hole, par-72 course. Greens fees, $100, include a cart and one bottle of water.

HORSEBACK RIDING

Rancho Punta Cana (⊠ *PuntaCana Resort & Club, Punta Cana* ☎ *809/959–2714* ⊕ *www.puntacana.com*) is across from the main entrance of the resort. A one-hour trail ride winds along the beach, the golf course, and through tropical forests. The two-hour jungle trail ride has a stopover at a lagoon fed by a natural spring, so wear your swimsuit under your long pants. You can also do a three-hour full-moon excursion or take riding lessons. The stock are Paso Fino horses.

Southfork Ranch (Rancho Pat) (⊠ *Hotel Sol de Plata, Bávaro* ☎ *809/223–8896*), on the north end of Bávaro, is the stable of choice for many visitors staying at resorts in Uvero Alto, Macao, and Arena Gorda, among others. Trail rides are offered along the beach and open country roads for about $25 per hour.

TENNIS

Most resorts have tennis courts where you can play for free during the day. Some have night lighting, but there's usually an extra charge to play after dark. If you're looking for a club atmosphere, PuntaCana Resort & Club has a tennis center open to nonguests; at this writing, there's also a racket center under construction at Cap Cana that will have tennis and squash courts open to the public.

PuntaCana Resort & Club (⊠ *Punta Cana* ☎ *809/959–2262 Ext. 7158; toll free U.S. & Canada, 888/442–2262*) has six clay courts and a full-scale operation, with professional instructors on hand for lessons or match-ups. Clinics, ball boys, racket rental, and racket stringing are among the other services available. There's also an exhibition stadium. Nonguests can play for two hours for $26; the courts close at 7 PM.

SHOPPING

Souvenirs and crafts are the focus of shopping in Punta Cana, and there are few outlets for high-end clothing or accessories. As in the rest of the country, the regional specialty products are cigars, coffee, larimar and amber jewelry, *mamajuana* (an herbal liqueur), and rum (especially the locally made premium Brugal).

Most resorts have a few retail shops, but prices are higher than what you would pay for similar goods in the nearby shopping plazas or at kiosks on the beach. Many vendors sell crafts and goods from neighboring Haiti, too, so if you're looking for something specifically Dominican, make sure that's what you're getting. Some resorts have a weekly Dominican theme night, which typically includes local vendors setting up their stalls in a central plaza, where guests can peruse the offerings and try to strike a bargain without ever leaving the resort.

Shopping in the plazas with outdoor kiosks, the sound track is the constant hum of greeting, searching, and haggling. Shopkeepers tend to be persistent when trying to lure you in, but are generally friendly. In regular stores prices are not negotiable, but bargaining is expected at the kiosks.

SHOPPING CENTERS

The colorful, bazaarlike atmosphere at **Bi2JH2O Artisanal Shopping Plaza** (⊠ *El Cortecito, Bávaro*), pronounced like *bibijagua,* makes it fun to browse through the rows of shopping stalls laid out in the sand on Bávaro Beach. Here you can find handicrafts, cigars, mamajuana, hand-made musical instruments, paintings, sculptures, wood carvings, and amber, larimar, and coral jewelry. Expect the spirited shopkeepers to beckon you into their kiosks; don't hesitate to look around before you settle on a purchase, as you might find a few pearls in what may at times seem like a sea of trinkets. Break out your bargaining tactics, as prices are not set in stone. There's a snack bar with Dominican munchies and restrooms nearby. The plaza is accessible on foot along the beach from a few hotels. Otherwise, grab a cab, and a camera.

Fodor's Choice
★

The **Galerias at PuntaCana Village** (⊠ *PuntaCana Resort & Club, Punta Cana*) lie within a still-blossoming shopping, dining, and residential complex built on the road to the airport. It was built to house employees of PuntaCana Resort & Club, but now it's also a tourist draw. The village houses a church, a school, and two banks (with two more planned). The commercial square also has an Oscar de la Renta shop, Portuguese and Italian restaurants, a bowling alley, beauty parlor, bagel shop, Baskin Robbins ice-cream shop, and an art gallery where you can find locally crafted items on display, including an exquisite wooden chess set with giant pieces carved to resemble classical musicians on one side and Dominican pop stars on the other. Free transportation is provided to guests at PuntaCana Resort & Club.

Fodor's Choice
★

A standout among the region's shopping centers, **Palma Real Shopping Village** (⊠ *Bávaro* ☎ 809/552–8725 ⊕ *www.palmarealshoppingvillage. com*) is a swanky, partially enclosed mall. Fountains and tropical plants infuse life into the bright and airy interior areas beneath the blue-tile roof. Music pipes through the stone-floor plaza in the center, where seating is available and security is tight. Upscale retail shops, which sell beachwear, clothing, skin-care products, and jewelry, line the walls. Several restaurants give visitors welcome dining alternatives beyond the gates of their resorts. There are two banks, ATMs, and a money exchange outlet. Stores are open 10–10, but the restaurants stay open later. Shuttle buses run to and from many of the hotels, with pick-ups every two hours. Punta Cana's first movie theater, **Palacio del Cine** (☎ 809/5592-8860), opened here in 2009, and has three screens showing current films in English with Spanish subtitles.

The sprawling **Plaza Bávaro Shopping Center** (⊠ *Bávaro* ☎ *No phone*) has dozens of shops spanning two sides of the main street that cuts through its center. On the side closest to the beach you can find clothing stores, jewelry, cigars, and crafts, as well as three money-exchange spots, a DHL shipping station, and a pharmacy, all laid out in a square; in the middle is a bar where you can take a break from the bustle. Across the street, most of the booths sell artwork and handicrafts, and if your hair is long enough, you'll likely be approached by women offering to braid it on the spot.

You won't find brand-name shops at **Plaza Uvero Alto** (⊠ *Carretera Uvero Alto, Uvero Alto*), which is a convenient shopping center for the hotels in the remote Uvero Alto area, with a bank and outdoor ATM, money exchange, Internet access, a small pharmacy, gift shops, and two mini-markets (one in the front, the other in the back row of booths). Here you can get sundries like suntan lotion and deodorant at prices much cheaper than in the hotels. Behind the first row of enclosed stores, visit the colorful kiosks full of handicrafts, paintings, ceramics, and other gift items; most shopkeepers here, although very friendly, don't speak much English, so knowing even a few words of Spanish will come in handy. For beautifully designed pieces with larimar and amber and other locally made novelties, visit **Tesoro Caribeño** (No. 5, front row of stores), where the owner speaks fluent English. There's also a branch of the Politur (tourist police) in the plaza.

SPECIALTY STORES

CIGARS

Hand-rolled cigars are available everywhere you turn in Punta Cana. Cigar lounges, where you can sample the aromatic flavors of the different tobaccos, are common, too. Dominican cigars—proudly touted as even better than Cubans—make great gifts for aficionados and are legal to bring back to the United States (100 per person max). Look for sellers with expertise and, of course, authentic products.

Before 6 PM you can watch cigars being made by hand at **Cig's Aficionados** (⊠ *Palma Real Shopping Village, Bávaro* ☎ *809/552–8754*), a reputable outlet for Dominican cigars. You can sample varieties at the shop, too, which is open daily, including Sunday, from 10 AM to 9:45 PM.

Near the airport, **La Tabaquería Cigar Club** (⊠ *La Plaza Bolera, Suite 10A, Punta Cana* ☎ *809/959–0040*) is a haven for cigar lovers, who can watch the production process or relax at the bar with a drink. Fine Dominican and Cuban cigars are for sale, as are humidors and related accessories, from 9 AM to 9 PM daily. You can call the store to arrange transportation.

JEWELRY

Two types of stones are popular in the Dominican Republic, and they both make exquisite pieces of jewelry. Larimar is a rare blue form of the mineral pecolite whose only known occurence in the world is in the southwestern Dominican Republic. The larimar mines tell a story of the island's emergence from solidifying rock beneath the ocean floor about 100 million years ago. Dominican amber, about 25 million years old, in some cases has life forms encapsulated inside it. Jewelers in Punta Cana showcase these stones as well as other precious gems.

★ It's hard to walk by the windows of **Harrison's Fine Jewelry** (⊠ *Palma Real Shopping Village, Bávaro* ☎ *809/552–8721*) without stepping in to admire the collection of jewelry, including a large selection of larimar and amber pieces in striking settings, as well as diamonds and other classic gems. Outlets of this renowned chain are also in several resorts of Punta Cana.

★ Browse through the museum showcases and panels depicting the fascinating history of the Dominican Republic's unique stones at **R&R Amber & Larimar Museum Jewelry** (✉ *Palma Real Shopping Village, Bávaro* ☎ *809/552–8710*), before stopping at the jewelry shop on the way out.

Samai Factory Jewelry (✉ *Plaza Bávaro, Store 39, Bávaro* ☎ *809/304–3770*) has some interesting amber and larimar pieces, as well as diamond and zirconium rings. Custom pieces can be made if you like a stone and want to change its setting.

Tesoro Caribeño (✉ *Plaza Uvero Alto, Local 5, Uvero Alto* ☎ *809/707–3355*) has a fine selection of amber and larimar jewelry and other stones amid the colorful shelves full of souvenirs and crafts. The same designers who create jewelry for the Harrison's chain craft the unique pieces, but they're generally cheaper here. The owner speaks fluent English.

Samaná Peninsula

WORD OF MOUTH

"[Cayo Leventado] is a very small island . . . nice for a day trip . . . but you'd be better off on the mainland if actually planning on staying over there."

—oldhippy

"The waterfall in Limón is beautiful. We did the first part of the mountain on horseback and then hiked back down to the waterfall. Be sure to swim through the falls as there is a cool little cave behind it."

—despina555

By Michael de Zayas

"One of the authors of the King James Bible traveled the Caribbean, and I often think that it was a place like Samaná that was on his mind when he sat down to pen the Eden chapters. For Eden it was, a blessed meridian where mar and sol and green have forged their union." —Junot Díaz, *The Brief Wondrous Life of Oscar Wao*

You need only squint a bit in the sun to imagine a tropical paradise with biblical attributes—a dramatically beautiful peninsula, like an island unto itself, of coconut trees stretching into the sea. It's something of a microcosm of the Dominican Republic: here you'll see poverty and fancy resorts, good and bad (and really bad) roads, verdant mountainsides, tropical forests, tiny villages lined with street-side fruit vendors, secluded beaches, and the radiant warmth of the Dominican people.

The green mountains teem with coconut trees and dramatic vistas of sea, full of hidden beaches reachable only on foot or by sea, protected coves, and undeveloped bays. There are also a number of all-inclusive resorts that claim territory to themselves, as well as quaint and low-key beachfront hotels and restaurants where you can find complete relaxation and tranquillity. Samaná (pronounced sah-mah-NAH) is the name of both the peninsula and its biggest town, as well as the bay to the south. It's worth noting that to locals, Samaná denotes only the biggest town, Santa Bárbara de Samaná, which makes a great departure point for whale-watching or an excursion to Los Haitises Park across the bay. The bay is home to some of the world's best whale-watching from mid-January to late March. If you're here during that time, don't miss it.

A visit to Samaná is really about two things: exploring its preserved natural wonders and relaxing at a small beachfront hotel. The latter is most readily accomplished in Las Terrenas, the only true tourist center, where you can find picturesque restaurants, accommodations of all types, and great beaches. Reach it by taking a winding road through the mountains from the town of Sánchez. At Las Terrenas you can enjoy peaceful *playas,* take advantage of the vibrant nightlife (including a casino), and make all your plans for expeditions on the peninsula. The other pleasures are solitary—quiet beaches, the massive national park Los Haitises, and water sports and hiking.

The Samaná peninsula is a great place just to explore. Two days would suffice to drive the entire length of the peninsula, but without much time for real relaxing. A full week would give you ample time to explore some of its more remote wonders. If you're here from mid-January to late March, definitely make a whale-watching cruise the primary focus of your itinerary.

TOP REASONS TO GO

■ **Independent travel.** In a country that overdoes the all-inclusive resort, you'll find a happy change of pace in this harder-to-reach corner.

■ **Boating to Parque Los Haitises.** Visit the coastline islands and grottoes, kayaking along the coastline and through mangroves to discover the wildly verdant coast.

■ **El Limón Waterfall.** A horseback ride into the forest ends in a dazzling cascade.

■ **Beachfront meal or drinks at Las Terrenas.** At a small stretch on the beach at the heart, Pueblo de los Pescadores, eight fun and romantic restaurants stand on small stilts above the sand.

■ **Pristine, secluded beaches.** Playa Rincón and about a dozen rarely seen beaches offer unspoiled mountainside views, perfect sands, and privacy. The best can be reached only by hiring a boat.

■ **The drive from Sánchez to Las Terrenas.** Winding across the mountain, you'll take in views of the entire bay and beyond, to Los Haitises National Park.

5

ORIENTATION AND PLANNING

GETTING ORIENTED

From the mainland, **Highway** 5 runs along the southern coast of the peninsula, passing the westernmost town of any size, Sánchez, along to the biggest town on the peninsula, Santa Bárbara de Samaná (called simply Samaná) in about an hour. From this main artery a couple of winding, poorly maintained roads traverse the mountains to the north shore, where you will find nearly all the public beaches. Off the southeastern corner of the peninsula lies the small island of Cayo Levantado, accessible only by boat. Highway 5 continues beyond Samaná to the northeastern beach outpost of Las Galeras. From here you'll want to rent a boat to reach the peninsula's best, and most secluded, beaches.

Las Terrenas. The only busy tourist spot on the peninsula can be delightful or a noisy mess, depending where you look. We highlight the wonderful beaches and eateries that can make a stay here a real joy: investigate, because there's bliss hereabouts.

Santa Bárbara de Samaná. There's little reason to linger in Samaná town. The port serves as a launching point for Cayo Levantado; whale-watching trips in the bay (Jan. to Mar.); and year-round expeditions to Los Haitises, a national park that's the peninsula's number one must-do.

Las Galeras. If you're an independent traveler, spend a happy day or two sleuthing out the pristine beaches that dot the coast here at the northeast tip of the peninsula. Las Galeras is a sleepy corner of the country, but one rich in quiet rewards for the adventurous.

PLANNING

GETTING HERE AND AROUND

AIR TRAVEL

American offers connections to El Catey Airport in Samaná from San Juan. All other flights come from other points in the Dominican Republic. Flights from other airports are relatively cheap and frequent.

The peninsula has two airports with regular service. El Catey (AZS) is a 30-minute drive from Las Terrenas and a 40-minute drive from Samaná town. El Portillo (EPS) is just a few miles east of Las Terrenas.

AeroDomca flies three times daily from Las Isabella domestic airport in Santo Domingo to El Portillo and back for $75 each way. AeroDomca offers charter flights to all airports in the Dominican Republic, as well as helicopter transfers to all Dominican airports.

Another small domestic airline, DominicanShuttles.com, flies daily from Punta Cana to El Catey for $149 and El Portillo for $149. All costs are for one-way service.

Information AeroDomca (✉ *Plaza El Paseo, Las Terrenas* ☎ *809/240-6571* ⊕ *www.aerodomca.com*). **Takeoff Destination Service** (☎ *809/552-1333* ⊕ *www.takeoffweb.com*).

BUS TRAVEL

Caribe Tours offers a four-hour bus service from the capital. There are stops in Sánchez, Las Terrenas, and Santa Bárbara de Samaná. There are six departures in each direction daily. From Santiago, Transporte PEPE runs four buses daily to Samaná, starting at 8 AM, with the last, at 3 PM, a nonstop route to Las Terrenas.

From Puerto Plata, Transporte Papagayo is a private bus service leaving at 6:45 AM from in front of the hospital. It goes as far as Sánchez, returning at 2 PM.

Information Caribe Tours (✉ *Av. 27 de Febrero, corner of Leopoldo Navarro, Santo Domingo* ☎ *809/221-4422*). **Transporte PEPE** (✉ *Calle Pedro Francisco Bonó, Santiago* ☎ *809/582-2134 or 809/582-5709*). **Transporte Papagayo** (✉ *Puerto Plata* ☎ *809/749-6415*).

CAR TRAVEL

Renting a car is the best way to get around the island, though driving in the Dominican Republic can be a hectic and even harrowing experience. Get a four-wheel drive if at all possible; you'll need to go through serious mud, puddles, and countless potholes. At the time of this writing, the roads had dramatically improved, but were still terrible from Samaná town to Las Galeras and in the Las Terrenas area.

Javier Inversiones Rent-a-Car, a local agency in Samaná, can put you in a Jeep or even a Toyota Camry, although there is not a large inventory of automatics. Expect to pay at least $50 a day—more for an automatic—but that does include insurance.

In Las Terrenas, consider Indianapolis Car Rental, which often has the best prices. Daihatsu Terios, which are rugged mini-SUVs, go for RD$2,300 a day or RD$1,800 a day based on a one-week rental. If you dare, you can also rent a scooter for RD$900 a day or RD$550 a day based on a week's rental.

Another inexpensive option in Las Terrenas is SAINAR.

Information **Indianapolis Car Rental** (⊠ *Av. Playa Popy, Las Terrenas* ☎ *809/875–6015*). **Javier Inversiones Rent-a-Car** (⊠ *Francisco Rosario Sánchez 7, Samaná* ☎ *809/249–5937*). **SAINAR** (⊠ *Calle Duarte 238, Las Terrenas* ☎ *809/252–9826*).

TAXI TRAVEL

Negotiate prices, and settle before getting in the taxi. To give you an idea of what to expect, a minivan that can take eight people will normally charges US$90 for the round-trip from Samaná town to Las Terrenas, including a two-hour wait while you explore or enjoy the beach. Similarly, you'll pay $80 round-trip to travel from Samaná to Las Galeras or Playa Rincón. Many of the drivers speak some English. Within town, motorcycle taxis, called *motoconchos,* are far less costly and are also fun. They're fine to get around town on, but don't even think about going the distance with them. If you are based in Las Terrenas, you can call Eddy's Taxi.

Contact **Eddy's Taxi** (☎ *809/252–7888* ⊕ *www.eddystaxi.com*).

INTERNET

You'll find several convenient Internet cafés in Santa Bárbara de Samaná, Las Galeras, and Las Terrenas. The cost to go online ranges between RD$30 and RD$80 per hour—inexpensive to be sure. Almost all hotels have Wi-Fi at least in their lobby areas.

Internet Cafés **Centro Llamada Edwards** (⊠ *4 Francisco Rosario Sánchez, Samaná* ☎ *809/538–2476*) has five computers and charges only RD$30 an hour to connect. **Deleon Communications** (⊠ *Maria Trinidad Sánchez 13, Samaná, across from landmark Palacio Justicia* ☎ *809/538–3538*) has six computers and four phone booths.

MONEY MATTERS

The most common foreign bank in the Dominican Republic is Scotiabank, with 54 branches throughout the country, including two on the Samaná peninsula. This is the most reliable place to change money or use an ATM. The branches are open weekdays 8:30–4:30 and Saturday 9–1. You won't find any ATMs at all anywhere east of Santa Bárbara de Samaná, including at Las Galeras, so if you're heading there, money up in Samaná first. Western Union has two offices here: one in Samaná town and one in Las Terrenas.

TOUR OPTIONS

There are a number of tour operators based in Las Terrenas. The best is Flora Tours, which will help you book all possible trips, rentals, and tours, including visits to Los Haitises and snorkel trips to Playa Jackson.

If seeing the sights from the air is more your style, AeroDomca offers 15-, 30-, and 45-minute helicopter tours from El Portillo Airfield (just east of Las Terrenas). Flights are inexpensive, starting at $25.

Samaná Tourist Service is a local travel agency that arranges flights, transportation, excursions, and hotel stays.

Contacts **AeroDomca** (⊠ *Plaza El Paseo, Las Terrenas* ☎ *809/240–6571* ⊕ *www.aerodomca.com*). **Flora Tours** (⊠ *Calle Principal Duarte, Las Terrenas* ☎ *809/360–2793* ⊕ *www.floratours.net*). **Samaná Tourist Service** (⊠ *Av. La Marina 6, Samaná* ☎ *809/538–2740*).

RESTAURANTS

You can stay busy finding your favorite restaurant at Las Terrenas, the town where you can find almost all the best restaurants on the peninsula. Particularly memorable is the collection of eight shoulder-to-shoulder restaurants on the beach called Pueblo de los Pescadores. These are on stilts above the sand, a few paces from the water.

Although you'll be able to get meat, fish is the specialty here, and is available far and wide. *Mero* (grouper) and *dorado* (mahimahi) are the most abundant—you can find the traditional Dominican preparation of *pescado al coco* (coconut fish) virtually everywhere. Shrimp and lobster also readily available. Passion fruit, called *chinola*, is an abundant staple, as well as bananas (*guineos*), oranges (*naranjas*), and giant papayas (*lechozas*). Chinola makes a great fresh-squeezed breakfast juice, especially when it's mixed with pineapple (*piña*).

All restaurants have bars, and serve as the nightlife focal points. Expect to pay around US$8 to $15 for most entrées in this chapter; restaurants in the Dominican Republic always charge in pesos, but you can sometimes pay in U.S. dollars.

HOTELS

The quintessential stay, the one that has the most local flavor and puts you in contact with the people and spirit of Samaná, is in one of the small beach hotels run by expats. These were the region's first tourist outposts, and the oldest opened in the mid- to late 1990s. In these small hotels you can find complete tranquillity: no TVs or phones, just a quiet, lush cabana haven with a footpath leading to the water. These hotels range from $50 to $140 per night, and are mainly concentrated in the towns of Las Terrenas and Las Galeras; rates in small hotels are often set in pesos, but as in some restaurants, you can sometimes pay in U.S. dollars. On a hill high above Playa Cosón is Peninsula House, one of the world's great luxury bed-and-breakfasts. It's new and almost unknown, and it's well worth the money if you can afford it.

There are five all-inclusive resorts in Samaná, with rates ranging from around $100 to $150 per person (AIs in the Dominican Republic almost always charge in U.S. dollars). Bahía Príncipe, a Spanish all-inclusive chain, has four resorts scattered across the peninsula. These are of a high caliber, though two are not included in this guide because of their less-than-choice locations. The fifth is the appealing Samaná Grand Paradise, at Las Galeras.

In Las Terrenas, Playa Bonita and Playa Cosón are the best places to stay; they are removed from the louder nightlife of Playa Las Terrenas. Be sure to ask whether your room has air-conditioning if that's important to you (or phones or TVs, for that matter). The weather is breezy and wonderful, and you may not find air-conditioning to be a necessity (many smaller hotels don't offer it), but if it's important, you'll want to clarify ahead of time.

WHAT IT COSTS IN U.S. DOLLARS AND DOMINICAN PESOS					
	¢	$	$$	$$$	$$$$
RESTAURANTS in dollars	under $8	$8–$12	$12–$20	$20–$30	over $30
RESTAURANTS in pesos	under RD$275	RD$275–RD$410	RD$410–RD$680	RD$680–RD$1,000	over RD$1,000
HOTELS*	under $80	$80–$150	$150–$250	$250–$350	over $350
HOTELS**	under $125	$125–$250	$250–$350	$350–$450	over $450

*EP, BP, CP **AI, FAP, MAP

Restaurant prices are per person for a main course at dinner and do not include the 16% tax (ITBIS) and 10% service charge (ley). Hotel prices are per night for a double room in high season, excluding 16% tax and 10% service charge.

LAS TERRENAS

22 mi (35 km) northwest of Santa Bárbara de Samaná.

Las Terrenas is the main tourist base on the Samaná Peninsula. It, rather than Santa Bárbara de Samaná, the peninsula's biggest town, is the true center of a visit to the region.

GETTING HERE AND AROUND

The main roads from the southern part of the peninsula end up at the busy center of town along the water, where you can find lots of bars and shopping. Some visitors looking to get away from civilization may find this section overcrowded, but others enjoy the variety of restaurants and nightlife.

EXPLORING LAS TERRENAS

A river outlet to the sea splits the center of town. To the east, the beach is known as Playa Punta Popy, and this is the least desirable of the five big **public beaches** in Las Terrenas. To the west is a charming conglomeration of restaurants along the beach called Pueblo de los Pescadores. These eight side-by-side restaurants are set up on wooden floorboards supported by stilts above the sand. Don't miss having a drink here at sunset, and then dinner at one of the restaurants. The bars and restaurants are set up about a foot over the sand, and the views and breezes are relaxing. It's one of the highlights of any trip to Samaná. The beach here is called Playa Las Terrenas. Beyond this, the beach becomes even less commercial and more attractive, stretching to where the road ends: this is Playa Ballenas, named for the offshore rock islands that appear to resemble humpback whales.

As nice as Playa Las Ballenas is, Playa Cosón and Playa Bonita are even quieter and less trafficked, since they're farther away from the town. At Playa Bonita you can bounce between the golden beach and one of the hotels directly across the rough road, where you can have lunch. Hotel Acaya, for instance, has an open-air restaurant and bar.

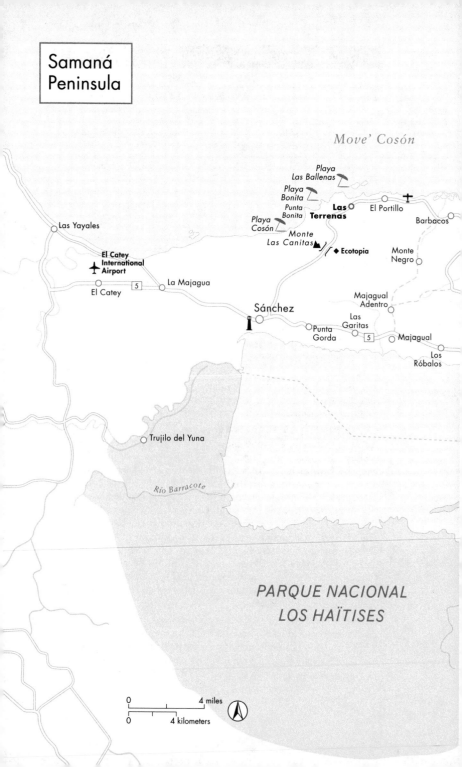

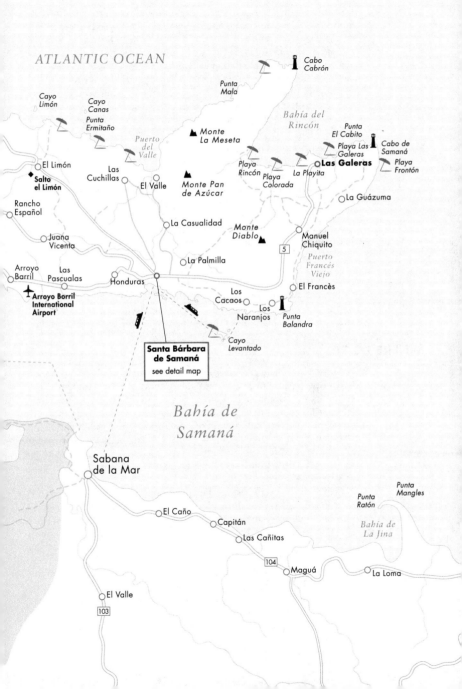

ATLANTIC OCEAN

Cabo
Cabrón

Punta
Mala

Bahía del
Rincón

Cayo
Limón

Cayo
Canas

Punta
Ermitaño

Puerto
del
Valle

Monte
La Meseta

Punta
El Cabito

Playa Las
Galeras

Cabo de
Samaná

El Limón

Las
Cuchillas

El Valle

Monte Pan
de Azúcar

Playa
Rincón

Playa
Colorada

Las Galeras

La Playita

Playa
Frontón

Salto
el Limón

Rancho
Español

La Casualidad

Monte
Diablo

Manuel
Chiquito

La Guázuma

Juana
Vicenta

5

Puerto
Francés
Viejo

Arroyo
Barril

Las
Pascualas

La Palmilla

Honduras

Los
Cacaos

El Francès

Arroyo Borril
International
Airport

Los
Naranjos

Punta
Balandra

Cayo
Levantado

Santa Bárbara
de Samaná
see detail map

Bahía de
Samaná

Sabana
de la Mar

Punta
Mangles

Punta
Ratón

El Caño

Capitán

Bahía de
La Jina

Las Cañitas

104

Maguá

La Loma

El Valle

103

Playa Cosón is an unspoiled 12-mi stretch of white sand, the best beach in Las Terrenas. There is one beachfront hotel here, Casa Cosón, and it's a fine stay, with a great restaurant called The Beach.

One mile southwest of Las Terrenas on the mountain road to Sánchez, **Ecotopia** (⊠ *Hoyo de Cacao, Las Terrenas* ☎ *809/350–4820 or 809/299–4820* ⊕ *www.ecotopia-dr.com* ⊠ *$2* ⊘ *Mon.–Sat. 8–5, Sun. 9–noon. Closed Mon. Jan.–May*), a private botanical park, fills a vital role in a region without a public botanical garden. In the 70-acre preserve you can hike along trails, learning about the many varieties of exotic plants. Highlights of the hikes include a panoramic lookout where you can see across mountains to a view down over Cosón and Bonita beaches. There's also a natural pool you can swim in. The real pleasure is just walking past valleys full of heliconia and other tropical flowers.

★ Provided that you're fit and willing to deal with a long and slippery path on horseback, an adventurous guided trip to the spectacular **Salto el Limón Waterfall** is a delight. The journey is done mostly on horseback, but includes some walking down rocky, sometimes muddy trails. You'll have to cross two rivers en route. Horse paths are slippery, and the trek is strenuous. The well-mannered horses take you across rivers and up mountains to El Limón, where you can find the 165-foot waterfall amid luxuriant vegetation. Some snacks and drinks are usually included in the guided trip, but a grilled chicken lunch is only a few more pesos. The outpost for the trek, a local guide service called Santi Rancho, is relatively difficult to find; it's best to ask your hotel for detailed directions or arrange a tour from an operator like Flora Tours in Las Terrenas. The trip to the waterfall by horseback takes 40 minutes each way; the entire excursion lasts about three hours. ⊠ *Santi Rancho, El Limón.*

WHERE TO EAT

¢–$ ✕ **Acaya Café.** There are a few inviting places to eat or have a drink on
SEAFOOD Playa Bonita. This one is beneath an attractive palapa (grass hut). The contemporary decor, all handmade by the former owner, includes long lanterns created from palm roots collected nearby. It's this attention to detail that gives this café a whiff of languorous style. Lounge chairs and settees make it inviting to curl up with a book, too; it's a beach, after all. The menu offers typical Samaná fare; it's almost always right to go for the grilled fresh fish. ⊠ *Hotel Acaya, Playa Bonita, Las Terrenas* ☎ *809/240–6161* ▤ *MC, V.*

$ ✕ **The Beach.** The very best food in all of Samaná is served up for lunch
SEAFOOD (and lunch only) at this little place on Playa Cosón, which is likely to
Fodor's Choice be a highlight of your trip. Hidden past a long lawn behind a grove of
★ coconut trees on this 12-mi stretch of virgin beach (reachable after a long, torturous drive), The Beach is a splendid mix of fancy and relaxed beach club: an old plantation-style hut with tables along the patio where you can linger in your swimsuit and sandy feet while receiving service on cotton linens, fine antique china, and crystal glassware. The daily changing menu is based on what fresh ingredients and fish are available. Cooking is refined, whether you opt for a hamburger or something a bit more elaborate, like beef fillet with pepper sauce. It's experiences

like this that help make vacations worthwhile. ✉ *Playa Cosón, Las Terrenas* ☎ *809/962–7447* 🖃 *No credit cards* ⊘ *Closed Mon. No dinner.*

$ ✕**La Terrasse.** The unassuming charm of this adorable whitewashed
MEDITERRANEAN restaurant can rival relaxed beachfront dining anywhere in the world.
★ What sets it apart from its similar brethren on Pueblo de los Pescadores is the care of its French and Spanish owners Denise Cheynesy and Willy Barrera. You can guess that it's Denise's hand in little touches like perfume in the bathroom, the ginger and bougainvillea on the tables, and the white wooden trim, a rare attempt at daintiness in the Dominican Republic. Specials are presented on a chalkboard with an ornamental border, and might feature "sun-inspired" dishes like sunny-yellow zucchini blossoms deep-fried until they're crispy and perfect. Tuna steak is served sesame-crusted with a soy-based sauce, along with ratatouille, green beans, and white rice. A surprisingly good wine selection is stored in a wine refrigerator. ✉ *Pueblo de los Pescadores, Las Terrenas* ☎ *809/240–6730* 🖃 *No credit cards.*

$$ ✕**L'Atlantico.** Prystasz Gerard, honorary French consul and former pri-
SEAFOOD vate chef to François Mitterrand, has camped out at this relaxed, thatch-
★ roofed outpost right on the beach at the far end of Playa Bonita. The vibe is casual, the food a cut above. Gerard can prepare food that no one else in Samaná can, including shrimp in cacao and whisky sauce and house-smoked fish. Dorado in champagne sauce? Mais oui. The fine local fish meets its fancy French fate, and you'll be glad for it. ✉ *Atlantis Hotel, Playa Bonita, Las Terrenas* ☎ *809/240–6111* 🖃 *AE, MC, V.*

WHERE TO STAY

$ 🏨**Casa Cosón.** This is the best lodging choice in La Terrenas if what you
HOTEL care about is proximity to a quiet beach. In fact, it's the only lodging option on Playa Cosón, the best of the beaches around—you'll feel like you own the place. The two-story house has four bedrooms, all with balconies that have ocean views, at $140 each. Behind the house are four thatch-roofed bungalows, better and more fun for families. Air-conditioning is $15 a night extra throughout the property. There's also a bar and a restaurant here, and a two-minute walk down the beach is another fine place to have lunch, The Beach restaurant. What this means is that you really don't have to leave much to enjoy a restful vacation. There's a nice pool and a wide lawn set with tables under coconut trees leading to the sands. **Pros:** beachfront setting amid miles of empty sands. **Cons:** bad roads mean a lot of tough driving into town. ✉ *Playa Cosón* ☎ *809/861–6288* ⊕ *www.casacoson.com* ⇱4 *rooms, 4 bungalows* ⌂ *In-room: no phone, safe, kitchen (some), refrigerator (some), no TV. In-hotel: restaurant, bar, pool, beachfront, laundry service.* 🖃 *AE, MC, V.*

¢ 🏨**Coyamar.** If you don't mind going without air-conditioning, it's hard
HOTEL not to love the hyper-relaxed atmosphere of this small, family-run hotel
★ on Playa Bonita. At $55 a night, Coyamar is the least expensive of the peninsula's languorous gems. A path wends its way across the yard of orange trees, coconut palms, and bamboo to the beach at the end of the lawn, which stands fifteen feet from the water. The restaurant, under an enormous thatch roof, serves fresh fish and is a wonderful place to

read a book. Coyamar is the creation (just like the name itself) of German expat owners Peter and Judith, who designed the environmentally sensitive hotel in the 1990s. Expect to see a shirtless Peter reading the papers while young son Tao cavorts with his chow chows. Rooms are bright, with peach and light greens. Red floor tiles extend from spacious terraces to the comfortable interiors, which have high ceilings and colorful art and radios. There is no air-conditioning, nor TVs or phones, but the shutters ensure breezy nights (there are ceiling fans). Don't like the overhead fluorescent lighting at night? Light the candle in your room, and take in the sounds of the surf by flickering light. Life doesn't get simpler. **Pros:** hands-on owners; green hotel; great value. **Cons:** no air-conditioning; fluorescent lights are dim. ⊠ *Playa Bonita 1, Las Terrenas* ☎ *809/240–5130* ⊕ *www.coyamar.com* ⇱ *10 rooms* ⌂ *In-room: no a/c, no phone, safe, no TV. In-hotel: restaurant, bar, pool, beachfront, Wi-Fi, some pets allowed* ▭ *MC, V* ⧖ *CP.*

¢   ⚏ **Hotel Acaya.** Ten steps from Playa Bonita, Acaya holds a beach-bum
HOTEL   vibe with touches of surprisingly tasteful decor—and the addition of air-conditioning, a rarity in these parts. Rooms are simple, with white-tile floors and queen beds with pastel linens; but high ceilings, light colors, and wood shutters create a feeling of lightness and space. Lamps are made from gourds collected on the property. Stay closer to the restaurant; doubles in the next building aren't quite as nice. A full breakfast, included in the price, is made fresh each morning, even if you sleep in until 3:00. You get beach chairs and cushions for a day on the sand, and if you're feeling ambitious, there's a surf shop on-site. Bathrooms are spacious, with two sinks, and are painted a cheery cerulean. The stylish restaurant and bar has hammocks and games that make it a relaxing place to hang out. Rooms are $75. **Pros:** inexpensive; bright. **Cons:** the tide sometimes covers up the small beach. ⊠ *Playa Bonita, Las Terrenas* ☎ *809/240–6161* ⊕ *www.hotelacaya.com* ⇱ *16 rooms* ⌂ *In-room: no phone, refrigerator, no TV, Wi-Fi. In-hotel: restaurant, bar, beachfront, water sports, laundry facilities, laundry service, Internet terminal, Wi-Fi hotspot* ▭ *MC, V* ⧖ *BP.*

¢–$ ⚏ **Hotel Playa Colibri.** With full kitchens and expansive balconies (actu-
HOTEL   ally bigger than the bedrooms) that overlook the beach, friendly and
⚙   relaxed Colibri is the best bet for families on Playa Las Ballenas, a few minutes from the hubbub of town. Rooms overlook the big pool and the ocean, and balconies are equipped with a table and chairs for outdoor dining. The interiors, however, suffer from overhead fluorescent lighting and artlessly assembled furnishings. The pool is one of the biggest around, and has a small kids' section and a whirlpool. Rooms come in three basic layouts: type C is only a few dollars cheaper and faces the rear, so focus on A or B rooms). The hotel, which has a bar directly on the beach under a thatched roof, provides beach towels for guests. **Pros:** on the quieter end of Playa Las Ballenas; easy for kids to enjoy the pool. **Cons:** most rooms do not have air-conditioning; rooms aren't anything to write home about. ⊠ *Playa Las Ballenas, Las Terrenas* ☎ *809/240–6434* ⊕ *www.playacolibri.com* ⇱ *41 rooms* ⌂ *In-room: a/c (some), no phone, safe, kitchen, refrigerator, DVD, no TV, Internet, Wi-Fi. In-hotel: restaurant, room service, bars, tennis courts, pool, gym,*

spa, beachfront, diving, water sports, bicycles, children's programs (ages 2–14), laundry facilities, laundry service, Internet terminal, Wi-Fi hotspot, some pets allowed ▭ AE, MC, V ⦿ EP.

$$$$
BED-AND-BREAKFAST
Fodor's Choice
★

🏠 **Peninsula House.** The gorgeous Victorian-style plantation house with wraparound verandas overlooks miles of coconut palms down to the ocean. Superlative in so many ways, a review should truly begin by establishing up front: this is one of the best bed-and-breakfasts in the world. If you can afford it, a stay here will reset your thinking on what a small luxury property can be. It's family run, showcasing generations' worth of museum-quality sculptures, paintings, and objects d'art, many of which were brought from Asia and the Middle East. The art elevates the rooms and common areas to a fascinating visual experience. Dinner, available only to guests, takes place in the central open-air brick courtyard. Dishes, linens, even the stationery is refined; to mention that rooms come with flat-screen TVs (the only ones on the Samaná Peninsula at this writing) would be missing the point. No expense has been spared: even the pool house has a world-class collection of African masks. Admittedly, more than $500 is a lot for a room, and it does not have full-fledged "resort" amenities, but we'd recommend that you consider saving now. In terms of international high-end travel, this is a real steal. The house doesn't advertise, and the secretive entrance is unmarked from off a long dirt road. **Pros:** quiet and remote; luxurious; impeccable guest attention. **Cons:** very expensive, but that's the only drawback we can find. ⊠ *Camino Cosón, Las Terrenas* ☎ *809/307–1827 or 809/882–7712* ⊕ *www.thepeninsulahouse.com* ⤶ *6 rooms* ⌂ *In-room: safe, DVD, Wi-Fi. In-hotel: bar, pool, spa, laundry service, Wi-Fi, no kids under 18* ▭ *AE, D, MC, V* ⦿ *BP.*

NIGHTLIFE

El Corazon (⊠ *Calle Duarte at intersection to Cosón Beach Road, Las Terrenas* ☎ *809/240–5329* ⊕ *micorazon.com*) is considered the best restaurant in the country by some Santo Domingo residents, but we're less impressed by the expensive menu of gussied up Dominican dishes like fish in coconut sauce and beef tenderloin. You should visit here for a drink, though, if you're in town for more than a couple of days. On one end of Calle Duarte, away from the beach, this three-story white edifice set around an interior courtyard has a pastry shop on the ground floor, the restaurant on the second floor, and atop the white walls and benches, this third-floor bar. This is the town taking itself seriously and acting self-consciously romantic: candles niched along walls with wrought-iron rails and Colonial-style lanterns. They're trying, but maybe too hard.

El Mosquito (⊠ *Pueblo de los Pescadores, Las Terrenas* ☎ *809/877–2844*) is the main bar at Pueblo de los Pescadores. It opens nightly at 6 PM and offers a small food menu; there's occasionally live music. There is a rotating set of pretty good art on its walls. Mainly, though, it's a wonderful place to enjoy drinks on the beach and gaze up at the stars.

El Toro Sobre El Techo (⊠ *Pueblo de los Pescadores, Las Terrenas* ☎ *809/240–6648*), another Pueblo de Pescadores favorite, is the busiest and most crowded scene in Las Terrenas, relative to its small size. Expect pulsing music and a singles-bar type crowd.

Gaia Club (⊠ *Pueblo de los Pescadores, Las Terrenas* ☎ *809/240–5133, gaiaclub.com*) is a new three-story bar and disco that has elevated the humble Terrenas nightlife scene. Each floor plays different music and has a different look. If you're looking to dance, cross the street from the beachside Pescadores bars and you've found your place.

★ **Syroz Bar** (⊠ *Pueblo de los Pescadores, Las Terrenas* ☎ *809/212–7217*) is a consistent nightlife favorite, known for its live jazz. Before dinner, you can take in the sunset from the beachfront stools; it's hard not to feel as if this is one of the best spots in the world. They also serve lunch and dinner.

SPORTS AND THE OUTDOORS

BEACHES

On **Playa Bonita** (⊠ *Las Terrenas*) you can bounce between the golden beach (BYO towel—no chaises) and one of the hotels and restaurants directly across the rough road, where you can have lunch. The beach can disappear during flooding and high tides. It's a quiet stretch of gold sand with leaning coconut trees.

Fodor's Choice **Playa Cosón** (⊠ *Las Terrenas*) is a long, wonderful stretch of white sand
★ and the best beach close to the town of Las Terrenas. At the time of this writing, it was completely undeveloped, but there are a dozen condo developments under construction, so that sense of solitude won't last. One restaurant, The Beach, serves the entire 15-mi shore.

★ **Playa Jackson** (⊠ *Approximately 10 km (6 mi) from Las Terrenas by boat*), a secluded beach with a coral reef just offshore, can be reached by hired boat from Las Terrenas or Las Galeras. It's a popular destination for snorkeling.

Playa Las Ballenas (⊠ *Las Terrenas*) is the westernmost of the three beaches at the town of Las Terrenas (the others are Terrenas and Punta Popy, all three of them forming a continuous stretch of beach with different names). Ballenas is the nicest stretch in town, since it's the quietest section. The western edge is undeveloped. Moderate hotels across the street provide chaises to their guests, and the Hotel Playa Colibri runs a little bar on the beach. The beach is named for the small whale-shaped cays in the distance.

Playa Punta Popy (⊠ *Las Terrenas*) is basically an undistinguishable continuation of Playa Terrenas to the east; this section is slightly cleaner and less crowded the farther east (away from town) you travel.

Playa Terrenas (⊠ *Las Terrenas*) is the most crowded (and dirtiest) of all the peninsula's beaches. As you approach the ocean from the town of Las Terrenas, a fork divides the road. To the west is Playa Las Ballenas, and to the east is this beach.

BOATING AND FISHING

Boats are a great way to see more secluded beaches. Playa Jackson, for example, is the best spot in the area for snorkeling, and can be reached only by boat. Flora Tours (*see* ⇨ *Tours, below*) is the only operator arranging snorkeling trips at the moment.

DIVING

In 1979 three atolls disappeared after a seaquake off Las Terrenas, providing an opportunity for truly memorable dives. Also just offshore from Las Terrenas are the Islas Las Ballenas (The Whale Islands), a cluster of four little islands with good snorkeling. A coral reef is off Playa Jackson, a beach accessible only by boat.

Las Terrenas Divers (⊠ *At hotel Bahía Las Ballenas, Playa Bonita, Las Terrenas* ☎ *809/889–2422* ⊕ *www.lt-divers.com*) offers diving lessons and trips. A dive is $38; daily diving equipment rentals are $10. Learn-to-dive programs are $80. It is closed Sunday.

HORSEBACK RIDING

Rancho Cedric (⊠ *Playa Las Terrenas, behind Hotel Las Cayenas, Las Terrenas* ☎ *809/847–4849*) offers rides on Playa Bonita for $18 and Playa Cosón or Las Terrenas for $45. **Club Hippique Las Terrenas** (☎ *829/962–4259*)has mountain and beach excursions.

SURFING

Surfing, windsurfing, wakeboarding, and kite surfing are popular in Las Terrenas. Playa Cosón has the best breaks. Playa Bonita is another popular spot, because, as on Cosón, there are no rocks. Two-hour lessons are $35, and a one-day board rental runs $25; it's usually $15 for half a day.

Carolina Surf School (⊠ *Hotel Acaya, Playa Bonita, Las Terrenas* ☎ *809/882-5467* ⊕ *www.carolinasurfschool.com*) rents surfboards and offers lessons.

Las Terrenas Divers (⊠ *Playa Bonita, Las Terrenas* ☎ *809/889–2422*) rents surf and Boogie boards and gives surfing lessons.

TOURS

★ **Flora Tours** (⊠ *Calle Principal Duarte, Las Terrenas* ☎ *809/360–2793* ⊕ *www.flora-tours.net*), the best operator in Las Terrenas, can arrange boating and hiking trips. To the El Limón waterfall the cost is $50 per person and includes taxi pickup at your hotel, round-trip transportation, a meal, tips for your guides, horse, and trip to the falls. They also arrange snorkeling trips to various beaches nearby. They have also created hiking trips up to cacao plantations and arrange trips to Los Haitises. Guided hikes cost $35 to $65. In addition, this well-established, safety-oriented company offers horseback riding on the beach and in the countryside for $40 for two hours, canyoning, and lots of other adventure sports.

SHOPPING

Shopping isn't a big draw in Samaná in general, but Las Terrenas has the most shops. They mainly sell trinkets aimed at tourists.

Haitian Caraïbes Art Gallery (⊠ *Calle Principal 233, Las Terrenas* ☎ *809/240–6250*) is the entire peninsula's main source for Haitian art. They also sell the best of the region's other souvenirs, including cigars as well as sarongs.

SANTA BÁRBARA DE SAMANÁ

22 mi (35 km) southeast of Las Terrenas.

The official name of the city is Santa Bárbara de Samaná; but these days it's just called "Samaná." An authentic port town, it's just getting its bearings as a tourist zone, and compared to Las Galeras and Las Terrenas there are very few reasons to spend time here. It has a typical *malecón* (seaside promenade) that's ideal for strolling and watching the boats in the harbor. A small but bustling town, Samaná is filled with friendly residents, skilled local craftsmen selling their wares, and a handful of outdoor restaurants.

A big all-inclusive resort, the Bahía Príncipe Cayacoa, is on one end of the bay road on a hill. Day passes are available (and the resort has the only beaches in town). The hotel also operates a block of new and colorful gift shops and a small casino. This group is the town's first (and so far only) attempt to capture cruise-ship-passenger money. It's the very colorful and new string of buildings called Pueblo Marina. Along Avenida del Malecón is Victoria Marine, ground zero for tours to see whales from January until late March, as well as the Los Haitises park across the bay.

EXPLORING SANTA BÁRBARA DE SAMANÁ

There are no public beaches in Samaná town, but you can hire a boat to take you to **Cayo Levantado,** which has a wonderful white-sand beach on an island in Samaná Bay. Today the small island has largely been turned into a commercial enterprise to accommodate the 1,500 cruise-ship passengers who dock here each day; it has dining facilities, bars, restrooms, and lounge chairs on the beautiful beach. Unfortunately, it's also a tacky tourist trap, especially when there's a ship in port. The company that runs cruise-ship services on the island also operates the public section of the island and is guilty of some bad decisions, including importing sea lions and charging tourists $8 to take a photo with them. It's this sort of practice that can make Cayo Levantado unpleasant, though the beaches are undeniably beautiful. The new Grand Bahía Príncipe Cayo Levantado, an upscale, all-inclusive resort, claims the eastern two-thirds of the island for its private use, and sells one-day passes that allow you to use the resort's facilities and get food and drinks for about $70. Day trips to Los Haitises often stop here for some beach time before returning to Santa Bárbara de Samaná. ⊠ *Samaná Bay* ☎ *No phone* 🎫 *Public beach free* ⏱ *Daily dawn–dusk.*

Back in 1824, a sailing vessel called the *Turtle Dove,* carrying several hundred slaves that had escaped from Philadelphia, was blown ashore in Samaná. The historic **Dominican Evangelical Church** is the oldest original building left in Samaná. The structure actually came across the ocean from England in 1881 in a hundred pieces and was reassembled

CLOSE UP

Expats in Paradise

If you spend any amount of time on the Samaná Peninsula, you'll meet a gaggle of unaffiliated expatriate entrepreneurs who have made Samaná their homemade paradise and who have created most of its tourism infrastructure. Here are three of their stories.

In the late 1990s two young Germans, Peter and Judith, decided they wanted to start a new life in a tropical setting. They ranked all the warm-weather nations of the world, considering critical factors like political stability and crime rates. "This was before the Internet, and involved a lot of dedicated research," said Peter. "The D.R. was at the very top of our list." Then they built their hotel in Las Terrenas. Today a visit to the beachfront Coyamar Hotel—which exudes a breeziness that's decidedly romantic—is a trip into their world. You'll probably meet soft-spoken Judith at reception, and you'll see a bare-chested Peter and their son, Tao, who was born here in 2001. "It's almost impossible to make a profit, but we enjoy our life," Peter said.

French-born Yvonne Bastian arrived in 1998 from the Central African Republic, where she'd run a restaurant that had served presidents and dignitaries. Revolution brought her to the Dominican Republic, and she's been the guiding gastronomic light in the main town of Santa Bárbara de Samaná sever since. (In 2007 the restaurant Xaman opened, and suddenly there were *two* good restaurants in town, but it closed not long after, and it's back to just Yvonne.) Yvonne's grown-up son runs the front of the house. The duo's care is evident in the tranquil, oasis-like interior.

In 2005 a family of three were in search of a new life project and a new place to live. Cari Guy had grown up in the kitchens of his family's Colorado restaurants and later found success operating a luxury bed-and-breakfast in Provence. There he met Marie-Claude Theibault, whose Parisian family had imported antiques from the Far East for generations. Her son Thomas Stamm grew up in the United States and South Africa. The three had sought out locales in Croatia, Spain, and beyond. "We came to the Dominican Republic visiting friends and knew we'd found our place when we saw Samaná," said Thiebault. "It was beautiful, and nothing like this had ever been done." The Peninsula House—their ultrarefined six-room hilltop property overlooking huge swaths of coconut forest to the sea—was built from scratch, using a French architect. Thomas handles guest relations, Marie-Claude tends the gardens, Cari oversees the cooking. The result is one of the world's most extraordinary small hotels.

5

here, serving the spiritual needs of the African-American freedman here. ⊠ *Calle Chaseurox, in front of Catholic church* ☎ *809/538–2579* 🖃 *Donations appreciated* ☺ *Daily dawn–dusk.*

En route to the Cayacoa hotel, the tiny **Whale Museum & Nature Center (Centro de Naturaleza)** is dedicated to the mighty mammals of the sea. Samaná has one of the largest marine mammal sanctuaries in the world, and is a center for whale-watching in the migration season. The CEBSE (Center for Conservation and Ecodevelopment of Samaná Bay and Its

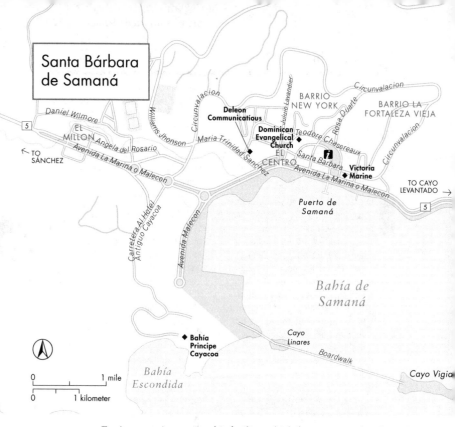

Santa Bárbara
de Samaná

Environment) manages this facility, which features a 40-foot humpback skeleton. ⊠ *Av. La Marina, Tiro al Blanco* ☎ *809/538–2042* ⊕ *Samana. org.do* ⚏ *RD$50* ⊙ *Daily 8–noon and 2–5.*

Fodor'sChoice
★
Los Haitises National Park. One of the highlights of a trip to the Dominican Republic—and probably the most extraordinary part of a visit to the Samaná Peninsula—is a chance to explore Los Haitises National Park. Los Haitises (pronounced High-*tee*-sis), which is across Samaná Bay from the peninsula, is famous for its karst limestone formations, caves, and grottoes filled with pictographs and petroglyphs left by the indigenous Taino, who inhabited this area before Columbus's arrival.

The park is accessible only by boat, and a professionally guided tour is highly recommended—especially so you can kayak along the shoreline (there's no place to rent a kayak without a guide). Another option is to hire a fisherman to take you over on a small boat, but then you'll miss the guidance that an experienced operator can provide.

On a trip you'll sail around dozens of the dramatic rock islands and spectacular cliff faces. Swirling around are hundreds of beautiful coastal birds that represent 121 different species, including Magnificent Frigate-birds, brown pelicans, brown booby, and varieties of egrets and herons. The sight of dozens of different birds continually gliding past the boat at any time is enough to make a bird-watcher out of anyone.

A good tour will let you visit the many caverns. Your flashlight will illuminate Taino and pre-Taino petroglyphs. You'll also find out how the forest slowly consumes the caves. But the best experience is being able to kayak here. Unlike mangrove kayaking trips in, say, the Florida Everglades, the mangroves here are dramatically flanked by the karst formations. It's a continual sensory delight. The islands rise dramatically and have wild growths of plant life and birds swooping around. ⊠ *Samaná Bay* ☏ *No phone* ✉ *Admission included with guided tour (required)* ☉ *Daily dawn–dusk.*

WHERE TO EAT

$

SEAFOOD

✕ **La Mata Rosada.** The French owner-chef of La Mata, Yvonne Bastian, has been luring local expats and foodies since the late 1990s. She sets tables with white linens in an all-white interior that includes an army of ceiling fans to keep you cool; breezes sneak in from the bay across the street. There's a plentiful array of choices, starting with a sea and country salad of conch, potatoes, greens, and bacon; or the "gourmet" plate, a mix of grilled lobster and other shellfish. Ceviche, a specialty of this port town, is made with *dorado* (mahimahi) and conch. Whether you go local or international, order the creole shrimp or a substantial salad, and you should leave satisfied. The desserts are also presented with pride. ⊠ *Av. Malecón 5B* ☏ *809/538–2388* ⊟ *AE, MC, V* ☉ *June–Nov., closed Tues.*

WHERE TO STAY

$$$

ALL-INCLUSIVE

☷ **Bahía Príncipe Cayacoa.** As you might expect of an all-inclusive built in the middle of immense natural beauty, this place combines the best and worst of everything. Of the four Gran Bahías on the peninsula, only this one doesn't make you feel like a prisoner (although you are still wearing a plastic ID bracelet), since town (and the good food you can find there) is just a five-minute walk away. The best that Cayacoa offers are the mesmerizing views: the ocean, the town, and the rolling green landscape all lie before you from this hilltop perch on the bay. Also, this is the only actual hotel in the town of Samaná. (The next closest, Gran Bahía Samaná, is 10 minutes away, but still feels unpleasantly isolated.) Day visitors can purchase a pass for $70 that includes all food and drinks and recreation (an excellent choice for cruise passengers). You need to stay a minimum of three nights to dine at the nonbuffet restaurants. Cayacoa has its own spa and disco. Snorkeling and kayaks are included. **Pros:** beautiful views; fun activities. **Cons:** bad food; forced to wear ID bracelet. ⊠ *Puerto Escondido, Santa Bárbara de Samaná* ☏ *809/538–3131* ⊕ *www.bahiaprincipe.com* ⇆ *209 rooms, 86 suites* ⌂ *In room: a/c, safe, refrigerator. In-hotel: 5 restaurants, room service, bars, pools, gym, spa, beachfront, diving, water sports, laundry service, Internet terminal, Wi-Fi* ⊟ *AE, D, DC, MC, V* ⊚ *AI.*

$$$

ALL-INCLUSIVE

★

☷ **Bahía Príncipe Cayo Levantado.** This all-inclusive resort—the most expensive and highest rated of the four Bahía Príncipes in Samaná—hogs two-thirds of the gorgeous island for itself. Whether that's good or bad, you can't deny that it has the best beaches, pools, and recreational choices

5

of any resort in the area. Twice-daily ferries shuttle you to the island from the mainland; you're welcomed with a beverage at reception and given a bracelet. Unfortunately, if you tire of tourists in Hawaiian shirts and bad food, you're stuck here until the next morning. Well, at least you've got a nice room to wait it out in: each has a balcony or terrace that looks out over the ocean, with a big canopy bed and a whirlpool bath separated by a glass partition from the bedroom. Service is a high point—and you will be treated with care by the hard-working local Dominican staff. The peppy "animation" team puts on shows each night. **Pros:** beautiful beach; new rooms with ocean views. **Cons:** bad food; expensive for this region; ID bracelet required; removed from reality. ⊠ *Cayo Levantado* ☎ *809/538–3232* ⊕ *www.bahiaprincipe.com* ⤴ *195 rooms* ⚄ *In-room: a/c, afe, refrigerator. In-hotel: 5 restaurants, room service, bars, pools, gym, spa, beachfront, diving, water sports, laundry service, Internet terminal, Wi-Fi hotspot* ▤ *AE, D, DC, MC, V* ⏝⃝ *AI.*

$ ⚄ **Hotel Las Ballenas Escondidas.** The English-speaking French couple who
HOTEL   run this place have created a small utopia of gardens and thatch-roof
Fodor's Choice   bungalows sloping down to the sea. If you're looking for a truly relax-
★   ing and peaceful setting with a private beach, this is your place. An infinity pool is in the middle of it all. Ballenas Escondidas is 15 minutes east of Santa Bárbara de Samaná, nearly halfway to Las Galeras. It's essentially in the middle of nowhere. But where the remoteness and the nice pool and restaurant might seem to imply an all-inclusive experience, there are no forced good times here. At night the ocean is the only music you'll hear. By day, a private terrace with two bamboo chairs overlooks the hibiscus, bougainvillea, coconut trees, and colorful pastels of the other bungalows; a few cats roam the grounds. The hotel offers boating excursions directly from its small beach. The rooms have new mattresses and ceiling fans, but no air-conditioning. **Pros:** private; quiet; beautiful. **Cons:** remote location; thin sheets; no air-conditioning, no credit cards. ⊠ *Los Naranjos* ☎ *809/495–0888 or 809/899–9781* ⊕ *www.hotelballenasescondidas.com* ⤴ *12 bungalows* ⚄ *In-room: no a/c, no phone, safe, refrigerator, no TV. In-hotel: restaurant, bar, pool, beachfront, laundry service* ▤ *No credit cards* ⏝⃝ *BP.*

SPORTS AND THE OUTDOORS

BEACHES

Although Santa Bárbara de Samaná has no public beaches, there is one private beach near town and one reachable by ferry.

Puerto Escondido (⊠ *Puerto Escondido, Santa Bárbara de Samaná*) is the beach at the Bahía Principe Cayacoa, and day visitors can enjoy the sands if they buy a $70 day-pass at the resort. Though crowded with guests, the beach offers great views of the bay, plenty of drinks, and the best strand on the south side of the peninsula.

To reach **Cayo Levantado** (⊠ *Samaná Bay* ✉ *Free* ☉ *Daily dawn–dusk*), you must hire a boat in town or take an excursion to Los Haitises that stops here. The beaches are overly commercialized but beautiful, though on days when cruise ships are in port they are packed with passengers.

BOATING AND FISHING

A new marina, Puerto Bahía, is west of town a few miles and serves Samaná Bay.

Cap Ocean (✉ *Puerto Bahía, Samaná* ☎ *809/803–5595* ⊕ *capocean.site. voila.fr*) has a 35-foot catamaran that operates out of the Puerto Bahía marina. Captains Fabrice and Christian specialize in elaborate (and expensive) fishing excursions

SPAS

The peninsula's only true public spa is run by the Bahía Príncipe Cayacoa hotel, across from the hotel's entrance in a separate building.

Bahía Spa (✉ *Bahía Príncipe Cayacoa, Carretera Camino Playa, Samaná* ☎ *809/538–3131 Ext. 1298* ⊕ *www.bahia-principe.com*) offers 50-minute "Caribbean Relaxing" massages for RD$1,800. The spa also offers a wide range of other body treatments, including waxing, facials, and hot stone therapy.

WHALE-WATCHING AND MARINE EXCURSIONS

Humpback whales come to Samaná Bay to mate and give birth each year for a relatively limited period, from approximately January 15 through March 30. Samaná Bay is considered one of the top 10 destinations in the world to watch humpbacks. If you're here during the brief season, this can be the experience of a lifetime. You can listen to the male humpback's solitary courting song and witness incredible displays as the whales flip their tails and breach (humpbacks are the most active species of whales in the Atlantic).

Victoria Marine/Whale Samaná (✉ *Across street from cement town dock, beside park, Samaná* ☎ *809/538–2494* ✎ *kim.beddall@usa.net* ⊕ *www.whaleSamaná.com*) is owned by Kim Beddall, a Canadian who is incredibly knowledgeable about whales and Samaná at large, having lived here for decades. Her operation is far and away the region's best, most professional, and environmentally sensitive. On board the *Victoria 11,* a 50-foot motor vessel, a marine mammal specialist narrates and answers questions in several languages. Kim herself conducts almost all the English-speaking trips. The $50 price does not include the RD$100 Marine Mammal Sanctuary entrance fee. Kim also welcomes cruise passengers, but requires advance reservations. You must be able to arrive on shore by 9 AM for the morning trip and by 1:30 PM for the afternoon trip.

She also conducts trips to Los Haitises National Park on Tuesday, Thursday, and Saturday on the *Mistral,* a 45-foot catamaran. Tours, which cost $25 per person, include a terrific lunch and last four to five hours. Kim's boat has a dozen kayaks in which teams of two explore the shoreline.

LAS GALERAS

14 mi (22 km) northeast of Santa Bárbara de Samaná.

Sleepy Las Galeras, a dot on the map between two protected and undeveloped green mountain capes, is the endearingly unkempt North Coast

Kim Saves the Whales

Samaná Bay is considered one of the top destinations in the world to watch whales. If you're here in season—humpback whales come to mate and give birth from mid-January for about 60 days—this can be the experience of a lifetime. Humpbacks are the most active species of whales in the Atlantic (Melville called them "the most lighthearted and gamesome of all the whales" in *Moby-Dick*). You can witness incredible displays as the whales breach over and over, spouting a column of air and water with each surface, and then sink with a graceful arc terminated by their beautiful and distinctive tails. If you're lucky, the humpbacks will sometimes leap out of the water acrobatically or slap their tails. You'll witness and learn about other maneuvers, too, like "logging" and "spy hopping," when the whales submerge themselves for about five minutes at a time. Playing scout and being the first to spot the site of the next breach is part of the fun. The real advantage of whale-watching in Samaná is the reliability—the sighting rate is 95% between January 20 and March 20, so you're practically guaranteed to see whales.

The first official whale watch was conducted in Samaná in 1983, and was led by a Canadian named Kim Beddall, who is now the peninsula's recognized whale expert. She's also a tireless advocate for natural causes and responsible growth. Kim arrived in 1983 from Toronto to teach diving. She got a look at the whales during her stay and was hooked: "The local fisherman told me that whales came here to drink freshwater. Nobody knew what species they were or really why they came to Samaná, but they were here and I was hooked."

Kim is responsible for the comanagement process of whale-watching to ensure responsible activity (and thus to make sure the whales keep returning). There are now 43 official permits for whale-watching, a number that's now fixed in perpetuity. The fewer the boats and the larger the size of the boats, the less stress on the whales. (The effect of large cruise ships that frequent the area on mating whales is still unknown.) The rules that Kim helped formalize (a continual bureaucratic and political process) includes minimum boat sizes, minimum distance from whales, viewing order, length of time each boat can be with a whale, and a ban on swimming with the whales.

Now a certified marine mammal specialist, Kim leads the regions' best trips. Her company is Victoria Marine/Whale Samaná.

sister of Las Terrenas. Despite its tucked-away location in eastern end of the Samaná Peninsula, the village maintains a pulse—thanks, mostly, to the hubbub created at the epicenter of the town, which abuts the shoreline. El Kiosko, a barebones grouping of local food merchants beneath a roof thatched with coconut fronds, serves up Presidentes for a crowd made up of equal parts locals, expats, and tourists. The beach itself is rocky and uneven, but you can bring your own towel and rent a white plastic chaise for RD$100 (about $3), accept the syncopated merengue blaring out of a parked car, and stare out toward the cays dotting the horizon.

The real joy of Las Galeras is its lineup of pristine beaches around the bend. To reach them you'll need to be an intrepid and resourceful navigator by car, or, better yet, hire a boat from the beach. The fellow manning the push cart stacked with glossy conch shells can make arrangements for a local fisherman to guide you on a wooden charter out to some of the most pristine beaches the peninsula has to offer, Rincón, Frontón, Colorado, La Playita, and Madama. You should be able to get a boat to Playa Rincón for about $15 per couple. You can spend the day there or go beach-hopping and snorkel off the shore.

GETTING HERE AND AROUND
To reach Las Galeras, continue past Samaná town on the only road along the southern coast, Highway 5, for about an hour, depending on the road conditions. At this writing, the entire road to Las Galeras was being redone, which may cut the travel time in the future. (By the way, the main reason for the lack of development of the northwest corner of the peninsula may have been the woeful state of this road.)

5

WHERE TO EAT

¢–$ ✕**Coconut Roy's Paradise Restaurant.** John Bomare of East Texas con-
SEAFOOD   structed a big grill on the main corner of town, a block from the beach, gave it a catchy name, and with his French wife Audrey serves smoked baby back ribs, steaks, grilled lobster, and seafood to hungry foreigners. The bar here also functions as the nighttime center of town, so if you're spending a night in Las Galeras, you're probably having a drink at Roy's. Expect to make friends with a young waitress from, say, New Zealand, and other folks making their way around the world—barebones bungalows on the property are offered at rock-bottom prices (they're still not worth it). ⊠ *Calle Principal, Las Galeras* ☎ *No phone* ⊟ *MC, V.*

$ ✕**El Cabito.** Don't forget your camera: a hundred feet over the edge of
SEAFOOD   seaside cliff, with views of nothing but jungle and endless sea, this bar and restaurant feels like one of the corners of the world. The simple, off-the-grid thatch palapa edging the cliff seems to exhale with a breezy, unbothered joviality that begins with the serene owners John and Catrin. You're likely to feel like a regular on your first trip, and the setting, perhaps more than any other spot in Samaná, is likely to lure you back. The food is standard fresh catch, nothing too different from any other decent seafood place on the beaches around here. But this is a remote $3 motor taxi ride down coastal dirt roads from Las Galeras beach to the middle of nowhere: it's beautiful, adventurous, or romantic, depending on your mood. Take a seat at the rail, looking straight down the cliff. If weather's stormy, the crashing ocean is spectacular. ⊠ *El Cabito* ☎ *829/697–9506* ⊕ *elcabito.net* ⊟ *Cash only* ⊙ *Closed Mon.*

$ ✕**El Kiosko.** Expect Yaquelín to come out and solicit you when she sees
CARIBBEAN   you trying to figure this place out. That's the charm of the kiosks, the collection of outdoor eateries that's the soul of Las Galeras. The amiable Yaquelín is the proprietress and most outgoing of eight owners of small kitchens that run independently (each represented by their own hand-painted wooden signs, with names like Cafeteria Coco Loco). Kiosko is the big straw hut at the end of the road just before the beach.

All the local vendors pretty much offer the same thing: beer, squid, pork, shrimp, and fish. Lobster served in the native coconut style runs RD$500 and is served with rice, potatoes, beans, and a salad. ⊠ *Calle Principal, Las Galeras* ☎ *No phone* ▤ *No credit cards.*

WHERE TO STAY

$ 🏨 **Grand Paradise Samaná.** There's only one all-inclusive on this side of
ALL-INCLUSIVE the island, and it's a really good one. Unpretentious and remote, with a great beach and a load of activities, the Grand Paradise is a great place to do all the things you want to do in Samaná, including snorkeling, diving, and visiting the virgin beaches. It's also a good base for heading out into the tropical wilderness. The clientele is mainly French and adventurous, and the tour operators that bring them in set up a slew of activities that you can participate in for free: archery, shuffleboard, soccer, volleyball, kayaking, bocce, you name it. All boating excursions depart directly from the shore. Rooms are basic, spread out over the large complex. **Pros:** great beachfront setting; relaxed atmosphere; lots of activities. **Cons:** all-inclusive means a lot of people; have to wear an ID bracelet; less interaction with town. ⊠ *Playa Casa Marina* ☎ *888/774–0040* ⊕ *www.grandparadiseSamana.com* ⤶ *284 rooms* ⚿ *In-room: safe, refrigerator. In-hotel: 3 restaurants, bars, tennis courts, pools, gym, beachfront, diving, water sports, children's programs (ages 4–12), Internet terminal* ▤ *AE, MC, V.* ⑩ *AI.*

¢   🏨 **Todo Blanco.** This is the kind of place—just a few people, beautiful
HOTEL beachfront, cheap, not much to do, a lawn overtaken by coconut trees, hammocks—where reading a good book is your highest priority. There's one housing structure here, a two-story white building with five rooms on each floor. Each room has a balcony of white wood (indeed, all is white, hence *"todo blanco"*). The setup is simple: a couple of beds of average quality, a wicker chair, a dresser, ruddy tiles. It's nothing luxurious—no phones, a TV in the lobby—and gets a little sloppier each year. But, oh, that view—and suddenly you have all the time in the world to finish that book. You pay $15 extra for air-conditioning, and breakfast is an additional $5. Todo Blanco is the second hotel to the right on the beach when you reach Las Galeras. **Pros:** simple, relaxed beachfront setting. **Cons:** not luxurious; landscaping needed; few on-site activities. ⊠ *Playa Las Galeras, Las Galeras* ☎ *809/538–0201* 🖷 *809/538–0064* ⊕ *www.hoteltodoblanco.com* ⤶ *10 rooms* ⚿ *In-room: a/c (some), no phone, no TV. In-hotel: bar, beachfront, laundry service, some pets allowed* ▤ *MC, V* ⑩ *EP.*

¢   🏨 **Villa La Plantación.** Remi Catinot is the exuberant owner and keeper
HOTEL of this castle—two two-story buildings set around a pool. He is rightly proud. While the location is not beachfront—you're about a block from the beach—these simple rooms provide a home base from which to explore Las Galeras for a song. Try for a second-floor room; they have their own terraces. Most rooms have brand-new mattresses and happen to provide the best sleep in town, regardless of the cost. Although rates are quoted in euros for the convenience of the mostly European clientele (it's €40, about $50, for a basic room in high season), you must actually pay in either pesos or U.S. dollars. **Pros:** pleasant, exuberant

owner on-site; good mattresses. **Cons:** not on the beach; not as fancy as the Web site makes it seem. ⊠ *Las Galeras* ☎ *809/538–0079* ⊕ *www. villalaplantacion.com* ⇩ *12 rooms* ⚑ *In-room: a/c (some), no phone, no TV. In-hotel: bar* ⊟ *No credit cards* ⧖ *EP.*

$ ⌂ **Villa Serena.** The best non-all-inclusive hotel choice (among AIs we
HOTEL   like Grand Paradise) in the eastern corner of the peninsula, Villa Serena
★   makes a wonderful, relaxed vacation in Samaná a breeze. You'll love the secluded location removed from the business of the main beach, but it's also nice being able to walk over to the main street to mix with locals and day-trippers. Included in the price are kayaks, bicycles, and snorkeling equipment—you can pack a picnic lunch, paddle out to the postcard-perfect little island not far offshore, and snorkel around the perimeter. (The continual views of "el cayito" directly ahead of you are a large part of the joy of staying here.) The sensational Room 17 has two balconies and a hammock overlooking the beach. Rooms have bamboo canopy beds with covering scrims. Excursions directly from the premises include the Dream Beach package for a reasonable $53 per couple—get a tour of all the area's secluded beaches and be dropped off for as long as you like at your favorite. This is worth doing, since the beach at this hotel is actually quite small. Prices include a full breakfast **Pros:** private beachfront; quiet and secluded property; fine staff; bicycles included. **Cons:** 8-minute walk to town; small beach. ⊠ *Las Galeras* ☎ *809/538–0000* ⊕ *www. villaserena.com* ⇩ *21 rooms* ⚑ *In-room: safe, refrigerator; a/c (some), no phone, no TV. In-hotel: restaurants, room service, bar, pool, beachfront, water sports, bicycles, laundry service, Wi-Fi* ⊟ *MC, V* ⧖ *BP.*

SPORTS AND THE OUTDOORS

BEACHES

Playa Casa Marina (⊠ *1 km [½ mi] by boat, 3 km [2 mi] by road from Las Galeras*)is named for the former name of Grand Paradise, an all-inclusive that's here. Though a sign here says it's private property, the beach is public and it's worth a visit. Boats leave the beach here (as they do from Playa Las Galeras) for all the nearby snorkeling spots and hidden beaches. Another reason to come here: boats leave from here three times a day to visit a small coral reef that's great for snorkeling called Aquario Natural. The quick boat trip over is $10, which includes the use of snorkeling gear. While you're there, the guides will drop food to draw in all the nearby fish. To reach the beach, you have to circle around the hotel property, and it's unsigned. It's simplest to take a motoconcho over from Playa Las Galeras.

Playa Colorada. The beach between La Playita and Playa Rincón is quite similar to the others: a haven for snorkeling, swimming, and solitude.

★   **Playa Frontón** (⊠ *5 km [3 mi] by boat, 5 km [3 mi] by foot from Las Galeras*) is a beach accessible only on foot or by boat. It's on the east side of the easternmost cape of the peninsula. As you might expect, this long uncluttered beach will have almost no one or nearly no one here.

★   **La Playita** (⊠ *2 km [1 mi] by boat, 5 km [3 mi] by road from Las Galeras*), or Little Beach, is a stunner that's a fifteen minute walk from the main Las Galeras beach. Here you'll find a small shack serving fresh fish, lounges for rent, and a beautiful small beach with few people. Coconut trees lean far out over the water, and the virgin stretch of Cabo Cabrón extends far along one side, providing incredible views and a sense of privacy and solitude.

Playa Las Galeras (✉ *Las Galeras*) is within this tiny coastal town, a 30-minute drive northeast from Samaná town. It's a lovely, long, and uncluttered beach. The sand is white, the Atlantic waters generally calm. It has been designated a "Blue Flag" beach, which means that it's crystal-clean with no pollution, though there are several small hotels here. This is a good snorkeling spot, too. That said, this is really just a departure point for the nearby virgin beaches closer to the cape to the west. Hire a boat and get to them!

Fodor's Choice ★ **Playa Rincón** (✉ *5 km [3 mi] by boat, 15 km [9 mi] by road from Las Galeras*), a beautiful, white-sand beach, is considered one of the top beaches in the Caribbean. It's relatively undeveloped, and at the far right end is a sheltered area where you can snorkel. At the other end, cliffs segue into the turquoise water of Caño Frio, an ice-cold river that runs down from the mountains and forms a splash pool, ideal for rinsing off the saltwater. There are no facilities per se, but local ladies will sell you the freshest lobster and fish in coconut sauce with rice, and other creole dishes as well as cold drinks. You can reach Playa Rincón by boat, bus, or car from Las Galeras. A boat is preferable; expect to pay about $15 *(see ⇨ Boating)*. Driving here takes about 50 minutes each way from town because of the distance and the deplorable state of the road. (Although the bad road does keep it even more private.)

BOATING

It would be a fine thing if, immediately arriving at Las Galeras, you headed straight to the beach, and the many small fishing boats lined there. "Take me to the beaches," should be enough to get you a wonderful tour of the remote beaches here, the best on the peninsula. Playa Rincón is the farthest from Las Galeras, about a 15-minute ride. La Playita is another gem, about 5 minutes by boat. **Excursiones Melo** (✉ *Playa Las Galeras, Las Galeras* ☎ *829/333–1805*) has a boat at the ready and will skiff two people off to Playa Rincón for RD$1,200 round-trip. You can be dropped off there and ask to be picked up at any time. A more complete tour of the area's other beaches will be slightly more money, but worth every penny.

DIVING

The shipwrecks and coral reefs a few minutes by boat off Las Galeras make for decent diving, though there aren't too many fish here. Las Galeras Divers has a little office in town as well as a stand at the beach at the town's only all-inclusive, which is still known locally as Casa Marina, even though the name has changed to Grand Paradise Samaná. The company's PADI-certified instructors are eager to take you out.

Las Galeras Divers (✉ *Playa Casa Marina and Calle Principal, Las Galeras* ☎ *809/538–0220* ⊕ *www.las-galeras-divers.com*) offers diving lessons and trips in English; diving equipment rentals start at $40, snorkeling equipment at $15 per day.

The North Coast

PUERTO PLATA, PLAYA DORADA,
SOSÚA, CABARETE & CABRERA

WORD OF MOUTH

"The North Coast in particular has beautiful beaches (some of the best in the Caribbean) and mountains. There are tons of activities, or you can do nothing at all. If you want to get away from the "touristy" towns, look into Cabrera. . . . Cabarete is nice, but it IS a party destination, as it is the kite-surfing capital of the world and the party crowd goes there. We could not believe how many U.S., Canadian, and European expats have moved to the Cabrera area. . . ."

—CaribbeanTraveler

"Playa Dorada all the way. Have a great time, folks."

—cvdoj

By Michael de Zayas

The Dominican Republic's northern coast, with mountains on one side, is also called the Amber Coast or the Amber Riviera because of the large quantities of golden amber found in the area. The sands on its 75 mi (121 km) of beach are also golden. As the area moves up on the luxury scale, the "Riviera" moniker seems more appropriate all the time.

Nicolás de Ovando, the island's first governor, founded Puerto Plata in 1502. Subsequently, in the colonial days, there were pirates, also called corsairs, skulking around almost every cove, to the degree that the city had to be abandoned in 1606. Nonetheless, because of that threat, tourists have San Felipe, an attractive fort, to tour. Puerto Plata is a typical Dominican city, but it has some unique appeal of its own, mainly because of the wooden houses with gingerbread fretwork from the Victorian era, which was its halcyon age.

The beaches of the Costa Dorada are along Puerto Plata's principal highway, where there is a large all-inclusive resort, Iberostar; Playa Dorada is the nearby, long-established resort area, where the Dominican Republic's first all-inclusive resorts were built—there are 14 there now. If you want rest and relaxation and a tan, you don't have to leave the golden beach. When you want to explore, within a two-hour radius are a plethora of towns, including Sosúa, Cabarete, Cabrera, and Santiago (see ⇨ Chapter 7, Santiago and the Cibao Valley). Each offers its own mix of Caribbean character and characters. The fun quotient is high in Sosúa and particularly Cabarete, where strong ocean breezes create the ideal conditions for kite- and windsurfing. The bar and restaurant scene here—you eat and drink right on the sand—is phenomenal.

The north country's more remote areas are like Eden, with remote beaches and rich, tropical vegetation that grows up the hillsides to the cliffs. Cabrera is a new hot spot, and with its upscale rental villas it's helping to redefine the Dominican vacation. And visitors are now beginning to discover the glorious, often unpopulated beaches between Río San Juan and Cabrera.

ORIENTATION AND PLANNING

GETTING ORIENTED

Most visitors to the North Coast fly into the International Gregorio Luperón Airport (POP) in Puerto Plata. The all-inclusive crowd settles in at Playa Dorada. Those heading east to Cabarete and beyond rent a car and explore from there.

Puerto Plata and Playa Dorada. The most well-established resort area on the North Coast is showing its age in some respects, but it still attracts the bulk of tourists to the area.

TOP REASONS TO GO

A meal at Playa Grande. The world-class beach of Playa Grande has few people, and is made even more memorable with a freshly caught meal right on the sand. Don't miss a piña colada served inside a ripe pineapple, or a "coco loco" served in a coconut brought right down from a tree.

Kite surfing. Try an adventure sport like kite surfing in Cabarete, or at least watch the kites and take the pictures. The sails are a form of flowing art.

Play 18 holes. Playa Dorada's Robert Trent Jones–designed course is

moderately priced, and its renovated clubhouse is a convivial place.

Cabarete's restaurants and nightlife. The night here starts early with happy hour at one of the beachfront restaurants. After dinner, when the dancing cranks up, it's another whole party. All of this happens right on the beach.

Discover lovely unknown beaches. Seek out the lesser-known, unpopulated beaches by taking a boat ride from Laguna Gri Gri or driving around Cabrera.

Sosúa. A little seedy, this small town with a great beach is a home base for lots of expats and other foreigners.

Cabarete. Surfing—kite- and windsurfing, too—and great dining and nightlife keep the young and sporty coming here.

Cabrera. An hour's drive due east from Cabarete, this remote area appeals to those who want a tranquil, upscale villa experience.

PLANNING

GETTING HERE AND AROUND

AIR TRAVEL

Although Gregorio Luperón International Airport in Puerto Plata is the usual airport here, it may be cheaper for you to fly into Cibao International Airport in Santiago (see ⇨ Chapter 7, Santiago and the Cibao Valley). That will require a two-hour drive to and from the airport if you're staying in Cabarete. If you're staying in Cabrera, you may be able to fly into El Catey International Airport in Samaná (see ⇨ Chapter 5, The Samaná Peninsula), though most regularly scheduled flights to that airport from the United States have been suspended.

It's also possible to take a domestic flight from Higüero Airport in Santo Domingo; there are also flights from La Romana and Punta Cana (either charter or regularly scheduled service). But given the added cost, it's rarely a good deal to make this kind of complicated connection.

AIRPORTS AND TRANSFERS Gregorio Luperón International Airport is about 7 mi (11 km) east of Playa Dorada. Cibao International Airport in Santiago receives an increasing number of international flights. El Catey is about 25 mi (40 km) west of Samaná.

If you book a package through a travel agent, your airport transfers will almost certainly be included in the price you pay, and even some private villas can arrange airport transfers. If you travel independently, you may have to take a taxi or rent a car.

Anticipate long lines and be sure to give yourself a full two hours for international check-in. Missing luggage, particularly if you're traveling American Airlines and making a connection in Miami, are common, but your bags will almost always be delivered to your hotel the next day, though theft can be a problem.

Contacts Cibao International Airport (STI ⊠ Santiago ☎ 809/582–4894). **Gregorio Luperón International Airport** (POP ⊠ Puerto Plata ☎ 809/586–0107 or 809/586–0219).

BUS TRAVEL

Privately owned air-conditioned buses are the cheapest way to get around the country and connect Puerto Plata with Santo Domingo. The one-way fare is about $7.50, and the trip takes 3½ hours. Just be aware that buses can be packed, especially on weekends and holidays. *For more information on these buses, see* ⇨ *Chapter 2, Santo Domingo.*

Contacts Caribe Tours (☎ 809/221–4422). **Linea Gladys** (☎ 809/565-1223 in Santo Domingo; 809/539–2134 in Puerto Plata). **Metro Buses** (☎ 809/566–7126 in Santo Domingo; 809/586–6062 in Puerto Plata; 809/587–4711 in Santiago).

CAR TRAVEL

The major car-rental companies operate in Puerto Plata, which has the airport of choice for most independent travelers. Phones below are for the airport location; Avis has a location just outside the Playa Dorada complex. Prices can be high (up to $600 per week). You'll save by making your car reservation in advance.

Major Agencies Avis (⊠ Gregorio Luperón International Airport, Puerto Plata ☎ 809/586–0214 ⊠ Carretera Luperón, Playa Dorada, Puerto Plata ☎ 809/586–4436 ⊠ Playa Dorada Plaza, Calle Duarte at Av. 30 de Marzo, Puerto Plata ☎ 809/320–4888). **Budget** (⊠ Gregorio Luperón International Airport, Puerto Plata ☎ 809/586–0413). **Europcar** (⊠ Gregorio Luperón International Airport, Puerto Plata ☎ 809/586-7979). **Hertz** (⊠ Puerto Plata ☎ 809/586–0200 ⊠ Gregorio Luperón International Airport, Puerto Plata ☎ 809/586–0285). **National** (⊠ Puerto Plata ☎ 809/586–0200 ⊠ Gregorio Luperón International Airport, Puerto Plata ☎ 809/586–0285).

TAXI TRAVEL

Taxis, which are government regulated, line up outside hotels and restaurants. They're unmetered, and the minimum fare is about $4, but you can bargain for less if you order a taxi away from the major hotels. Though they are more expensive, hotel taxis are the nicest and the safest option. Freelance taxis aren't allowed to pick up from hotels, so they hang out on the street in front of them. They can be half the cost per ride depending on the distance. Carry some small bills, because drivers rarely seem to have change.

Motoconchos are a popular, inexpensive mode of transportation in such areas as Puerto Plata, Sosúa, and Cabarete. You can flag down one of these motorcycle taxis along rural roads and in town; rates vary from

RD$20 per person for a short run to as much as RD$100 to RD$150 between Cabarete and Sosúa (double that after 6 PM).

Taxi Companies **Taxi-Cabarete** (☎ *809/571–0767 in Cabarete*).**Taxi-Sosúa** (☎ *809/571–3097 in Sosúa*).**Tecni-Taxi** (☎ *809/320–7621 in Puerto Plata*).

INTERNET

At the Playa Dorada Internet Center, computers cost US$4.99 for one hour, US$2.99 for a half-hour, US$1.99 for 15 minutes. It's expensive, but cheaper than the others nearby.

Alf's Internet Center in Sosúa is next door to Alf's Tours, and run by the same good people. You can buy nice refreshing juices, coffee, and snacks as you surf the Internet. Price wise, it's the going rate, about RD$60 per hour.

In Cabarete, @ Internet Café has a bank of computers and several phones. Expect to pay RD$30 for a half-hour, RD$45 for 45 minutes, and RD$60 per hour. Its open daily from 9 AM to 11 PM.

Internet Cafés **Alf's Tours Internet** (✉ *Calle Pedro Clisante, Sosúa* ☎ *809/571–1013* ⊕ *www.alftour.com*). @ **Internet Café** (✉ *Calle Principal, Cabarete* ☎ *809/571–0006*). **Playa Dorada Internet Center** (✉ *Playa Dorada Plaza, near children's playground, Playa Dorada*).

Post Offices **Post Office** (✉ *Calle 12 de Julio at Separación, 2 blocks north of Parque Central, Puerto Plata*).

Shipping Companies **Sosúa Business Services** (✉ *Ocean Dream Plaza, Suite 8, Cabarete* ☎ *809/571–0668* ✉ *Calle Pedro Clisante, Sosúa* ☎ *809/571–3451*).

TOURS

Most North Coast travelers arrange their activities and tours through the company that sold their travel package. Most such companies do a decent job, but there are also a few independent tour operators in the region.

In Sosúa, multilingual Alf's Tours has been a mainstay for years. Iguana Mama, in Cabarete, specializes in adventure sports, having a reputation for being the most safety-oriented, reliable, and fun tour company.

Tours, Trips, Treks & Travel, founded by a veteran Iguana Mama trip leader who adheres to the tenet of experiential learning, specializes in educational, adventure, and other programs for groups; the company does cultural tours that employ local experts.

Brianda Tours, in Abreu, services the area from Playa Grande all the way to Cabrera, and will take smaller groups than Iguana Mama. The trilingual staff takes clients to Gri Gri Lagoon for diving and snorkeling, on horseback riding excursions, on fishing trips, and on sightseeing tours that might include stops at local villages where you can meet the locals. Prices are moderate, and can be customized for groups.

Outback Safari in Puerto Plata operates the wildly decorated open trucks that take groups into the Dominican countryside, stopping at fruit plantations, schools, and local homes to see how people live. This will get you out of the AI compound or your luxury villa and give you more of a feel for what the countryside is like. These touristy trips may not be to the liking of everyone: they're booze buses with loud music, though many kids seem to like them. Outback goes as far as the Playa Grande area, and villa guests staying in Abreu or Cabrera can meet up with them there. Given substantial advance notice, they may provide pickup even in Cabrera. Tours leave at either 8 or 9 AM and return at 4 or 4:30 PM; expect to pay $79.

Private tours are another option. You should expect to pay $125 a day for a guide, and figure $100 for the transportation, which can be a reasonable cost for a group of four or more. Personalized tours can include beautiful waterfalls, freshwater lagoons, secret jungle paths, or almost any other adventure you can name. Your hotel or rental villa management company will be able to hook you up with good drivers and English-speaking guides.

Information **Alf's Tours** (⊠ *Calle Pedro Clisante 12, across from North Coast Dive Center, El Batey, Sosúa* ☎ *809/571–9904 or 809/571–1013* ⊕ *www. alftour.com*). **Brianda Tours** (⊠ *Carretera Cabrera–Río San Juan, Km 8, Abreu* ☎ *809/707–6096* ⊕ *www.briandatours.com*). **Iguana Mama** (⊠ *Calle Principal, Cabarete* ☎ *809/571–0908* ⊕ *www.iguanamama.com*). **Outback Safaris** (⊠ *Plaza Turisol, Local 7, Av. Luperón, Km 2.5, Puerto Plata* ☎ *809/244–4886* ⊕ *www.outbacksafari.com.do*) **Tours, Trips, Treks & Travel** (⊠ *Cabarete* ☎ *809/867–8884* ⊕ *www.4Tdomrep.com*).

RESTAURANTS

You can find lots of independent restaurants in Cabarete and Sosúa, which draw a larger contingent of independent travelers. Since Playa Dorada is primarily an all-inclusive compound, there are not too many choices outside the resorts, but we list a couple as well.

The price of food here keeps escalating, and that is as true in grocery stores as much as in restaurants. Generally, restaurants in Cabarete are priced higher than those in Sosúa. The good news is that the quality of the food on the North Coast is on the rise. Not all restaurants take credit cards (and hardly any take American Express), so be sure to ask in advance if that matters, and if they do take credit cards, there's usually a 4% or 5% surcharge. The tax and service (which usually totals 26%) are often not included in the menu prices, so be sure to ask about that as well. In supermarkets you'll pay 16% tax on most of your purchases. If you shop the *colmados (grocery stores)*, tax is not usually added, but prices are higher. The Dominican Republic is no longer a cheap place to dine out; now, as in the rest of the Caribbean, you'll save greatly on your food bill by staying at an all-inclusive resort, especially if the food there is good.

HOTELS

Playa Dorada was one of the first resort areas in the Dominican Republic to be developed, and it still has a dozen or so all-inclusive resorts, along with one deluxe boutique hotel, Casa Colonial. What's interesting is how these older resorts are evolving in order to compete with their increasingly upscale competition to the east. The transformation of the Blue Bay Villas Dorada into an adults-only resort was also a major happening; it's spa-oriented and well priced. Allegro Puerto Plata (formerly Jack Tar Village, then Holiday Village Golden Beach) has taken the

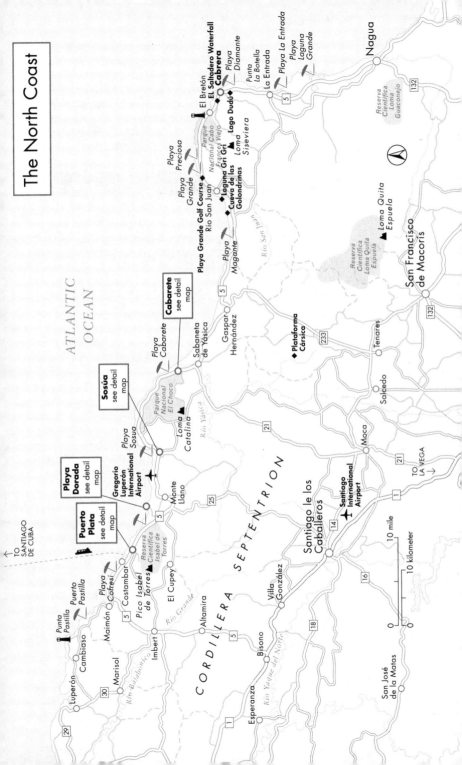

club-within-a-club concierge concept to a budget resort. And perched on a mountain ridge, the new Tubagua Plantation Village appeals to budget travelers and groups.

Cabarete and Sosúa were once proud to say that they were the strongholds of the small, casual hotel. Nowadays there are as many rooms in all-inclusive resorts as in the small independents. Condos have also come to Cabarete in particular, and many are luxurious complexes on the oceanfront. Farther out, in Cabrera and Abreu, luxury villas in exclusive gated communities are the draw.

WHAT IT COSTS IN U.S. DOLLARS					
	¢	$	$$	$$$	$$$$
RESTAURANTS	under $8	$8–$12	$12–$20	$20–$30	over $30
HOTELS*	under $80	$80–$150	$150–$250	$250–$350	over $350
HOTELS**	under $125	$125–$250	$250–$350	$350–$450	over $450

*EP, BP, CP **AI, FAP, MAP

Restaurant prices are per person for a main course at dinner and do not include the 16% tax and 10% service charge. Hotel prices are per night for a double room in high season, excluding 16% tax and 10% service charge.

VISITOR INFORMATION

Contacts **Oficina de Turismo** (✉ Jose del Carmen Ariza 46, Puerto Plata ☎ 809/586–3676).

PUERTO PLATA AND PLAYA DORADA

Puerto Plata is 18 km (11 mi) west of Gregory Luperón International Airport; Playa Dorada is 13 km (8 mi) east of Puerto Plata.

A port founded in 1502, Puerto Plata's name was inspired by the shimmering silver (*plata*) color of its coast at sunset. The city is cradled between the colonial harbor and Mt. Isabel de Torres, which provides a dramatic backdrop. The largest city on the North Coast, its charm is the extent and variety of its Victorian architecture, unrivaled by any other Dominican city. The gingerbread fretwork and pastel colors of its houses and public buildings convey the romantic aura of an earlier time. These vestiges of its halcyon days now house mostly tourist-oriented businesses—galleries, shops, bars, restaurants, and clubs.

Although Puerto Plata seems to have been sleeping for decades, this was a dynamic city both in colonial times and the Victorian era, and it's on the way back now. You can get a feeling for this past in the magnificent Victorian gazebo in the central **Parque Independencia**; the beautification of the park and its gazebo is a work in progress. The **Fortaleza de San Felipe** protected the city from many a pirate attack, and was later used as a political prison. The nearby **lighthouse** has been restored, which it desperately needed. On the Malecón, new streetlights have been erected and the construction here and on the main highway is finally finished. Organization has come to the Malecón, and the many food carts are being replaced by a more hygienic *parador* (which in the Dominican Republic is a small, roadside restaurant serving up local specialties). Similarly, the vendors selling souvenirs and crafts now congregate in a *modelo* (market).

Big changes are afoot in this town, which is realizing what it needs to do to become a tourist destination. The Office of Cultural Patrimony, which has done an admirable job of pulling Santo Domingo's Zona Colonial from the darkness, is at work on Puerto Plata. Simultaneously, a group of private business owners and investors have developed a long-term plan for beautifying the city to take advantage of its hundreds of classic, wooden gingerbread buildings. A new museum for the country's heroes will be in the former family home of Independence hero, Gregory Luperón, in the old town. Most of these houses, painted in pastels with wooden, gingerbread fretwork, are found around the central park—to the northeast and for about eight blocks east and down to the ocean.

GETTING HERE AND AROUND

From Playa Dorada drive five minutes' west into the heart of town. Driving can be a little tricky here, however, so if you're staying in Playa Dorada there's no need to rent a car. Getting a drive from your resort and the airport should be all you need.

6

Numbers in the margin correspond to points of interest on the Puerto Plata map.

EXPLORING PUERTO PLATA

2 **Casa de La Cultura.** Drop by here when you're strolling through the park. An art gallery has revolving exhibits that will help you understand how much talent there is in this country. You may even wish to buy from a budding artist. This Victorian building also has workshops for those talented in dance and music. ⊠ *Parque Central, Calle Separación, near Duarte* 🕾 *809/261–2731* 🎫 *Free* ⊗ *Weekdays 9–noon and 3–5.*

1 **Fortaleza de San Felipe.** The only remaining vestige of the colonial era in Puerto Plata was built in the mid-16th century to defend the city against pirates bent on pillaging the growing wealth from its shipping port. In 1605 the fort was dismantled, and it was rebuilt in 1739. It has a moat and a small museum with some historical artifacts—nothing fascinating, though there are pieces from the period. The thick walls and interior moat made it ideal as a prison, which is exactly how the fort was used. Kids will enjoy the opportunity to run around and explore, but it's not a must-see attraction, certainly not for adults. The views of the bay are excellent, and a grassy knoll provides a pleasant place to sit. The fort is included on most city tours. A restored lighthouse is adjacent, and is included in the entry fee for the fort. ⊠ *At eastern end of Av. Circunvalación, on peninsula in Bahía de Puerto Plata* 🕾 *No phone* 🎫 *RD$40* ⊗ *Daily 9–5.*

4 **Mt. Isabel de Torres.** Southwest of Puerto Plata, this mountain soars 2,600 feet above sea level and is notable for its huge statue of Christ. Up there also are botanical gardens that, despite efforts, still are not memorable. You can choose to hire a knowledgeable English-speaking guide for

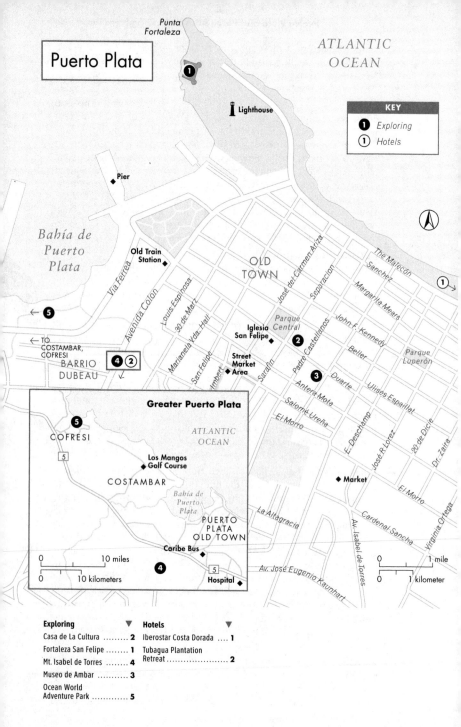

Puerto Plata

Punta Fortaleza

ATLANTIC OCEAN

KEY
- ❶ *Exploring*
- ① *Hotels*

Lighthouse

Pier

Bahía de Puerto Plata

Old Train Station

OLD TOWN

The Malecón

Sanchez

Margarita Mears

José del Carmen Ariza

Separacion

John F. Kennedy

Parque Central

Parque Luperón

Iglesia San Felipe

Street Market Area

Padre Castellanos

Beller

Duarte

Ulises Espaillat

Antera Mota

Salomé Ureña

E. Deschamp

José R. Lorez

20 de Dicie.

Dr. Zaira

El Morro

← TO COSTAMBAR, COFRESI

BARRIO DUBEAU

Via Ferrea

Avenida Colón

Louis Espinosa

30 de Marz.

Marianela Vda. Hall.

San Felipe

Sardín

El Morro

◆ Market

Cardenal Sancha

Virginia Ortega

Av. Isabel de Torres

Av. José Eugenio Kaunhart

Greater Puerto Plata

ATLANTIC OCEAN

COFRESI

Los Mangos Golf Course

COSTAMBAR

Bahía de Puerto Plata

PUERTO PLATA OLD TOWN

Caribe Bus

Hospital

0 — 10 miles
0 — 10 kilometers

0 — 1 mile
0 — 1 kilometer

$5 a person. A cable car takes you to the top for a spectacular view. The cars usually wait until filled to capacity before going up—which makes them cozy; and should the electricity happen to go off, there is no backup generator. You should visit in the morning, preferably by 9 AM; by afternoon, the cloud cover rolls in, and you can see practically nothing. ■ TIP→ The vendors are particularly tenacious here. ⊠ *Off Auto-pista Duarte, follow signs* ☎ *No phone* 🖃 *Cable car RD$250* ⊙ *Mon., Tues., and Thurs.–Sun. 9–5.*

❸ **Museo de Ambar Dominicano (Dominican Amber Museum).** In a lovely old galleried mansion, this museum displays and sells the Dominican Republic's national stone: semiprecious, translucent amber. Amber is essentially prehistoric hardened tree sap, and Dominican amber is considered the best in the world. Many pieces are fascinating for what they have trapped inside, and the museum contains a piece with a lizard reported to be 50 million years old, give or take a few millennia. The museum's English text is informative. Shops on the museum's first floor sell amber, souvenirs, and ceramics. ⊠ *Calle Duarte 61* ☎ *809/261–3610* 🖃 *RD$50* ⊙ *Mon.–Fri. 9–5, Sat 9–noon.*

❺ **Ocean World Adventure Park.** Billing itself as "the biggest attraction in the Caribbean," this multimillion-dollar aquatic park in Cofresí has marine and wildlife interactive programs, including dolphin and sea lion shows and encounters, a tropical reef aquarium, stingrays, shark tanks, a rain forest, and a Tiger Grotto inhabited by Bengal tigers. With sea views, the buffet lunch is delightful but not included in the entrance fee. You don't have to come on a tour, but you must make advance reservations if you want to participate in one of the swims or encounters. For example, if you are brave enough for the shark encounter ($70), you will feed them and touch them in the shark lagoon; the stingray encounter is included as well. If you're staying in the Puerto Plata or Cabarete area, ask at your hotel for tour schedules; if you are at nearby Lifestyle resorts, transfers are free. Children must be at least age six to do the dolphin swim, and a photo lab and video service can capture the moment. A private beach, locker room, splashy marina, Las Vegas–style casino, and fine-dining restaurant make for a fascinating mix (⇨ *Casinos and Boating*). (Note that many animal welfare groups, including the World Society for Protection of Animals, consider keeping dolphins in captivity a form of abuse.) ⊠ *Calle Principal 3, Cofresí* ☎ *809/291–1000 or 809/291–1111* ⊕ *www.oceanworldadventurepark. com* 🖃 *$55, kids $40, with many supplements for additional activities and encounters* ⊙ *Daily 9–5.*

NEED A BREAK? Colorful flying flags from many a country, that's to let you know that "fureners" are welcome at Sam's Bar & Grill (⊠ *Jose del Carmen Ariza 34* ☎ 809/586-7267). The place has character, and many Caribbean characters. Sit down, have a cold one and something family like a Philly steak sandwich, and get the latest skinny on the goings on around town.

6

WHERE TO EAT

$$ ✕ **Al Fresco.** If you're near the Playa Dorada Plaza (just behind Heming-
SEAFOOD   way's bar), Al Fresco is the best food choice. It's an intimate restaurant
where you can dine on a terrace embellished with hanging plants.
The sushi and grilled lobster are reason enough to come. And you
may want to return—even if you have paid for an all-inclusive pack-
age—because this is a sanctuary away from that frenetic pace, with
heady music and fine wine. Ondina, a professional manager and caring
owner, will see that your order is served well, be it the penne puttan-
esca or porcini risotto, whether you dine alfresco or inside (with air-
conditioning). If you want to keep it light, the salads are exceptional,
especially the house salad with goat cheese, arugula, grilled shrimp,
and nuts. ⊠ *Playa Dorada Plaza, Calle Duarte at Av. 30 de Marzo, left
of Hemingway's Café, Playa Dorada, Puerto Plata* ☎ *809/320–1137*
▤ *AE, MC, V* ⊘ *No lunch.*

$$$ ✕ **Lucía.** New life has been breathed into Lucía by one of the most inno-
CONTINENTAL   vative chefs in the country, Angel Mejia. His menu is comprehensive
★   and contemporary. The setting is as artistic as a gallery—befitting its
location within Casa Colonial, a refined boutique hotel. Picture orchids
galore, crisp white linens, and attentive waiters in white guayabera
shirts. Guests love the one-of-a-kind appetizers, like the Tris-Viche, a
seviche of Chilean sea bass, tuna, and lobster. A main course headliner
is the Duck Connection—a grilled breast, crispy leg confit, and foie gras
served with rum-mango sauce and mashed pumpkin. Carnivores with
more basic tastes can order an Angus fillet. The molten chocolate volcano with vanilla ice cream is the dessert you want. When the digestif
cart is rolled over, be daring with a Brunello grappa or the local Brugal
Unico rum, and look out to the orchids clinging to the trees and the
tropical mangrove garden. It's the good life at Lucía. ⊠ *Casa Colonial,
Playa Dorada* ☎ *809/320–3232* ▤ *AE, MC, V.*

WHERE TO STAY

$ ⊞ **Allegro Puerto Plata.** One of Playa Dorada's first resorts (formerly the
ALL-INCLUSIVE   Jack Tar Village, and then Holiday Village Golden Beach), Allegro is a
budget-oriented all-inclusive that's great for kids. Fun waterslides and
pools for tots, as well as kids' clubs, will keep the young ones happy.
The 44 units in the Royal Club section include an adults-only pool and
bar. The spacious grounds of the entire property make the whole seem
like a big park. That all said, the age of the property is evident—it's not
fancy by any stretch. **Pros:** four good specialty restaurants, including a
Caribbean one on the beach; well-known public casino and disco are
on premises; price is very right. **Cons:** infrastructure is not top-drawer;
only a few of the villas have water views; buffet's food is not generally
memorable. ⊠ *Playa Dorada, Puerto Plata* ☎ *809/320–3800* ⊕ *www.
occidentalhotels.com* ⇥ *179 rooms, 37 deluxe rooms, 38 family rooms,
10 family suites, 7 suites* ⚴ *In-room: a/c, safe, refrigerator, DVD (some).
In-hotel: 5 restaurants, bars, tennis courts, pools, beachfront, water
sports, children's programs (ages 4 months–16), laundry facilities, laun-*

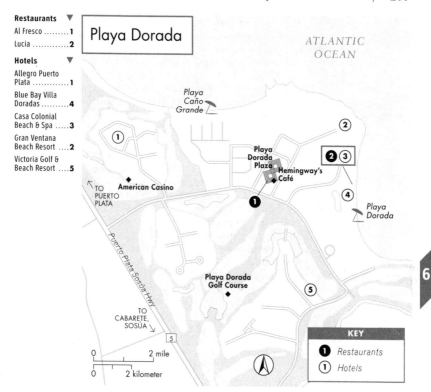

dry service, Internet terminal, Wi-Fi hotspot, parking (free) ▤ AE, D, DC, MC, V ⓘ⃝ AI.

$
ALL-INCLUSIVE

🏨 **Blue Bay Villas Doradas.** The stunning grand entrance (a Sara Garcia design) at this adults-only resort with its slender white pillars uses white fabric to shelter the lobby from tropical rainfalls. Cushy woven lounge furniture with bright and floral pillows, the boutique with its tropical whites, and a staff in tropical whites all make for one attractive island scenario. It provides the backdrop for the weekly manager's party that may be the country's best: a stellar five-piece band, mimosas, and delicious hors d'oeuvres. The exuberant management leads the way to an admirable display of abundance, including all the à la carte Asian and seafood restaurants as well as the international buffet, from raw oysters to a real turkey dinner. The focus is on healthy food. Fitness classes include aqua aerobics by a certified instructor, with live music (a sax and a trumpet) three times a week. Learning-oriented activities are the norm here, be they Spanish classes, cooking and cocktail classes, even casino gambling instructions. This is an adults-only resort—no children allowed. Upgrade your room if you can afford it; the bungalows with private Jacuzzis are the best. **Pros:** great spa; handsome beach club and stellar beachfront; yoga and golf classes included. **Cons:** standard and standard-plus rooms are not luxurious; rooms near the stage can be noisy until 11 PM. ⊠ *Playa Dorada, Puerto Plata* ☎ *809/320–3000,*

809/320–1600 for reservations ⊕ www.bluebayresorts.com ⇦ 245 rooms, 4 suites ⚒ In-room: a/c, safe, refrigerator. In-hotel: 4 restaurants, bars, tennis courts, pools, gym, spa, beachfront, water sports, bicycles, laundry service, Internet terminal, Wi-Fi hotspot, parking (free) ▤ AE, D, DC, MC, V ⃝⃝ AI.

$$$$
HOTEL
Fodor's Choice
★

Casa Colonial Beach & Spa. Done in the clean, sophisticated, contemporary style of a boutique hotel, Casa Colonial is a surprise among the chockablock all-inclusives of Playa Dorada. Gorgeously designed by Sara Garcia, the small property exudes refinement and relaxation amid tropical gardens that lead to the quietest end of the long beach here. In comparison to the exquisite neo-colonial architecture and landscaping, the suites fall flat. They are very comfortable—with Frette linens and the inviting open bath-to-bedroom floor plan pioneered by Mandarin Oriental—but the rooms lack pizzazz, with furnishings pushed into corners. The lobby feels more like a great Manhattan lounge, with a stellar bar. Lucía, the designer gourmet restaurant, is also beautiful to look at. Upscale spa devotees will savor the Baqua Spa, with its Vichy showers, body wraps, inventory of massages and facials, and refreshing juices. The rooftop sundeck is close to heaven—an infinity pool and four warm Jacuzzis overlooking the ocean as well as an eatery here and on the ground floor facing the ocean. In short, if you like exclusive boutique hotels, this is the choice on the North Coast. **Pros:** architectural gem offering the full luxury boutique experience; glorious spa and dining choices. **Cons:** can feel empty during the low season; the large suites are a little blah and need a designer's direction. ✉ Playa Dorada, Puerto Plata ☎ 809/320–3232 ⊕ www.casacolonialhotel.com ⇦ 50 suites ⚒ In-room: a/c, refrigerator, Internet, Wi-Fi. In-hotel: 2 restaurants, bar, pool, gym, spa, beachfront, laundry service, Wi-Fi hotspot ▤ AE, MC, V ⃝⃝ EP.

$–$$
ALL-INCLUSIVE
☾

Gran Ventana Beach Resort. This all-inclusive is filled with Americans who like its renovated, clean, colorful grounds and easy beach access. The lobby, with pottery and local drums suspended from the walls, is a contemporary study in Caribbean colors, with a fountain as a focal point. The beach is on a point with unobstructed views to the left. Families are a good share of the market, and this resort is solid as far as the tour operators are concerned, with service and food improving each season. Many couples prefer the larger rooms (sans good ocean views, unfortunately) that surround the active pool scene. A Victorian-style wedding gazebo is popular for nuptials. **Pros:** consistently good food and service for this price point; plenty of activities for the whole family. **Cons:** feels busy year-round; the buffet is often better than the freestanding dining rooms. ✉ Playa Dorada, Puerto Plata ☎ 809/320–2111 ⊕ www.vhhr.com ⇦ 499 rooms, 2 suites, 1 penthouse ⚒ In-room: a/c, safe, refrigerator. In-hotel: 5 restaurants, bars, tennis court, pools, gym, beachfront, water sports, bicycles, children's programs (ages 4–12), Internet terminal ▤ AE, MC, V ⃝⃝ AI.

$–$$
ALL-INCLUSIVE
★

Iberostar Costa Dorada. This resort will dazzle you with its sprawling lobby, its hardwood benches and sculptures, and its curvaceous pool with a central Jacuzzi encircled by Roman pillars. As you swim along, you can see the mountains and the beach. Other all-inclusives could

Sarah Garcia—A Dominicana Role Model

Sarah Garcia is revered as an architect, considered by many to be the top designer on the North Coast, if not in the entire country. She has become the architect of choice for the moneyed owners of Sea Horse Ranch. Her contemporary homes are showpieces in their gated communities. But she also designs resorts, and a prime example is the boutique hotel Casa Colonial, which was challenging because of its odd-shape oceanfront setting in Playa Dorada.

Garcia is one of five daughters of Don Isidro Garcia, a poor boy from rural Río San Juan. When he was a boy, her father sold small packets of rice to neighbors, traveling on horseback. But from these humble beginnings he grew up to become a land baron, making his fortune in cacao and cattle; in 1986 he began to invest in resorts. Don Isidro recently passed away at the age of 82, leaving his daughters to manage his estate. As Sarah says: "My father was my hero. I couldn't believe that he could die. We were all girls, and he raised us to be proud and to be strong together, as well as individuals. This is a country of men, and I worked so hard to develop

myself. In New York it is difficult to make a name for yourself; imagine here? Dominican women use their 'weapons' (sensuality); I let my work speak for itself. People say that I am the best, but the most important thing is to compete with yourself. Thank God, the clients come to me now. I don't have time to knock the doors!"

Garcia's advanced education took her to the United States, England, France, and finally Italy, and it was in the latter where she became accredited in interior design and where she met her husband, Roberto Casoni, who is the vice-president for the Victoria Hotel Group. "As for Roberto," she says, "we have love and we are partners, too. I was lucky to find the other half of my orange! He understands my desire to work and to continue to reinvent myself. I feel that makes me both a better wife and mother."

Garcia volunteered her services to redesign the family home of Independence hero Gregorian Luperón, to create a museum for national heroes. It's in the old town of Puerto Plata, the city of her birth, and is expected to open in 2011.

learn from Iberostar's excellent buffet; of the à la carte restaurants, the Brazilian is the standout and the Mexican is highly authentic. The rooms are somewhat dated but attractive, with woven wall hangings and bright colors. Many of the staffers speak English here, and the resort itself is close to Puerto Plata, so you can have more contact with real Dominican life. At night you can watch the entertainment (the music is especially good) from the outdoor seating in the garden. **Pros:** good management makes for a happy staff and a fun resort; good spot along the beach; top-shelf liquor in the lobby bar. **Cons:** popularity translates to high-occupancy year-round; no Wi-Fi; pool can be very noisy. ⊠ *Playa Costa Dorada, Carretera Luperón, Km 4, Marapica* ☎ *809/320–1000 or 888/923–2722* ⊕ *www.iberostar.com* ⟳ *498 rooms, 18 junior suites* ⚙ *In-room: a/c, safe, refrigerator. In-hotel: 4 restaurants, bars, tennis courts, pools, gym, spa, beachfront, diving, water* sports, children's programs (ages 4–12), Internet terminal ▤ AE, MC, V ▮◎▮ AI.

¢   ▦ **Tubagua Plantation Eco-Village.**
HOSTEL If you're an independent traveler turned off by the all-inclusive experience, this 12-acre mountaintop property, set on the first inland ridge some 1,000 feet above sea level, will give you some contact with nature and elicit an appreciative sigh. The rustic, palapa-style accommodations, which are focused on ecotourism and sustainable development, have long views of the countryside leading far to the ocean: it's spec-

tacular. These rustic, back-to-the-earth lodgings (including camping-style bathroom and showering setup) make a brilliant base for exploring the country, since your host here is Canadian consul Tim Hall. Santiago is less than an hour's drive along a spectacular, winding mountain road. There are private lockers, shared bathroom facilities, a game room, and hiking trails; beach access is 15 minutes away. Shared lodging is $25, with mosquito-netted beds lined up in one longhouse, but a shared private palapa is only $35. **Pros:** authentic rural setting that's still 15 minutes from Puerto Plata airport; all the necessary facilities and services, including clean, hot water, power, and Wi-Fi; spectacular views; pools. **Cons:** bathing facilities are shared; remote location, with limited public transportation options. ⊠ *Km 19, Carretera Turística, Tubagua* ☏ *809/696–6932* ⊕ *www.Tubagua.com* ⤳ 5 private double palapas, 1 longhouse with 8 beds shared quarters ⚹ *In-room: no a/c, no phone, no TV. In-hotel: restaurant, bar, pool, Wi-Fi hotspot* ▤ *No credit cards* ▮◎▮ *EP.*

$ ▦ **VH Victoria Resort.** Owned and designed by the same family that did
ALL-INCLUSIVE Casa Colonial and the neighboring Gran Ventana, Victoria shares with
★   the others their good looks and a reputation for providing a comfortable stay. Unfortunately, it's across the street from these, so you'll need to walk about 300 yards to reach the nice private beach area set up for Victoria guests. Victoria's niche is clear: couples, honeymooners, and golfers—the resort overlooks the golf club. Although you can get a breakfast-only plan, you can go all-inclusive for just a few dollars more: the buffet is better than the norm, and service is super. The resort is quieter than the beachfront all-inclusives, which can be a plus, and you can latch on to those activities at Gran Ventana when you want. There's a spa suite here where guests can enjoy massages and other services. Weddings can be amazingly affordable here. **Pros:** has a Cristal Certificate for food hygiene; two great pools, including a "chill" pool with a soothing cascade. **Cons:** not on the beach; needs another standalone restaurant; might be too quiet for some. ⊠ *Playa Dorada Box 22, Puerto Plata* ☏ *809/320–1200* ⊕ *www.victoriagolfhotel.com* ⤳ 164 rooms, 26 suites, 3 2-bedroom villas ⚹ *In-room:a/c, safe, refrigerator.*

In-hotel: 3 restaurants, bars, tennis court, pools, gym, diving, water sports, bicycles, Internet terminal ⊟ AE, D, MC, V ⚏ AI.

NIGHTLIFE AND THE ARTS

BARS

Celuisina Tropicale (⊠ *Playa Nacho Resort, Playa Dorada* ☎ *809/320–6226*) doesn't crank up until after midnight, but it keeps rolling until 4 AM. Locals and tourists dance to hip-hop together.

Hemingway's Cafe (⊠ *Playa Dorada Plaza, Puerto Plata* ☎ *809/320–2230*) has long been the rockin' spot for the young and young at heart who love to party. There's rock or reggae by DJs or live bands, but only big-name merengue bands require a cover charge. On Saturday night there's a Latin fiesta, and on Thursday the mike is taken over by karaoke singers. The kitchen, which doesn't close until 2 AM, serves American-style fun food that includes good burgers, with fajitas a specialty.

Bravissimo (⊠ *Ocean World, Cofresí* ☎ *809/291–0000*) is unique in the Dominican Republic. The nightly open-air show outside the casino complex at Ocean World is a spectacle of beautiful dancing girls and guys with incredible voices. Its more-or-less amateur take on Vegas glitz could easily pass for camp. But with 30 dancers on stage and 120 costumes, the blur, shake, and whirl is memorable. (The unlimited beer and rum provided as part of the $45 per couple package helps.) A souvenir photo is included in the price, as is round-trip transportation.

CASINOS

Puerto Plata has most of the casinos on the North Coast. There is also one in Cabarete. On Playa Dorada there were two casinos with the same name; at the time of this writing, only one was open. **The American Casino** (*Allegro Puerto Plata* ⊠ *Puerto Plata* ☎ *809/320–1046* ⊕ *www.amcasgroup.com/puerto-plata*) is connected to the Allegro Puerto Plata but is open to all. It has one Texas Hold 'Em table and about a dozen table games, including blackjack and roulette, as well as dozens of slots, in one large room.

Ocean World Casino (⊠ *Calle Principal 3, 3 mi [5 km] west of Puerto Plata, Cofresí* ☎ *809/291–0000* ⊕ *www.oceanworldcasino.com*) is slightly bigger than the other casinos on the North Coast, and a touch flashier. It's still small by Vegas standards, housed entirely in just one big, circular room with the casino basics: a Texas Hold 'Em table (sometimes two, and there are $60 entry tournaments Saturdays at 7 PM), slots, roulette, and blackjack. What sets Ocean World apart is the array of other things to do: a nocturnal tour of the complex can include a sunset happy hour at the Lighthouse Lounge, dinner at Poseidón, and then a Las Vegas–style review, *Bravissimo*. If you want the night to continue even later, there's the Lighthouse Disco upstairs.

BEACHES

Many beaches on the North Coast are accessible to the public and may tempt you to stop for a swim. (In theory, all beaches in this country, from the high-water mark down, are open to everyone.) That's part

Tim Hall—A Quintessential Expat

Tim Hall first came to the Dominican Republic in 1983 as a journalist to write a feature for the *Toronto Star* about Playa Dorada, the new tourist destination in Puerto Plata. He was a young Canadian lad, who, like so many who have chosen the expat life, came back again and again until he finally stayed.

Tim began by writing for the country's only English-language newspaper, *Santo Domingo News*. He went on to publish a local Spanish-language newspaper and to produce a tourism-related TV show. Although his talents as a scribe are still in demand, Tim has learned the lesson of the Caribbean: survival depends on wearing more than one hat.

His restaurant, Café Cito, gained renown during its time as a fun, funky expat hangout. In 2008 he opened the doors of the Tubagua Plantation Eco-Village in the mountains behind Puerto Plata. He is also the North Coast's Canadian Honorary Consul. As he explains, "I was appointed in 1988, after a phone call that woke me up on my 30th birthday. It's been two decades now and there's lots of stories to tell."

As he recalls, "In 1982 charter flights started bringing planeloads of tourists to Playa Dorada, to this virgin region where they built the country's first all-inclusive resorts. During that first tidal wave of tourists, local fishermen were getting pulled off their boats to wait on tables, delivering dinners like surf 'n' turf, and getting raked over coals by some fancy tourist when a steak wasn't medium rare. At the time, nobody knew about medium rare. Yet Dominicans have amazing resilience,

and the ability to smile, whether the tip is 10 pesos or 10 dollars."

Today, interesting new things are happening in the region, he says. "People are learning this isn't just a beach resort destination; there is a growing interest in ecotourism, and people are discovering the real Dominican Republic. They're also realizing that there's a real sense of community for visitors on the North Coast." Tax and cost-of-living benefits are attracting more expat retirees, including a strong contingent of boomers. And Tim is a central figure in the area.

"One of the things I enjoy most is sharing the things I've discovered living here...the best local rums and the hand-rolled cigars that are among the top in the world...the fresh foods and local recipes...the hidden-away places that most tourists don't get to see." For example, his standing offer at his Tubagua Eco Village is that if you spend your first two days there, Tim will use his insider's knowledge to help custom-plan the rest of your trip and loan you a cell phone for 24/7 trip support.

Tim lives with his Dominican wife, Beatriz, and their four children at their 12-acre eco-resort. Thinking over the life he has built for himself, he says, "Living in the islands doesn't provide typical financial security, such as a pension to look forward to. And I haven't afforded a BMW, but my life pretty much belongs to me." And his future plans? "This ecovillage is turning out to be as funky and fun as Café Cito—but with a spa and cabanas and a knockout view. Now that it's up and running, I might take off a few hats."

of the uninhibited joy of this country. Do be careful, though: some have dangerously strong currents, which may be the reason why they're undeveloped.

Cofresí Beach (⊠ *Calle Pincipal, Cofresí, Puerto Plata, 4.3 mi west of town center*) offers a long stretch of golden sand that's good for swimming, but with some wave action as well. Locals mainly use it. On the other side of the public area are Ocean World and its marina.

Playa Dorada (⊠ *Off Autopista Luperón, Puerto Plata, approximately 10-min drive east of town*) is the primary beach destination on the North Coast and one of the Dominican Republic's most established resort areas. Each hotel has its own slice of the beach, which is covered with soft sand, nearly white now thanks to its participation in a $6 million beach rejuvenation. Lots of reefs for snorkeling are right offshore. Gran Ventana Beach Resort, which is on a point, marks the easternmost end of the beach, followed by Casa Colonial and Blue Bay. If you're not staying at one of the resorts in the Playa Dorada complex, then it's best to enter the beach before this point. Zealous hotel security guards try to keep you off "their" stretch of beach, but by law they cannot if you walk along the water's edge. They can keep you off the chaise longues and from coming into the resort's property, though. The Atlantic waters are great for windsurfing, waterskiing, and fishing.

6

SPORTS AND THE OUTDOORS

BIKING

A number of resorts in Playa Dorada have bicycles available for no charge. They are often not the best wheels you'll ever spin, but it's really delightful to cruise around Playa Dorada on two wheels. It's safe enough since cars go slowly, and you can wave to the drivers of the horse carriages as you pass them by.

BOATING

Ocean World Marina (⊠ *Cofresí, 3 mi [5 km] west of Puerto Plata* ☎ *809/970–3373 or 809/291–1111* ⊕ *www.oceanworldmarina.com*) is a state-of-the art marina strategically positioned between the heavily traveled Florida-Bahamas region and the Puerto Rico–eastern Caribbean region. It has filled a large 300-mi (480-km) void on the North Coast where no full-service marina previously existed. The 35-acre complex has 120 slips that accommodate sailboats of up to 200 feet. It is a port of entry with its own immigration and customs office, concierge, laundry and shower facilities, duty-free shop, food and liquor store, car-rental service (even hourly rentals), and marina store with fishing supplies, as well as an entertainment clubhouse, nightclub, and casino.

DIVING

Dressel Divers (⊠ *Playa Costa Dorada, Carretera Luperón, Km 4, in front of Iberostar, Marapica, Puerto Plata* ☎ *809/320–1000 Ext. 1364* ⊕ *www.dresseldivers.com*) is one of the best of the area dive centers. Spanish-owned, it has an international staff and PADI five-star rating. Dressel offers it all, from one- and two-tank dives in the region's best dive spots, such as Sosúa Bay, to night dives, instruction, and advanced certification. Nondivers can rent snorkeling gear. The company will arrange a pickup at resorts other than Iberostar.

GOLF

Los Mangos Golf Course (⌧ *Carretera John F. Kennedy 2, Costambar, Puerto Plata* ☎ *809/970–3073 or 809/696–2858*) is about 5 km (3 mi) west of Puerto Plata and is much less crowded and more tranquil than many of the large resort areas, and that is even more true of Cofresí, which is a bit farther west. Costambar is right off the Puerto Plata–Santiago Highway. You'll see a large overhead sign on the right. Go to the security gate and say you're coming to check out the golf course. Greens fees at Los Mangos Golf & Beach Resort are $30 for 18 holes, $20 for 9, and you can enjoy a couple of cold ones at the little clubhouse. The course is open from 9 to 6 daily.

Golf Digest has named **Playa Dorada Golf Club** (⌧ *Playa Dorada, Puerto Plata, next door to Victoria Resort* ☎ *809/320–3472* ⊕ *www. playadoradagolf.com*) one of the top 100 courses outside the United States. It's open to guests of all the hotels in the area. Greens fees for 9 holes are $58, 18 holes $87; caddies are mandatory for foursomes and will cost about $15 for 18 holes, $8 for 9; carts are optional, at $20 and $15, for 18 or 9 holes, respectively. Guests at certain hotels in the Playa Dorada complex, particularly the Victoria Golf & Beach Resort, get discounts.

TENNIS

Occidental Tennis Academy (⌧ *Occidental Club on the Green, Playa Dorada, Puerto Plata* ☎ *809/320–1111 for hotel's main switchboard* ⊕ *www.occidentalhotels.com*) was the first tennis academy in the Caribbean. It's equipped with seven Har-Tru clay and hard courts (night lighted), as well as a gym, pool, social club, and pro shop. Classes are given and supervised by pros. Programs are for adults and children five and over. You can get private ($13 an hour) or group classes ($8), in English or Spanish, for beginners to professionals. Nonguests can also rent courts.

Playa Naco Resort & Spa (⌧ *Playa Dorada* ☎ *809/320–6226 Ext. 2568*) allows nonguests to play on its four clay courts for $10 an hour by day, $20 at night. Lessons from the pro cost $23 an hour plus the cost of the court.

SHOPPING

In Puerto Plata you can find enough interesting stores to both quell your shopping urge and pick up a few funky gifts, like *mamajuana*, the Dominican herbal liqueur. A popular shopping street for costume jewelry and souvenirs is **Calle Beller.**

Playa Dorada Plaza (⌧ *Calle Duarte at Av. 30 de Marzo, Puerto Plata*) is a shopping center in the American tradition; stores here sell everything from cigars, rum, coffee, and herbal remedies to ceramics, trinkets, American clothing brands, Oscar de la Renta tops, and Gottex bathing suits.

DISCOUNT STORES

Discount Plaza (✉ *Playa Dorada Plaza, Calle Duarte at Av. 30 de Marzo, Puerto Plata* ☎ *809/320–6645*) is the local equivalent of Wal-Mart, though on a small scale. The clothes you can find here are of the same caliber—bathing suits, flip-flops, baseball caps, and the like. You can choose from a pretty good selection of toiletries if you have forgotten anything, as well as rum. There are also cheap Dominican souvenirs. You can buy phone cards here, as well as make long-distance calls in private booths and exchange currency.

HANDICRAFTS

Collector's Corner Gallery & Gift Shop (✉ *Playa Dorada Plaza, Calle Duarte at Av. 30 de Marzo, Puerto Plata* ☎ *No phone*) has souvenirs, including many made of amber.

JEWELRY

Harrisons (✉ *Playa Dorada Plaza, Calle Duarte at Av. 30 de Marzo, Puerto Plata* ☎ *809/586–3933*) doesn't sell trinkets but rather high-end jewelry, most likely at better prices than in your hometown. For quality larimar and amber with well-designed settings, many in platinum, this is it. Branches can be found in many touristy zones, including Cabarete and Sosúa.

6

SOSÚA

16 mi (25 km) east of Puerto Plata.

Six hundred Austrian and German Jewish refugees settled this small community during World War II. After the war many of them returned to Europe or went to the United States, and most who remained married Dominicans. Only a few Jewish families reside in the community today, and there's only the original one-room wooden synagogue. Sosúa is called Puerto Plata's little sister, and consists of two communities—El Batey, the modern hotel and expat residential neighborhood, and Los Charamicos, the dense Dominican quarter—separated by a cove with one of the island's prettiest beaches. The sand is soft and the color of light amber, the water clear and calm. The walkway above the beach is packed with tents filled with souvenirs, pizzas, and even clothing for sale. The town developed a reputation for prostitution in the 1990s, but much continues to be done to eliminate that and to clean up the more garish element, and it continues to have a seedy nightlife.

With numerous supermarkets, banks, pharmacies, restaurants, schools, and all the necessities for day-to-day living, the town lends itself well to the expat lifestyle. Sosúa has the Dominican Republic's largest concentration of German residents and tourists, and it sometimes seems that you can get schnitzel here more easily than sancocho.

The up-and-coming Dominican families are coming back to the big houses on the bay, even as upscale condos and hotels are springing up to cater to higher-paying tourists. An example is Sea Horse Ranch, a community just two miles out of town with a rental pool of villas with private pools and landscaped yards.

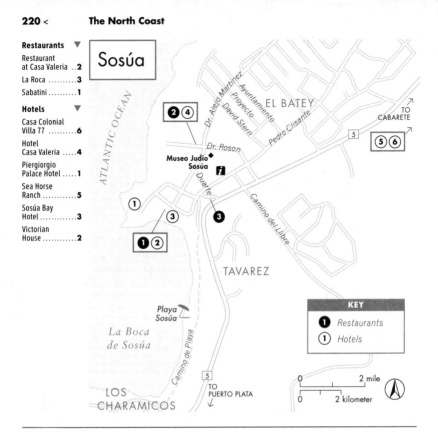

EXPLORING

Museo Judio Sosúa. Sosúa is not a destination known for its sights. However, this museum stands as an exception, chronicling the immigration and settlement of the Jewish refugees in the 1940s. This is a fascinating place, and depending on the docent, you may hear that the Jewish settlers experienced a certain amount of prejudice here when they arrived. The adjacent small wooden synagogue is the wedding spot for many Jewish couples from abroad. ⊠ *Calle Dr. Rosen at David Stern* ☎ *809/571–1386* ✉ *RD$75* ⊘ *Weekdays 9–1 and 2–4.*

WHERE TO EAT

$–$$ ✕ **La Roca.** Where are you, Key West or Sosúa? Hemingway would like
CONTINENTAL   this place that's smack in the middle of town. With its old wooden doors and gingerbread trim, and an inviting open-air porch hung with cascading plants, you'll want to hang out here, too. Grab one of the sidewalk tables laminated with nautical maps and American movie posters from the '90s and watch the people of Sosúa go by. There's a chalkboard for daily specials, but you can always count on a grilled *dorado* (mahimahi) for 500 pesos. It's served with a choice of sides, and like all the dishes here, it starts with a basket of freshly grilled garlic bread. At night,

CLOSE UP

A Caribbean Jewish Refuge

One of the best things the infamous dictator Rafael Trujillo ever did for his country was to inaugurate an immigration plan for certain ethnic groups, including Jewish refugees fleeing Nazi persecution. In 1938 he granted visas to about 5,000 Jews from Nazi-occupied lands in Europe. In 1939 the Dominican Republic Settlement Association (DORSA) acquired land held by the United Fruit Company, and in 1940 the first refugees arrived and settled the land, followed by many others in the coming years. After World War II ended in 1945, many of the refugees left the island for the United States, Mexico, or Europe to seek professional employment. Those who remained turned their attention to dairy farming, which was their primary means of employment in Sosúa. The families that stayed prospered, and a few of the families live on in Sosúa today.

La Roca makes a pleasing spot to have a drink, with two pool tables. There's also free Wi-Fi. Friday nights from 6 to 10 there's an all-you-can-eat barbecue for 375 pesos. ⊠ *Calle Pedro Clisante 1, El Batey, Sosúa* ☎ *809/571–3893* ⊟ *MC, V*

$
CONTINENTAL

✕ **Restaurant at Casa Valeria.** A wave of pink adobe, sculpted in a Mexican hacienda design—that's what this restaurant and its accompanying hotel are like. A palm tree snakes its way through the thatched roof, and a hand-painted mural of a happy local scene takes up one wall. From the tiny kitchen such classics as salade Niçoise and escargots provençales emerge, as well as inimitable pastas such as a carbonara with a splash of Amaretto as the special ingredient. Guests brag about the filet mignon bordelaise with caramelized onions. Chill with the soothing CDs as you move on to crêpes with French bitter orange and Grand Marnier confit. Pricing is an incredible value for the peso. Breakfast is also very popular here. ⊠ *Calle Dr. Rosen 28, El Batey, Sosúa* ☎ *809/463–3710* ⊟ *MC, V* ⊙ *No lunch or dinner Wed.*

$
MEDITERRANEAN

✕ **Sabatini.** On a hill at one end of Sosúa Beach is Victoria Inn, a hotel with three restaurants on three levels (the others are Viva Zapata, serving Mexican; and Asiatico, serving Asian). The three are open on alternating nights; Sabatini is open Tuesdays, Thursdays, and Saturdays. Forget the food here—the reason to come is the open-air panoramic vista of Sosúa Bay, which is *fabuloso* as the night lights dance across the rippling tide. Grab one of the two tables in the corner Victorian turrets. Then you can eat: an Italian classic like beef carpaccio can be your starter, or you can have something more innovative like grouper carpaccio or a mixed salad with shrimp, avocado, and pineapple. Similarly, there are classics like veal scaloppine in white-wine sauce or a luscious gnocchi in Gorgonzola sauce with walnuts. Veteran waiters give laudable service. ⊠ *Calle Alejo Martinez 1, El Batey, Sosúa* ☎ *809/571–4000* ⚑ *Reservations essential* ⊟ *AE, D, DC, MC, V* ⊙ *Closed Sun.–Mon., Wed., Fri. No lunch.*

6

WHERE TO STAY

$$$$
PRIVATE VILLA

Casa Colonial Villa 77. Families and groups like this sophisticated villa that combines character with the latest in home decor and materials for an up-to-date but still traditional environment. The decor shifts between more iron grillwork to dramatic contemporary art; the smoky-green wood cabinets in the impressive kitchen and the sea-grass sleigh beds all combine to make this vacation rental feel more like a real home. The state-of-the-art home theater surrounds an Italian L-shaped sofa. The wonderful pool complex has a dive rock, submerged basking platform, and a big whirlpool. Amid palms and birds-of-paradise is the palapa gazebo, which makes this place feel like your own private all-inclusive resort; it's equipped with two wonderful egg-shaped, wicker sitting hammocks. **Pros:** flat-screen TVs and iPod docks in all the rooms; use of a four-seater golf cart is included. **Cons:** close but not on the ocean; not one of the latest megamansions. ⊠ *Sea Horse Ranch, Las Palmas, Cabarete* ☎ *809/571–3880* ⊕ *www.sea-horse-ranch.com* ⤶ *4 bedrooms, 4 bathrooms* ⚏ *In-room: a/c, safe, DVD. In-hotel: pool, laundry facilities* ⊟ *AE, MC, V* ¡◎¡ *BP.*

¢
HOTEL

Hotel Casa Valeria. Evoking Mexico, this pink adobe, housing a hotel and a restaurant, is a standout in this quiet neighborhood. Wrought-iron gates open to a courtyard that's candlelit by night, and most of the simple accommodations face the pool in the rear garden. The proud owners are a Dutch couple. Some of the rooms have hand-painted tropical murals; poolside rooms are the best and have patios. This inn may be cheap, but it's not sleazy, and is a great value. Airport transfers are included if you stay a week. **Pros:** nicely renovated; the owners will transfer you to the airport for half the price of a taxi; rooms have cable TV. **Cons:** service is limited; no ocean views. ⊠ *Calle Dr. Rosen 28, El Batey, Sosúa* ☎ *809/571–3536* ⊕ *www.hotelcasavaleria.com* ⤶ *9 rooms* ⚏ *In-room: a/c, no phone, kitchen (some), refrigerator. In-hotel: restaurant, pool* ⊟ *MC, V* ¡◎¡ *EP.*

$
HOTEL

Piergiorgio Palace Hotel. Italian fashion designer Piergorgio has passed away, but his widow is carrying on running his hotel without any major alterations. This Victorian-style inn, with its wraparound veranda and intricate fretwork, is definitely in need of renovation, but ask for the six newest rooms or the cliffside suite (No. 500s). They have the same white-wicker furniture as other rooms, but colorful drapes and comforters from Europe cover the beds instead of pinks and florals. The hotel's location is the draw—the gazebo has breathtaking bay views, as does the outdoor restaurant. Honeymooners love its romanticism, fostered by the charming, strolling guitarist, and ladies appreciate the salon and spa services (men, too, for that matter). **Pros:** good alfresco breakfast; none of the aggravating elements of an all-inclusive; views are incredible, especially from the penthouse terraces. **Cons:** dated furnishings and surroundings; most of the staff speaks little English; small pool. ⊠ *Calle La Puntilla 1, El Batey, Sosúa* ☎ *809/571–2626* 🖷 *809/571–2786* ⊕ *www.piergiorgiohotel.com* ⤶ *55 rooms, 3 apartments, 2 penthouses* ⚏ *In-room: a/c, safe, kitchen (some), refrigerator, Wi-Fi. In-hotel: 2 restaurants, bars, pools, spa, Internet terminal, Wi-Fi hotspot* ⊟ *AE, MC, V* ¡◎¡ *BP.*

$$$$
VILLA RESORT
★

⬚ **Sea Horse Ranch.** This enclave of 105 private homes, each with large front and back yard and private pool, opened in 1993 as an elite bastion of private homes set within a vast country club–like setting. Today 14 of those homes are available as rentals, with houses starting at just under $1,000 a week (they are also available by the night). It all resembles an upscale American suburb, with a short drive to reach two tiny communal beaches. The equestrian center, with dozens of horses grazing on wide expanses, is the most stellar feature. There are five groomed clay tennis courts as well (ball boys are included). Three of the houses at Sea Horse are reviewed separately here. Though all include a housekeeper who cooks breakfast (you supply the groceries) and a gardener, a chef can also be requested. Sea Horse Ranch will buy food for your villa for $50 and also has a nanny service. The beach club restaurant overlooking a dramatic cove delivers. **Pros:** one of the most organized, well-managed groups of villas in the country; potent security makes your vacation worry-free; location close to Puerto Plata and the airport. **Cons:** not much sense of place (you could be in an upscale neighborhood in Florida or Southern California); not all villas have Wi-Fi, and DSL is very expensive; small beaches. ⊠ *Cabarete* ☎ *809/571–3880 or 800/635–0991* ⊕ *www.sea-horse-ranch.com* ⟿ *75 villas* ⌂ *In-room: a/c, safe (some), kitchen, Wi-Fi (some). In-hotel: restaurant, bar, tennis courts, pool, beachfront, parking (free)* ⊟ *AE, MC, V* ⟿ *2-night minimum* ⑽ *EP.*

¢
HOTEL

⬚ **Sosúa Bay Hotel.** The clean, basic rooms here start at $65. And for the money, the views, overlooking Playa Sosúa from a rise to the side, can't be beat (rooms in oceanfront Buildings 3 and 4 have the best views). The hotel also has a small pool that provides panoramic views of the bay; it shares this pool with the Victorian House next door. The rotunda buffets are a cut above—particularly on Seafood Night—and even better than the stand-alone restaurants. There's a small casino across the street. **Pros:** fun atmosphere; steps away from town but mercifully quiet; caring, efficient, and good-humored management and staff. **Cons:** no top-shelf liquor at the bar; balconies are small and have just chairs, no chaises; guest rooms not as attractive as lobby and public areas. ⊠ *Calle Dr. Alejo Martinez 1, El Batey, Sosúa* ☎ *809/571–4000* ⊕ *www. sosuabayresort.com* ⟿ *193 rooms* ⌂ *In-room: a/c, safe, refrigerator. Inhotel: 5 restaurants, bars, pools, gym, beachfront, diving, water sports, bicycles, children's programs (ages 4–12), laundry facilities, Internet terminal, Wi-Fi hotspot* ⊟ *MC, V* ⑽ *AI.*

$
HOTEL
★

⬚ **Victorian House.** On a cliff above breathtaking Sosúa Bay, this boutique hotel is an appealing replica of a Victorian gingerbread house. It's much more low-key and not as densely populated as its sister property next door, the Sosúa Bay Hotel. (You can join its all-inclusive plan for an additional $55 per person.) Check-in is at a white-pillared cottage, originally a settlement house for Jewish refugees in the 1940s. Multilingual concierges pamper independent travelers. Terraces have teak lounge chairs and ottomans, as well as ever-changing knockout views. **Pros:** bilevel penthouses are outstanding; consistently good service; tiein meal plan can be a good option. **Cons:** lack of elevators can be hard if you're on a higher floor; latest renovation not entirely successful.

6

⊠ *Calle Dr. Alejo Martinez 1, El Batey, Sosúa* ☎ *809/571–4000* 📞 *32 rooms, 7 junior suites, 8 suites, 3 penthouses* ⚿ *In-room: a/c, safe, kitchen (some), refrigerator. In-hotel: 5 restaurants, room service, bars, pools, gym, beachfront, diving, water sports, bicycles, children's programs (ages 4–12), laundry facilities* ▤ *MC, V* 🍽 *BP.*

$$$$
PRIVATE VILLA
Fodor's Choice
★

⌂ **Villa Catalina.** This 3½-acre, beachfront estate is the best site in Sea Horse Ranch, having been designed by the famed architect Sara Garcia in 2006. The style might be best described as Tuscany meets Manhattan. The sprawling rose-colored stucco mansion looks like an Italian palazzo, while the contemporary interior is filled with quality artwork. An unexpected cartoon sculpture on the front lawn is just one of many whimsical art pieces here (others are an Adam and Eve on glass, a massive painting of a zebra pair, and a Sopranos pinball machine, all framed by neutral and white furnishings). There is more color in the five bedrooms, including a blue-and-white room with cobalt ocean views and yes, more art. **Pros:** both a private (with cavern) and semiprivate beach, so large that it would not feel crowded even if there were a crowd. **Cons:** beach nearly disappears when the tide is high; lacks traditional warmth. ⊠ *1 Sea Horse Ranch, Los Corales, Cabarete* ☎ *809/571–3880* ⊕ *www.villa-catalina.com* 📞 *5 bedrooms, 6 bathrooms* ⚿ *In-room: a/c, safe, DVD. In-hotel: pool, beachfront, laundry facilities* ▤ *AE, MC, V* 🍽 *BP.*

$$$$
PRIVATE VILLA

⌂ **Villa Windsong 129.** Unique among the Sea Horse Ranch collection, this sprawling vacation home is not only on one of the most enviable beachfronts, it's Balinese in design, utilizing the most natural construction materials: palapa roofs, native coralina and fieldstone floors, round white stones, and hemp ropes on the high-ceilinged rafters. Individual bedrooms flank the main building, which has an open-air living room, extending to an indoor dream kitchen in stainless steel. A wood-burning pizza oven is indicative that this is ideal for casual fun, and especially good for family reunions. Past the infinity pool, an Asian-influenced gazebo looks onto the beach with its tidal pools. The indoor-outdoor environment provides a natural high. **Pros:** sandals and pareos suit this villa; bedrooms have their own patios, and one has a baby's nursery. **Cons:** not as many cushy creature comforts as some expensive mansions here; lacks a formality or elegance that some upscale clients would want; very expensive. ⊠ *Sea Horse Ranch, Las Olas, Cabarete* ☎ *809/571–3880* ⊕ *www.sea-horse-ranch.com* 📞 *4 bedrooms, 4 bathrooms* ⚿ *In-room: a/c, safe, DVD. In-hotel: pool, beachfront, laundry facilities* ▤ *AE, MC, V* 🍽 *BP.*

NIGHTLIFE AND THE ARTS

Nightlife in Sosúa often consists of lolling around your hotel bar and lobby, as some, like the Sosúa Bay Hotel, have live entertainment or music playing. Walking into town and hanging at one of the bars or restaurants, such as La Roca, or taking a coffee at one of the cafés, is another option. If you're here because you heard that the place was ripe for sex tourism, you'll find that the less savory elements of Sosúa are now relegated to the east end of town, including the seedy Merengue Bar, which has a popular disco upstairs.

The best expat bar was begun by a Canadian pop star who named it Voodoo Lounge; it's called Beecher's. Tourists sometimes motor on over to the little casino at Playa Chiquita.

Club 59 (⊠ *Pedro Clisante, corner of Calle Dr. Rosen, El Batey* ☎ *No phone*) is atop the infamous Merengue Bar, a red-light landmark. If you want to dance where the girls are, or at least gyrate to the Afro beat from your bar stool, then climb the stairs to 59. It has a long bar and is attractive, almost tasteful. There is usually no cover, but drinks cost more here than in other bars. Early on, around 10 PM, you'll see about 10 scantily dressed Dominican and Haitian *chicas* to each guy. As the night progresses, the men—mainly older white guys—come in ever greater numbers.

> **LOCALLY MADE IN SOSÚA**
>
> The cooperative through which the early Jewish immigrants sold their products is still around today. Named Sosúa Productos, they include unsalted butter, yogurt, and fruit-flavored yogurt drinks as well as cheese and sausage. The quality is excellent, and they're available in every store of any size in the area, as well as in *colmados y supermercados* from Juan Dolio to Barahona.

6

Beecher's Rock N Blues. (⊠ *Pedro Clisante corner of Calle Arzeno, last building in Sosúa Bay complex, Sosúa* ☎ *No phone*) was once the Voodoo Lounge and then Ruby's Lounge, and now belongs to Canadian Beecher Miller. The upstairs bar is a lounge, while the main level is friendly, inviting bar. Live bands play on weekends, and Tuesday is open-jam night. The bar also has a karaoke-on-demand system.

Sosúa Bay Grand Casino (*Sosúa* ☎ *809/571–4075* ⊕ *www.sosuabaygrandcasino.com)* has over 80 slots, a Texas Hold 'Em table, and a dozen table games.

BEACHES

Playa Sosúa (⊠ *Carretera Puerto Plata–Sosúa, El Batey, Sosúa*), the gorgeous beach on Sosúa Bay, is renowned for its coral reefs and dive sites, and is about a 20-minute drive east of Puerto Plata. Here, calm waters gently lap at a shore of soft, golden sand. Swimming is delightful—except after a heavy rain, when litter often floats in. But beware of sea urchins in the shallow water (they attach themselves to large rocks). From the beach you can see mountains in the background, the cliffs that surround the bay, and seemingly miles of coastline. Snorkeling from the beach can be good, but the best spots are offshore, closer to the reefs. The beach is backed by a string of tents where hawkers push souvenirs, snacks, drinks, and water-sports equipment rentals. Lounge chairs can usually be had for RD$60, so bargain. The scene here on a weekend is incredible—local families pack the beach, and the roar of Dominican fun fills the air.

SPORTS AND THE OUTDOORS

DIVING

There's good snorkeling in Sosúa Bay right off the beach, but you can also take a dive boat to a sandy beach and have a look-see underwater at the colorful gardens and reefs abundant here. The North Coast is dotted with numerous reefs, walls, wrecks, and caverns, making this a good destination for divers. In the waters off Sosúa alone, you can find a dozen dive sites (for all levels of ability) with such catchy names as Airport Wall (98 feet) and Pyramids (50 feet). You can book a cavern dive for Gri Gri Lagoon and be transported by van to Río San Juan.

Several dive schools are near Sosúa Beach, but you're always better off enjoying the quality and dependability provided by a PADI five-star dive shop. The Sosúa hotels have dive shops on-site or can arrange trips for you. Rental equipment, dive packages, and courses are available for every level, from introductory to instructor.

Northern Coast Aquasports (⊠ *Sosúa* ☎ *809/571–1028* ⊕ *www.northern-coastdiving.com*) is a five-star, Gold Palm PADI dive center; it's also the only National Geographic diver certification site in the Dominican Republic. Professionalism is apparent in the initial classroom and pool practice, as well as in the selection of legendary dive sites around beautiful Sosúa Bay, where you can explore the reefs, walls, wrecks, and swim-throughs, from 25 to 130 feet. Successful completion of a three-day course and $350 earns you a PADI Open Water Certification card. Classrooms have air-conditioning and DVDs. On Friday nights the British owners host a curry supper and beer party for their clients.

SHOPPING

If you need to know anything about anything in Sosúa, stop by and meet Patrick at **Patrick's Silvermithy** (⊠ *Calle Pedro Clisante 3, El Batey, Sosúa* ☎ *809/571–2121*). Here for decades, he is kind about aiding gringos and has a sense of humor. He also makes tasteful silver jewelry if you are looking for a souvenir of your time here.

CABARETE

10 mi (15 km) east of Sosúa.

Of the towns within easy reach of the Puerto Plata airport, Cabarete has the best dining, the longest beaches, and the most youthful spirit. The main street is crowded with colorful signage and speeding traffic, and smoky with the fumes of motoconchos, but it's easy to ignore these potential annoyances when you're having so much fun. A hot destination, especially for the young—and more and more for retired baby boomers as well—one of its main claims to fame is the wind. Nowhere on the island can you find such perfect conditions for kite surfing. If there's a good breeze, the shoreline flares with bright sails. An annual international competition, Master of the Ocean (⊕ *www.masteroftheocean.com*), takes place the last weekend in February. It's a triathlon of windsurfing, kite surfing, and surfing.

The Reef Ball Foundation

If you think the Reef Ball Foundation sounds like some annual charity event at a yacht club, it most assuredly is not. It's a nonprofit organization founded in 1993 to help restore and protect the natural reef systems throughout the world, including the reef in Sosúa Bay, by dropping reef-enhancing balls of concrete.

After deploying a reef ball, a team of trained divers, called a Coral Team, transplants imperiled corals on to the artificial reef. Eventually, coral growth covers the Reef Ball, leaving nothing exposed except a healthy natural reef.

The foundation workers have taught local dive operators and resort staff the art of constructing and deploying these balls to provide the infrastructure needed to rehabilitate coral habitats devastated by pollution, over-fishing, and severe storms.

The **Reef Ball Foundation, Inc.** (⊕ www.reefball.org) is a publicly supported nonprofit group that has placed Reef Balls in numerous countries. Their projects include artificial reefs, estuary restoration, red mangrove plantings, coral propagation, erosion control (often on the beach), and education on preserving natural reefs.

6

Those who are afraid to ride the waves or to soar like an eagle propelled by a piece of lightweight fabric can still watch and enjoy these colorful goings-on across the blue horizon. Later, chat up the water adventurers as they barhop and dance the night away. A dozen chockablock bars and restaurants have created a creative and relaxing setup of tables and lounges right atop the sand on the main beach in town, creating a coast's best beachfront dining and nightlife experience.

GETTING HERE AND AROUND

Cabarete is the next down on Route 5 after Sosúa. The condo developments hug the shore, first along Kite Beach and the then a mile or so later along the main strip in town, Cabarete Beach.

NEED A BREAK?

Claro (⊠ *Calle Principal, just past Velero Beach Resort, at sign for Casa Blanca* ☎ *809/867–8884*) is a true local's secret. It's down a driveway just off the main drag, but still away from the noise and a little hard to find. You can enjoy a variety of breakfast choices from 10 to 2 (though it's closed Monday). If you're looking for lunch, have a wrap, the weekly special (which might be couscous), or the good cheeseburger. Claro has a kids' menu with surprising variety that includes chicken fingers and pigs in blankets.

WHERE TO EAT

Americans tend to leave at least 10% over and above the 10% service charge (which goes to everyone working in the restaurant). Servers have become accustomed to that and are starting to expect it from English-speaking customers. So now with 16% tax, you should expect to pay a whopping 36% on top of the menu prices for your meals.

Many restaurants in Cabarete only take cash, or if they do take plastic, will charge you 4% to 5% more for the privilege. Always ask, and come with money in your pocket. You can also leave your American Express card home, because most restaurants won't take it unless they're very pricey or are within an expensive hotel.

$$
AMERICAN
CASUAL
✕ **Ali's Surf Camp.** You sit at long tables with a disparate group of strangers from at least three different countries, surrounded by bulrushes poking up from a lagoon. (Many of those eating here are kiters in residence at the adjacent surf camp, considered Cabarete's best.) You can have a good meal for around 10 to 15 bucks. Try grilled, sweet barbecued ribs with fries and a Dominican salad, or the house special, *churrasco* (grilledskirt steak, Argentineanstyle). There's always a shooter of *mamajuana*. The German owner, Ali, changes offerings often, but at this writing, German rotisserie chicken is the designated Saturday special. For lunch, try the Austrian schnitzel burger. If you want to do breakfast, offerings are limited. It may simply be pancakes, and there's fresh-squeezed juice, that is, if you do the squeezing. The palapa roof gives the terrace shelter, but you'd best douse yourself with mosquito repellent. ⊠ *Procab Cabarete, Cabarete* ☎ *809/571–0733* ▤ *No credit cards.*

$
CAFÉ
✕ **Cabahá.** The hip decor and the hot-pink wall paint at this diminutive café a few steps from the beach illustrate the same good taste as the music, top-shelf liquor, fresh-fruit drinks, and healthy fare. The fresh mango juice with añejo rum and triple sec may be the best cocktail you'll have in the Dominican Republic—unless you try the special-recipe mojitos with crushed ice. Breakfast can be anything from fresh smoothies to muesli. Organic salads and sandwiches, such as smoked salmon and cream cheese on dark bread, are on the lunch menu. *Picaderas* (finger foods) and fish seviche are on offer for dinner. A must-try is the hummus with a drizzle of house-made pepper oil. Most everything is low-calorie, and there are no fried foods on the menu, which leaves room for decadent desserts such as double chocolate cake. The Chilean chef-proprietress Haudy (pronounced *how*-dy) Retamal has a loyal following. ⊠ *Paseo Don Chiche 14, across from Fred's, Cabarete* ☎ *809/963–8397* ▤ *No credit cards* ☹ *Closed Tues.*

$$
SEAFOOD
✕ **Casita de Papi.** Cabarete Beach is awash in trendy beach restaurants, where you can see plenty of sexy young customers. But the reason this decade-old family restaurant, owned by a retired French chef, has made the cut is that a couple of its specialties are true pleasures. The food will help you overlook the dated polyester tablecloths and the service. They do try, but it's just not quite there. But here's the deal: order the sizzling cauldrons of either 16 large *camarones* (shrimp) or *langostinos* (small lobsters) in a creamy sauce. True, this is the most expensive thing

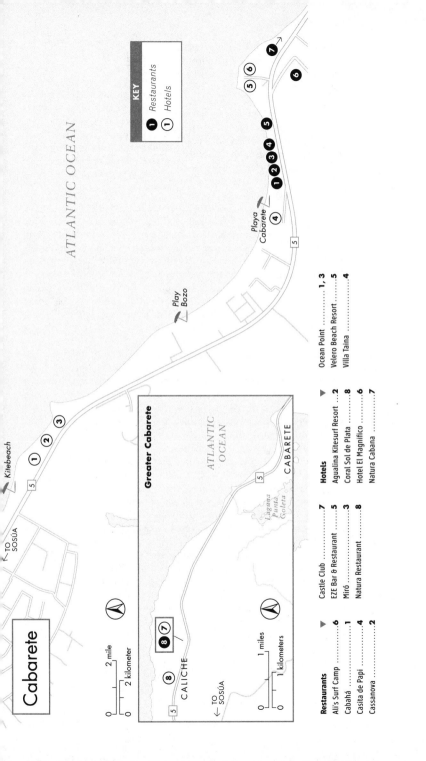

Cabarete

ATLANTIC OCEAN

TO SOSÚA

Kitebeach

Play Bozo

Playa Cabarete

KEY

① Restaurants

① Hotels

0   2 mile

0   2 kilometer

Greater Cabarete

ATLANTIC OCEAN

Laguna Punta Goleta

CABARETE

CALICHE

TO SOSÚA

0   1 miles

0   1 kilometers

Restaurants ▶

Ali's Surf Camp **6**

Cabahá **1**

Casita de Papi **4**

Cassanova **2**

Castle Club **7**

EZE Bar & Restaurant **5**

Miró **3**

Natura Restaurant **8**

Hotels ▶

Agualina Kitesurf Resort ...**2**

Coral Sol de Plata **8**

Hotel El Magnifico **6**

Natura Cabana **7**

Ocean Point **1, 3**

Velero Beach Resort **5**

Villa Taina **4**

on the menu (800 pesos), but two people can easily share a cauldron (trust us), and you can spread the wealth even wider if you order the fish quenelles, too. The sign on the beach says LA CASITA DE DON ALFREDO PAPI. On an exotic beach where you'd like to have a week to eat at each restaurant, this is the place to feast. ⊠ *Cabarete Beach, Cabarete* ☎ *No phone* ▤ *No credit cards.*

$

INTERNATIONAL

✕ **Cassanova.** This Southeast Asian–inspired restaurant has lots of glitz and a large Buddha head at the entrance. On the beach are kite-shaped lights in the palms, a flaming torch, and Dominican musicians serenading. Few local residents brag about the food on the extensive menu, though. The most popular items are the Thai red chicken curry and the shrimp with pastis. You can also order some tapas like the peanut chicken satay or the symphony of fish. Service is quite good. But if you hit the restaurant for happy hour or a late nightcap (the kitchen closes at midnight, but the crowd stays on), you can have your beers or blender drinks and people-watch. It's the scene you're here for, after all. ⊠ *Cabarete Beach, Cabarete* ☎ *809/571–0806* ▤ *AE, MC, V.*

$$$$

CARIBBEAN

✕ **Castle Club.** A man's home is his castle. In this one, Doug Beers prepares creative lunches and dinners for guests who cross the rocky driveway to enjoy this one-of-a-kind experience. His wife, Marguerite, is the gracious hostess, who shows patrons their expansive mountain home and the artwork strategically positioned between the many open-air arches. Served on antique lace tablecloths strewn with bougainvillea, the well-orchestrated dinner might consist of canapés, carrot-ginger soup, Thai salad, grouper with a ginger–passion fruit sauce, fiesta rice, cold lemon soufflé, and coffee. After dinner, Doug lights a fire in the great room and offers guests a liqueur to warm their interiors. You must make reservations in advance, since this meal is cooked in the owner's own house. ⊠ *Mocha Rd. between Jamao and Los Brazos, 20 mins from Cabarete* ☎ *809/357–8334, 809/223–0601, or 809/223–0601* ✎ *castleclub@hotmail.com* ⚏ *Reservations essential* ▤ *No credit cards.*

$–$$

AMERICAN

✕ **EZE Bar & Restaurant.** This little place, at the far end of the beach, doesn't look like much, but it has an intensely loyal following, from wallet-watching windsurfers to wealthy *capitaleño* (from Santo Domingo) families. Menu names, reflecting the jargon of the surfers who frequent the place, include Bluebird's Salad (chicken tenders over mixed greens with a sweet chili salsa), the EZE Club Dude (curried grilled chicken), and the Rocker (grilled, marinated beef with onions, peppers, tomato, and tzitiki on a soft pita). Frosty, tropical cocktails are excellent, and you can get an energy kick from yogurt-and-mango smoothies. The blenders also churn out healthful, organic vegetable drinks. Conversely, if you need a bacon-cheeseburger fix, this is the place. Dinner is priced similarly to lunch, with more refined specials, like calamari or even lobster. Also on the menu are some *nueva criolla* (contemporary takes on local creole dishes), open for breakfast through dinner; the kitchen is often open until midnight. ⊠ *Cabarete Beach in front of Carib Wind Center, Cabarete* ☎ *809/880–8779* ▭ *No credit cards.*

$–$$

ECLECTIC

✕ **Miró Gallery & Restaurant.** Chef-owner Lydia Wazana, of Canadian–Moroccan descent, knows many artists, and there is always art on the walls, accompanying imaginative offerings like Moroccan chicken tagine or Asian seared tuna. Grazers can share tapas such as the Middle Eastern hummus, baba ghanoush, and grilled veggies. Look for items that pair with the incredible curry aioli or spicy pineapple-chutney-and-wasabi-potato puree. The master sushi maker and menu—classic sashimi and sushi, as well as some fab innovations that include shrimp tempura rolls—from Lydia's former restaurant, Wabi Sabi, are here now. Lounge at a table on top of the beach or curl up with your buddies or beaus on the king-size Balinese sun bed. ⊠ *Cabarete Beach, Cabarete* ☎ *809/853–6848* ▭ *No credit cards* ☾ *Closed Oct. 15–Nov. 15. No lunch.*

$$

SEAFOOD

★

✕ **Natura Restaurant at Natura Cabana.** If you're staying at this remote thatch-hut eco resort on the beach, you'll be lucky enough to have all your meals here. If not, it's definitely worth a trip, not only for the very good seafood, but to take in the private beach that stretches out before you. Seafood is at the heart of the menu here, and appropriately so, because diners listen to the sounds of the waves crashing on coral rock as they fork the catch of the day with a buttery pistachio sauce. Start with the octopus in mint vinaigrette and then go for the lobster scampi. It all tastes so fresh. The filet mignon with mixed mushroom sauce is perfection. For dessert, enjoy a classic such as a pear poached in red wine à la mode. The wines are French, Spanish, and Chilean (go for the *reservas*). Tables are set with geometric plates, laced linens, and oversize wine glasses. Service is warm, caring, and efficient, the international music atmospheric. ⊠ *At Natura Cabana, Perla Marina, Cabarete* ☎ *809/858–5822 or 809/571–1507* ⚑ *Reservations essential* ▭ *AE, MC, V.*

6

WHERE TO STAY

Each year the number of deluxe accommodations seems to be on the rise even as the less expensive lodgings, from $50-a-night surf camps to cheap hotels and apartment complexes, dwindle. However, Cabarete is still one of the few holdouts against all-inclusives, making it friendly to independent travelers. There are a couple of AIs outside of town, but villas and condominiums have become the choice of increasingly affluent visitors and second-home buyers. In the town itself are two long, connected beaches: Kite Beach is farther from the nightlife. Here you will find Ocean Point and Agualina. Cabarete Beach, in the thick of things, is where you'll find Villa Taina, Velero, and El Magnifico.

HOTELS AND RESORTS

$

HOTEL

▦ **Agualina Kitesurf Resort.** Compared to the digs many surfers occupy, this small, clean mid-rise hotel at the east end of Kite Beach, right beside Ocean Point One, is a deluxe address. In fact, many of the occupants, particularly in low season and on weekends, are well-to-do Dominican families, who often take the penthouses or the units with kitchens. The young kite surfers usually live on breakfast, burgers, and burritos from the Dare2fly bar, right in front, where the kite school is. A small pool is to the left, and the tiny lobby has a free public computer. It's all modern and moderately priced. A small bar and grill is right on the beach here, too. **Pros:** all rooms have balconies and incredible views of the sea and the kite action; excellent two-for-one rum cocktails during happy hour. **Cons:** everything feels small; the hotel, grounds, pool, beachfront, can be noisy on weekends in high season. ⊠ *Kite Beach, Cabarete* 🕾 *809/571–0787* ⊕ *www.agualina.com* ⤳ *7 rooms, 8 studios, 4 junior suites, 3 apartments* ⟳ *In-room: a/c, kitchen (some), refrigerator. In-hotel: restaurant, bar, pool, beachfront, water sports, laundry service, Internet terminal, public Wi-Fi, parking (free)* ⊟ *MC, V* ⟨◎⟩ *EP.*

$
ALL-INCLUSIVE
☾

⌗ **Coral Sol de Plata.** Two miles east of Sosúa towards Cabarete, this former Breezes is one of the few 24-hour all-inclusives on the North Coast. On 62 acres with an extensive beach and quietly removed from the highway noise by a long driveway, it's highly family-friendly, with nine (somewhat sloppy) holes of golf, and a private beach and a fun, winding pool. The newer hotel buildings, 10 and 11, have bilevel master suites furnished with rough-hewn four-posters and woven wall hangings. The sprawling resort has the Lighthouse Spa, which is consistently good. The casino was closed at the time of this writing, as was an inviting rock-climbing feature. There's an Italian and a Japanese restaurant, plus a buffet and beach eatery. A Dominican family favorite on weekends and during low season, the resort is also frequented by Europeans and Americans, who prevail in the winter season. **Pros:** fun pool; nice beach; quiet spots even when the resort is full; good breakfast buffet. **Cons:** other than breakfast, the food is not super; rock climbing closed at time of writing; clientele can be rowdy. ⊠ *Carretera Cabarete, Cabarete* 🕾 *809/320–3600* ⊕ *www.coralhotels.com/english/ hotels/sol_de_plata* ⤳ *436 rooms, 22 junior suites, 8 2-bedroom suites* ⟳ *In-room: a/c, safe, refrigerator. In-hotel: 5 restaurants, bars, tennis courts, pools, gym, spa, beachfront, water sports, children's programs (ages 4–12), laundry service, Internet terminal, golf (9 holes), parking (free)* ⊟ *AE, D, DC, MC, V* ⟨◎⟩ *AI.*

$
HOTEL

⌗ **Hotel El Magnifico.** Coral-stone paths wind you around the exquisite tropical gardens of cactus and orchids at this serene luxury boutique condo-hotel just a gravel driveway from the dusty, noisy highway into town. The open reception area, backed by an artistic screen, is flanked by a quiet seating or "swinging" area (there's a comfy hammock) that whispers tranquillity. The lush gardens hold a pair each of pools and Jacuzzis. For your accommodations, try to get the newest Building 6, with beach and water views. The stonework surrounding it and the walkways to the warm, oceanfront Jacuzzi are eye popping. Further, the glow from the lanterns leading to the water makes it a fantasia. Gerhard Hebert, creator of "The Magnificent," is a charming French Canadian, an early surfer who arrived in 1984 and has a following. **Pros:** never feels crowded; the interior decor is très chic; the spaces are large and contemporary; children under 15 stay free. **Cons:** steep spiral staircases and no elevators; no restaurant or bar; no in-room phones and no way to communicate with reception unless you have a cell phone or rent one here. ☒ *Calle del Cementario, Cabarete* ☎ *809/571–0868* ⊕ *www.hotelmagnifico.com* ⟿ *7 rooms, 10 1-bedrooms, 6 2-bedrooms, 1 3-bedroom, 6 2-bedroom penthouses* ♿ *In-room: a/c, no phone, kitchen (some), refrigerator, Wi-Fi. In-hotel: pool, hot tub, beachfront, parking (free)* ▭ *MC, V* ⭐ *EP.*

$$
RESORT
Fodor's Choice
★

☷ **Natura Cabana.** If your idea of perfection is thatch-roof cabanas and a quiet, private beach among the trees, then this is the North Coast's top choice: an oceanfront ecoparadise. The ten cabanas here are made from bamboo, artistic brick, and stonework. All baths have stones that feel wonderful underfoot and have enormous rain-shower showerheads. The property was designed to blend into the environment without disturbing its beauty, and this draws a nature-loving crowd; you might find yourself next to a surfer, a young neurologist, or a yoga aficionado. Lole, the *dueña* (owner), and her caring, bilingual staff promote camaraderie. Healthy breakfasts and lunches are served in one of the two waterfront restaurants (breakfast and lunch in one, dinner in the other). The food is great, and mellow music serves as the backdrop for backgammon and conversation. The artistically designed Attabeyra Spa has services like chocolate wraps and massage on the beach. The splendid yoga pavilion is a *palacio*: it's also the setting for retreats and weddings. The pool gazebo, with its colorful Indian sarongs, is the setting for romantic dinners. There's a special discount if you pay in cash. **Pros:** natural, peaceful beachfront stay; good food; caring owner; spa; treehouse for kids. **Cons:** car is almost a requirement; outside of town (a one-hour walk by the beach); no air-conditioning, but sea breezes. ☒ *Playa Perla Marina, Cabarete* ☎ *809/571–1507* ⊕ *www.naturacabana.com* ⟿ *10 bungalows* ♿ *In-room: no a/c, no phone, kitchen (some), refrigerator, Wi-Fi, no TV. In-hotel: 2 restaurants, bar, pool, spa, beachfront, Wi-Fi, parking (free)* ▭ *AE, MC, V* ⭐ *CP.*

$$$
VACATION
CONDO

☷ **Ocean Point.** Enjoy the good life at this upscale condo complex, the snazziest on Kite Beach, as you sit at the pool, shaded by a golden market umbrella, and watch the parade of multicolored surf-kites over the big blue ocean. You can take out a kayak or bodyboard or just bob around with a pool noodle. The attractive, modern condos have expansive terraces and outdoor dining areas. The interiors are even better, with fully equipped Italian designer kitchens that are great for those who want to stay in for dinner. The four-bedroom, four-bath, 4,000-square-foot penthouses are tastefully luxurious and worth the extra money if you have a larger family or group. Mind you, even the two-bedroom condos are 1,800 square feet. A concierge can arrange pre-arrival grocery

---

RAMILIFE—BREAK FOR A WELLNESS DAY

The staff of **RamiLife** (☎ *809/710–1221* ⊕ *www. RamiLife.com*) offer a day of health for the area's resort guests to help them recover from many all-inclusive days of too much food and too many rum drinks. Treatments are structured around the RAM-Energy-Median massage (REM). Services are offered at Natura Cabanas every Monday and Friday in the glorious, outdoor yoga pavilion.

6

stocking and nanny service. **Pros:** great beach location; nice pool; gorgeous views; high-quality building materials. **Cons:** a 20-minute beach walk to most restaurants; no breakfast or meals available on-site (one small, good, and inexpensive restaurant next door, the Kite Club Grill, serves breakfast and lunch). ⊠ *Kite Beach, Carretera Principal, Cabarete* ☎ *809/571–0030* ⊕ *www. oceanpointdr.com* ⇥ *28 2-bedroom condos, 10 4-bedroom penthouses* ⌂ *In-room: a/c, safe, refrigerator, kitchen, Internet, Wi-Fi. In-hotel: pool, beachfront, water sports, laundry facilities* ▤ *AE, D, DC, MC, V* ⏝◎⏝ *EP.*

$ ▦ **Velero Beach Resort.** Laze in the

RESORT   hammock or swing on the palm that bends over the beach while you

THE SANTIAGO ALTERNATIVE

Check out airfares to Santiago, which has numerous direct flights from New York, Newark, and Miami. JetBlue has rates as low as $130 one-way. Some flights arrive around 3:30 AM, but you can bunk at the spiffy Courtyard by Marriott Santiago five minutes from the airport, spend the day at Centro León, and take a bus or taxi to the North Coast towns of Puerto Plata, Sosúa, and Cabarete. Since JetBlue prices by segments, you may want to fly out of another destination, which won't require paying a penalty.

watch the kite surfers work to become airborne, and you'll appreciate Velero's location, just a few minutes' walk east of the noise of town yet also just minutes from the happening bars. (It's across a small path from Hotel El Magnifico). Spacious suites with full kitchens are the best deals; the basic unit has two full bedrooms, but room dividers can turn one larger unit into two smaller ones. Guests in standard rooms (without kitchens) get a complimentary breakfast at the private beach restaurant. You might ask for the art deco Building 111, which has all been repainted. The views from the penthouses are knockout, and an excellent value if three couples share. Ask about the 10% discount for cash. **Pros:** blenders, microwaves, and DVDs in the junior suites and above; draped Balinese sun beds at the pool are wonderful. **Cons:** no elevators—it's a climb up the spiral staircases; standard rooms are not spacious. ⊠ *Calle la Punta 1, Cabarete* ☎ *809/571–9727* ⊕ *www. velerobeach.com* ⇥ *22 2-bedroom suites, 7 penthouses* ⌂ *In-room: a/c, safe, kitchen (some), refrigerator, Wi-Fi (some). In-hotel: restaurant, pool, beachfront, Internet terminal, Wi-Fi* ▤ *MC, V* ⏝◎⏝ *EP.*

¢   ▦ **Villa Taina.** Smack amid the action, steps down from the main drag,

INN   this small, German-owned inn encapsulates the original spirit of Cabarete. It caters to the independent traveler and the young and sporty who want bigger digs than a surf camp. Included in the room rate is an ample breakfast at Serenada, the beachside restaurant adjacent to the kite- and windsurfing center; your fellow coffee drinkers may be shielded by German and French newspapers. By night, the revamped restaurant serves international cuisine, with special buffet theme nights, cool sounds, and a fun crowd. There's also a cute bar with live music. The room interiors (a standard-issue tile floor, wicker furnishings) are nothing to write home about, but this beach hotel is a solid value. Request the quiet rooms (the second floor up to the penthouses) that front the beach. **Pros:** great location; efficient and caring owner. **Cons:** small pool; noise of town can be heard in the buildings closest to the street; standard rooms are on the small side. ⊠ *Calle Principal, Cabarete* ☎ *809/571–0722* ⊕ *www.villataina.com* ⌐ *56 rooms, 1 apartment* ⌂ *In-room: a/c, refrigerator, Internet. In-hotel: restaurant, bar, pool, beachfront, water sports* ⊟ *MC, V* ⌐⌐ *BP.*

NIGHTLIFE AND THE ARTS

All around the country and in many foreign ports, the nightlife in Cabarete is known as the big beach party. And so it is. Barhopping is the name of the game here. The open-air bars and restaurants that line the beachfront mainly attract the young and restless, but anyone who is fun-loving is made welcome. It starts at happy hour, which, as at Onno's, might include half-price tapas from 4 to 7; factor in the half-price local drinks from 6 to 8. The best advice is to walk the beach and see which bars offer the best discounts (and when), then make your plans. Curfews mean that bars close at 3 AM on weekends, helping to curb after-party crime. △ **Nevertheless, after midnight exercise your street sense on the beach. Watch your back as well as your purse or wallet. And don't walk the beach alone after dark, especially deserted stretches.** Be wary of moto-conchos, which zip down the streets with little notice of pedestrians. Men may be approached by prostitutes, or younger tourists by drug dealers. We recommend that you avoid both.

BARS AND CAFÉS

★ **Lax** (⊠ *Cabarete Beach, Cabarete* ☎ *809/915–4842*) is a perennially popular open-air bar that really comes alive by night. You can sit in the sand in lounge chairs or jump into the action under the palapa, where a DJ will be spinning madly or a live band will be playing. There's good grazing chow, too, and special theme nights like Thai (it's not bad, either). Carefully made mojitos and other drinks (two-for-one specials from 5 to 7) mean you must be patient: getting one can take time when the bar backs up. It's next to a small hotel, so it must close early, around 1 AM.

DANCE CLUBS

Onno's Bar (⊠ *Cabarete Beach, Cabarete* ☎ *809/571–0461*), right next to Lax, remains a serious party place. It is usually wall-to-wall and back-to-back as the young and fit pack the dance floor and groove to techno sounds while other multinational youth sit at the tables in the sand. It's easier to get served at the beach bar than the main one, and as you chill, people will pass by, introduce themselves, chat, and then move on. It's fun and friendly, although on Friday and Saturday nights in high season, when it stays open until 3 AM, the scene can be rowdy.

BEACHES

The wonderful expanse of Atlantic beach that is Cabarete has been made not only more aesthetically pleasing but more user-friendly since its beach rejuvenation. Morning is best for swimmers and children, when the wind is light and the water calmer. Most of the beaches are soft sand, with few rocks. No motorized water sports or scuba diving are allowed at any of these beaches, but since this is a prime windsurfing area, especially in front of Carib Wind Center on the east end of Playa Cabarete, swimmers should be on guard for surfers of various kinds.

Kite Beach (⊠ *Sosúa–Cabarete Rd., 1.2 mi [2 km] west of town, Cabarete*), named for all the kite surfing that goes on here, is therefore fairly hazardous for those who just want to swim. On the sand you'll see instructors teaching new students how to work the lines that hold the wind foil—the colorful "kite." Experienced kiters are like poetry in motion, and it's mesmerizing to watch them. The windy month of March is prime time. Kite Beach passes a sandy peninsula at its east end and becomes Playa Cabarete.

Playa Cabarete (⊠ *Sosúa–Cabarete Rd., Cabarete*) is the main business district of this town. If you follow the coastal road east from Playa Dorada, you can't miss it. The beach, which has strong waves after a calm entrance, and ideal, steady wind (from 15 to 20 knots), is an integral part of the international windsurfing circuit. Segments of this long beach are strips of sand punctuated only by palm trees. The regeneration of Cabarete Beach was a massive engineering project that made the beach some 115 feet wider, adding an infusion of white sand. In the most commercial area, restaurants and bars are back-to-back, spilling onto the sand. The informal scene is young and fun, with expats and tourists from everywhere.

Playa Encuentro (⊠ *Sosúa–Cabarete Rd., 3.7 mi [6 km] west of Cabarete Beach, Cabarete*) is the area's main surfing beach because the waves here are large. The original ride-the-waves type of surfing on a fiberglass board is the ideal activity here. However, you need to be a strong swimmer, for currents are mighty, and you must be careful of the rocks. For general beaching, the other two in town are the ones to see.

SPORTS AND THE OUTDOORS

BIKING AND HIKING

Cabarete, backed by forested mountains, is the perfect starting point for outdoor adventures. You can have a spectacular mountain-biking adventure for a half or full day through the interior of the Dominican Republic. A 3,000-foot downhill ride on winding mountain roads can be great fun for all levels of athletes. A guided ride that includes a support vehicle makes the trip safer, and may help to alleviate the anxiety of the less experienced biker. Things look different from atop a bicycle seat; it's an exhilarating way to get into the heart of the country and learn about Dominican culture and vegetation, biking through Dominican villages, refreshing yourself with tropical fruits, and taking an invigorating swim in the Jamao River.

Hiking is another way to get in touch with the Dominican countryside. You can explore one of the newest national parks in the country, El Choco, an incredible 77 square mi of jungle, lagoons, caves, forests, and open backcountry outside Cabarete.

The more adventurous might want to make the cascade hike to the 27 Waterfalls of Damajagua, although this nontechnical climb is quite physically demanding, and you must be able to swim. You'll face a labyrinth of tunnels, caves, and natural pools. Watersliding and jumping down rock formations can be challenging, but will give you a sense of pride when it's over.

Fodor's Choice **Iguana Mama** (✉ *Calle Principal 74, Cabarete* ☎ *809/571–0908 or*
★ *809/571–0228* ⊕ *www.iguanamama.com and cariberush.com*) has traditional and mountain bikes, and will take you on guided rides on the flats or test your mettle on the steep grades in the mountains. Their "Cascading" tour takes you to 27 waterfalls on a full-day trip that includes climbing up and jumping off various waterfalls. Downhill bike rides, which include a taxi up to the foothills, breakfast, and lunch, cost $99 for a full-day trip, $65 for a half-day trip. Advanced rides, on and off roads, are $40 to $50. Guided hikes cost $35 to $70. In addition, this well-established, safety-oriented company offers horseback riding on the beach and in the countryside for $40 for two hours, canyoning, eco-tours, and a lots of other adventure sports.

BOATING

★ **Carib Wind Center** (✉ *Cabarete* ☎ *809/571–0640* ⊕ *www.caribwind. com*) is a renowned windsurfing center (known for decades as Carib BIC Center) that also rents Lasers, 17-foot catamarans, bodyboards, and sea kayaks. It has an Olympic Laser training center with a former racing instructor. Experts—even champions—come to train here.

HORSEBACK RIDING

Horseback riding is a delightful way to experience the beach and see the interior. It's best to go with an operation that maintains a certain caliber of mounts, equipment, and guides. Some of the local ad hoc guys will take you for less and let you gallop the beach, but if the tack breaks 10 minutes out and you bite the sand, don't expect to get your money refunded. Iguana Mama also offers horseback-riding trips, both on the beach and in the countryside (*see* ⇨ *Biking and Hiking, above*).

The **Sea Horse Ranch Equestrian Center** (✉ *Cabarete* ☎ *809/571–3880 or 809/571–4462*) is a professional, well-staffed operation. The competition ring is built to international regulations, and there is a large schooling ring. The Dominican Equestrian Federation sanctions an annual invitational jumping event. Lessons, including dressage instruction, start at $35 an hour, and endurance rides are $30 for 90 minutes, $50 for three hours, including drinks and snacks—but make reservations. The most popular ride includes stretches of beach and a bridle path across a neighboring farm's pasture that's full of wildflowers and butterflies. Feel free to tie your horse to a palm tree and jump into the waves.

TENNIS

Sea Horse Ranch (✉ *Cabarete* ☎ *809/571–2902*) has a tennis center with five clay courts, illuminated for night play and open to nonguests. Court time is $20 per person an hour, which includes ball boys, with an additional fee of $7 for night play. Instructions, available in four languages, cost $20.

WIND AND KITE SURFING

Fodor's Choice
★

Between June and October, Cabarete Beach has what many consider to be optimal windsurfing conditions: wind speeds at 20 to 25 knots (they come from the side shore) and 3- to-10-foot Atlantic waves. This also makes Cabarete a safer alternative, since the wind always blows toward the shore here, a plus for both novices and the weary, who will always drift back toward the beach rather than out to sea. The Professional Boardsurfers Association has included Cabarete in its international windsurfing slalom competition. The novice is also welcome to learn and train on wider boards with light sails.

> **DID YOU KNOW?**
>
> It's said that when kite surfing was just in its fledgling stage, one of the pioneers of the sport was swooped from the ocean by a mighty gust, becoming airborne. As dazed comrades looked up (and after many anguished minutes), his kite snagged on a tree, and he landed on the roof of the local *supermercado*. Word traveled fast, and children giggled as they squinted in the sun to see such a sight. Before long the whole town came to witness this averted tragedy. Of course, it made newspaper headlines the next day.

In kite surfing, the board—smaller than a traditional windsurfing board—is attached to a parachute-like "kite." Those who are proficient can literally fly through the air. It's a heady, adrenaline-spiked ocean adventure. One fortysomething novice explained that if you have surfed, it should only take about three hours to get the hang of it. As for the fear factor, it's there, but you will learn to control your kite. Novices can learn and train on wider boards with lighter sails.

Although one place offers an initial come-on for $20, which is just a trial run on the sand, real lessons in kite surfing don't come cheap. For private lessons, you should expect to pay $459 for 3 days (9 hours) or less; $612 or 4 days (12 hours). Group lessons can be cheaper; if you have a friend, you can take 3 days (9 hours) for $382 each, 4 days (12 hours) for $510 each.

Carib Wind Center (✉ *Cabarete* ☎ *809/571–0640* ⊕ *www.caribwind. com*) carries a number of brands, including many Olympic Laser boards. Equipment and instruction are offered, and lessons are generally $30 to $35 an hour; boards rent for $20 an hour. A gem of a windsurfing club, this family-owned business has many repeat clients and is open year-round. In the complex is its beach bar, EZE, as well as a retail shop. It has all the paraphernalia for surfing and a good variety of sunglasses, including Maui Jim's, and some of the best bikinis, cute miniskirts, and dresses in town.

★ **Kite Club** (✉ *Kite Beach, next to Ocean Point, Cabarete* ☎ *809/571–9748 or 809/972–6609* ⊕ *www.kiteclubcabarete.com*), an International Kitesurfing Organization (IKO) Certification Center, is a fraternal sports club that has multilingual lessons, from beginner to instructor certification. Prospective students generally book in advance online. Those kiters (and part-time residents) who have their own gear pay inexpensive, weekly dues to belong. This covers the use of the beach furniture and the rescue boat if needed. Equipment can be rented, too, and the adjacent snack shop is open to all. Credit cards are accepted.

Kitexcite (⊠ *Kite Beach Hotel, Kite Beach, Cabarete* ☎ *809/571–9509, 809/913–0827, or 809/914–9745* ⊕ *www.kiteclub.com*) operates a large school. (Fuel up at the adjacent Kite Club Grill.)

Laurel Eastman Kiteboarding (⊠ *Playa Bozo, in front of Ocean Dream, Cabarete* ☎ *809/571–0564* ⊕ *www.laureleastman.com*) is one of the best-known and respected schools, offering a free lesson with certified instructors from 10:30 to 11 AM daily. In four days, beginners can learn the theory of the wind and start using the smaller kite trainers. It may be exhilarating, but it isn't cheap. Four days of lessons (the amount of time it takes to be able to kiteboard on your own) costs $460. A hotel complex at this school allows adults to place kids at an on-site Montessori camp while you learn.

SHOPPING

In Cabarete, shopping is mainly for trinkets and souvenirs, Dominican cigars, beachy resort wear, jewelry, and surfing paraphernalia.

ART GALLERIES

Lisa Kirkman Gallery (⊠ *Ocean One Plaza, next to Banco Santa Cruz, Cabarete* ☎ *809/571–0108*) has a great selection of nationally acclaimed contemporary masters, up-and-coming artists, and works from the winners of the last art festival (held in Santo Domingo) and of the Eduardo León Jimenez national competition for contemporary artists. The gallery buzzes when there's an art opening, and the Indo-Caribbean furnishings (also for sale) create a loungelike atmosphere. Many of the artworks and accessories could be carried on a plane, or shipping can be arranged.

At **Miró Gallery & Restaurant** (⊠ *Cabarete Beach, Cabarete* ☎ *809/571–0888*) you can find rotating exhibitions of contemporary art with an emphasis on Latino artists and photographers, especially from the Dominican Republic and Cuba. Opening soirees are social events.

CLOTHING

Rata Surf Shop (⊠ *Calle Principal, across from blue Victorian building with gingerbread fretwork, Cabarete* ☎ *809/571–0863*) sells some of the town's best swimsuits, as well as sundresses, pareos, and crinkly miniskirts. There's a large selection of quality flip-flops and sandals, men's swimsuits and jams, plus T-shirts. Come here for chic, straw sun hats (Panama-style and more) and baseball caps.

GIFTS

Gary's Gift Shop (⊠ *Calle Principal, across from Supermercado Albertico, Cabarete* ☎ *No phone*) is just one of the many no-name souvenir shops selling knickknacks. There's no sign, but if you find it, you'll discover that among the better gift items are handmade candles in the shape of a dugout boat, key rings, pink shell necklaces, colorfully painted wooden turtles, photo albums and picture frames made with sand and fiber, flip-flops, and inexpensive Panama hats, caps, and visors. And this is where the locals go to buy their cigars.

JEWELRY

Beach Box Boutique (⊠ *Paseo Don Chiche 5, Cabarete* ☎ *809/571–0673; 809/399–7628 cell*), the sister shop to Fred Joyas, has colorful and utilitarian beach bags, pareos, organdy sun hats, shell jewelry, and wide silver bracelets.

Fred (⊠ *Paseo Don Chiche 3, turn at green BHD sign for ATM, Cabarete* ☎ *809/571–0673 or 809/399–7628*). *Joyas* is Spanish for jewelry. Here it's silver jewelry coupled with the island's semiprecious stones— larimar, amber, and black onyx—as well as shells and beads. Fred is the proprietress, a savvy Frenchwoman with great taste.

CABRERA

60 mi (96 km) east of Cabarete.

Cabrera, Abreu, Río San Juan, and the Playa Grande area are largely unspoiled and pristine coastal areas. There's a raw beauty, with some beaches that are still completely undeveloped, soaring cliffs overlooking pounding ocean waves, and towering inland hills with sweeping vistas not seen elsewhere on the North Coast. In addition, there are some of the most luxurious villa choices in the country. These high-end holiday homes, which are far away from the action and the bustle of Sosúa and Cabarete, will appeal primarily to those who wish to avoid noise. The area in general attracts a more moneyed crowd—mostly baby boomers—who want an upscale experience, as well as couples or friends who want to share a house and enjoy the amazing beaches.

GETTING HERE AND AROUND

It's an hour's drive to the east past Cabarete. If you're coming here directly, it's almost the same drive—about two hours—from Santo Domingo on the new highway as it is from the Puerto Plata airport.

EXPLORING CABRERA

Cabrera itself is still a sleepy, dusty Dominican town centered on its central square, which is remarkably clean. Tourists can safely mingle with townies in the park, and can stop for a drink at one of the adjacent restaurants, such as the thatched-roof Town Square Bar. In a land of warm, friendly people, Cabrerans are among the sweetest. Nearly 50 local and expat children now attend the new International Academy here, soon to expand to a secondary school.

The area is known more for its beaches and golf course than anything else. Playa Grande is one of the top tourist pleasures in the country—an unspoiled beach framed by verdant tropical jungle. Best of all, you can order fresh fish dishes from the shacks near the parking lot and eat them on the sand. Get a piña colada, and it's served inside a fresh pineapple—one of the best drinks you'll ever have. The adjacent beach, Playa Preciosa, is perhaps even more beautiful. You can also golf at the Playa Grande Golf Course, a famous Robert Trent Jones Jr. design that has most of its holes lining dramatic ocean cliffs (Hole 13 looks out high over Playa Grande itself).

★ **El Saltadero Waterfall**. Past the towns of Abreu and El Bretón, just west of the entrance to Cabrera, this 50-foot cascade empties into the icy pool at the bottom. You're likely to encounter local kids who jump down the falls into the pool for tips. You can scoot down the embankment to swim in it, too, but proceed with caution. The moss makes the rocks slippery.

Lago Dudú. This memorable natural wonder is a small complex of three natural features a few miles west of Cabrera (admission 50 pesos). There is a lagoon here that you can swim in—try the rope that swings into it. Then walk over to explore a nearby natural cave (bring your own flashlight if you remember). Then, across the way take stairs down into a spring that flows inside a cave.

★ **Laguna Gri Gri**. In the town of Río San Juan is this river-fed estuary leading to the ocean. Greeting you at the water is a picturesque collection of fishing boats. Here you hire a driver and boat from a cooperative (☎ 809/589–2277 ⌚ daily 8–6) for a 90-minute trip (1,000 pesos for two people, cheaper with larger groups) down a mangrove outlet that teems with tropical seabirds. Once in the ocean, the boats follow the shore until reaching a tiny cave, Cueva de las Golondrinas, which is named for the swallows that flitter about. You can then swim to a series of virgin beaches. Bring snorkeling gear if you have it.

6

WHERE TO EAT

A synopsis of the Cabrera dining scene includes the rustic Babanuco as well as the hilltop Hotel La Catalina's terrace dining room. In between, there are some recommendable, middle-of-the-road restaurants where you get a tasty Dominican meal with a full complement of seafood, including conch and octopus, for $6 to $15 for a main course.

The Carretera Río San Juan–Cabrera is lined with many other modest restaurants serving mainly Dominican food, as well as a few Italian spots. As most are open-air with thatched roofs, they can be noisy, even dusty, but welcoming. In town around the central park are another handful of local restaurants, including a pizza place where you can get your pie to go.

$ ✕ **Babanuco Bar & Restaurant**. You want rustic? This is genuine. Furniture
CARIBBEAN   might be a tree stump, decoration a cow horn; tablecloths are raw burlap. The floor is dirt. In the bar hang vintage license plates from French Canada, the United States, and the Netherlands. The food served up by chef-owner Juan Alberto is flavorful and authentic, with seafood a specialty of the house. Try langoustines and lambi (conch), *pulpo* (octopus), land crab, and fillet of fresh, fresh fish. And Juan goes that extra mile, past the ubiquitous creole sauce, like conch in mushroom sauce with fried green bananas and salad. It's cheaper and even more fun if you come with a group. Make a party, and with some notice he can hire musicians for you. ⊠ *Off Carretera Río San Juan–Cabrera Entrada de Saltadero, Cabrera* ☎ *809/223–7928* ▭ *No credit cards.*

$ ✕ **Restaurant at Hotel La Catalina**. If you're keen on local and fresh ingre-
INTERNATIONAL   dients, you'll love this restaurant, where all the fruits and vegetables are grown on-site, and everything else except for the meats is grown within

a mile. What's more, it's romantic, high on a hill overlooking the ocean amid tropical gardens you're sure to stroll through. Arrive early for a cocktail at the bar, accompany it with house-made pâté, and sway to international music as you gaze down the cliff to the ocean. The menu offers chicken, fish, shrimp, pork, beef, and a vegetarian choice, and each day a chef's special (lobster one day, barbecue another) is added. Starters are particularly well priced (as are desserts), with flavorful soups starting at $3.50. A meal here has an air of camaraderie and conviviality—so much so that it can sometimes feel like a house party. It's also a great place for breakfast. ⊠ *Las Farallones, off Carretera Río San Juan–Cabrera, 4 km (2.5 mi) east of Cabrera* ✥ *Turn at sign for Catalina, go another 1.5 km (0.9 mi) up hill to sign for Catalina, and then turn left. Go straight into gated community of Las Farallones, where restaurant is on right* ☎ *809/589–7700* ▭ *AE, MC, V.*

WHERE TO STAY

$$$–$$$$

RESORT

🏠 **Caliente Caribe.** This 130-acre clothing-optional resort, which has jokingly been called a "naughty place," has turned out to be very nice indeed. Upon entering the reception-lobby, which flows into the main dining room, you'll first notice the naked people, but then you see the sweep of sand with primitive rock paintings. Though there are a few (nude) activities such as kayaking, snorkeling, pool volleyball, tennis, and aqua aerobics, guests are often content simply doing (and wearing) nothing. Accommodations are in the main building, as well as four tiers of one- to two-bedroom villas. The latter are spacious, with rattan furnishings and some pleasing, hand-painted murals of palm trees. The meals, which are primarily served à la carte, are very impressive. If you want to sample this lifestyle, you can buy a day pass for $75. Airport transfers are included from either El Catey or Puerto Plata airports. **Pros:** the guests are amazingly friendly and the camaraderie contagious; caring and efficient (and clothed) staff; much repeat business. **Cons:** fairly isolated (a $30 round-trip taxi from Cabrera); Seacliff rooms (least expensive) are a hike from the main facilities; guests can be nude at dinner. ⊠ *Cabrera–Río San Juan Hwy., Km 8, Abreu* ☎ *809/589–7750* ⊕ *www.calienteresorts.com* ⇗ *48 rooms, 12 studios, 62 1-bedroom villas, 4 2-bedroom villas* ⚌ *In-room: a/c, safe, kitchen (some), Wi-Fi. In-hotel: 2 restaurants, bars, tennis courts, pools, gym, spa, beachfront, water sports, laundry facilities, laundry service, Internet terminal, Wi-Fi hotspot, parking (free), no kids under 18* ▭ *MC, V* ⦿|*AI.*

$$$$

PRIVATE VILLA

Fodor's Choice

★

🏠 **Casita Callahan.** This little seaside house makes a great find for couples looking for a quiet, private getaway for about $200 a night. The pluses here include an infinity pool and the sound of the ocean 24/7. Unfortunately, the little beach here down the steps beyond the hammock is too rocky for swimming, though you can snorkel if you're skilled. (Otherwise head to one of the amazing public beaches nearby.) At your private pool, which looks straight out to the ocean, you can lounge on a raft or rest on the attractive garden patio furniture. Fine details include a sunshade that draws down over a portion of the patio. Inside the casita, set up as a one-room studio with high ceilings, you'll find custom-made dark mahogany furniture; air-conditioning; a small kitchen with gas

The Villa Alternative

One of the hottest tropical destinations in the Caribbean, the Dominican Republic has always been known as a cheap date because of its many all-inclusive resorts, which began in Playa Dorada and really took hold in Punta Cana. The European crowd was the first to grab on to the all-you-can-eat-and-drink concept; Americans followed suit, and at first almost everyone was happy. But AI resorts are no longer the only show in town.

Villas now provide a popular alternative. You can have the services and amenities of a five-star hotel, as well as a well-trained staff dedicated solely to your needs. And you don't have to elbow your way through a throng of strangers to get a cocktail. Vacation villas are privately owned homes and may be moderately priced or luxurious. Most have three or more bedrooms (larger homes have as many as 10) and are perfect for group trips, including family reunions, corporate retreats, and destination weddings.

Villa vacations are best for savvy travelers who seek a personalized vacation experience with privacy a priority, particularly around the pool and in dining areas. However, the Dominican Republic offers many gated villa communities with resortlike amenities and restaurants that offer the privacy of a villa with the services of a resort. Some villas are right in town, so that you can interact daily with local residents and have a more genuine experience in the country.

Price is always a factor, but while all-inclusive resorts offer savings on food and drinks, the shared facilities are often crowded, with food and drink that's often mediocre. If more people crowd into a room, the cost goes up,

while comfort goes down. A midrange AI resort can still offer a tremendous value, and is almost always cheaper than a comparable room in a luxury resort.

Villas typically offer a single price for the entire villa, including its complement of staff, features, and amenities. If all of the bedrooms are occupied and the total costs shared, the per-person cost of staying in a villa (even considering the added cost of provisioning) can be about the same as the cost of a room at a luxury resort.

For example, a large beachfront villa in Cabrera's Orchid Bay Estates can accommodate 16 people and costs $2,600 per night. This is about $160 per person per night, which is the equivalent price of an upper midrange all-inclusive resort in the Dominican Republic but much less than a comparable luxury room at a resort on almost any other island. If you're willing to pay double that, you can have an ultraluxurious contemporary villa, also right on the water.

While provisioning is almost never included in the villa rental price, it often can be added for a moderate daily supplement. Many villas offer breakfast and even lunch preparation as a part of your maid's daily duties (some charge a relatively small additional fee). Personal chefs can be engaged to prepare and serve dinner in most villas. And the cost of these services as well as food is usually considerably less than the cost of restaurant meals at a luxury resort.

6

range and microwave (there are outdoor grills as well); a stone-and-seashell-tiled shower; down pillows and comfortable queen bed; and a flat-screen TV with a great collection of DVDs (no cable). When you arrive, the French property manager will show you where you can buy groceries—and where to get fresh eggs from a nearby farmer. Daily maid service is optional. To get here, ask for Cabo Fino, a well-known villa next door. **Pros:** rare find in small private rental house for two; high-quality contemporary furnishings; great pool. **Cons:** rocky beach isn't good for swimming; no activities other than the pool. ⊠ *2 mi east of El Breton, Cabrera* ⊕ *www.preferredpropertiesdr.com* ↰ *1 house* ⌂ *In-room: a/c, kitchen, refrigerator, DVD, Wi-Fi. In-hotel: pool, beachfront, laundry facilities* ▭ *AE, MC, V* ⋈| *EP.*

¢
HOTEL
Hotel La Catalina. Few things soothe like a tropical garden in the sky. So although you're far from a beach here (a 5-minute drive), you're also far from the madding crowd. Some 4 mi from the ocean, this hillside retreat does have a panoramic view of the ocean blue all the same. The adult-oriented getaway was carved from the cliffs in the 1980s by a French Canadian and has evolved over the years, with condominiums added gradually. However, it still retains an air of refinement and tranquillity. The hotel was purchased in 2007 by American cousins, and resident owner Tim Moller, after years of living in the Dominican Republic, communicates equally as well with his moneyed Dominican clients, the embassy crowds, Europeans, and American golfers as he does with the local people. Reception is more like a boutique, where handsome jewelry and crafts, which were made by the courteous, long-term employees, are sold. Airport transfers (which can cost as much as $200) are included with a week's stay, as is a beach shuttle. Massages and pedicures can be arranged on-site. The property is split between condos on one half and hotel rooms on the other. The hotel rooms are cheaper, but not nice. Stick to the condos. **Pros:** rooms are pristine and clean; convivial bar serves top-shelf liquors; grounds are appealing, with mature landscaping; airport transfers included with a week's stay. **Cons:** under 10 minutes from beaches and the golf course; decor is outdated; far (80 minutes) from Puerto Plata airport. ⊠ *Las Farrallones, off Carretera Río San Juan–Cabrera, 4 km (2.5 mi) east of Cabrera, Cabrera* ⌖ *Turn at sign for Catalina, then continue 1.5 km, (0.9 mi) up hill to sign for Catalina, and turn left; go straight into gated community of Las Farrallones* ☎ *809/589–7700* 🖷 *809/589–7550* ⊕ *www.lacatalina.com* ↰ *36 rooms, 6 1-bedroom condos, 11 2-bedroom condos* ⌂ *In-room: a/c (some), no phone, kitchen (some), no TV. In-hotel: restaurant, bar, tennis court, pools, laundry service, Internet terminal, Wi-Fi hotspot* ▭ *AE, MC, V* ⋈| *MAP.*

$$$$
PRIVATE VILLA
Fodor's Choice
★
Sunrise Villa. Dozens of coco palms and almond trees make for a truly wonderful beach; staff will set up bonfires here. The luxurious beachfront compound, designed in a Balinese style by architect Sara Garcia, is a collection of individual structures that house five suites, with the main house as a focal point. Spread over two lush acres, the exotic architecture and interior design make it a romantic getaway destination, a photographer's dream, the perfect island wedding venue, or a super home for fun-filled family reunions, with each person or couple having

an individual cabana. There are cribs and booster seats, a billiard room, and a giant chess set. The vacation atmosphere is laid-back, relaxing, and luxurious without being pretentious. There's even a house bar. The staff is well managed by Chris Quinlivan, one of the American owners. Rates are based on the number of guest rooms you plan to use. The meal plan is an additional $50 per person per day, and airport transfers can be arranged. **Pros:** one of the best locations on Orchid Beach; beautiful golden sands; villa comes with a full staff. **Cons:** most rooms are in separate buildings, so if it rains you'd better have an umbrella handy; the ocean air has aged the structures somewhat since they were built in 2002; meal plan is mandatory. ⊠ *Orchid Bay Estates 26, Orchid Beach* ⌂ *Plaza Commercial Maria, Av. Maria Gomez 10, Carbrera* ☎ *809/589–8054; 866/845–5210* ⊕ *www.sunrise-villa.com* ⇒ *8 bedrooms, 9 bathrooms* ⌂ *In-room: a/c, safe, DVD, Wi-Fi. In-hotel: pool, gym, beachfront, bicycles, laundry facilities, public internet; some pets allowed* ⊟ *AE, MC, V* ⓘⓄⓘ *EP* ☞ *4-night minimum.*

$$$–$$$$
PRIVATE VILLA

⌂ **Villa Cantamar.** This low-rise, ultracontemporary, 11,000 square-foot home in a minimalist, Asian style, has a sweeping expanse of verdant lawn that ends abruptly at a rock cliff soaring above the beach below. A free-form infinity pool and Euro-style outdoor furniture are a knockout. This luxurious oceanfront estate, which sits on 2.5 acres within a prestigious gated community, enjoys rare privacy, since it's flanked by undeveloped land. If you love innovative design by a premier architect (Sara Garcia), and sleek, minimalist decor, all in a secluded, romantic setting, this could be your dream villa. Although children are allowed, this home is remote and geared to adults. Airport pickups can be arranged. A meal plan of $55 per person per day is mandatory and additional to the rental cost. **Pros:** staff are a cut above; well priced; VIP airport reception available at Puerto Plata (POP). **Cons:** some might not like the isolation; decor not glamorous or ornate; beach is beautiful but relatively inaccessible, so guests usually drive to one of the known beaches; mandatory meal plan. ⊠ *Seatree Estates 1, Abreu* ⌂ *Plaza Commercial Maria, Av. Maria Gomez 10, Cabrera* ☎ *809/589–8083; 809/710–1078 cell; 610/429–9616 for reservations in U.S.; 866/845–5210* ⊕ *www.villacantamar.com* ⇒ *4 bedrooms, 5 bathrooms* ⌂ *In-room: a/c safe, DVD, Wi-Fi. In-hotel: pool, beachfront, laundry facilities, some pets allowed* ⊟ *AE, MC, V* ⓘⓄⓘ *EP* ☞ *4-night minimum.*

$$$$
PRIVATE VILLA
Fodor's Choice
★

⌂ **Villa Castellamonte.** This is one of the jewels in the string of lavish vacation homes collectively known as Orchid Bay Estates. Its Italianate design, ceiling paintings, and original art by Guillermo Estrada raise it to the level of palazzo. Guests can swim in the large pool, bubble in the Jacuzzi, or descend the stairway that leads to a semiprivate, golden beach. The home offers as many diversions and amenities as a beach resort (including a well-stocked wine cellar); the caring staff makes it feel like home. Kids are welcome and love the game room, karaoke, shuffleboard, and more. This is truly opulent and unforgettable, be it for a destination wedding, small conference, or a reunion. With eight bedrooms, even these rates can be affordable if you bring enough paying friends. Airport transfers are available from Puerto Plata; the mandatory meal plan is $65 per person per day. **Pros:** for all its grandeur and

6

size, it's as laid-back as a garden hammock; sumptuous master suites have gas fireplaces; an English baker provides scones, fresh-baked cookies, breads, and cakes. **Cons:** beach is rocky and requires reef shoes; two Great Danes live on-site; the staff of eight can be a bit much. ⊠ *Orchid Bay Estates 10, Orchid Bay* ⊕ *Plaza Commercial Maria, Av. Maria Gomez 10, Cabrera* ☎ *809/589–8083; 809/710–1078 cell; 610/429–9616 for U.S. reservations office; 866/845–5210* ⊕ *www. northcoastmanagement.com* ⇗ *8 bedrooms, 10 bathrooms* ⚭ *In-room: a/c, safe, DVD, Wi-Fi. In-hotel: pool, gym, beachfront, bicycles, laundry facilities* ☰ *AE, MC, V* ⧀ *EP* ⌂ *4-night minimum.*

BEACHES

Independent travelers, true beach lovers, and those in the know have discovered the incredible beaches in this relatively isolated area west of Cabarete. Some travelers may even want to rent a car and take a day trip from the Puerto Plata, Sosúa, or Cabarete resorts, while others opt to stay in this pristine area.

Lago Dudú (⊠ *Carretera Río San Juan, Km 21, Cabrera*) is a large freshwater lake fed by an underground spring, just off the main road and hidden in the bush. The lake is so deep that scuba divers go down regularly, but rumor has it that no one has ever located the bottom. You'll be greeted by great rope swings and really cold water throughout the year. There's also a cave you can swim into.

Orchid Bay Beach (⊠ *Carretera Río San Juan, Km 17, Cabrera*) is the large public beach within Orchid Bay Estates. It's seldom used by anyone but the residents of Orchid Bay villas, but there is a public road just to the left of the ORCHID BAY sign. Very picturesque, it's swimmable in a couple of choice locations.

Playa Caletón (⊠ *Carretera Río San Juan–Cabrera, Km 1, Río San Juan*) has virtually no waves and is superb for snorkeling, with caves nearby. It's a favorite for just playing around in the water. There are local food stands and souvenir shops on the beach as well.

★ **Playa Diamante** (⊠ *Carretera Río San Juan–Cabrera, Km 19, Cabrera*) is
☾ a very pretty beach that was formed from an estuary where an underground river sends freshwater into the ocean. The result is a broad beach that is very shallow for up to 200 feet into the ocean. This is an excellent beach if you have small children: it has easy drive-up access, no waves, and it's very shallow. There's also a mysterious trail of air bubbles in the mucky sand that kids will love. There's a small restaurant here, and you can rent kayaks.

Playa El Bretón (⊠ *Carretera Río San Juan–Cabrera, Km 14, Río San Juan*) is close to Cabrera within Parque Nacional Cabo Francis. It's the perfect beach for swimming, playing, searching for seashells, and snorkeling. It has no facilities and is quiet and uncluttered.

Playa Entrada (⊠ *Carretera Río San Juan–Cabrera, Km 21, La Entrada*) is one of the longest beaches on the North Coast, and has been too remote for many years. However, that means the beach is exceptionally pristine and unspoiled, and the site of several movie location shoots, which have taken advantage of its remoteness. Though technically in La Entrada, it's part of the municipality of Cabrera. You'll find a few beach shacks that sell cold drinks and Dominican snacks.

Fodor's Choice ★ **Playa Grande** (⊠ *Carretera Río San Juan–Cabrera, Km 12, Río San Juan*) is next to the famous golf course of the same name. This beach has been named one of the top beaches in the world. It's a gorgeous stretch of sand with food stands and souvenir shops. More development is on the table at this writing.

Playa Preciosa (⊠ *Carretera Río San Juan–Cabrera, Km 12, Río San Juan*) is next to Playa Grande. It's a favorite of the locals because it's so beautiful. You have to descend a sandy bank to reach the completely open beach, which has excellent conditions for surfing (be careful). There are no facilities, though the views are stunning.

SPORTS AND THE OUTDOORS

Those staying in and around Cabrera will have many opportunities to get out and enjoy the sporting life, whether it's on horseback or under the sea. Gri Gri Lagoon in Río San Juan is a great diving and snorkeling destination. Most guests in the region make all arrangements through their villa management company. **North Coast Management** (☎ *888/589–8455 or 809/589–7065* ⊕ *northcoastmanagement.com*), the primary agent in these parts, has a reputation for knowing all the best local operators. Iguana Mama will allow guests staying in the Cabrera area to join their organized tours and activities, but they will not come out just for small groups. Other dive and activity outfitters in Sosúa and Cabarete offer trips to the Cabrera area.

DIVING AND SNORKELING

Gri Gri Lagoon in Río San Juan is the region's best dive and snorkeling destination. There are some exciting caves to explore, and most of the top dive operators out of Sosúa offer trips here, which you can join. Brianda Tours *(see ⇨ Tours in Planning, above)* also offers trips here. After snorkeling and/or diving near or into some sea caves and then visiting a beach and snorkeling in a quiet cove, your boat will return for a brief and quiet ride through the mangrove swamp, which teems with tropical seabirds. There are some 20 dive sites in the area with amazing coral, caves, and underwater mountains, as well as a wide variety of colorful sea life. Expect to pay $85 for two dives, $50 if you're just snorkeling. While snorkelers can also negotiate with the local boatmen to take them out into the lagoon, if you opt to do this, try to find one that comes recommended.

GOLF

Playa Grande Golf Course (⊠ *Carretera Río San Juan–Cabrera, Km 9* ☎ *809/582–0860* ⊕ *www.playagrande.com*), between Río San Juan and Cabrera on the North Coast, is sometimes described as the Pebble Beach of the Caribbean, with 10 holes along 60-ft cliffs overlooking the Atlantic Ocean. It carries the signature of Robert Trent Jones Sr. At this writing a much-delayed plan to privatize the area into a golf-themed residential complex still hadn't come to pass. Greens fees to play the

18-hole, par-72 course are $110 ($65 for 9 holes); all fees include the cost of a mandatory cart. Caddies, also mandatory, are an additional $30 for 18 holes, $22 for 9. Dress code dictates no tank tops, bikinis, or cutoffs. There's an open-air restaurant here offering a few dishes, including fish and burgers.

HORSEBACK RIDING

This is ranch country, and taking a horse through the countryside just seems like the right thing to do. Local *ranchos* have horses on-site, but to arrange a ride you'll need to go through your villa management company or contact Iguana Mama *(see ⇨ Biking and Hiking in Sports and the Outdoors, in Cabarete, above)*. Transportation will be included. You'll trek through the countryside and rain forest on a two- to three-hour horse ride (depending on your stamina), either in the morning or late afternoon, with an English-speaking guide. Refreshments are included; an adult must accompany children under 12. Expect to pay about $35 for an adult, $25 for a child.

NIGHTLIFE

Most of Cabrera's bars are local places, not really aimed at *turistas*. But since dancing rather than baseball is the true Dominican passion, you'll be able to shake your booty all night if you're willing to search out the latest local hot spots. The restaurant at Hotel La Catalina has a vocalist on Friday night, and you can have dinner and just drinks in the lounge. Babanuco also has a fun bar scene *(see ⇨ Where to Eat, above)*. Every town in the Dominican Republic has a patron saint, and in Cabrera the annual **Patronales Festival** in late September lasts for nine days. The whole town comes out for loud music and live bands on a makeshift stage. The entertainment can be top-notch, and there are also carnival rides and a festive atmosphere that will appeal to kids.

Santiago and the Cibao Valley

SANTIAGO, LA VEGA VIEJA,
JARABACOA, CONSTANZA

WORD OF MOUTH

"We took a day trip to Santiago. There we visited a cigar factory and a ranch located in the mountains. We had lunch, went horseback riding, and then sped down a river on an inner tube."

—Michel

"We drove 2.5 hours each way to a very interesting 'mountain' lodge for a night. It was a drive through simple rural areas, which were also fascinating. We saw cocoa beans, coffee beans, avocados, oranges, palm trees, sugarcane, honey, and all sorts of little farms. Really charming, though very poor and simple. The people were so welcoming and eager to explain their work to us."

— PeaceOut

By Eileen Robinson Smith

Santiago, which is in the province of the same name, is in the agricultural heart of this developing Caribbean country. The Dominican Republic's second city has a population of some 750,000; it's the intellectual, educational, and cultural center of the region. It's also the economic center of the fertile Cibao Valley, where most of the country's sugar, tobacco, and coffee are grown.

The city itself has many centuries-old buildings, including architectural vestiges of its Victorian heyday. There's also a dominating cathedral, an authentic fort (now a museum), fascinating side streets, and a festive covered market dating from the 1940s. Visitors often take scenic horse-drawn carriage tours to soak up the atmosphere.

This charming provincial city can be home base for exploring the Dominican Republic's mountainous Cordillera Central, including the towns of Jarabacoa, Constanza, and the national park area of Valle Nuevo. Nearest to Santiago is La Vega, the somewhat quaint center of lower Cibao Valley. (La Vega Vieja was one of the oldest settlements in the New World.) If you head up to the mountains, plan on staying a couple of days in one of the atmospheric rustic lodges, and pack warm clothing for temperatures that can feel more like fall in New England. These mountains offer a respite from the island's hot temperatures and are a complete change of pace. The air is crisp and pine-scented, and around every turn in the mountain roads is a panoramic view. It can be a glorious and unexpected experience in a Caribbean island best known for its beach resorts.

ORIENTATION AND PLANNING

GETTING ORIENTED

This diverse area is a special part of the Dominican world, and if you have sufficient time, it's worth the effort to go here. You can fly directly into Santiago's airport or drive up from Puerto Plata or Santo Domingo. Santiago is worth at least a day of exploring, but if you spend the night, you can then head for the hills in the morning. Beyond, in the Cordillera Mountains, are Jarabacoa, Constanza, and Valle Nuevo. From Constanza to Valle Nuevo and the cottage complex of Villa Pajon, you follow the carretera to San Jose de Ocoa, then take the turnoff to Valle Nuevo; the total distance is about 24 km (15 mi).

Santiago. The Dominican Republic's second city is roughly 90 minutes south of Cabarete on the scenic Autopista Duarte.

La Vega. Less than a half hour by car from Santiago, La Vega is usually a sleepy farm town. It bursts to life during Carnaval.

TOP REASONS TO GO

Centro de Leon. Santiago's impressive art museum is worth several hours of your time, and your visit can include lunch and a tour of the replicated cigar factory, circa 1900.

Head to the water. An excursion to the Dominican Republic's mountainous Cordillera Central can include white-water rafting and visits to waterfalls.

Exploring Santiago. The relatively slow-paced city has an impressive district of buildings, a few from the

Colonial era and a number from Victorian times. Spanish ancestry is more apparent here than anywhere else in the country

Carnaval in Santiago or La Vega. Carnival in Santiago or La Vega is one of the quintessential Dominican experiences. It's wild, but if you have the right spirit, it can be a fun, memorable party.

Jarabacoa. This mountainous region is known for its outdoor activities. The town is 36 km (22 mi) southwest of Santiago.

Constanza. Farmland and cool mountain breezes make the area surrounding this small town memorable. It's 36 km (22 mi) south of Jarabacoa.

7

PLANNING

GETTING HERE AND AROUND

Many of the towns are reachable by *guaguas*, the local public buses and minivans, but the trip will be much more pleasant if you have your own transportation (preferably four-wheel drive, which is an absolute requirement if you plan to visit Villa Pajon), so you can meander around and up the mountain roads to spectacular waterfalls. Even though the distances do not sound far, you have to allow twice as much time as you would normally because of the steep, winding mountain roads. Once you arrive, you will be glad you made the effort and understand why Santo Domingoans, particularly, consider this a slice of heaven.

AIR TRAVEL

Cibao International Airport in Santiago is the gateway to the entire Cibao Valley. With service from JetBlue and others, it's definitely the best airport if you're visiting only this area. It's also possible to fly into the Gregorio Luperón International Airport in Puerto Plata, but that will add almost two hours onto your drive after arrival.

Airports Cibao International Airport (*STI* ✉ *Santiago* ☎ *809/582–4894*). **Gregorio Luperón International Airport** (*POP* ✉ *Puerto Plata* ☎ *809/586–0107 or 809/586–0219*).

BUS TRAVEL

Metro Bus and Caribe Tours have frequent service from both Puerto Plata and Santo Domingo to Santiago. Metro is a comfortable, upscale bus line. Its service from Santo Domingo is hourly, between 6 AM and 7:45 PM, and the trip takes about 2 hours and costs about $8. Between

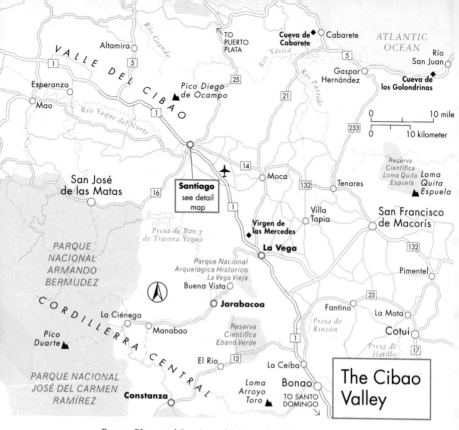

Puerto Plata and Santiago the trip takes about 1¼ hours and costs about $3. Schedules change, but for now buses leave Puerto Plata about every 2 hours, at 9, 11, 1, 4, and 6. Caribe Tours takes longer than Metro to get to Santo Domingo, 2½ hours with many local stops, but it also costs slightly less, about $6; there are about 25 runs daily between 6 AM and 8:15 PM. Caribe Tours also stops in La Vega, a trip that takes another 45 minutes. From there you can transfer for a bus to Jarabacoa for about $6. There are two bus stations in Santiago, so make sure your bus is leaving from Las Colinas Terminal. Caribe Tours service from Puerto Plata is good, too, hourly between 6 AM and 9:30 PM. The cost is about $3, and it takes 1¼ hours; that same bus continues on to Sosúa, which takes another 45 minutes and costs about $1 more. If you need to get to Cabarete, you will need to take a taxi or hop a motoconcho (motorcycle taxi).

Linea Gladys runs between Santo Domingo and Constanza.

Bus Companies Caribe Tours (☎ 809/576–0790 in Santiago; 809/221–4422 in Santo Domingo; 809/574–3796 in Jarabacoa). **Linea Gladys** (☎ 809/565–1223 in Santo Domingo). **Metro Buses** (☎ 809/582–9111 in Santiago; 809/566–7126 in Santo Domingo; 809/586–6062 in Puerto Plata).

CAR TRAVEL

It's certainly easier to get around the area if you have your own transportation. Just remember that some places are only reachable with a four-wheel-drive vehicle, which can be very expensive in these parts. You could take the bus out of Santo Domingo and make a reservation with Francis Rent a Car, in Jarabacoa. Have them pick you up at the bus station. This way you can avoid driving in the capital, with its unnerving traffic and reckless drivers.

Car Rentals Avis (⊠ *Cibao International Airport, Santiago* ☎ *809/223–8153).*
Francis Rent A Car (⊠ *Carretera a Salto Jimenoa Dos, Km 2, Jarabacoa*
☎ *809/574–2981).* **Hertz** (⊠ *Cibao International Airport, Santiago* ☎ *809/612–*
3380). **Honda** (⊠ *Cibao International Airport, Santiago* ☎ *809/233–8179).*

TRAVEL BY TAXI

Taxi-Queen is the company that works through the Santiago hotels; drivers have passed security checks and wear their ID tags around their necks. Their cars are not wonderful, and drivers are unlikely to speak English, but their prices are very reasonable. Taxi-Tourismo, the company that services the Cibao Airport in Santiago, has safer, bigger vehicles (mostly SUVs and minivans) but higher rates.

Contacts Taxi-Queen (☎ *809/570–0000; 809/233–3333 in Santiago).* **Taxi-**
Tourismo (☎ *809/829–3007 in Santiago).*

INTERNET

Camber Net, in Santiago, is quite a good place; its computers are newer than most, its prices better (RD$50 per hour), and some of the employees speak English. It stays open until 10 PM. Centro de Copiado y Papelería, in Jarabacoa, offers both Internet computers and some business services like photocopying and office supplies. It's also inexpensive, at RD$45 an hour. Ciber Bibilotec Emy is in Constanza, and is about RD$50 an hour.

Contacts Camber Net (⊠ *Calle Espana 41, near Av. Restauración, Santiago*
☎ *809/734–2232).* **Centro de Copiado y Papelería** (⊠ *Calle Duarte, near*
Indepedencia, Jarabacoa ☎ *809/574–2902).* **Ciber Bibilotec Emy** (⊠ *Opposite*
children's baseball field, Constanza ☎ *No phone).*

TOURS

In Santiago, freelance guides hang out at the Heroes Monument and can give tours in English for about $25 for an hour. Make certain that they are wearing government-issued IDs. Vacation Tours, a travel agency with an office in the Hotel Gran Almirante in Santiago, can also arrange city tours.

Contacts Vacation Tours (⊠ *Hotel Gran Almirante & Casino, Los Jardines, San-*
tiago ☎ *809/825–1996 Ext. 252* ⊕ *www.vacationtours.com.do).*

VISITOR INFORMATION

Contacts Oficina de Turismo Constanza (⊠ *Calle Matilde Viná near San*
Miguel Andrés Abreu, 2nd fl., Constanza ☎ *809/539–2900).* **Oficina de Turismo**
Jarabacoa (⊠ *Plaza Ramirez, across from west side of central park, 2nd fl.,*
Jarabacoa ☎ *809/574–7287).***Oficina de Turismo Santiago** (⊠ *Parque Duarte,*
Calle de Sol, 2nd fl., Edificio de Santiago, Santiago ☎ *809/582–5885).*

RESTAURANTS

Santiago lacks Santo Domingo's vibrant restaurant scene. With the exception of Puerto del Sol, even the city's few fine-dining establishments stick to the classics. The restaurants in Hotel Gran Almirante are generally good, with one serving a good selection of tapas and another serving a fusion menu. A TGI Fridays, which opened next door to the city's best hotel, is emblematic of the local love of American chain restaurants. Many restaurants and cafés line the Calle del Sol, starting at the central Parque Duarte; most have outdoor seating that is great for people-watching. Similarly, down the Avenida de Monumento from the landmark Heroes Monument, there are restaurants that are lively and fun, serving mainly Dominican or simple fare. In the mountains you'll find Dominican specialties served at the simple *comedors* (local restaurants), as well as some atmospheric restaurants where rabbit and other game are specialties and fresh vegetables taste as if they came straight from the earth. Constanza is strawberry country, so fresh strawberries are usually on the menu in some form.

HOTELS

In Santiago you can find a sophisticated city hotel and, near the airport, the laudable American chain-style Hodelpa Garden Court. Camp David Ranch, a restaurant and hotel in an upscale suburb is better than most of the properties in town, where the pickings are slim. In the nearby mountain towns of Jarabacoha, Constanza, and Valle Nuevo you can have a relaxing getaway in rustic lodges, with fireplaces to take off the chill.

WHAT IT COSTS IN U.S. DOLLARS					
	¢	$	$$	$$$	$$$$
RESTAURANTS	under $8	$8–$12	$12–$20	$20–$30	over $30
HOTELS*	under $80	$80–$150	$150–$250	$250–$350	over $350
HOTELS**	under $125	$125–$250	$250–$350	$350–$450	over $450

*EP, BP, CP **AI, FAP, MAP

Restaurant prices are per person for a main course at dinner and do not include the 16% tax and 10% service charge. Hotel prices are per night for a double room in high season, excluding 16% tax and 10% service charge.

SANTIAGO

145 km (90 mi) northwest of Santo Domingo, 55 km (34 mi) south of Puerto Plata, 60 km (37 mi) south of Cabarete.

The second city of the Dominican Republic, where many past presidents were born, is reached by the Autopista Duarte, the four-lane highway from Puerto Plata that follows a centuries-old trade route that is still dotted with sugar mills, some of which are being renovated by the Office of Cultural Patrimony and the Brugal Rum company. This industrial center still feels charming, provincial, and a little genteel—it has a slower pace and less crime than the capital. The families of sugar barons, who have been making their fortunes from rum for centuries, cigar kings, and bankers dominate the city; there is a hierarchy of moneyed families in this city, and they make their presence and influence felt. The women of Santiago are said to be among the fairest and best looking in the country, and the men are true *caballeros* (gentlemen), often donning Panama hats. Santiago's full name—Santiago de los Caballeros—comes from the fact that it was founded by a group of 30 Spanish noblemen.

Generations of Italian and Cuban immigrants, including the famous cigar-making Fuentes, have become successful in everything from the restaurant business to cigar manufacturing, adding flavor to the ethnic mix. Like Santo Domingo, Santiago is a city of real Dominicans—entire generations—not just the transplants who live in hotel housing in resort areas like Punta Cana, which never had an identity before it was developed.

Santiago is still relatively new to the tourist scene, but already has several thriving restaurants and hotels. It's definitely worth setting aside some time to explore the city. Some colonial-style buildings—with wrought-iron details and tiled porticos—date from as far back as the 1500s. Others are from the Victorian era, with the requisite gingerbread and fanciful colors, while more recent construction is often designed in a Victorian style. Old Town Santiago covers roughly the area from the central park, Parque Duarte, to the fort, and then to the monument.

Santiago is the center of the island's cigar industry, and the Arturo Fuente factory is in the free zone here. Cafés and restaurants abound on the Calle del Sol, and on weekends the outdoor cafés allow you to watch the world of Santiago go by. This is a great, feel-good city that is often overlooked. Inland, there are no pearl-white beaches, but in the nearby foothills and mountains of the Cordillera chain there are icy rivers and little natural *balnearios* (swimming pools).

GETTING HERE AND AROUND

A relaxing and popular way to see the sights of Santiago is on a horse-and-buggy ride. This is definitely slow travel, but it's very atmospheric to be closer to street level and not locked up in a bus or taxi. You get a real sense of what life must have been life in a more genteel era. Horse-and-buggy drivers congregate around both Duarte Park and the Heroes Monument. Expect to pay about $20 for a 30-minute ride (bargain for $15 if your Spanish can manage it) and settle on the price before you start trotting.

EXPLORING

Numbers in the margin correspond to points of interest on the Santiago map.

7 **Bermudez Rum Distillery.** This is a rum-making island, and some tourists look forward to the free booze that comes with a tour of one of the factories. As one of the Dominican Republic's three Bs—Brugal and Barcelo being the other two major rum producers—Bermudez used to be numero uno, but it now, reputedly, holds the third spot based on

Bathroom Break

All the *capitaleños* (Santa Domingoans) stop at **Parador Jaracanda** (✉ *Autopista Duarte, between Santo Domingo and Santiago, at northern edge of Bonao* ☎ *809/525–5590*) on their journey between Santo Domingo and Santiago because it has some of the cleanest and most well-maintained restrooms on the highway. It's accessible whether you're traveling north (on the left) or south (on the right). You can also get food.

Dominicans prefer their own heavy specialties from the buffet, but lighter eaters may prefer yogurt, cheese, fresh-baked goods, tea, or coffee to go. You can also get sandwiches. There's an attached hotel if you need to stop for the night, and it's a fine place for that, with the 22 rooms costing less than $40 a double. It's a possible accommodation for a Carnaval overnight if you can't get a room in Santiago.

sales. On your tour you'll learn that there are three types of rum; first is white rum (the least expensive variety), then gold or amber, and finally *anejo* (aged rum, which is often sipped like brandy and coupled with a choice Dominican cigar). It's easiest to tour this processing and bottling plant as part of a city tour, because a visit is by appointment only. The tour itself is not very exciting unless someone on the line misses a beat and the bottles go crashing into each other and everyone claps. ✉ *Pueblo Nuevo* ☎ *809/947–4201* ⚑ *Free* ☉ *Weekdays 9–noon and 2–5; independent travelers by appointment only*

❷ Catedral de Santiago Apóstol. Santiago's cathedral dominates the south side of Parque Duarte. The lovely pink stucco adds to the calming effect that the park has on this part of the old city. Its construction took from 1868 to 1895, and it replaced an earlier cathedral destroyed by an earthquake in 1842. The end result is a mix of Gothic and neoclassical architecture. The most noteworthy features are the stained-glass windows, which are actually modern-day designs by Dominican artist Dincón Mora. In the cathedral lie the remains (in a marble tomb) of a Santiago native son, dictator Ulises Heureaux (1845–1899). ✉ *Parque Duarte, Calles 16 de Agosto to Benito Monción* ☎ *No phone* ⚑ *Free* ☉ *Mon.–Sat. 7 AM–9 AM, Sun. 7 AM–8 PM.*

❾ Centro León. Without question, this is a world-class cultural center for the Dominican arts. A postmodern building with an interior space full of light from a crystal dome, the center includes several attractions, including a multimedia biodiversity show, a museum dedicated to the history of the Dominican Republic, a simulated local market, a dramatic showcase of Dominican art and sculpture, galleries for special exhibits, a sculpture garden, an aviary, classrooms, and a replica of the León family's first cigar factory, where a dozen cigar rollers turn out handmade cigars. There's even a first-rate cafeteria and a museum shop where you can buy high-quality, artsy souvenirs and jewelry. Check the Web site for activities and night events. It can be a fine way to meet Santiagoans who have a high level of fluency in English. ✉ *Av. 27 de Febrero 146, Villa Progresso* ☎ *809/582–2315* ⊕ *www.centroleon.org.do* ⚑ *RD$50,*

Fodor's Choice
★

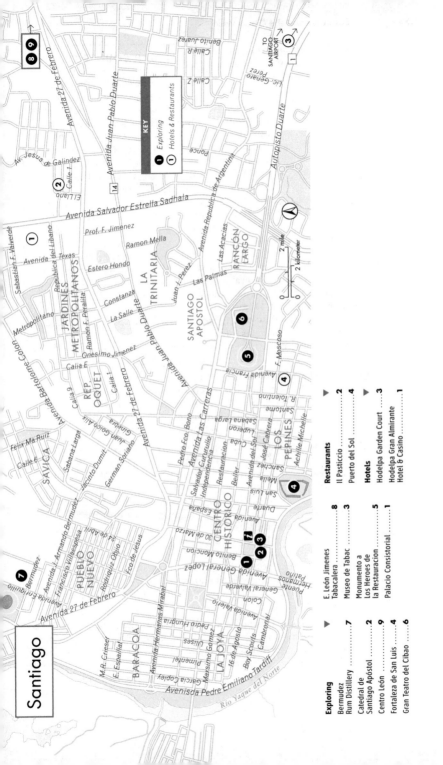

Santiago

KEY
1 Exploring
1 Hotels & Restaurants

▶ **Exploring**

Bermudez Rum Distillery	7
Catedral de Santiago Apóstol	2
Centro León	9
Fortaleza de San Luis	4
Gran Teatro del Cibao	6

▶

E. León Jimenes Tabacalera	8
Museo de Tabac	3
Monumento a Los Heroes de la Restauracion	5
Palacio Consistorial	1

▶ **Restaurants**

Il Pasticcio	2
Puerto del Sol	4

▶ **Hotels**

Hodelpa Garden Court	3
Hodelpa Gran Almirante	3
Hotel & Casino	1

TO SANTIAGO AIRPORT

RD$150 guides in English ☺ Exhibitions Tues.–Sun. 9–6, public areas daily 9–9.

④ **Fortaleza de San Luis.** The fort was a military stronghold from the late 17th century right up through the 1970s, when it became a prison. Its most recent reincarnation is as a museum showcasing Air Force weaponry from World Wars I and II, as well as weapons and artifacts from colonial days, including a collection of Spanish coins. The artwork is not stellar, but there are some Taino artifacts and primitive art and some Trujillo-era art from the 1950s. The generalissimo was rumored to have an insatiable sexual appetite, and was nicknamed el Chivo ("the Goat") for that reason: there are some fascinating caricatures of him in that guise. The city's 19th-century clock tower is also here. ⊠ *Calle San Luis at Calle Boy Scouts* ☎ *809/724–7276* 🖃 *Free* ☺ *Daily 9–5.*

> **CIGAR COUNTRY**
>
> The Dominican Republic ranks first in the world in terms of tobacco cultivation. And the whole process of tobacco growing and cigar manufacture affects the final quality of the cigars, from the selection of the ground to the artisans who roll them. The tobacco must be harvested, dried, and well fermented. Dominican cigars have conquered the most demanding and knowledgeable smokers. Santiago is the home of the internationally famous Arturo Fuente Cigars. Leon Jimenes and its brand, La Aurora, Davidoff, and General cigars are other names known to cigarro aficionados.

⑥ **Gran Teatro del Cibao.** Santiago's main performing arts theater was built in the 1980s. Not much happens in the mammoth landmark these days, and it's not so beautiful. Tours are not allowed, though you can always attend the occasional theater or opera production. ⊠ *Av. Monumento, across from Parque Monumento and Monumento a Los Heroes.*

⑧ **E. León Jimenes Tabacalera.** You can gain an appreciation for the art and skill of Dominican cigar making by taking a tour of this company's cigar factories, which are among the best offered. Also known as La Aurora Cigar Factory, it's a hard-working Dominican institution (since 1903) that exports some of the world's best cigars to the United States, Puerto Rico, Canada, Mexico, and Europe. A premier Santiago family, who run a classy tour, owns it. You will marvel as you watch the cigar rollers roll those leaves, glue, cut, tap, and then move on to the next one. It's fascinating if you've never seen it done. Almost everyone ends up buying some beautifully packaged cigars in the factory store. The tour takes approximately 90 minutes. ⊠ *Av. 27 de Febrero 146, Villa Progreso* ☎ *809/563–1111 or 809/535–5555* 🖃 *Free* ☺ *Tues.–Fri. 9–noon and 2–5:30.*

③ **Museo de Tabac.** This museum, which is in an old tobacco warehouse, is a tribute to this cigar-producing region and a good historical introduction to an important Dominican business. Visitors will learn everything that they didn't know about tobacco, from when it's a leaf in the ground to when it's hand-rolled into excellent cigars. If you're in town and interested in the subject, it's worth the time. ⊠ *Parque Duarte,*

A Cigar Family's Charitable Trust

What you see when you drive the dirt road to Chateau de la Fuente, the tobacco plantation of Arturo Fuente Cigars, looks like a dream vision. Rising from an uncultivated field is a pristine yellow-and-white complex that includes a primary school, a high school, medical clinic, laboratory, pharmacy, multiuse community center, baseball stadium, and basketball and volleyball courts. The Arturo Sandoval School of Music is now open and a source of joy for the students. The Cigar Family Charitable Foundation built this rural miracle, and the United Nations has recognized it as a prototype for schools in the Caribbean.

In 1992, when Carlos Fuente Jr. (Carlito) and his father, Carlos Fuente, bought these cow pastures, they were nothing but mud; the road was nearly impassable. Ragged children would run alongside the car and beg, an activity that continued until 2004, when the Fuente family charity and the Newman family, their distribution partners in the United States, built this complex.

Additional donations have been received, including a bus from Metro Bus Company; a communal kitchen from a major restaurant group; and a baseball stadium, sponsored by Marvin Shanken, publisher of *Cigar Aficionado*. In a country where litter is omnipresent and schools are dirty and

scrawled with graffiti, this one still looks brand-new, with landscaping as attractive as that of a gated, residential community. The school houses 448 students, and has added a 12th grade; the first high-school graduation was in 2009.

The Foundation's generosity extends to the community, with an astounding litany of outreach projects already completed: construction of clean-water stations; extension of electricity to homes, new bridges over rivers; the road paved; new sanitation programs; repairs to existing community health facilities and schools; nutrition, prenatal, and preventative medicine programs.

Unlike many other organizations, 100% of every dollar contributed goes directly to the charitable projects. The Fuentes and Newman families underwrite all administrative, legal, accounting, office, and marketing costs.

Carlito Fuente is a deeply caring, sensitive, and sincere person who transmits his energy and passion to those he encounters. "There is no greater love than that of family," Carlito says ardently. Now he has an extended family with two branches—his cigar family of friends and associates, who have helped make all this possible, and the children and families within some 11 communities who consider him their beloved patriarch.

7

Calle 30 de Marzo at Calle Aug. 16 ☎ *No phone* ✉ *Free* ☺ *Tues.–Fri. 9–noon and 2–5:30.*

5 **Monumento a Los Heroes de la Restauracion** *(Monument to the Heroes)* is
Fodor's Choice ★ a huge attraction here. Vela Zanetti painted the murals that decorate its walls, and they show the distinct influences of Diego Rivera. The topmost observation level gives an impressive view of the sprawling city. After a recent renovation, there are also dioramas, a Carnaval costume display, and statues of the heroes done in a bronze-look-alike

composition. Although it was built in the 1940s as a monument to the dictator Trujillo, the government that followed changed the name and focused on Trujillo's assassination, rededicating it to those heroes who died between 1863 and 1865 in the war to free the country from Spain. In the lovely park that surrounds the monument, similar sculptures sit whimsically on park benches. ⊠ *Av. Monumento* ☎ *No phone* 🎫 *Free* ⊙ *Tues.–Sun. 9–6.*

❶ **Palacio Consistorial.** This is another tribute to Trujillo's love of opulence, and in this case the city is grateful to have such a grand example of European neoclassical architecture. The former town hall has become an integral thread in the fabric of life here. Old men sit outside and play dominoes, directing *turistas* into the building, which is the local headquarters of the Ministry of Culture and a center for cultural programs. It hosts some fascinating contemporary art exhibits as well as a little museum that tells the story of the city. Annually during Carnival, winning masks are hung for all to see. El Palacio is one of the landmarks that sit smack on the tree-shaded central park and next to a revered, private social club, Sociedad Centro de Recreo, an old haunt of Trujillo's (established in 1894, it's still owned by the Bermudez Rum family). ⊠ *Parque Duarte, Calle de Sol and Benito Monción* ☎ *No phone* 🎫 *Free* ⊙ *Tues.–Fri. 9–noon and 2:30–6.*

OFF THE BEATEN PATH

Natura Bella. Take a coffee break! Dominicans always do, and this one is free. This coffee factory is on the Autopista Duarte between Puerto Plata and Santiago, just south of the town of Navarette on your right if you're headed toward Santiago (on the left if you're headed toward Puerto Plata). Take a break and have a sample of any of their organic (USDA-certified) coffees or an espresso. If you truly want to gain some coffee knowledge, call ahead—the Italian owner speaks English—and request a coffee tasting. The South American quality-control expert will teach you a thing or two, including how certain blends have a citrusy taste. Of course, they would like it if you would purchase a pound or two (though there is no pressure). And why not? It's a good product, and the artsy packaging makes it an even better gift. When you call to make your tasting reservation, you can ask for more detailed directions. ⊠ *Villa Gonzalez, Autopista Santiago-Navarrete, Las Lavas* ☎ *809/880–4144* 🎫 *Free* ⊙ *Mon.–Sat. 9–5.*

WHERE TO EAT

$–$$
INTERNATIONAL

✕ **Camp David Ranch.** This well-established landmark restaurant and hotel is in an upscale neighborhood in the hills about 20 minutes outside Santiago. Jose M. Bermudez, a businessman, collector, and newspaper writer, opened the restaurant in 1989. Though it was never a ranch, nor a camp, his son's name is David. You may be surprised by the urban chic decor, with ultrasuede couches and Wi-Fi. Lunches here are especially delicious, and this is the best time to see the magnificent views. Sit on the terrace, enjoy the sophisticated music, and experience the seamless service. Recommended on the menu are the cream of pumpkin soup to counteract the cool breezes, followed by a shellfish paella, a lobster with coconut curry sauce, or grilled rack of lamb with a choice of sauces.

Dominican specialties are present as well, including sides like a puree of yucca. The menu, which is reviewed every six months, is the same at dinner, when the nocturnal view includes so many twinkling lights below. Be sure to see the vintage car collection, which once belonged to Trujillo. ⊠ *Carretera Luperón, Km 7.5, and follow signs, Gurabo* ☎ *809/276–6400* ⊕ *www.campdavidranch.com* ⊟ *AE, D, MC, V.*

$ ✗ **Il Pasticcio.** Everyone from college students to cigar kings, presidents
ITALIAN   and politicos, movie producers and stars, packs this eccentrically deco-
★   rated culinary landmark, which opened in 1995. Tourists take photos of the bathrooms, with their ornate mirrors and Romanesque plaster sinks. Chef-owner Paolo, a true *paisano*, makes this bungalow a personality palace. A living art gallery, it is where the artists, poets, and intelligentsia hang. His mouthwatering creations are authentic and fresh. Ask about the *menu degustacion* (tasting menu, $17). Or try the great antipasto selections; commence with the pasticcio salad, which might have smoked salmon, mozzarella, anchovies, capers, and baby arugula. Even the bread service comes with three sauces, one is like pesto, there's a pomodoro, and the best is a creamy anchovy sauce. They can all be had on pasta, too. And if it's too dim to read the menu, just look up—the menu's also written on the ceiling. Who said Paolo is off the wall? Finish with a shot of limoncello and cheesecake or handmade gelato with strawberries marinated in wine. The value here is remarkable. ⊠ *Calle 3, No. 5, at Av. Del Llano, Cerros de Gurabo* ☎ *809/582–6061* ⊟ *AE, MC, V* ☉ *Closed Mon. and between 3:30 and 7:00 pm.*

$–$$ ✗ **Puerto del Sol.** This landmark restaurant closed for too long, and
INTERNATIONAL   when it reopened under new ownership it gained an edgy, contemporary attitude. The other restaurants in this touristy area are lively and fun, serving mainly Dominican or simple, classic dishes, but Puerto del Sol is something more. It has three sections: a major liquor store in the front; an expanded, open-air terrace serving light fare nearby; and a glass-walled, air-conditioned salon in back that serves an international fusion menu. The terrace is a Wi-Fi hotspot, and is heavily patronized by student types and guys who come to watch the game on the widescreen TVs or listen to live music. Others watch the world that is Santiago go by. The patio is known to have icy cerveza (beer) that pairs well with the pizza served there. The young and talented Dominican-Italian chef, Marco Modolo, cooks great Italian dishes. His English is fluent—something he picked up at a ski resort in Utah, where he was taught the latest culinary trends. He couples that knowledge with top-quality products that can be paired with a savvy selection of wines. (Remember the liquor store?) His style is clean and healthy, and he can prepare a fresh lobster with a delicate citrus sauce, and a creative mélange of vegetables, all beautifully presented. The accomplished servers keep the Chilean sauvignon blanc on ice, a reserve to be sure. Puerto is open late, until midnight Sunday through Thursday and until 2 AM on Friday and Saturday. ⊠ *Calle del Sol 23, corner of Daniel Espinal, Area Monumental* ☎ *809/947–1414* ⊟ *AE, MC, V*

$ ✗ **Tipico Bonao.** Two identically named restaurants stand on opposite
CARIBBEAN   sides of the highway outside Santiago so they can catch drivers coming from either direction. Savvy Dominican city dwellers recommend the

7

sisters, saying that they are the offspring of a caring family and that service is professional. The best news for travelers: the restrooms are clean and well supplied. You can get a good breakfast here: Dominican (fried salami, cheese, eggs, etc.), American (pancakes), or French (croissants and cappuccino). The five-page menu includes nearly every typical Dominican dish, with highlights being roast pork and *asopao* (stew) with crab claw meat. ⊠ *Autopista Duarte, Km 90, Monseñor Nouel* ☎ *809/296–6000* ⊠ *Autopista Duarte, Km 83* ☎ *809/525–3941* 🖃 *MC, V.*

WHERE TO STAY

¢   ▦ **Camp David Ranch.** In a suburban area 20 minutes outside Santiago,
INN this hotel and restaurant complex offers gorgeous views of the Cibao Valley. Though well known as a restaurant, not everyone tells you that it has three floors of hotel rooms, too; a number of which have just been tastefully updated to include flat-screen TVs. (Request one of those.) Daughter Nicole Bermudez and several of the staffers speak English fluently. Hotel guests can have their breakfast at the adjoining restaurant or delivered to their room. The tastefully decorated, oversize rooms have balconies, most with incomparable views of the city and the valley. It's best to have a rental car here (the hotel is well signposted), but if you don't feel like driving, the sum you will save on accommodations will make the taxi fares worthwhile. **Pros:** clean air and manicured grounds; no noise; excellent value. **Cons:** far from town; hotel has only the one restaurant; first-floor rooms do not have views. ⊠ *Carretera Luperón, Km 7.5, Gurabo* ☎ *809/276–6400* ⊕ *www.campdavidranch.com* ⤳ *35 rooms* ⌂ *In-room: a/c, Internet (some), Wi-Fi (some).* ⌂ *In-hotel: restaurant, room service, laundry service, Wi-Fi hotspot, parking (free)* 🖃 *AE, D, MC, V.* ⧗ *EP.*

$ ▦ **Hodelpa Garden Court.** This
HOTEL squeaky-clean, American-style midsize hotel, once a Courtyard by Marriott, is now owned by the growing Hodelpa Hotel Group, which owns the Gran Almirante Hotel & Casino downtown. Since the purchase, there have been few changes—unless it is that the employees are even more hospitable now. The plush bedding and bevy of pillows in the contemporary rooms are normally found only in the priciest resorts, and the thick wall-to-wall carpeting is certainly not the norm either. Breakfast is an ample buffet, and the food in the restaurant, generally quite good, includes great cheeseburgers with imported U.S. beef. Although it's up to 15 minutes from downtown,

TRUJILLO'S CADDIES

A magnetic attraction for Camp David—particularly for car lovers and those who remember the 1950s—is a unique collection made up of Cadillacs and Jeeps that once belonged to Dictator Trujillo and his son. Vintage models include Trujillo's renowned 1956 black Cadillac Fleetwood, with two horns mounted on its left flank, and a smashing yellow and black Caddie, as well as his son Ramis's army Jeep, a 1954 Willy's Jeep C63. (Ramis was commander in chief of the armed services.) All are parked in the contemporary cocktail lounge.

it just takes a few skinny minutes to reach the Santiago Airport, making it handy for businesspeople: they fly into Santiago, catch the free shuttle, utilize the meeting rooms and 24-hour business center, and take out cash from the ATM here. Leisure guests appreciate the creature comforts for the moderate price, too. **Pros:** many staffers speak English; personalized service is the norm; discounted weekend rates; lovely pool area. **Cons:** no fine-dining restaurant; not in the middle of town. ⊠ *Autopista Duarte, Km 9, Santiago* ☎ *809/612–7000* ⊕ *www.hodelpa.com* ⤳ *138 rooms, 33 suites* ⚂ *In-room: a/c, safe, refrigerator, Internet, Wi-Fi. In-hotel: restaurant, room service, pool, laundry service, Internet terminal, Wi-Fi hotspot, parking (free)* ▭ *AE, MC, V* ⧦ *EP.*

$–$$

HOTEL

★

The Hodelpa Gran Almirante Hotel & Casino. The best hotel in downtown Santiago attracts business travelers with its great business center and executive level with panoramic city views, but the pool and sundeck, fitness room, steam and sauna, and the Asian-inspired massage services are equally attractive to tourists. Guest rooms are large but utilitarian, and could use some colorful and cheery accessories. Yet new bedding and plush pillows let you sleep with the angels. It's worth the supplement to stay on the executive floor: the rooms have been given a clean, modern look, and a 30-minute massage and a free nightly happy hour with hors d'oeuvres are among the extra perks. A most appealing breakfast buffet with excellent service is an option; by night, you can enjoy a meal or Spanish-style tapas in the Bar & Meson. Boka serves a fusion menu at night. **Pros:** free shuttle to the airport; fun casino; great pool with warm Jacuzzi. **Cons:** service from the friendly staff occasionally inconsistent; hotel lacks the elegance of a grand hotel. ⊠ *Av. Estrella Sadhala, corner of Calle 10, Santiago* ☎ *809/580–1992* ⊕ *www.hodelpa.com* ⤳ *151 rooms, 4 suites* ⚂ *In-room: a/c, safe, refrigerator, Wi-Fi. In-hotel: 3 restaurants, room service, bars, pool, spa, gym, laundry facilities, Internet terminal, Wi-Fi hotspot, parking (free)* ▭ *AE, MC, V* ⧦ *EP.*

EN
ROUTE

About 3 mi (5 km) north of La Vega is Santo Cerro (the Holy Mount), site of a miraculous apparition of the Virgin and the destination for many local pilgrimages. The Convent of La Merced is here, and the views of the Cibao Valley are breathtaking. The town's remarkable Concepción de la Vega Church was constructed in 1992 to commemorate the 500th anniversary of the discovery of America. The unusual modern Gothic style—all curvaceous concrete columns, arches, and buttresses—is striking.

NIGHTLIFE

Santiago does not have the number of nightspots that the capital has, but there are a few good ones, as Santiagoans like to dress up, go out, and feel their dances. The city is under the same curfew restrictions as Santo Domingo, so nightspots must close at midnight during the week and 2 AM on Friday and Saturday nights; casinos in hotels do not have to abide by the curfew. It's not unusual to see a parade of cars, the majority SUVs, beelining it to the Hotel Hodelpa Gran Almirante at 2 AM to play the tables at its casino. There aren't that many "in" places, so those that are get traffic by all age groups, not just the young and good-looking. In addition to those listed, Il Pasticcio, reviewed here as a restaurant, is also a nightly gathering place. Patrons are open and welcoming, none more so than the owner. People tablehop, and it's easy to make new friends. The resurrected Puerto del Sol restaurant also doubles as a social networking hotspot, particularly on its open-air terrace, where live music plays.

BARS

Moma Bar (✉ *Centro Plaza Internacional, Av. Juan Pablo Duarte at Calle Ponce* ☎ *809/724–6781*), aptly named after New York City's Museum of Modern art, has a contemporary design, just as sleek as the jazz, Spanish rock, and electronic music that plays.

CASINOS

The **Casino at Hotel Gran Almirante** (✉ *Hotel Gran Almirante & Casino, Av. Estrella Sadhala, corner of Calle 10* ☎ *829/582–7304*) is similar to a small Vegas casino, offering craps, poker, roulette, blackjack, Texas Hold 'em, and slot machines. It's well managed, and service is particularly good; drinks are served to players. The casino stays open nightly until 5 AM. Special activities have included various casino promotions, live bands, and even dominoes competitions, popular among older Dominican men. The casino is independent of the hotel, so guests can't transfer tabs to their room.

DANCE CLUBS

La Dolce Lounge (✉ *Plaza Zona Rosa, Av. Juan Pablo Duarte at La Salle St.* ☎ *809/971–0415*) has modern decor and an excellent environment for partying, but on some weekend nights, when live bands play on the expansive stage, the crowds can be wild and the atmosphere best for just the young.

LA VEGA

50 mi (80 km) south of Puerto Plata, 25 mi (40 km) southeast of Santiago.

Founded in 1495 by Christopher Columbus, La Vega is the site of one of the oldest settlements in the New World. The Spanish discovered gold here in the 1490s, and they also established the first mint in the New World here. The original settlement, now referred to as La Vega Vieja, was destroyed by a hurricane. El Parque de Flores, the town's central park, has a delightful, contemporary fountain. The brightly painted, centuries-old buildings surrounding it are being slowly restored, under a beautification project of President Leonel Fernández. Plans are to have an ongoing exhibition of Carnaval masks in one of them.

A commercial center for the surrounding farms, it's not a tourist magnet except in February, when La Vegas is justly celebrated for its Carnaval, probably the best in the country. The celebration dates back to the first Spanish settlers, and at this time the normally reserved, hardworking townspeople can become rowdy, especially when joined by nearly 100,000 fellow Dominicans and tourists. The Presidente flows faster than the water in the fountain during Carnaval, so be careful on the road during this time—drunk driving is a problem. In general, it's a pretty safe party, with good security, and it's fun. As with any event with large crowds, carry little of value on you, and make certain that your camera is around your neck and in a case with a wide, sturdy strap. Book accommodations far in advance, since even Santiago is busy during this time with its own Carnaval.

Crowds sit in bleachers erected along the parade route or join the organized, costumed groups who are the official marchers. Costumes can be lavish, heavy, and wildly decorated—otherworldly, even. La Vega is known for its distinctively haunting devil masks. These creations are intricate, fanciful gargoyles painted in surreal colors; spiked horns and cows' teeth (once real but now simulated) lend an eerie authenticity. Several artisans work in dark, cramped studios throughout the area, their skills having been passed down for generations.

⚠ **Before you dance wildly in the street, be forewarned that some of the young male marchers snap leather whips, so you need to stay clear. Their buddies wield hard rubber, faux animal bladders and whack people in the butt, so watch your back.**

JARABACOA

43 mi (70 km) south of Santiago.

Nature lovers should consider a trip to Jarabacoa, in the mountainous region known rather wistfully as the Dominican Alps (altitude 2,666 feet). The town is not pristine like a real Alpine village, though some of the buildings strive for the look. The clean mountain air is contaminated by the many *motoconchos* (motorcycle taxis) that scoot around the downtown. It's far more hectic than you imagine it will be, and the only peace and tranquillity is found outside of town. Still, the buzz of activity and the European visitors all make Jarabacoa a fun place to visit. The central park is quite pleasant, and some decent restaurants surround it, as well as a pretty Catholic church.

But a lot of the joy of visiting Jarabacoa is the opportunity to take excursions on foot, horseback, or by motorcycle taxi to the surrounding waterfalls and forests—quite incongruous in such a tropical country. Other activities include adventure tours, particularly white-water rafting or canoe trips, canyoning, Jeep safaris, and paragliding, trekking, and mountain biking. Unless you plan to climb Pico Duarte, most of these excursions are more tourist adventures than solitary ecotours.

WHERE TO EAT AND STAY

$–$$ ✕ **El Bambu.** The region's rocky, fast-flowing rivers are much of the

INTERNATIONAL appeal of Jarabacoa. This social club along the Yaque del Norte River has a suspension bridge leading to terrace seating, walkways, inviting pools, and a bar, all along the river. In addition to the main restaurant, there's a large pavilion where a DJ plays, as well as a piano bar. Sunday lunch is the busiest time here, and if you like overflowing buffets, your music loud, and your parties fierce, this is the time to come. If you are looking for a quieter meal, come midweek for a long lunch, when you

Mask Maker

Just days before Carnaval, young mask maker Miguel Morine Morte was still working feverishly to finish some masks for a La Vegan troupe. His older brother and mentor, Melvin Antonio Morte, was off to get a visa for a European trip (he and his masks would be part of a contingent promoting the Dominican Republic as a tourist destination).

Miguel dries the *diablo conjuelo* (limping devil) masks on a clothesline after they have been painted. (Diablo Conjuelo is the name of one of the local Carnaval groups, which has some 160 members, and each member requires a mask.) The devil had immense horns like barbed branches, an elongated nose, and a leering smile and rows of long teeth. The mask was painted in that year's colors, white and apple green. Such an art object costs US$1,030, which is not bad compared to the heavy, ornate costumes priced at more than US$4,000. The prices are high because each mask takes the artisan and his assistants seven days to make. This is good money in a country where the poorest citizens don't make that much in an entire year.

The 20-year-old, who had started painting for his brother when he was six, insisted that his business wasn't just about the money: "The *conetos* (masks typical of La Vega's Carnaval) are a cultural tradition, not just in my country but in many others around the world like Brazil, even Germany." He went on to explain the process of fabricating a mask. First a clay mold is sculpted and secured with nails through the head. Then a mixture of gesso (plaster of paris) and acrylic is applied and allowed to dry. It's painted and dried again. Miguel even produced a set of dental work: "In earlier times, they would use real cows' teeth, but now we have a mold for them, too."

How might a tourist acquire such a mask? Miguel says, "*Turistas* can ask a wearer when the parade is over if they would like to sell theirs. Some do. The going rate is half of what it cost, say $500."

---

can enjoy the music of the river. The menu is largely upscale Dominican cuisine, and some of the standouts include pumpkin soup, yucca croquettes, sea bass in garlic sauce, and the house specialty—rabbit in red wine sauce. It's delicious indeed, although you may find as many bones as meat. Side dishes are extra. ⊠ *Jarabacoa River Club & Resort, Carretera Jarabacoa, Manabao, Km 2½, 16 mi (26 km) north of Jarabacoa* ☎ 809/656–0026 or 809/501–3020 ⊕ *www.jarabacoariverclub. com* ⌂ *Reservations essential* ☰ AE, MC, V.

$ | **Hotel Gran Jimenoa.** On the river of the same name, this is an upscale
HOTEL | hotel with a central pool that segues into gardens ornamented with a small waterfall that mimics the river's. Overlooking the river is the hotel's restaurant, Piedras Del Río. A narrow suspension bridge leads to a palapa-roofed karaoke bar that's only open erratically. It's just as well, since the sound of the rushing river is what you want to hear at the restaurant. (By dinnertime, the weather can go from fresh and crisp to damp and chilly, so dress appropriately.) The hotel's choice rooms are in the Río building, which is set back but offers river views;

the primo ones are on the second and third floors. (River-view rooms are the same price, so request one.) Rooms are large and simply decorated. Rates go up on Friday and Saturday nights, and in summer and holidays expect higher prices and mandatory meal plans. It's joyful to open your patio door in the early morning and watch and listen to the river. You may also see a ranch hand on horseback herding his cattle into the white foam for a breakfast drink. **Pros:** caring staff

> **DID YOU KNOW?**
>
> You may think that you have tasted new potatoes, but unless you live in Idaho, you probably have never tasted a really fresh potato until you have had one straight from the fields of Constanza and Valle Nuevo. It's an amazing difference. You can peel it, sprinkle salt on it, and eat it raw like a radish.

and (young) management; nice sauna. **Cons:** rooms have dated decor and some maintenance issues; a sizeable conference center means that big business groups tend to take over midweek, public Wi-Fi is unreliable; guests are not told when the hot water will be turned off. ⊠ *Av. Confluenzia, at entrance to Los Corrilitos, Jarabacoa* ☎ *809/574–6304 or 809/574–4345* 🖷 *809/574–4177* ⊕ *www.granjimenoa.com* 🖙 *60 rooms, 1 suite, 2 apartments* ⚴ *In-room: a/c, safe (some). In-hotel: restaurant, room service, bar, pool, laundry service, Internet terminal, Wi-Fi hotspot, parking (free), some pets allowed* ⊟ *AE, MC, V* ⦿ *BP.*

ADVENTURE TOURS

Iguana Mama (⊠ *Cabarete* ☎ *809/571–0908* ⊕ *www.iguanamama.com*), the adventure-tour operator based in Cabarete, offers a large variety of tours and activities in the Jarabacoa area. The same young and sporty types who come to Cabarete for their adventure sports want to go to the mountains to try their brand of adrenaline. This experienced, highly recommended company is a good choice if you're staying in Puerto Plata or Cabarete and do not wish to make the trip to Jarabacoa on your own. They will take care of all of the transportation details for you, using Rancho Jarabacoa as their outfitter. *For more information, see ⇨ Biking and Hiking under Sports and the Outdoors in Cabarete in Chapter 5, The North Coast.*

In Jarabacoa, safety and professionalism can mean the difference between life and death in the mountains and on the rivers. The largest reliable adventure operator is **Rancho Baiguate** (⊠ *La Joya, Jarabacoa* ☎ *809/574–4940* ⊕ *www.ranchobaiguate.com*). Their roster of activities includes canyoning, river rafting, and mountain biking, not to mention trekking on foot or horseback. The company will even help you do the strenuous climb up Pico Duarte, which is attempted by only a few hardy souls every year. Mules are utilized, and experienced mountain guides accompany climbers. The company offers lodging on its ranch, but the facilities may be a bit too rustic for typical American travelers.

MotoCaribe (⊕ *www.motocaribe.com*) is a one-of-a kind adventure tour done on V-Strom 650s Suzuki motorcycles. An American, Richard Cooper, created it, and it's run by his Dominican wife, Alida. Riders are followed by a van/trailer that carries supplies. Motorcyclists can opt for a one- or two-week adventure in "living large." These exciting sojourns are planned for several regions within the country, including Samaná and the Southwest, with most of them starting in Jarabacoa. The utmost care and caution is exercised; the bikes are late or new models and exceptionally comfortable for long days in the saddle (as much as six hours.) As a rule the groups avoid the large autopistas, driving instead on less trafficked country and mountain roads. Lunch stops can be in quaint mountain resorts such as Mi Vista (⊕ *mivista.biz*), with shorter breaks at coffee producersand the like.

Rancho Jarabacoa (⊠ *A Carretera Division, Sabeneta* ☎ *809/222–3202]* ⊕ *www.ranchojarabacoa.net*), a small family-owned operation, organizes white-water rafting in the fast-moving Yaque Del Norte River. Other adventure activities include horseback riding, paragliding, rapelling, canyoning, and kayaking (for the experienced), or one can just come and have lunch and pass the day at the ranch, on the banks of the Río Jemenoa.

CONSTANZA

22 mi (36 km) south of Jarabacoa, 45 mi (72 km) south of Santiago.

The road south of Jarabacoa takes you higher up in the mountains until you reach Constanza, which has an altitude of 4,264 feet. However, since you are in the Cibao Valley you do not feel that high. The town is surrounded by farmland, which gives you the impression of being on level ground. Although Constanza has approximately the same number of residents as Jarabacoa—slightly fewer than 30,000—it has a much more small-town feel, with a less crowded downtown. However, in some ways it's not as attractive as Jarabacoa, particularly because its central park is not as appealing. Town folk seem friendlier, however, with more time for you. Without many adventure tours here, the real reason you go to Constanza is to breath in some fresh, cool mountain air and just relax, which you can do in a couple of nearby lodges.

GETTING HERE AND AROUND

There are no buses between Constanza and Jarabacoa. The only "public" transportation is the beat-up pick-up trucks that hang out by Constanza's central park. They wait for enough passengers to make the hour-run to Jarabacoa, and it can be a very uncomfortable, dusty ride. As a tourist, you may have to pay up to $25 each way. If you want the front seat and a modicum of comfort and a little extra room, pay for two (you will also pay for two people if you have a large suitcase). The driver may not budge if he doesn't have enough passengers to pay for the gas, and he may also try to hit up the tourists for more money.

NEED A BREAK?

Constanza's Q Liquor Store (⊠ *Calle Antonio Maria Garcia 2, Constanza* ☎ *809/539–2680*) is unexpectedly hip, carrying top-shelf brands like Grey Goose. Seat yourself at the tables outside and people-watch. The proprietors are friendly to visitors, and there is some English spoken.

WHERE TO EAT

¢ ✕ **Mi Casa.** The Acosta family, Jose and wife Estela, have run this restau-
CARIBBEAN rant and hotel for decades. Papa is still on the floor, and Estela is still in
the kitchen, but she now receives some help from their son. The interior
is rustic, pine-paneled, and homey, and the comfort food on the menu
is prepared with love. You can always have the flavorful chicken soup
or garlic soup that will cure anything and a litany of fresh fruit juices,
including strawberry and carrot. Dominican specialties prevail, including at breakfast, which has become an occasion for locals and tourists to
meet; the same is true during the busy lunch period. Try the goat with
a sweet potato puree or the plump rabbit. You'll wonder if it was fat-
tened up on Constanza's plus-size carrots. The Acostas have 13 simple,
inexpensive guest rooms ($25–$40), recently renovated. The first-floor
rooms have attractive plaid coverlets; the back room is particularly
inviting, with rustic timbers and tile work. However, the second floor
rooms are tacky, and not where you want to stay. ⊠ *Calle Luperón,
corner of Calle Sanchez, Constanza* ☎ *809/539–2764* ▤ *MC, V.*

$ ✕ **Restaurant Delenia.** Stop here when you're looking for something
CARIBBEAN healthier and with a bit more atmosphere than the locally popular
comedors, the typical cinder-block restaurants serving up enormous
portions of hearty Dominican fare. This pleasantly rustic restaurant,
built with pine and lots of love, has both indoor and outdoor seating.
You can ask for a large salad with fresh, curly lettuce and an array of
vegetables, or vegetable juice. You can have your main meal, by day or
night, including lamb in creole sauce or a small rabbit or guinea hen in
a red-wine sauce. The owners are accommodating, and use quality, fresh
produce. There are also rooms here, but they aren't anything special,
and they lack the feel-good ambience of the restaurant. ⊠ *Gaston Fer-
nandez Delenia, corner of Reyes, Constanza* ☎ *809/539–2213* ▤ *AE,
D, DC, MC, V* ☺ *No dinner Mon.*

WHERE TO STAY

¢ ⌸ **Altocerro Villas, Hotel & Camping.** Close to town, this family-run ran-
VACATION VILLAS cho is in a bucolic setting, surrounded by vegetable fields and down a
country road. The central communal areas are good-looking. They, like
the second-floor restaurant and 10 hotel rooms, are done in a country
motif. The adjacent minimarket has a good selection, from Pringles to
vodka, but is pricey. The villas, which look like two-story town houses,
are in tiers on a hillside, and the most desirable have working fireplaces.
The aroma of the wood fire—priceless. All the villas have well-equipped
kitchens and balconies and views of the Constanza Valley. You won't
be roughing it here, not with cable TV and Wi-Fi, too. More outdoorsy
types may choose to stay in the separate campground, but even it is
commodious, with clean restrooms, barbecue, and bonfire areas, a playground, and rustic gazebos. The new convention center here is bringing
in some interesting groups, like an orchid society. A spa and gym is under
construction and should be operational by early 2011. **Pros:** good value
for money, although rates increase on weekends; bi-level two-bedroom
villas are particularly attractive and spacious; scenic country setting.

Japanese Colonists and Constanza—A Success Story

In the foreground of a black-and-white photo of the first ship carrying Japanese colonists to their new home in the Dominican Republic in 1956, a father, Hitoshi Waki, holds his tiny son (Teruki, age one) while his little daughter (Yumiko, age two) plays next to them. The picture is in the book *Más Relatos Sobre Constanza* by Constancio Cassá, his second book on the subject.

Generalissimo Rafael L. Trujillo embarked on a program to bring in new immigrants to the Dominican Republic in the 1950s. His invitation was extended to Japanese, Spanish, Hungarian, and Lebanese colonists; in the 1940s he had invited Jewish refugees from Europe to settle in Sosúa. Japan, which was suffering from overpopulation and an economic and social crisis following World War II, sent a total of 1,282 colonists, who entered the Dominican Republic between 1956 and 1959.

Trujillo's government scattered the settlers in different regions of the country, but 201 individuals from 30 Japanese families put down their roots in Constanza. Their mission was to make it a premier agricultural area, which it still is today. They were sold fertile land dirt-cheap. It's said, also, that while Trujillo wanted more "white blood" in his country, he later approved of the Japanese immigrants, as they proved themselves industrious yet docile.

As is common in Japanese culture, several generations of the Waki family live under the same roof, including Teruki's teenage daughter and son. The home itself is one of the largest and most attractive on the periphery of the original Colonia Japonese

(Japanese Colony). Today it's the poorer Dominicans who live in the converted barracks originally constructed for the Colonia Japonese.

In Spanish, Choko Waki (wife of the late Hitoshi) explains that in order to be accepted into the country initially, a family had to have four adults capable of working, and they had to sign a work contract. Neither she nor her daughter Yumiko remembers any prejudice being shown against them. Yet their culture was so different from that of the local Dominicans. Initially, the Japanese married only among themselves and with others they met at the island-wide reunions every year in the capital. There were also family-arranged marriages and "mail order" brides from the fatherland. However, as time passed, children were baptized in the Catholic Church and intermarriage with Dominicans began.

The Waki family lived in the colony housing for 12 long years; Hitoshi eventually owned a florist shop in Santo Domingo and commuted. This large, durable home was constructed in the late 1960s, and looks out to fields planted with vegetables and strawberries and to a greenhouse. Teruki, assisted by his sister, makes their primary living by growing the greenery used by florists. During the spring cherry blossom festival they do the artistic floral displays. Japanese food is also sold.

Surprisingly, there are no Japanese restaurants in Constanza, despite the long history. Yumiko interjects: "A relative and I have been thinking about opening a takeout place. What do you think?"

Cons: not a whole lot of personality or charisma; units have dated decor. *Colonia Kennedy, Constanza* ☎ *809/539–1553,809/539–1429; 809/530–6192 reservations only* ⊕ *www.altocerro.com* ◄ *10 rooms, 4 suites, 10 1-bedroom villas, 14 2-bedroom villas, 6 3-bedroom villas* ◊ *In-room: no a/c, kitchen (some), Wi-Fi. In-hotel: restaurant, Wi-Fi hotspot, parking (free)* ⊟ *AE, D, DC, MC, V* ⓘ *BP.*

¢ 🏨 **Hotel/Restaurant Vista Del Valle.**

HOTEL If you come into town and want something centrally located and inexpensive for the night, you'll be safe, warm, and dry at this family-run hotel. Some attractive rustic touches include rough-hewn furniture and hall lights fashioned from rope, twigs, and branches. Popular with European budget travelers on weekends, the hotel is usually filled with business travelers during the week. You do get some views of the surrounding countryside, particularly from the third-floor front rooms (back rooms have no views, but are more removed from the street and motorcycle racket below). The owners, the Garcia family, have opened a steak house around the corner, where breakfast is served for RD$100. For lunch and dinner, you can have a small, medium or large Angus steak with a baked potato or *tostones* (fried green plantains) and salad. **Pros:** great location; cheap but not sleazy; interesting rustic decor. **Cons:** rooms are small, with few amenities; stairs are steep. ⊠ *Antonio María Garcia 41, corner of Matilde Viñas, Constanza* ☎ *809/539–2071 or 829/447–4010* ⊕ *www. hotelvistadelvalle* ◄ *12 rooms* ◊ *In-room: no phone, no a/c* ⊟ *No credit cards* ⓘ *EP.*

¢ 🏨 **Villa Pajon.** With the smoke rising from the chimneys, this hideaway

AGRITOURISM could be in the North Carolina mountains. If it were, it might be used
★ for a photo shoot in a country-home glossy—it's all done in great taste. You'll find fieldstone fireplaces in the communal dining room and in each of the cabins, which have white-stucco walls crisscrossed by beams, lots of lodgepole pine, and gingham and plaid fabric. You can fling open the green shutters to reveal gardens of calla lilies, hydrangeas, and purple agapanthus. This 1,000-acre property (at 7,150 feet elevation) was first a lumber mill, then a flower plantation. It's now a potato farm as well as a vacation haven for savvy urban dwellers, romantic couples, families, and tourists. Each cabin has a well-equipped kitchen with a gas range; there are dining tables on the front porches and barbecues. Transportation can be arranged if you don't have a car to handle the rough road, and cooking or maid service can be provided for an additional charge. The best rates can be found during midweek and in summer. A hiking trail has been created. **Pros:** the true simple country life; horses are available to take over logging trails; the owners speak English and are genuinely hospitable and fun; hiking trail.

7

Cons: limited electricity (there are battery-operated inverters, powered by solar panels); dirt road from town requires a four-wheel drive; guests must bring all their own supplies. ⊠ *Take Calle de Constanza to San Jose Ocoa, 15 mi (24 km) from Constanza Valle Nuevo* ☎ *809/412–5210* 🖷 *809/619–1945* ⊕ *www.villapajon.com* 🛏 *1 1-bedroom cabin, 3 2-bedrooms cabins, 3 3-bedrooms cabins* ♿ *In-room: no a/c, no phone, kitchen, no TV* ⊟ *No credit cards* ⑩ *EP.*

DID YOU KNOW?

Much of the land surrounding Valle Nuevo is now part of the Parque Nacional de Valle Nuevo. Since the Guzman family has owned their land and the structures of their Villa Pajon for generations, they were grandfathered in.

Travel Smart
Dominican Republic

GETTING HERE AND AROUND

It was once said that all roads lead to Rome. In the Dominican Republic, the same could be said for the capital, Santo Domingo. All of the island's major highways radiate from the capital, so this is the place from which bus and air service are the best. Puerto Plata and Santiago are key cities in the north, while Punta Cana and La Romana are the key destinations in the southeast. While the Dominican Republic has some excellent highways and secondary roads, some roads are still in bad repair, and driving can be hazardous. Choose your airport of entry carefully, however. You may find it's cheaper to fly into Santo Domingo, but the trip on to your final destination could still take several hours.

TRAVEL TIMES FROM SANTO DOMINGO		
To	By Air	By Bus
La Romana	30 mins	1.5–2 hrs
Punta Cana/ Bávaro	45 mins	3–4 hrs
Santiago	30 mins	2.25–3 hrs
Puerto Plata	45 mins	3.5–4 hrs
Santa Bárbara de Samaná	40 mins	2.5–3 hrs
Barahona	45 mins	3.5–4 hrs

▌AIR TRAVEL

The Dominican Republic has more international airports than any other island in the Caribbean, but it's important that you fly into the airport that is closest to your resort. You don't want to fly into Santo Domingo if you're staying in Punta Cana, since this can be an expensive drive that takes over three hours. Here are some sample flight times to the Dominican Republic: New York to Santo Domingo: 3 hours, 15 mins; or Puerto Plata: 3 hours; Miami to Santo Domingo: 1 hour, 50 mins; Miami to Puerto Plata 1 hour, 45 mins; San Juan to Punta Cana: 1 hour.

Domestic flights are less numerous than in years' past, and at present there are no domestic flights between Santo Domingo and Puerto Plata. To make this trip, you must charter a plane, take a bus from downtown Santo Domingo, rent a car for the drive, pay over $150 for a taxi, or hire a private car/shuttle service, like Dominican Shuttles.com with its Mercedes service. With the new highway completed, drive time (not bus time) is now about 3 hours 15 mins to Puerto Plata, 3 hours to Sosua, and 2 hours 45 mins to Cabarete.

There are a lot of flights between Punta Cana and La Isabela, and they are only rarely cancelled. However, passengers must be aware that if they have a connection in SDQ it is about an hour's drive between La Isabela and Las Américas Airport, and traffic can be horrible. Also, flights that use 3- or 5-seater planes are often cancelled because of meteorological conditions or insufficient passengers, so always check and recheck your reservation. Also, the amount of luggage is often an issue because of limited space.

AIRPORTS

The Dominican Republic has seven major international airports and one major domestic airport, including Cibao International Airport in Santiago (STI), which is convenient to the North Coast and central mountain regions of the island; Gregorio Luperón International Airport (POP) in Puerto Plata, about 7 mi (11 km) east of Playa Dorada; the La Isabela International Dr. Joaquin Balaguer Airport (JBQ), about 10 mi (16 km) north of Santo Domingo (you'll hear it called Higüero Airport and even Isabela, and it's used mainly for domestic flights, with just a few international ones); La Romana–Casa de Campo International Airport (LRM) in La Romana, which is being used increasingly for international flights; Las Américas International Airport (SDQ), about 15 mi (24 km) east of Santo Domingo, which has been beautified and improved over the past few years; El Catey International Airport (AZS), the impressive international airport about 25 mi (40 km) west of Samaná (as of yet no regularly scheduled airlines from the states, just charters); and Punta Cana International Airport (PUJ, the island's busiest, handling some 1.5 million passengers a year).

Security checks and check-in at Dominican airports can be slow, so you definitely must arrive 2 hours before an international flight. Anticipate long lines like those at major U.S. city airports.

Airport Contacts Cibao International Airport (STI ⊠ Santiago ☎ 809/582–4894). Gregorio Luperón International Airport (POP ⊠ Puerto Plata ☎ 809/586–0107 or 809/586–0219). La Isabela International Dr. Joaquin Balaguer (DHG ⊠ Higüero ☎ 809/826–4003). La Romana/Casa de Campo International Airport (LRM ⊠ La Romana ☎ 809/556–5565). Las Américas International Airport (SDQ ⊠ Santo Domingo ☎ 809/412–5888). President Juan Bosch International Airport (AZS ⊠ El Catay ☎ 809/338–0150). Punta Cana International Airport (PUJ ⊠ Punta Cana ☎ 809/686–8790).

FLIGHTS TO AND FROM THE DOMINICAN REPUBLIC

Most major airlines now have service to the Dominican Republic, including American Airlines/American Eagle, Continental, Delta, JetBlue (to Santiago, Puerto Plata, and Santo Domingo only), Spirit (to Santo Domingo, mainly in high season and some months to Punta Cana), and US Airways.

Many visitors fly nonstop on charter flights directly from the East Coast and Midwest, particularly into Punta Cana. These charters are generally part of a package, and can only be booked through a travel agent.

Air Caraïbes and Air Antilles Express connect to the French West Indies, both

Guadeloupe and Martinique; LIAT connects the Dominican Republic mainly to the English-speaking Caribbean islands.

Incidents of theft, especially at Las Américas airport in Santo Domingo, are much less of a problem than in the past. At this writing, flights into Puerto Plata (particularly those connecting in Miami) have the worst reputation for pilfered baggage. Shrink-wrap your luggage whenever possible at the airports.

U.S. Airlines American Airlines/American Eagle (☎ 809/200–5151, 809/959–2420, 800/433–7300, or 809/542–5151 in Puerto Plata). Continental (☎ 809/262–1060 in D.R., 800/231–0856 in U.S.). Delta (☎ 809/200–9191, 809/233–8485, or 809/955–1500 in D.R., 800/221–1212 in U.S.). JetBlue (☎ 809/200–9898, 809/549–1793 in D.R., 800/538–2583 in U.S.). Spirit (☎ 809/381–4111 in D.R., 800/772–7117 in U.S.). US Airways (☎ 809/540–0505, 809/549–0165 in D.R., 800/428–4322, or 800/622–1015 in U.S.).

Caribbean & Regional Airlines Air Antilles Express (☎ 809/621–8888). Air Caraïbes (☎ 809/621–8888, 0590/82–47–00 in Guadeloupe). LIAT (☎ 809/621–8888).

FLIGHTS WITHIN THE DOMINICAN REPUBLIC

Aerodomca and Air Century, flying out of La Isabela Airport in Higüero Santo Domingo, offer charters and transfers. Aerodomca also services Punta Cana, Puerto Plata, La Romana, Santiago, and Samaná. Helidosa Helicopters offers both charter flights and aerial sightseeing excursions. In addition to charter flights, DominicanShuttles.com (formerly Takeoff Destination Service) has flights from Higüero, El Portillo (near Las Terrenas), Punta Cana, and Puerto Plata. It also offers a service called "Flights and Shuttles," which lets you book a shuttle to your hotel at the same time you get a flight. For example, it offers travelers who fly into Punta Cana a shuttle service in a Mercedes, to Samaná or even Puerto Plata.

Domestic Airlines **Aerodomca** (✉ *La Isabela International Dr. Joaquin Balaguer, Higüero* ☎ *809/567–1195*). **Air Century** (✉ *La Isabela International Dr. Joaquin Balaguer, Higüero* ☎ *809/566–0888* ⊕ *www.aircentury.com*). **DominicanShuttles.com** ✉ *Las Américas* ☎ *809/738–3014; 809/481-0707* ⊕ *www. DominicanShuttles.com*). **Helidosa Helicopters** (✉ *Punta Cana* ☎ *809/688-0744* ✉ *Puerto Plata* ☎ *809/320-2009* ⊕ *www. helidosa.com*).

▮ BUS TRAVEL

Privately owned air-conditioned buses are the cheapest way to get around the country. They make regular runs to Santiago, Puerto Plata, Punta Cana, and other destinations from Santo Domingo. One-way bus fare from Santo Domingo to Puerto Plata is about $7.50, and it takes 3½ hours. Metro's deluxe buses have more of an upscale clientele; however, there are no movies. Caribe Tours sometimes shows bilingual movies, keeps the air-conditioning on frigid, and is favored by locals and families. Buses are often filled to capacity, especially on weekends and holidays.

If you're going north, both Metro and Caribe Tours offer hourly service from Santo Domingo to Santiago, Puerto Plata, and Sosúa. The bus music will be Dominican-loud. Caribe Tours also runs buses to Las Américas International Airport and the mountain town of Jarabacoa from Santo Domingo. Linia Gladys is a small bus line that will get you from the capital to Constanza; if you are in the town of Constanza, call them, and they might even pick you up at your hotel.

Espreso Bavaró buses depart from Plaza Los Girasoles at Avenida Máximo Gómez at Juan Sánchez Ruiz; the buses are not the best, but the price is right, and the American movies current. If you're going to one of the Punta Cana resorts, you get off at the stop before the last and take a cab waiting at the taxi stand.

Frequent service from Santo Domingo to the town of La Romana is provided by Express Bus. Buses depart from Ravelo Street, in front of Enriquillo Park, every hour on the hour from 5 AM to 9 PM; the schedule is exactly the same from La Romana, where they leave from Camino Avenue. In Santo Domingo, there's no office and no phone, but a ticket taker will take your $4 just before departure. Travel time is about 1¾ hours. Once in town, you can take a taxi from the bus stop to Casa de Campo ($25), and to the Dominicus and Bayahibe resorts for from $40 to $45, depending on the distance.

Bus Information **Caribe Tours** (☎ *809/221–4422* ⊕ *www.caribetours.com.do*). **Espreso Bavaró** (☎ *809/682–9670*). **Express Bus** (☎ *809/556–4192, 809/550–4585*) **Linea Gladys** (☎ *809/565–1223 in Santo Domingo, or 809/539–2134*). **Metro Buses** (☎ *809/566–7126 in Santo Domingo, 809/586–6062 in Puerto Plata, 809/587–4711 in Santiago* ⊕ *www.metrotours-viajes.com*).

▮ CAR TRAVEL

Driving in the Dominican Republic can be a harrowing and expensive experience, and the typical vacationer will not want to rent a car. We especially caution tourists against driving outside the major cities at night. Watch out for pedestrians, stray cows, goats, or horses, bicycles, and motorcycles. Some vehicles will not have headlights, and others will be riding on the shoulders, often against oncoming traffic.

If you limit your driving to a daylong excursion, you can probably manage in the Southeast and in Punta Cana. Similarly, on the North Coast villa renters (especially those in the Cabrera area) may need to rent a car if their villa manager does not offer a good shuttle service. If you're traveling to the Southwest, you will probably need a car if you plan to do extensive independent exploring, and you may also need a four-wheel-drive vehicle (which must usually be rented in Santo Domingo or at Las Américas Airport). Prices and service may both be lower if you rent from a local company. Local car-rental companies do not always maintain their vehicles, although some are reputable. For a day's car rental you can almost certainly go with a local. However, if you need a car for a full week, it's best to go with a major company, especially one that offers 24-hour roadside assistance.

Most major companies have outlets at Las Américas Airport outside Santo Domingo and at Gregorio Luperón International Airport in Puerto Plata, the airports of choice for most independent travelers who are likely to rent cars.

To rent a car in the Dominican Republic, you will need a valid driver's license, passport, and credit card; you must be between the ages of 25 and 80. In season you can expect to pay between $45 and $83 (Kia Picanto) for an automatic with insurance from a major company like Budget, which is one of the more reasonably priced companies. SUVs can cost as much as US$160 daily (about $130 in low season) including insurance.

Take advantage of corporate rates, advance booking discounts, or a hotel discounts. Also, inquire whether you can rent a car that takes diesel, which is generally cheaper than gasoline. If you want to rent a car for a day, you can often do so at a car-rental desk at your resort and have it delivered.

GASOLINE

Fill up—and watch—the gas tank; stations are few and far between in rural areas. Prices are usually a couple of dollars more expensive than those in the United States. Make certain that attendants don't reach for the super pump, which is even costlier. Also, watch as the attendant starts the pump to see that it reads 000; when he is finished make certain it matches the amount you are supposed to pay. (Certain stations plan to inaugurate self-service soon, as they are aware of the abuses.)

ROAD CONDITIONS

Although some roads are still full of potholes, the route between Santo Domingo and Santiago is a modern, four-lane, divided highway, and the road between Santiago and Puerto Plata is a smooth blacktop. The highway from Santo Domingo to Casa de Campo, and from there to Punta Cana, is also a fairly smooth ride. A new highway between Santo Domingo and the Samaná Peninsula has been completed, cutting the driving time there in half, to about two and a half hours. Surprisingly, many of the scenic secondary roads, such as the "high road" between Playa Dorada and Santiago, are in good shape. Conversely, some in more remote areas are not only unlighted but have no lines.

ROADSIDE EMERGENCIES

It's particularly important to rent from an agency that offers emergency roadside assistance. For car theft, you can call 911 for the national police. For a simple flat tire, which is a common occurrence, you can have the tire repaired at almost every *bomba* (gas station) until around 7 PM, but it's best to look for a *gomero* (tire shop), which will give you the best service.

RULES OF THE ROAD

Driving is on the right, the 80-kph (50-mph) speed limit is strictly enforced, seat belts are mandatory. Otherwise, driving rules are similar to those in most of the United States. Right turns are allowed on red after you stop.

There are certain issues with driving in the Dominican Republic. Drunk driving is a problem, and the laws are not well enforced. The allowable blood alcohol level of 0.10 is higher than in most other countries, but it's particularly unwise to drink and drive in an unfamiliar place. You'll need to have all your wits when those around you don't.

Dominicans can be reckless drivers. They do not always stop at red lights, they often pass in a no-passing zone, and they don't always use their headlights at night.

Police corruption can also be a problem. You may see police officers standing on the side of the road, waving you down. You should always stop. One officer may smile and tell you that you were speeding or have made some other small violation, even if you have not. Always be polite, and speak as much Spanish as you can muster. He will do the same in his limited English. You can say something like: *"Que puedo hacer?"* (What can I do?). He may tell you that you can pay the fine directly to him; if he agrees, discreetly pull out RD$150 (less than five bucks). Hopefully, he isn't too greedy. Otherwise, offer more in small increments, about RD$50 at a time, and work it out. Unfortunately, that's the way these things are done here.

Under no circumstances should you drive across the Dominican border into Haiti.

CAR RENTAL

At the major agencies you'll have a choice of compact, midsize, and large vehicles (including minivans and quite a few SUVs). They're usually all automatics with air-conditioning. The condition of these vehicles can vary greatly, but they may not be of the same quality as cars you would rent in the United States. You'll need a four-wheel-drive SUV to reach more remote areas, like the hills west of Barahona or the mountainous regions beyond Jarabacoa. The Hotel El Quemaito, in Juan Estaban, 15 minutes from Barahona, has a few cars, trucks, and 4x4s, but they are in high demand. Reserve ahead of time, or rent at Las Américas or in Santo Domingo.

The week between Christmas and New Year's and Easter Week are typically the busiest times of the year for car-rental companies, so make your reservations far in advance.

A U.S. driver's license is sufficient to rent a car in the Dominican Republic. Renters must be between the ages of 25 and 80. Infant car seats are difficult to get and can be expensive (as much as a car during busy periods). You'll be better off if you bring your own. Laws are similar to those in the United States, though they are not well enforced. If you need a car seat, always reserve it with your car.

Allow plenty of time to drop off your rental car at any airport. It may be a breeze to drop off a car at a small airport such as La Romana, but at Las Américas you must allow 45 minutes to an hour, 30 minutes in Punta Cana. The agency will tell you how far in advance to arrive at the airport, and follow those estimates, since things rarely move as quickly in the Dominican Republic as in the United States.

Major Agencies Avis (☎ 800/331–1084 ⊕ www.avis.com ✉ Las Américas Airport ☎ 809/549–0468 ✉ Gregorio Luperón International Airport, Puerto Plata ☎ 809/586–0214 ✉ Castillo Marquez, corner Duarte, La Romana ☎ 809/550–0600). **Budget** (☎ 800/472–3325 ⊕ www.budget.com ✉ Las Américas Airport ☎ 809/549–0351 ✉ Gregorio Luperón International Airport, Puerto Plata ☎ 809/586–0413). **Europcar** (✉ Las Américas Airport ☎ 809/549–0942 ✉ Gregorio Luperón International Airport, Puerto Plata ☎ 809/586–7979 ✉ Punta Cana International Airport, Bavaro, Punta Cana ☎ 809/686–2861). **Hertz** (☎ 800/654–3001 ⊕ www.hertz.com ✉ Las Américas Airport ☎ 809/549–0454 ✉ Puerto Plata ☎ 809/586–0200).

Local Agencies Hotel El Quemaito (✉ Km 10, Carretera Barahona–Paraiso, Juan Estaban ☎ 809/649–7631 ⊕ www.hotelelquemaito.com). **MC Auto Rental Car** (✉ Las Américas Airport ☎ 809/549–8911 ⊕ www.mccarrental.com). **McBeal** (✉ Santo Domingo ☎ 809/688–6518). **Nelly Rent-a-Car** (✉ Las Américas Airport ☎ 809/530–0036, 800/526–6684 in U.S.)

RENTAL CAR INSURANCE

Unless you have a separate car-rental insurance policy, you should buy the collision damage waiver (CDW) or loss/damage waiver (LDW) from your agency in the Dominican Republic. These two waivers, essentially the same, prevent a car-rental company from suing you should the rental be damaged. Generally, the cost of a CDW or LDW is not included in the quoted price, and it will add substantially to your costs. For example, Budget rents an intermediate-size car for $41.58 per day during shoulder season, but CDW will cost an additional $21.95 per day, but this is not significantly different from the cost of insurance in the United States and also covers you for theft. You can often get insurance through your credit card—or even through a separate car-rental insurance policy—for significantly less. Most U.S. car-insurance policies that cover you for rentals do not cover you in the Dominican Republic; if you are unsure what your own policy covers, be sure to call and ask before your trip.

■ MOTOCONCHO TRAVEL

Motoconchos are a popular and inexpensive mode of transportation in such areas as Puerto Plata, Sosúa, Cabarete, and Jarabacoa. You can flag down one of these motorcycle taxis along rural roads and in town; rates vary from RD$20 per person for a short run to as much as RD$100 to RD$150 between Cabarete and Sosúa (double after 6 PM).

■ TAXI TRAVEL

Taxis, which are government-regulated, line up outside hotels and restaurants. They're unmetered, so ask about the rates before entering. Though they are more expensive, hotel taxis are the nicest and the safest option. Freelance taxis aren't allowed to pick up from hotels, so they hang out on the street in front of them. Carry some small bills because drivers rarely seem to have change.

Recommendable radio-taxi companies in Santo Domingo are Tecni-Taxi (which also operates in Puerto Plata) and Apolo. Tecni is the cheapest, quoting RD$80 as a minimum per trip, Apolo RD$90. Hiring a taxi by the hour—with unlimited stops and a minimum of two hours—is often a better option if you're doing a substantial sightseeing trip. Tecni charges RD$240

per hour but will offer hourly rates only before 6 PM; Apolo charges RD$280 per hour, day or night. When booking an hourly rate, be sure to establish clearly the time that you start.

You can use taxis to travel to out-of-town destinations at quoted rates. Check with your hotel or the dispatcher at the airport. For example, from the Colonial Zone in Santo Domingo to Playa Dorado with Tecni-Taxi is $150. If you book through your hotel concierge, it can be more.

Taxi-Queen is a company that works through the Santiago hotels. Drivers have passed security checks and wear their ID tags around their necks. Their cars are not wonderful, and the drivers are unlikely to speak English, but prices are especially reasonable. Also, they'll take you the distance to Sosúa for $45 and Cabarete for $10 more. The going rate for a taxi between Sosúa and Cabarete is $12. However, the rate is the same for one or five persons, night or day. Taxi-Tourismo, the company that services the Cibao Airport in Santiago, charges $80 to Sosúa, $90 to Cabarete, but has safer, bigger vehicles, mostly SUVs and minivans.

Information Apolo Taxi (☎ *809/537–0000, 809/537–1245 for a limo, which must be booked far in advance).* **Taxi-Cabarete** (☎ *809/571–0767 in Cabarete).* **Taxi-Queen** (☎ *809/570–0000, 809/233–3333 in Santiago).* **Taxi-Sosúa** (☎ *809/571–3097 in Sosúa).* **Taxi-Tourismo** (☎ *809/829–3007 in Santiago).* **Tecni-Taxi** (☎ *809/567–2010, 809/566–7272 in Santo Domingo, 809/320–7621 in Puerto Plata).*

ESSENTIALS

▍ ACCOMMODATIONS

The government rates hotels with a star system, doling out one to six stars. Star ratings take into consideration the facilities that the property has to offer, including restaurants, spas, tennis courts, bathroom amenities, and service, but the ratings are not qualitative judgments. Therefore, a so-called five-star resort in the Dominican Republic may not be up to the same standards as a similarly rated resort in Mexico or the United States. Generally, Americans may not be satisfied with any resort having a rating lower than four stars. To be safe, go with five stars. Six is a new designation, so few hotels have it. Those that do are mainly the most expensive all-inclusives and luxurious boutique hotels.

WHAT IT COSTS IN U.S. DOLLARS		
¢	under $80	under $125
$	$80–$150	$125–$250
$$	$150–$250	$250–$350
$$$	$250–$350	$350–$450
$$$$	over $350*	over $450**

*EP, BP, CP **AI, FAP, MAP

Hotel prices are per night for a double room in high season, excluding 16% tax, customary 10% service charge, and meal plans (except at all-inclusives).

▌TIP➔ Assume that hotels operate on the European Plan (EP, no meals) unless we specify that they use the Breakfast Plan (BP, with full breakfast), Continental Plan (CP, continental breakfast), Full American Plan (FAP, all meals), or Modified American Plan (MAP, breakfast and dinner), or are all-inclusive (AI, all meals and most activities).

APARTMENT AND HOUSE RENTALS

In Santo Domingo apartment rentals by the week do exist, but they are scarce. They're usually filled by word of mouth, with no "shingle" out in front. Renting an apartment can be risky unless you know the parties involved. At the very least, check out the situation in person before you hand over any money.

In the Southwest, foreign visitors who decide they want to be expats for a few weeks or months seem to have good luck in the towns of Los Blancos and Los Patos. Again, apartment rentals are usually found by asking around. Expats who have already found their rental in the sun are a good source. Realtors and owners sometimes prefer to have a good tenant in homes that are for sale, to ward off vandals or pests.

Rental condos or townhouses (often called villas) in the Dominican Republic are often the second homes of wealthy absentee owners. In some resorts like Casa de Campo they are the norm, though more often there are freestanding houses.

In Juan Dolio you can find a wide variety of villas in the Metro Country Club; Metro also has oceanfront condos in "new" Juan Dolio, also known as the Villas del Mar section. In "old" Juan Dolio there are more moderately priced apartments and homes for rent, many of which are suitable for singles or long-term renters.

On the North Coast much of the new high-end construction is designed to be privately owned but entered into a rental pool that is managed by the developers. Apartments are more common in Cabarete. The new oceanfront Seawinds Condominiums, at Punta Goleta, is one of the most luxurious such developments. The well-established Sea Horse Ranch development, between Sosúa and Cabarete, is a prestigious residential enclave with a beach club and restaurant, pool complex, and world-class equestrian center. In the Cabrera/Abreu area, about an hour west of Cabarete, the properties are in luxurious gated communities, where most rentals are managed by North Coast Management (NCM), a Cabrera-based agency. NCM is now renting less expensive homes and accommodations by the night, the week, or longer.

HOTELS

The Dominican Republic is best known for its all-inclusive resorts, which offer all you can eat, drink, and do for one moderate rate. These hotels, especially in the Punta Cana area, continue to be the big draw for this Caribbean island. Even though the escalating cost of food has driven costs up, they are still a great value, keeping the Dominican Republic at the forefront of cheap destinations in the Caribbean. But newer hotel developments are increasingly luxurious (and have high prices to match).

Perfectly nice, small, independent bed-and-breakfasts still exist in the Southwest near Barahona and are well priced, offering a more personal experience. In the mountain areas surrounding Jarabacoa, Constanza, and Valle Nuevo, rustic complexes—often with fireplaces—are the favored lodgings.

In Santo Domingo most of the better hotels are on or near the Malecón, with a growing collection of small, desirable properties in the trendy Colonial Zone, allowing you to feel part of that magical Old World neighborhood. But these hotels are still among the cheapest in the Caribbean.

▮ COMMUNICATIONS

INTERNET

Paid Internet access of some kind is available in almost every hotel, though you may sometimes have access to only one slow and old terminal in the lobby, maybe with a Spanish keyboard. Many all-inclusives have concessionaires who operate a bank of computers in either a separate room or in the back of one of the shops, but you will likely pay as much as $5 for only 30 minutes.

Wi-Fi is becoming more prevalent in the better hotels, particularly in Santo Domingo; it's usually free, but generally available only in the lobby and some public areas rather than in your room. Internet cafés are common in almost all the major resort areas.

Contacts Cybercafes (⊕ *www.cybercafes. com*) lists over 4,000 Internet cafés worldwide.

PHONES

Calling from a hotel is almost always the most expensive option; hotels usually add huge surcharges to all calls, particularly international ones. In some countries you can phone from call centers or even the post office. Calling cards usually keep costs to a minimum, but only if you purchase them locally. And then there are mobile phones (⇨ *below*), which are sometimes more prevalent—particularly in the developing world—than landlines; as expensive as mobile phone calls can be, they are still usually a much cheaper option than calling from your hotel.

To call the Dominican Republic from the United States, dial 1, then the area code 809 and the local number.

CALLING WITHIN THE DOMINICAN REPUBLIC

To make a local call, you must dial 809 plus the seven-digit number (dial 1-809 or 1-829 if you're calling a cell phone). Directory assistance is 1411. Rates for calling within the Dominican Republic vary by the hotel, but local calls are sometimes only a few pesos per minute. Sometimes calling at a hotel is cheaper than it would be to use a Dominican cell phone, which is usually charged by the minute.

CALLING OUTSIDE THE DOMINICAN REPUBLIC

From the Dominican Republic, just dial 1 plus the area code and number to call the United States or Canada. Some, but not all, U.S. toll-free numbers can be dialed from the Dominican Republic by dialing 1-880.

Many savvy travelers these days now use Skype, the international calling program that you can download directly to your laptop. It's a fraction of the cost of traditional options. If you don't want to lug your notebook, many of the better Internet centers and cafés have Skype on their computers and have headphones, too.

Access Codes MCI (☎ *800/888–8000*). **Sprint** (☎ *800/266–2255*).

CALLING CARDS

Phone cards, which are sold at gift shops and supermarkets, can usually give you considerable savings if you're calling the United States or Canada—a call for which a hotel might charge as much as $1 to $2 a minute. Codetel Comminicards can be used in most hotels (but check to see whether you will incur a connection or other fee). Codetel calling centers have equally good rates to the States, about 35¢ a minute, but you'll have to pay cash.

You don't hear of that many visitors using calling cards from U.S. companies in the Dominican Republic. That's because many hotels block these numbers to force you to go through the international telephone operator. Some hotels charge a connection fee that might range from $1.75 to a ludicrous $10 (be sure to verify with your resort whether there is a connection fee before using a calling card). Calling cards can be used successfully from pay phones, when you can find one that works (such as in the airport).

MOBILE PHONES

If you have a quad-band GSM phone, you can probably use your phone in the Dominican Republic, though roaming fees can be steep (and you pay international toll charges for incoming calls).

■TIP➔ **If you travel internationally frequently, save one of your old mobile phones or buy a cheap one on the Internet; ask your cell phone company to unlock it for you, and take it with you as a travel phone, buying a new SIM card with pay-as-you-go service in each destination.**

Orange and CLARO (the mobile communication division of Codetel) are the two major cell-phone companies. If you have a tri-band GSM phone, it will probably work on the island. Mobile phones in the Dominican Republic operate at 1900 MHZ frequency, the North American standard.

If you're spending more than a week or two in the Dominican Republic, you can also get a local phone. You cannot rent from Orange, but you can from CLARO; however, it's more economical to buy a phone for less than $50 and prepaid phone cards of various denominations for airtime. These are sold at pharmacies, supermarkets, and *colmados* (small local grocery stores.) You can then use the Dominican phone to call locally or long distance within the country. Or you could ask your provider to unlock your own phone and simply buy a local SIM card in the D.R.

Contacts Cellular Abroad (☎ *800/287–5072* ⊕ *www.cellularabroad.com*) rents and sells GSM phones and sells SIM cards that work in many countries. **Mobal** (☎ *888/888–9162* ⊕ *www.mobalrental.com*) rents mobiles and sells GSM phones (starting at $49) that will operate in 140 countries. Per-call rates vary throughout the world. **Planet Fone** (☎ *888/988–4777* ⊕ *www.planetfone.com*) rents cell phones, but the per-minute rates are expensive.

▮ CUSTOMS AND DUTIES

Customs inspections on arrival in the Dominican Republic are usually over quickly and painlessly. All travelers to the Dominican Republic are allowed to bring in one liter of alcohol, 200 cigarettes, and gifts not to exceed $100 in value. If you're carrying prescription medication—particularly controlled substances—be sure that you have a copy of the prescription and are carrying only enough for your personal use. Duties are particularly high for new electronic goods, and you'll be charged import duties if the customs inspector believes you're bringing, say, a new laptop to someone in the Dominican Republic.

If you buy antiques on your trip, carry the sales receipt with you. You can legally buy antique coins, including Spanish pieces of eight that are centuries old, from jewelry stores such as Everett Designs in the Casa de Campo Marina. Just produce your receipt and declare them as you exit the country.

Pets accompanying travelers from the United States must have a health certificate from a U.S. veterinarian signed within 15 days of your arrival. Dogs must have current rabies and parvo vaccinations. Airlines have other specific requirements, which you should inquire about before traveling to the Dominican Republic.

U.S. Information U.S. Customs and Border Protection (⊕ www.cbp.gov).

▌EATING OUT

The country's culinary repertoire includes Spanish, Italian, Middle Eastern, Indian, Japanese, American, certainly Dominican, and *nueva cocina Dominicana* (contemporary Dominican cuisine). Depending on where you go, you can usually find restaurants at all levels, low, moderate, and high. Santo Domingo, the country's capital, has the best dining scene, as cosmopolitan as any in the Caribbean, with many ethnic restaurants, Italian prevailing. Fresh seafood is universal in the country, the exception being in the mountain areas, where meat, including rabbit, is more the norm.

Restaurants that cater solely to tourists, as do many in the Colonial Zone, often dole out mediocre fare with poor service, yet their prices are escalating. Some of the best choices are in the business districts of the modern cities and in the upscale residential neighborhoods, where the menu prices offer a far better value.

Beach shacks serving simple but fresh seafood can be a fine way to make a great beach day even better. The quality of the food is usually fine, but you should always avoid ice and water unless it's bottled. Go with a cold beer in the bottle rather than a cocktail. Stands that serve cheap eats are an integral part of the culture and landscape, but eat street food at your own risk.

Dominican food does not have a stellar reputation, and it's doubtful that, despite some fusion movements, it will ever be world-class. Rice dishes prevail, and they're usually only "seasoned" with chicken or meat as well as tomato paste. Starchy root vegetables, such as yucca, as well as plantains, are staples, again with just a small amount of meat, and usually the less expensive cuts. *Mofango,* which consists of mashed green, roasted plantains mixed with shredded pork (or chicken), is very popular. *Moro,* a combination of seasoned rice and beans (usually brown pigeon peas) is ubiquitous. Soups can be the most flavorful, and the best thick stew is *sancocho,* usually made with five meats and poultry and served with white rice and avocado slices.

True vegetarian cuisine is rare in the Dominican Republic, but vegetarians can usually make do with the vegetable offerings, though you must always ask if such dishes have any meat in them. In *el campo* (the countryside) if you say that you don't want meat or that you never eat it, they will think that you are an Americano weirdo. People here only eat small amounts of meat because that is all they can afford.

If you eat dairy, one of the best Dominican specialties is *queso frito* (fried cheese). Children's menus are about as lackluster as they are in the States, usually listing chicken or fish fingers and *hamburgeresas.* *For information on food-related health issues, see* ⇨ *Health below.*

MEALS AND MEALTIMES
As in most Spanish-speaking countries, breakfast is called *desayuno,* lunch *almuerzo,* and dinner *cena.* Breakfast can

begin as early as 6 AM in a hotel, but usually it's 7 and will run until 10 or 10:30. Many hotel rates include some kind of breakfast, and in major properties a buffet is the norm. Some are elaborate, such as the breakfast buffet at the Hostal Nicolas Ovando in Santo Domingo. Breakfast at the Iberostar resorts is among the best at the all-inclusives.

A Dominican breakfast is usually fresh fruit and/or juice, eggs scrambled with cold cuts like ham or salami, mashed green plantains, and dark Dominican coffee. The European-owned bed-and-breakfasts are more likely to serve a continental breakfast with a selection of cheeses and cold meats, German bread or French croissants, and yogurt. Out on the street, breakfast is harder to come by, but you can always find a cup of strong coffee—often too strong for norteamericanos, especially since the coffee has often sat in the pot for hours.

Almuerzo can begin as early as 11 AM in the less-expensive eateries, where a daily *plato* is a mound of moro with chicken for $3 to $4; you'll pay the same price for a bland ham and cheese sandwich on white bread. Restaurants that cater more to tourists and businesspeople usually serve from noon to 2:30 or 3. These will offer a more upscale Dominican special (but most people still want their moro at lunch), as well as lighter fare for the younger crowd.

For dinner your hotel dining rooms and better establishments will open as early as 6 PM, but Americans may be the only patrons until 8:30 or 9, when the Dominicans start to roll in. Restaurants in the capital and its Colonial Zone, as well as those in Cabarete and Sosúa, may serve as late as 11 or midnight during the week, even later on Friday and Saturday. Restaurants in the Zone's Plaza España often will not take reservations on a Friday or Saturday night, or even answer the phone. Many independent restaurants are closed on Sunday night, since the main meal on Sunday is usually in the afternoon. When

all else fails, you can hit a *colmado* (grocery) or gas station that has a minimart.

Unless otherwise noted, the restaurants listed in this guide are open daily for lunch and dinner.

PAYING

Credit cards are widely accepted in upscale restaurants, particularly in the capital. Most of the restaurants in Cabarete and some in Sosúa, whether expensive or cheap, don't take them. It's the same situation in the Southwest and in the resort towns of Jarabacoa and Cabarete. Always ask in advance, and keep in mind that even if a restaurant is near an ATM, the machine may be out of money on a weekend. Elsewhere, small local restaurants rarely accept credit cards. American Express is usually only taken in the more expensive restaurants and in hotel dining rooms.

WHAT IT COSTS IN U.S. DOLLARS	
¢	under $8
$	$8–$12
$$	$12–$20
$$$	$20–$30
$$$$	over $30

Restaurant prices are for an average main course at dinner and do not include 16% tax or 10% service charge.

RESERVATIONS AND DRESS

Regardless of where you are, it's a good idea to make a reservation if you can. We only mention reservations specifically when they are essential (there's no other way you'll ever get a table) or when they are not accepted. (Large parties should always call ahead to check the reservations policy.) We mention dress only when men are required to wear a jacket or a jacket and tie.

WINE, BEER, AND SPIRITS

The three Bs dominate the Dominican market—Brugal, Barceló, and Bermudez—all very popular brands of locally made rum. Presidente is the most widely known and distributed local beer. It comes in green bottles and is sometimes called *agua verde* (green water). Brahma and Bohemia beers are the other two *cervezas* brewed here. Local Dominican restaurants may only serve rum and beer, or they may have a full bar, but if it's an inexpensive place, you may be able to get only cheaper, domestic brands. Small, local *colmados* also sell wine and liquor. Upscale restaurants usually have only international brands, with the exception of the national rums and beers.

The official drinking age is 18, but usually no one is counting, except at the hip clubs, which attempt to adhere to the law for fear of losing their club license. In Santo Domingo a curfew allows bars and restaurants to serve only until midnight during the week, until 2 AM on Friday and Saturday; exceptions are bars, clubs, and casinos in tourist hotels. That is why a lot of young people have adopted clubs like LED in the Hotel Hispaniola. All-inclusive resorts can serve alcohol 24 hours a day. In Cabarete some beachfront clubs must now close as early as 1 AM if they're next to a hotel; all bars must close by 3 AM.

ELECTRICITY

The current is 110–120 volts/60 cycles just as in North America. Electrical blackouts occur less frequently than in the past, and tend to last only one to two minutes (when they're over, everyone claps), but most hotels and restaurants have generators. It's a good idea to be considerate to your hotel hosts, especially those running small ones, and turn off lights, TVs, etc. when they're not needed. The Dominican Republic has one of the highest electricity rates in the world.

EMERGENCIES

In Santo Domingo and major destinations, 911 is the general emergency number; you'll normally find an operator who can speak some English.

If you need to speak to the police, contact Politur, a police force that has been created and specially trained to aid tourists. Most officers speak some English, are polite, and are not as accustomed to thinking about getting money on the side—although it happens. The telephone numbers for local Politur offices are given in each regional chapter.

A private ambulance service now exists in Santo Domingo, Puerto Plata, La Romana, and Santiago, and they will sometimes go to outlying areas. Movi Med will inform you when you call that they will want to be paid in cash—cash on delivery, so to speak. Just say okay. When the victim is delivered to a hospital, there is usually an ATM inside. If not, tell the driver to take you to one.

Aero Ambulancia, a division of Helidosa Helicopters, a well-established company for tours and transfers, now has a medivac service as well as insurance you can buy to safeguard yourself in case you should need their services during an emergency.

Santo Domingo and Santiago have the best medical facilities in the country. These cities have 24-hour pharmacies. It's rare to find them outside these cities. You'll be able to recognize *farmacias* by their large red or green crosses. In most places, 9 PM is closing time for pharmacies.

Emergencies **Movi Med** (📞 *809/532–000 in Santo Domingo, 1–200–0911 elsewhere in D.R.*).

Aero Ambulancia (☎ 809/552–6069, or 809/552–6066; 829/345–7236 cell for emergencies ✍ serviciocliente@helidosa.com)

U.S. Embassies & Consulates U.S. Consulate (✉ Calle Cesar Nicolas Penson, corner of Maximo Gomez, La Esperilla, Santo Domingo ☎ 809/221–2171). **United States Embassy** (✉ Leopoldo Navarro, at Calle Cesar Nicolas Penson, Gascue, Santo Domingo ☎ 809/221–2171).

▌ ETIQUETTE & BEHAVIOR

Wearing shorts, short skirts, and halter tops in churches is considered inappropriate. Men in Santo Domingo never wear shorts. If you have to go to a government office and are wearing shorts, a clerk, who might have her blouse unbuttoned to show cleavage, may refuse entry to you.

Security at hotels and resorts is tight, particularly regarding having guests in your room, especially if they're Dominican and of the opposite sex. Indeed, if you do have one overnight, you may find that you're charged double.

▌ HEALTH

Water sanitation is a constant problem across the island, and you should never drink water from the tap in the Dominican Republic. Many travelers choose to brush their teeth with bottled water, which is a reasonable precaution. Reports of foodborne illnesses in the Dominican Republic are down, primarily as a direct result of the Cristal program of food safety; look for resorts and restaurants with a Cristal certificate to indicate that the current food-safety procedures are followed. At most upscale resorts and restaurants, ice is made from purified water, and drinking water served to you is either bottled or purified (insist on bottled water if you're concerned). If you have a stomach ailment, see a physician immediately. If, for instance, you ingest some malignant creature in tainted food, getting tested right away and going on antibiotics can prevent

the parasites reproducing and making you sicker. Stray dogs and cats can be a problem; do not pet or feed these animals. If you are bitten or scratched, attend to the wound immediately. Do not hesitate to see a doctor if infection is evident.

Sexually transmitted diseases such as Hepatitis B and AIDS (known as SIDA in the Dominican Republic) are prevalent among the local prostitutes, yet another reason why it is unwise to choose the Dominican Republic for a sex-tourism vacation. Certainly, men should always use a latex condom, and women should insist that their local sex partners use a condom. Because the quality of condoms in the Dominican Republic can be questionable, you should always bring some from home.

Most often, however, the worst malady that tourists are affected by is bad sunburn. Be smart, and protect your skin. Wear a hat, visor, or cap, and apply sunscreen (SPF 30 and up) on your body and face (especially your nose and ears). Reapply lotion after swimming. As for lying on the chaise getting that tan, avoid acting like a mad Englishmen and stay out of the noonday sun. Most markets and pharmacies sell sunscreen, but expect to pay twice what you would pay at home, and that's often for a local brand.

Large resorts will have a medical clinic on-site. You'll have to pay a fee (about $65) to use the services of the physician, but if you have travel medical insurance, you can often have this amount reimbursed. Medications can be expensive, because they are often imported from the United States. If you have a more serious issue, you'll find private clinics and hospitals in the capital and most major tourist areas. You'll have to pay for services up front, but your medical insurance (or travel medical insurance) may reimburse you for out-of-pocket expenses. Some private clinics accept credit cards.

Mosquito coils are available in supermarkets, but you'll only need those if you're renting a house. Do buy your mosquito repellent (with DEET) before you leave home; the same major U.S. brands are sold in the Dominican Republic, but you'll pay double the price. It's important to protect yourself from mosquitoes and the illnesses they can carry. If you do get a mosquito bite, do what the locals do and rub a fresh lime on it to take out the itch.

MEDICAL INSURANCE AND ASSISTANCE

Consider buying trip insurance with medical-only coverage. Neither Medicare nor some private insurers cover medical expenses anywhere outside the United States. Medical-only policies typically reimburse you for medical care (excluding that related to preexisting conditions) and hospitalization abroad, and provide for evacuation. You still have to pay the bills and await reimbursement from the insurer, though.

Another option is to sign up with a medical-evacuation assistance company. A membership in one of these companies gets you doctor referrals, emergency evacuation or repatriation, 24-hour hotlines for medical consultation, and other assistance. International SOS Assistance Emergency and AirMed International provide evacuation services and medical referrals. MedjetAssist offers medical evacuation.

Medical Assistance Companies AirMed International (⊕ www.airmed.com). **MedjetAssist** (⊕ www.medjetassist.com).

Medical-Only Insurers International Medical Group (☏ 800/628–4664 ⊕ www.imglobal.com). **International SOS** (⊕ www.internationalsos.com). **Wallach & Company** (☏ 800/237–6615 or 540/687–3166 ⊕ www.wallach.com).

SHOTS AND IMMUNIZATIONS

At this writing, there are no required immunizations for adults or children traveling to the Dominican Republic.

Especially after heavy tropical storms or hurricanes, dengue fever has been reported, and in recent years more and more cases have been diagnosed. Unlike most others, the black aedes mosquitoes that carry dengue do their biting during the day. To ward them off, wear long sleeves, socks, and shoes, and apply a strong repellent containing DEET to exposed areas. Malaria has also been reported in the Dominican Republic after hurricanes, but at this writing there was no current malaria alert from the CDC regarding the Dominican Republic. Some years back, avian or bird flu was reported in certain areas of the Dominican Republic (it was associated with fighting cocks), but there have not been any new incidents.

Health Information National Centers for Disease Control & Prevention (*CDC* ☏ 877/394–8747 international travelers' health line ⊕ www.cdc.gov/travel). **World Health Organization** (*WHO* ⊕ www.who.int).

OVER-THE-COUNTER REMEDIES

You can find the usual over-the-counter medications in *farmacias* (pharmacies), in some *supermercados* (supermarkets), and even some essentials in the local *colmados* (small grocery stores). Look for the discount store California, which is the Dominican equivalent to Wal-Mart. One is on Calle Conde in Santo Domingo's Colonial Zone.

▮ HOURS OF OPERATION

Banks are open weekdays from 8:30 to 4:00 or 4:30, sometimes later on Fridays. Post offices are open weekdays from 7:30 to 2:30. Offices and shops are open weekdays from 8 to noon and 2 to 6, Saturday from 8 to noon. About half the stores stay open all day, no longer closing for siesta.

▮ LANGUAGE

Spanish is spoken in the Dominican Republic. Staff at major tourist attractions and front-desk personnel in most major hotels speak some English, but you may have difficulty making yourself understood. Outside the popular tourist establishments, restaurant menus are in Spanish, as are traffic signs everywhere. Using smiles and gestures will help, and though you can manage with just English, people are even more courteous, kind, and hospitable if you try to speak their language. It's a matter of respect. Buy one of those skinny phrase books or get Spanish audio discs from the library, and just try, *si*?

▌MONEY

The cost of a week's vacation in the Dominican Republic will vary widely. A package that includes airfare and an all-inclusive resort will usually be the best value, but this can vary from $4,000 per person for a week at a luxurious resort in Uvero Alto to less than $2,000 per person for a week at a less luxurious resort in Playa Dorada. It's also possible to do the trip for a much cheaper price if you go during the off-season (September to October) or lower your standards. But these days, the teaser offers of $1,000 usually have a lot of fine print (and are usually limited to three-night stays). You will not need any local currency if you're staying at an all-inclusive resort. But if you're traveling independently, cash is definitely king in the Dominican Republic; however, don't carry more than $100 on your person unless you're on your way to an upscale restaurant that does not take credit cards. Large hotels, upscale restaurants in major cities, and expensive stores take credit cards (though Amex is not accepted as often), but some local establishments will take credit cards only if you pay a 3% to 4% supplement.

ITEM	AVERAGE COST (IN US$)
Cup of Coffee	$1
Glass of Wine	$7
Glass of Beer	$2.50
Sandwich	$4.50
One-Mile Taxi Ride in Capital City	$4.50
Museum Admission	$1.50

Prices throughout this guide are given for adults. Substantially reduced fees are almost always available for children, students, and senior citizens.

ATMS AND BANKS

ATMs are widely available in the capital and iin tourist towns like Cabarete. As you get out into the country, they become scarce. In the Southwest, for example, there are several in the main city of Barahona but none in the countryside, and barely any in the hill towns. Banco Popular has many locations throughout the country, as do BHT and Scotiabank. Most ATMs—called ATHs or *cajeros automaticos* in the Dominican Republic—are members of Cirrus, PLUS, or other international networks. They will give you pesos.

At nearly all ATMs you'll have a choice of language, so just choose English. For years, 10,000 pesos was the maximum you could take out at one time. Scotia-Bank still uses that as its maximo. Now, due to ATM fraud, most banks only allow you to obtain RD$4,000 to RD$5,000 at a time. However, if you need more than this, you can do up to two separate transactions in one day.

The commands on the machine itself are self-explanatory, with the exception of "Valid" or Validate," which is the equivalent of hitting "Enter." Sometimes, however, ATMs may seem to have their own agenda. The buttons may not line up and you can become bewildered as to why your transaction cancelled. If your debit card normally draws from your checking account and does not process, you may be able to take funds from your savings account instead. Hit the button to get your card back; if you don't take your debit card immediately, the machine may take it back.

Always think safety. It's best to go to ATMs that are inside or just outside banks, during daylight hours only and when the bank is open. Avoid having to go on weekends. The safety reasons are obvious, but if the machine swallows your card, you immediately have some recourse other than to call the number for the bank the next day. Most banks do have security guards next to the outdoor ATMs at night, but always shield your PIN as you enter it.

CREDIT CARDS

Throughout this guide, the following abbreviations are used: **AE**, American Express; **D**, Discover; **DC**, Diners Club; **MC**, MasterCard; and **V**, Visa.

It's a good idea to inform your credit-card company before you travel, especially if you're going abroad and don't travel internationally very often. Otherwise, the credit-card company might put a hold on your card owing to unusual activity—not a good thing halfway through your trip. Record all your credit-card numbers— as well as the phone numbers to call if your cards are lost or stolen—in a safe place, so you're prepared should something go wrong. Both MasterCard and Visa have general numbers you can call (collect if you're abroad) if your card is lost, but you're better off calling the number of your issuing bank, since Master-Card and Visa usually just transfer you to your bank; your bank's number is usually printed on your card.

If you plan to use your credit card for cash advances, you'll need to apply for a PIN at least two weeks before your trip. Although it's usually cheaper (and safer) to use a credit card abroad for large purchases (so you can cancel payments or be reimbursed if there's a problem), note that some credit-card companies *and* the banks that issue them add substantial percentages to all foreign transactions, whether they're in a foreign currency or not. Check on these fees before leaving home, so there won't be any surprises when you get the bill.

Major credit cards (American Express not as often) are accepted at most hotels, large stores, and restaurants. Use them with care in the Dominican Republic.

There have been reports that merchants are duplicating credit cards. If you are traveling, you may not find out about the fraud until you are back home. One American living in Santo Domingo has had his credit cards duplicated four different times Therefore, it makes sense to only use credit cards at well-known hotels and resign yourself to hitting ATMs more frequently.

Reporting Lost Cards American Express (☎ 809/227–3190 in Santo Domingo, 866/751–2797 in other provinces [24 hours], 336/393–1111 collect from abroad ⊕ www.americanexpress.com). **Diners Club** (☎ 800/234–6377 in U.S., 303/799–1504 collect from abroad ⊕ www.dinersclub.com). **Discover** (☎ 800/347–2683 in U.S., 801/902–3100 collect from abroad ⊕ www.discovercard.com). **MasterCard** (☎ 800/627–8372 in U.S., 636/722-7111 collect from abroad ⊕ www.mastercard.com). **Visa** (☎ 800/847–2911 in U.S., 410/581–9994 collect from abroad ⊕ www.visa.com).

CURRENCY AND EXCHANGE

You may need to change some money, particularly if you're not staying in an all-inclusive resort, where dollars are usually accepted. Prices quoted in this chapter are in U.S. dollars unless noted otherwise. The coin of the realm is the Dominican peso (written RD$). At this writing, the exchange rate was approximately RD$36 to US$1.

Independent merchants willingly accept U.S. dollars, but because the peso can fluctuate, change will be in pesos. In recent years the Dominican peso has remained fairly stable, hovering between RD$32 and RD$36 to the dollar since 2006. Always make certain you know in which currency any transaction is taking place, and carry a pocket calculator.

You can find *cambios* (currency exchange offices) at the airports, as well as on the street, and in major shopping areas throughout the island. A passport is usually required to cash traveler's checks, if they're taken at all. Save some of the official receipts with the exchange transaction, so if you end up with too many pesos when you are ready to leave the country, you can turn them in for dollars. Do this before you leave, because in U.S. airports like Miami you may be charged as much as $7.50 a transaction, no matter how small, and then be given a bad rate of exchange for your trouble. Some hotels provide exchange services, but, as a rule, hotels and restaurants will not give you favorable rates—casino cages do.

▌ PACKING

Even though this is a Caribbean country, you should always bring some kind of warm clothing (a light shawl or hooded sweatshirt) appropriate for frigid, air-conditioned cars and buses. From September through November, be sure to have a good and strong folding umbrella.

If you'll be spending time in Santo Domingo, you'll find that residents dress up more. Women, in particular, dress up every day; high heels are the norm, and women never wear sneakers, flip-flops, or shorts, always a dress, skirt, or slacks and stylish shoes (more often with 3"–6" heels). In fact, some museums and churches will not allow tourists to enter if they're wearing skimpy tops or shorts. Similarly, men will find that a *guayabera* shirt will take them anywhere, but Dominican men never wear shorts or flip-flops, reserving those for the beach. In offices and in fine-dining restaurants, it's not unusual to see white starched shirts, ties, and dark suits. Younger Dominican men may wear designer jeans and polo shorts. And the tropical fedora is back in style, with girls and some of their dates, wearing the smaller version of these Panama hats. But the more casually you dress, the more you'll be sniffed at as a *turista*.

The North Coast is typically cooler and windier, particularly from December to March. At night you'll want long sleeves and perhaps even a jacket. Along the Southeast Coast and in Punta Cana, the weather is warm year-round, but you may still want something to protect yourself from the chill of nighttime air-conditioning.

If you're going to the mountain areas such as Jarabacoa, Constanza, or Valle Nuevo, you must be prepared for chilly weather at night because of the elevation. In Constanza and Valle Nuevo in the winter you will need hats, ski parkas, gloves, and scarves. In the hilly parts of the Southwest temperatures are not as cold, but they certainly drop at night, when winds pick up. But during the day it can be unbearably hot.

Generally, public restrooms in the Dominican Republic are unsanitary and do not have toilet paper. Always pack small tissue packets, travel-size wipes, and hand sanitizer.

If you'll be shopping for groceries, bring a tote bag; plastic bags at supermarkets and drug stores tear easily, as they are poor quality, when they're available at all.

Cosmetics and toiletries, sunscreen, and mosquito repellent are difficult to find if you want the usual American brands, and they are much more expensive than in the United States (expect to pay two to three times what you would normally pay). Over-the-counter medications, baby formula, disposable diapers, tampons, and contact lens supplies are similarly expensive, and sometimes you have to try several shops. (Major supermarkets such as Nacional, or the California department store(s) carry most of these things).

■TIP→ **Bring earplugs. The Dominican Republic may be the noisiest country that you've ever visited. In addition to the constant honking and incessant drone of the motorcycles, there's always high-volume Dominican music. By night, the music at the colmodons (general stores/bars) can be heard for a mile. And earplugs are almost impossible to buy in the Dominican Republic. Of course, an iPod can also help you drown out your surroundings.**

PASSPORTS AND VISAS

For a stay of 30 days or less, U.S. citizens entering the Dominican Republic must have a valid passport with six months of validity remaining. The new passport card is *not* sufficient for travel by air to the Dominican Republic. Upon arrival, you must purchase a Tourist Card for US$10, which is valid for a maximum of 30 days (after that you must appear in person at the airport to extend your visa, a process that requires another $10 fee and much paperwork). If you chose not to bother, you risk getting a fine when leaving the country. The fine will be higher the longer you overstayed your welcome. Still, it's not so much. Some tour operators include the tourist card in packages, so ask about that when you make your booking. Business travelers must always get a business visa at a diplomatic mission or consulate in their home country.

A nonparent or single parent traveling with a child must have a notarized statement of permission from the absent parent(s).

▌PROSTITUTION

Although the Dominican Republic has long had a reputation for prostitution and sex tourism, officials are making efforts to curb the problem. In the late 1990s, Sosúa was like one big red-light district, with European male travelers coming specifically for sex tourism. Town fathers have made vigorous efforts to clean things up—and they have—but prostitution still exists in the now designated *Zona Rojas*. It's traditionally been a different story in Cabarete, where young, local surfer boys target northern European girls, who end up paying the freight. The real action goes down in Punta Cana, with the infamous gigolo-like "sanky panky" boys—resort employees, often waiters, bartenders, and animation staff (those in charge of the entertainment, games and sports at resorts)—who seek out single female guests, especially older ones, lavishing attention on them, saying, "Meet me in the disco." Such a rendezvous often ends up in a seedy, drive-up, by-the-hour motel. What some unsuspecting ladies don't realize is that not only will they have to pay for the room but for the boy's services as well. Other sanky pankys may wait until marks have returned home to e-mail or phone them with a sob story about sick relatives or about losing their job.

In Santo Domingo, prostitutes are alive and not always well (diseases are a real threat). They ply their trade, roaming casinos and hotels, though top properties vigilantly thwart their efforts. Throughout the Dominican Republic, sex bars are usually called "gentlemen's clubs." There's substantial gay prostitution as well. Child prostitution has almost been stamped out, but not entirely, and the government will prosecute tourists who have sex with minors (under age 18), and they may also be prosecuted in their own country. It is not uncommon in certain areas, like Boca Chica, to see European men over sixty with girls who could be their granddaughters.

▌SAFETY

The Dominican Republic is one of the safer islands in the Caribbean. A first impression may make you think otherwise. Although the Dominican Republic is a very poor country—and crime does happen—violent crime against foreigners is rare. And even though you may hear warnings about pickpockets and purse snatching by motorcycle-riding thieves, both are relatively unusual. In fact, you may find Dominican honesty refreshing.

However, petty theft (particularly of cell phones), pickpocketing, and purse snatching (thieves usually work in pairs) is not rare and is most frequent in Santo Domingo. Pay attention, especially when leaving a bank, a cambio, or a casino, despite the very visible police. Crime has even come to Santiago, so be cautious at night, and lock the doors of your car or taxi. Armed private security guards are a common sight at clubs and restaurants.

The best tactic for dealing with the Dominican Republic is not to be paranoid, just cautious, and as in any area with a crime problem, only carry the credit cards and money that you actually need. Keep the rest in your hotel safe.

If you are the victim of a crime, you may have to offer the police "gas money" and a reward to really get some help. With the Politur (tourist police), it's less likely to happen, but it still does. Should you find yourself in that predicament, consult a savvy, English-speaking Dominican and ask what amount would be appropriate; this transaction always works best when you have a translator.

Each area in the Dominican Republic has its own safety concerns. For example, avoid walking in Cabarete after midnight, as much to protect yourself from speeding motoconchos as from criminals. Prostitution can be an annoyance there, as can drug dealers. "Bad boys" have been known to follow lucky winners at casinos. They can also be waiting behind a palm tree when one of their women slows you down to ask if you need "company." Wise tourists avoid such complications, particularly drugs; trust us when we tell you that you do not want to have to spend time in a Dominican jail. One hears stories of friends and relatives having to come up with US$10,000 to bribe a jailer to spring a young man who was cuffed and incarcerated for smoking a joint on the street. As for the security at all-inclusive resorts, the good news is that in general it's really good.

In Punta Cana, which is one of the safest regions, muggings or robberies have occurred when turistas have come out of a casino stumbling drunk and bragging about their winnings.

As for Santo Domingo, even though it's considerably safer in the tourist zones now, it's still a large metropolitan city, with higher crime rates than smaller towns. Muggings and thefts rise during street parties, such as Carnaval.

Regardless of where you are, if you leave your resort, take hotel-recommended taxis at night. When driving, always lock your car and never leave valuables in it, even when doors are locked. If you have a safe in your hotel room, use it; many can now accommodate a laptop. If it doesn't, camouflage it or secure it with a laptop lock to a pipe or immovable piece of furniture. If a computer costs $600 in the states, it would be worth twice as much in the Dominican Republic.

GOVERNMENT INFORMATION AND ADVISORIES

Advisories U.S. Department of State (⊕ *travel.state.gov*).

▮ TAXES

Departure tax—separate from the $10 tourist card you must purchase on entering the country—is $20 and almost always included in the price of your ticket. The government tax (*ITBIS*) is a whopping 16% and is added to almost everything—bills at restaurants, hotels, sports activities, rental cars, and items at the supermercados that are not considered basic, including imports. It's not a VAT, as it's paid in addition to the price.

▮ TIME

Atlantic Standard Time is observed year-round. From November to March, when it's 9 AM in New York, Boston, and Miami, it's 10 AM in the Dominican Republic. The Dominican Republic does not observe Daylight Savings Time: so during months when Daylight Savings Time is in effect back in the States, it's the same time on the island as it is on the East Coast.

▮ TIPPING

Generally a 10% service charge is included in all hotel and restaurant bills; it's the Dominican law. In restaurants, the bill will say *propino incluido* or simply *servis*. When in doubt, ask. Even then, it's still expected that you will tip an extra 5% to 10% if the service was to your liking. In resorts, it's customary to leave at least a dollar per day (or the peso equivalent) for the hotel maid. Taxi drivers expect a 10% tip, especially if they've had to lift luggage or to wait for you. Skycaps and hotel porters expect at least $1 per bag. Attendants in restrooms should be given something for that sometimes distasteful job. Anything from 10 pesos on up will get you a big "Gracias!"

Some guests have started to tip other service staff at all-inclusive resorts, even though tipping is supposed to be included in the cost of your trip. Bellboys, waiters, concierges, and bartenders (who may have a tip cup) are starting to expect a dollar, and they tend to give far better service to those who ante up. Remember, you're under no obligation to do this, but many travelers bring a stack of U.S. singles for this purpose. If you leave a present for your maid, write a note with it so they can show security that it was a *regalo* (gift).

The staff at a private villa also expects some kind of a gratuity. The management company from which you rent should be able to give you an idea of the tip expected, but it's usually about 10% of the total cost of the villa.

▌ TRIP INSURANCE

Comprehensive trip insurance is valuable if you're booking a very expensive or complicated trip (particularly to an isolated region) or if you're booking far in advance. Comprehensive policies typically cover trip cancellation and interruption, letting you cancel or cut your trip short because of illness, or, in some cases, acts of terrorism and acts of God, like earthquakes. Such policies might also cover evacuation and medical care. (For international trips you should at least have medical-only coverage. *See* ⇨ *Medical Insurance and Assistance under Health.*).

Some also cover you for trip delays because of bad weather or mechanical problems as well as for lost or delayed luggage.

Another type of coverage to consider is financial default—that is, when your trip is disrupted because a tour operator, airline, or cruise line goes out of business. Generally you must buy this when you book your trip or shortly thereafter, and it's available to you only if your operator isn't on a list of excluded companies.

Always read the fine print of your policy to make sure that you're covered for the risks that most concern you. Compare several policies to be sure you're getting the best price and range of coverage available.

Insurance Comparison Info Insure My Trip (☎ 800/487-4722 ⊕ www.insuremytrip.com). **Square Mouth** (☎ 800/240-0369 ⊕ www.squaremouth.com).

Comprehensive Insurers Access America (☎ 800/284-8300 ⊕ www.accessamerica.com). **AIG Travel Guard** (☎ 800/826-4919 ⊕ www.travelguard.com). **CSA Travel Protection** (☎ 800/873-9855 ⊕ www.csatravelprotection.com). **Travelex Insurance** (☎ 800/228-9792 ⊕ www.travelex-insurance.com). **Travel Insured International** (☎ 800/243-3174 ⊕ www.travelinsured.com).

▌ VISITOR INFORMATION

Information Dominican Republic One (⊕ www.dr1.com) is a "trusted site" of the Secretariat de Turismo. It's written by bilingual staffers at the ministry and delivers the official word on the latest news, travel, and airline information. **Dominican Republic Tourist Office** (⊕ www.godominicanrepublic.com ☎ 212/588-1012, 888/374-6361 in New York City, 305/444-4592, or 888/358-9594 in Miami).

▮ WEDDINGS

The relative ease of getting married in the Dominican Republic has made it a major destination for Caribbean weddings. There are no residency requirements nor are blood tests mandatory. Original birth certificates and passports are required. The Dominican consulate must stamp divorce certificates. If a woman has been divorced, it must have been at least 10 months ago. That same consulate must stamp single certificates that indicate the bride and groom are indeed single. If either party is widowed, a death certificate must be produced along with the previous marriage certificate. These documents must be translated into Spanish and legalized. You must usually submit documents at least two weeks in advance of your wedding, and the cost for processing is at least $100 per person.

As elsewhere in the Caribbean, civil ceremonies, performed by a judge, are easier and require less documentation than those performed in churches. They'll be in Spanish unless you arrange for an English translator. Similarly, the legalized wedding certificate will be in Spanish and may not be delivered for a week or more. Most couples arrange their wedding ceremonies through a wedding coordinator at their resort. (The all-inclusive resorts are seasoned at handling wedding celebrations, with some like Sunscape and Dreams resorts having wedding coordinators who earn kudos from the brides and their mothers.)

A number of resorts cater to the wedding market and provide a gorgeous backdrop for the occasion. The famed Casa de Campo has handpicked staffers who are near magicians at coordinating celebrity weddings, often in secrecy. Conversely, many young couples have married here surrounded by family and friends hosted in a handful of villas.

At Natura Cabana, in Cabarete, you can be married in the palatial, ocean-front yoga pavilion or on the beach. This ecolodge lends itself to creative, offbeat, wedding celebrations. In nearby Sosúa, Piergiorgio's (Palace Hotel) is a romantic Victorianesque inn with an amazing view of Sosúa Bay from a white rotunda, its picturesque wedding gazebo.

For those wanting a more intimate a high-end venue, ultraluxurious vacation villas on the beach provide a lifetime of memories. In Cabrera's Orchid Bay Estates, Villa Castellamonte is designed like an Italian palazzo. Its dedicated wedding coordinator performs magical transformations at this 15,000 square-foot mansion with eight bedrooms, a resort-size pool complex and golden beach. A neighbor in this gated community, Flor de Cabrera, is a multilevel (18,500 square foot) 10-bedroom, exquisitely furnished with a separate master casita for the bride and groom.

INDEX

PHOTO CREDITS

NOTES

ABOUT OUR WRITERS

Elise Rosen, who updated our Punta Cana chapter after writing it initially, has been working for Fodor's for a decade, covering such disparate destinations as Aruba, Bonaire, Curaçao, and Israel. She's a writer and editor based in New York City.

Eileen Robinson Smith was the lead contributor for this new guide to the Dominican Republic. Eileen, who moved from the Caribbean to Charleston, South Carolina, has lived all over the Virgin Islands and has written about food and travel for *Sky, Caribbean Travel & Life, and Condé Nast Traveler.* She updated our coverage for Santo Domingo, the Southwest, the Southeast Coast, and the Cibao Valley.

Michael de Zayas has covered destinations on five continents for Fodor's, updating or writing original coverage of Miami, New England, New York City, Spain, the Caribbean, and Chile. He's been based in New York City for over a decade. For this edition, Michael updated our coverage of the Samaná Peninsula and the North Coast.

NOTES